PRESIDENTIAL COMMISSIONS

A Da Capo Press Reprint Series

STUDIES IN AMERICAN HISTORY AND GOVERNMENT

GENERAL EDITOR: LEONARD W. LEVY

Claremont Graduate School

PRESIDENTIAL COMMISSIONS

By Carl Marcy

DA CAPO PRESS · NEW YORK · 1973

Library of Congress Cataloging in Publication Data

Marcy, Carl Milton, 1913-
   Presidential commissions.

   (Studies in American history and government)
   Originally presented as the author's thesis, Columbia, 1945.
   Includes bibliographical references.
   1. Governmental investigations—United States. I. Title.
JK516.M35   1973   353'.09   72-8109
ISBN 0-306-70532-X

This Da Capo Press edition of *Presidential Commissions*
is an unabridged republication of the first edition
published in New York in 1945. It is reprinted
by special arrangement with the author.

Published by Da Capo Press, Inc.
A Subsidiary of Plenum Publishing Corporation
227 West 17th Street, New York, New York 10011

PRESIDENTIAL

COMMISSIONS

PRESIDENTIAL COMMISSIONS

Carl Marcy

MORNINGSIDE HEIGHTS - NEW YORK

KING'S CROWN PRESS

1945

PREFACE

PRESIDENTIAL commissions created by the President upon his own authority and for his own purposes are governmental devices of increasing importance. Presidents rely on them more today than in the past. Their activities are news and their findings may profoundly affect the life of the nation. They have been used by Presidents as instruments to guide public opinion and to influence the Congress. They have also been used by Presidents to confuse the public and to avoid important issues.

Presidential commissions have not received the attention as an instrument of government that their importance and influence warrant. Studies of such commissions have been sporadic in appearance and incomplete in context. The few articles on this subject which have been published have usually been motivated by the creation and activities of a particular commission.

The present study is a survey of presidential commissions which have been created between the years of 1900 and 1940, with the addition of a few samples of commissions created before or after their period when their importance or characteristics so warranted.

Surveys always present their authors with the choice of whether to be general or particular. The present study touches on many commissions briefly rather than on a few commissions at length. The survey approach has been chosen because it lends itself better to a determination of the origin, the importance, and the future of presidential commissions.

I wish to thank Professors Lindsay Rogers, Arthur W. Macmahon, and Allan Nevins for their suggestions and criticism. I also wish to thank the following publishers for permissions to make quotations from publications within their copyrights: D. Appleton-Century Company; Harvard University Press; *The New York Times;* The United States News, an independent weekly magazine on national affairs published at Washington, D.C.; Yale University Press.

C. M.

TABLE OF CONTENTS

Table of Contents

PRESIDENTIAL

COMMISSIONS

1

THE IMPORTANCE OF PRESIDENTIAL
COMMISSIONS

Analysis of any phase of present-day government in the United States
must inevitably be made in the light or the shadow cast by the totali-
tarian-democratic conflict. This is true whether the study be of local
machine politics or of presidential commissions. Democracy for the past decade has been on the defensive because people judge their forms of government by the ability of those governments to satisfy their wants or at least maintain conditions under which man can satisfy his wants by his own labor. As
someone has remarked, the masses of Europe held up their hands and asked
to be manacled. The totalitarian state may have satisfied some wants, but at
the expense of freedoms which many men hold dear. Military victory will be
no positive assurance that democracy can survive. It cannot survive as a form
of government unless it makes man the master of his economic destinies instead of the servant. Whether democracy can meet the challenge will be determined in the decade after the war when people will demand that their
government enable them to attain the promise of the post-war world. To give
democracy the virility needed there must be an appraisal of the good and the
bad in government.

Democracy assumes that "the electorate is able to dispose of controversial
issues in the light of rational appraisal of relevant data. Such an assumption
. . . presupposes not only judgment, but also adequate information." [1] But
at this time when the responsibilities of democratic government are becoming
increasingly acute, new economic complexities make it increasingly difficult
to provide the public with the mass information which is necessary for a democracy to discharge its governmental obligations. The totalitarian states substituted the judgment of one or the few, for mass judgment; they substituted
state controlled "facts" for mass information. The governments which resulted were authoritarian regimes capable of swift and violent dealing with
the "new complexities." Democracies with their periodic elections have relied

on the assumption that mass judgment based on mass information will provide the state with the best guidance in broad paths of policy. If that assumption is to be well founded, unprejudiced information and facts must be accessible to the people.

President Hoover told the Gridiron Club in 1929,

> My conception of government leads me to the firm conviction that we have arrived at a time in our history, because of the increasing complexity of our civilization and the delicacy of its adjustments, when we must make doubly certain that we discover the truth. It is necessary that we make the fullest use of the best brains and the best judgment and the best leadership in our country before we determine upon policies which affect the welfare of a hundred and twenty million people.[2]

The value in the use of commissions, committees, boards and similarly designated multi-partite bodies as instruments of government has long been recognized.[3] They have been used by almost every unit and level of government for nearly every conceivable task.

The use which Congress has made of fact-finding and investigating committees to prepare the ground for legislation, to bring malodorous practices into the spotlight, or to whip legislation into shape has received much attention from students of government. The President, who is more and more commonly the source of legislation, and who more and more frequently uses commissions created by him on his own authority and for his own purposes, has received little attention from students of government in his role as creator of commissions.

Although broadly speaking, the purpose for the creation of both congressional and presidential commissions is to find facts, the executive branch of government tends to be fearful of congressional commissions and the legislative branch of government is in turn apprehensive of presidential commissions. There is little that the President can do to curtail the creation and activity of congressional commissions. Congress, on the other hand, can and has, as will be shown, placed legislative barriers in the way of the President's creation of commissions.

In New York State, however, the Executive has been encouraged to establish his own fact-finding agencies by an act of legislation known as the Moreland Act. This Act, as will be noted later, invites the Executive to have his own fact-finding surveys when and where he wants them and provides him with a fund upon which the commissioner may draw for his expenses. The executive commission is apparently a device of government which does not induce identical reactions in legislative bodies.

There can be little doubt that the President needs commissions to help him. "No high executive in this country is equal to the complexities of his task," was the comment of a Supreme Court Justice noted for his objections to bigness.[4] Certainly when the President of the United States determines policy, recommends policy, or administers policy, he must have facts and expert advice.

Not only must the President have facts upon which to base his policies, he must have knowledge of how policy is being administered by his executive agents. In the days when government was a town meeting and when federal employees were numbered by the hundred, administration was simple. But when government numbers its agencies by the hundreds and its employees by the millions, the job of administration is overwhelming. Since faulty administration reflects on the President, he must be able to assure the effective execution of policy. The President must be able to find out what the executive departments are doing, and how effectively they are carrying out policy. Presidentially inspired administrative investigating commissions are needed now and then to implement the regular lines of control that run to the President.

Furthermore, the increased size and complexity of government means the President is now unable to do many tasks which in earlier times he could have done himself. Today it is necessary for him to delegate many executive functions to various boards and committees. Thus in the early days of our government the coordination of governmental activities presented no problem. Coordination was automatic because the President knew what each department was doing and could coordinate their activities himself. Today the coordination of policy is beyond the capacity of any one man.

No matter how inexorable the logic for the creation of presidential commissions in the Federal Government, they have encountered a considerable amount of criticism. President Hoover's aforementioned argument for the appointment of fact-finding commissions encountered much criticism. "Sins of Commissions," "another commission Hoovering over us," and congressional attacks hampered Hoover's use of commissions.[5] The democratic state has feared too much bureaucracy and has identified government commissions, especially executive commissions, with the trend toward a totalitarian state. Those who oppose presidential commissions have not let the American public forget the Star Chamber.[6] Notwithstanding criticism of governmental commissions, there has been no surcease in their creation. From September 4,

1901 when President Theodore Roosevelt succeeded to office until March 4, 1929, there were no less than 471 federal commissions, committees, boards and similar bodies created . . . better than one and one-half per month.[7]

In 1930 President Hoover admitted that during his administration, which then totaled 16 months, there had been some 62 commissions, boards, and similar bodies appointed.[8] While there are no completely reliable figures on the number of similar bodies appointed during the administration of Franklin D. Roosevelt, the commissions mentioned in this study total more than 100, up to and including the year 1940.[9]

The increased use of commissions by the President has not meant an increase in their prestige. Their findings more frequently gather dust than lead to action.[10]

Nowhere in our American Government do we have a fact-finding body which approaches the prestige of the British royal commissions. We have had some notable commissions of inquiry but "by and large, the experience and tradition of the British royal commissions are lacking in the United States." [11] Dimock has pointed out the need for commissions of specialists with only a small portion drawn from the legislative body to find facts and study basic problems.[12] "Royal commissions," according to W. F. Willoughby, "are recognized as one of the most effective means for the handling of complicated questions requiring legislative action and the harmonizing of conflicting interests." [13] Royal commissions have been criticized [14] as well as praised, but their tradition now is established not only as effective fact-finding devices, but as catalysts in major social conflicts.

What stands in the way of the development of a similar instrument of government in the United States? [15] Court decisions have recognized that Congress has a broad authority to create commissions. There is little doubt that Congress can engineer as broad an investigation as any royal commission. One difficulty with legislative commissions, however, is that in the United States they have exhibited a "definitely partisan and political bias alike in their membership, their proceedings, and their reports." [16] Not only are legislative commissions set up for personal or partisan motives, but such commissions tend to be overloaded with congressmen and scarce on experts.

A second difficulty in the United States in the development of any fact-finding instrumentality similar to the royal commission can be traced to the principle of the separation of powers. In England, royal commissions bear a relationship to the executive and to the legislature which cannot be duplicated in a compartmentalized government like our own. The Cabinet is either the master or the servant of Parliament. The two can never be at odds for long.

No royal commission operates without the actual or implied consent of Parliament; no royal commission would be suggested by the Cabinet unless Parliament would approve. In the United States, Congress is free to have its own commissions but lacks both the tradition and the perspective for great success. The President can, within limits, engineer his own investigations but proposals for legislation which may grow out of such investigations may be met by an indifferent Congress—made so perhaps by reason of the feeling that the President has encroached on a legislative prerogative.

While presidential commissions might in time build up tradition and perspective and merit the respect which is accorded royal commissions, presidential authority to create commissions is severely limited. Congress has expressly provided that no part of the public moneys is to be used for commissions unless they are authorized by law. The President is prevented from using officers from the executive departments for any other purpose than the carrying out of duties which fall within their respective departments.[17] Congress is free to go about its fact-finding but the President must come to Congress before he can do much fact-finding—unless he can get a private grant of funds for his work. The American President has no special fund upon which he may draw for the expenses of commissions which he may want for legitimate executive purposes. The result is that Presidents have on occasion relied on money from private sources to finance their fact-finding commissions. It has been estimated that President Hoover received private grants for his commissions of over $2,000,000 and this figure is probably conservative.[18] One of Hoover's supporters in Congress proudly explained that many of Hoover's commissions had cost the government nothing.[19] One of his critics wrote that "their findings are not worth what they cost the taxpayer." [20] This is an anomalous situation. If presidential commissions are of any value to government, they should be supported by the government. There should be no taint of "private money" in presidentially sponsored fact-finding commissions. If they are not worth what they cost, that fact should be known.

In New York State, the Moreland Act is a standing invitation for the Governor to appoint commissions "to examine and investigate the management and affairs of any department, board, bureau or commission of the state." [21] Money is provided to pay the salaries of the commissioners and the expenses of the investigations. The New York Governor is supplied with an adequate fact-finding investigative instrument of his own—an instrument which assists him in his duty of faithfully executing the laws. The Moreland Act gives the commissioner or commission authority to subpoena both persons and records and to swear witnesses. The President of the United States charged with a like duty has no power similar to that of the New York Governor, unless it be under another guise. The President does not have this power in his own right and he cannot give it to his agents.

It may be suggested that the President has his executive departments from which he can get information and that there is no need for a "royal commission" device in the United States. President Hoover thought not. Over and beyond the problems handled by the executive departments, he believed,

> there are a thousand problems; where truth must be searched from a multitude of facts; where individual and regional experience must be had; where new ideas must be recruited from the kaleidoscope of a great shifting mass of humanity; where judgment must be distilled from many minds; where common agreement must be secured from conflicting sources; where assurance must be given to the people of the correctness of conclusions; and where their experience must be secured. . . .[22]

Whether or not one believes that royal commissions are examples of what commissions in the United States should attempt to become, our knowledge of commissions needs to be augmented by a survey of their use by the President. Once this study has been made it may be easier to evaluate presidential commissions as a governmental device and it may be possible to make some suggestions with regard to their future development.

It has been suggested by Gustavus A. Weber that a study of inquiries by the executive departments and on the order of the President, such as the present one, is both impracticable and purposeless.

> It is manifestly impracticable even to list, much less to describe in detail, all such inquiries, many of which are recorded only in manuscripts filed in the bureaus or departments to which they are related. Little useful purpose, moreover, would be served by attempting to do so, since most of them relate to conditions which have long since passed away.[23]

While it may be impracticable to list and to describe all such inquiries, the more important presidentially sponsored commissions have left reports, or taken action, which are subject to analysis. It is believed that a study of these commissions will reveal facts about them which are not generally known and that these facts will be valuable in appraising presidential commissions as a device of democratic government.

2

THE LEGAL BASIS OF PRESIDENTIAL COMMISSIONS

I. POWER TO CREATE

THE ability of the President to create commissions on his own authority and for his own purposes reveals to some extent his ability to influence legislation, to supervise the executive departments, and to discharge effectively his responsibilities.[1]

In delineating the *sources of power* for the creation of presidential commissions, one must keep in mind the *purposes* for which commissions have been created. These purposes broadly described are, first, to supply the President with facts and advice upon which he may recommend legislation or base his own policy—this is the informative function; second, to investigate the administration of the laws by the executive departments—this is the inquisitorial or supervisory function; and, third, to act as the agent of the President in either foreign or domestic affairs. The authority cited by the President for the creation of a commission occasionally will depend upon the function of the body. Thus, the authority for creating an "informative" commission may be the constitutional duty of the President to recommend to Congress "such measures as he shall judge necessary and expedient." [2] On the other hand, authority to appoint an "investigative" commission may be the presidential duty to take care that the laws be faithfully executed. The authority of the President to create commissions for his own purposes stems from no single source. In the following pages a number of the sources of presidential authority for the creation of commissions are discussed.

(A) TAKE CARE THAT THE LAWS BE FAITHFULLY EXECUTED

The constitutional obligation upon the President to "take care that the laws be faithfully executed," gives him a body of undefined inherent powers.[3] Whether among these powers there is to be found authority to appoint commissions to aid the President in the execution of the laws the courts have not said. Practice, however, has supplied an answer in the continued creation by the President of commissions unauthorized by statute law.

President Tyler was apparently the first President to have to justify to Congress the creation of a presidential commission created upon his own authority, although he was not the first to appoint such a body.[4] A House Resolution of February 7, 1842 requested the President to inform the House "under what authority," "for what purposes and objects," and "out of what fund" a commission to investigate the New York Customs House was operating.[5] Tyler's reply, paraphrasing Article 2, Section 3 of the Constitution, laid the basis not only for presidential investigating commissions but also for fact-finding commissions with legislative objects in view. He wrote

> I have to state that the authority for instituting the commission . . . is the authority vested in the President of the United States to "take care that the laws be faithfully executed, and to give to Congress from time to time information on the state of the Union, and to recommend to their consideration such measures as he shall judge necessary and expedient." The expediency, if not the necessity, of inquiries into the transactions of our customs-houses, especially in cases where abuses and malpractices are alleged, must be obvious to Congress. . . .[6]

In correspondence with one of the commission members, President Tyler made it clear that the report was for his benefit and not for Congress

> . . . the report of the commission is now wanted, by me, *for my own information*. I do not doubt but that it will contain many suggestions . . . most worthy to be recommended by me to Congress. . . . Whether, when made, I shall deem it best to communicate the entire report to Congress, or otherwise make it public . . . will be for my own decision. . . .[7]

President Theodore Roosevelt was subject to congressional criticism for his liberal creation of "volunteer unpaid commissions." One congressman objected to the great number of commissions "working under authority for the executive department alone, and employing a great many people in the various departments; . . . all being done without authority of law."[8] A section of the Sundry Civil Act of 1909[9] sought to prevent the creation of such commissions by the President. Roosevelt signed the bill, but in the belief that he was not bound thereby.[10]

Senator Borah before the Foreign Relations Committee in 1930 expressed a like view. "I think," he said, the President "has a right to appoint a commission or an agent to make any investigation he desires. . . . That has been the practice." [11]

That Senator Borah expressed the point of view generally accepted is indicated by the fact that objection to Hoover's commissions was directed not at their legality but at their futility, expense, and political character.[12] In 1941, the *New York Times* editorially remarked that the President is the "one man who . . . does have the power to appoint a Presidential Commission" to find facts and recommend legislation.[13]

In domestic affairs the President's power to create commissions to assist him in the faithful execution of the law appears in theory at least to be unlimited.

It has been objected that appointments to presidential commissions must be with the advice and consent of the Senate. If this were true, there would be a material check upon the President's power to create such commissions. Professor Corwin points out that the practice of constituting "volunteer unpaid commissions" is apparently justified on the theory that these assignments "are not 'offices' in the sense of the Constitution, being only for specific, temporary purposes. . . ." [14] Governmentally paid presidential commissions, on the other hand, are often created as a result of a congressional grant of appointing power in terms which do not require the consent of the Senate.[15]

Caleb Cushing propounded the general rule that

> the clause requiring the President to see to the execution of the laws, and to give information to Congress on the state of the Union, was imperative on the President, and constituted an obligation, by the omission of which he violated the Constitution and his oath of office, and was thereby liable to impeachment. . . .

And since the Constitution did not set forth a method for the performance of this imperative duty, the President could use commissions if he wished.[16] While it is easier to imagine a President impeached because of appointing too many commissions rather than too few, the reasoning seems unobjectionable and precedent has today served to establish the validity of Mr. Cushing's remarks.[17]

But as long as presidential commissions confine themselves to fact-finding, advice and investigation, and engage in no affirmative executive, legislative or judicial action on their own account, cases cannot arise and the courts cannot interfere with their activities. If the commissions are voluntary, funds are supplied from outside sources, and no federal employees are used, Congress, short of impeachment, can do nothing.

(B) CABINET COMMITTEES

In addition to the inherent power of the President to create commissions to assist him in seeing that the laws are faithfully executed, a second source of power is to be found in the relationship which exists between the President and the heads of the executive departments. Article II, Section II of the Constitution provides that the President "may require the opinion, in writing, of the principal officer in each of the executive departments upon any subject relating to the duties of their respective offices. . . ." Out of this grant of authority has grown the Cabinet—unprovided for in law, and in a sense, a presidential commission since it is created by the President for his own purposes and subject to his control. The fact that the Senate has accorded the President great freedom in the selection of his official family contributes to the control the President has over the Cabinet. The Cabinet is usually thought of as a semi-official advisory body and if it functions at all, it is in the advisory capacity. Occasionally, however, the President delegates fact-finding functions to cabinet officers. In 1933, for example, President Roosevelt asked the Secretaries of State and Labor and the Attorney General to act as members of the *Cabinet Committee to Review the Nationality Laws of the United States*.[18] The draft code submitted by the Cabinet Committee became the basis of the Nationality Act of 1940.[19] The appointment of a Cabinet Committee means of course that the "footwork" will be delegated to subordinates within the respective departments. Furthermore, each of the departments may be assisted by committees set up within the individual department.

Somewhat similar in organization to the Nationality Committee was the *Cabinet Committee to Study Prices* set up by the President in 1934 to study the price policies of various federal agencies.[20]

The shortcomings of this source of power for the creation of presidential commissions are found in the fact that the members of the bodies are government employees and thus act without lay experience, and, secondly, that the committees are so close to the President that despite all efforts to the contrary, their work will be colored by the President's political presence—a danger which confronts all presidential commissions.

(C) COMMISSIONS AS "COMMANDER IN CHIEF"

Another source of power for the creation of presidential commissions is derived from the President's position as "Commander in Chief of the Army and Navy of the United States." [21]

As Commander in Chief, the President is restricted in the purposes for which he can use officers of the armed forces. In general, assignments must pertain to military matters. Congress, for example, has provided that no Army officer on the active list "shall hold any civil office," "have an appointment in the Foreign Service," or "be employed on civil works or internal improvements . . . if it shall interfere with the performance of the military duties proper."[22] Nor can any reserve officer be assigned to active duty except as provided by law.[23] Thus the power which one might expect in the use of army officers by the Commander in Chief is hedged in by restrictions. If officers are to act outside of their military capacity, there must be statutory authority for such special duties.[24] In discussing the President's appointment of Lieutenant Col. Philip B. Fleming of the Army Engineering Corps as "assistant to the Acting Wages and Hours Administrator" without statutory authority and without the consent of the Senate, Professor Corwin says the President took "a totally untenable position."[25] The President did not maintain this position for long. To have done so would "have set a precedent that would enable his successors gradually to replace the whole civil establishment with army officers." There have been other similar instances.[26]

For example, President Coolidge nominated Brigadier General Frank R. McCoy to head a commission to supervise the Nicaraguan presidential elections of 1929.[27] Although the actual appointment was made by the President of Nicaragua, the case illustrates the breadth of the President's power as Commander in Chief to assign officers to duties which may have no close relation with military functions.

Although one may agree with Professor Corwin that the President occupies a "totally untenable position" when he assigns army and navy officers to civilian tasks without statutory authority, the appropriate reaction might well be "so what?" Even if the officer wants to object to such an assignment he is subject to military law and is not in a position to test the constitutionality of the President's order. Congress might try to control the President by cutting military appropriations, but as long as there are armed forces the relationship of officer to Commander in Chief will exist. This constitutional relationship cannot be abridged by an act of Congress and it does not appear that a case might arise whereby the courts could test the President's authority to order officers where he pleases.

The one man in our government who might stand in the way of a President bent on systematic replacement of civilian officers with military officers is the Comptroller-General. By a refusal to authorize salary payments for military officers engaged in civil functions, he might be able to forestall such a move.[28]

Thus far the discussion has been confined to the authority of the Commander in Chief to assign military men to civilian or semi-civilian functions. There seems to be no question of the President's authority to assign military men to commissions for purposes within the regular scope of their activities. Thus the convocation of a Board of Inquiry for the investigation of a naval disaster, although authorized by law, would also appear to be within the scope of the President's authority as Commander in Chief.[29]

Occasionally, however, the President's position as Commander in Chief is used to justify the appointment of civilian commissions. Senators who commented on the appointment of the Morrow Aircraft Board and on the President's authority to investigate the sinking of the submarine the S4, expressed approval of the appointment of civilians to commissions created pursuant to the President's authority as Commander in Chief. "I have no doubt that the Commander in Chief has full authority to make such an investigation as he sees fit," said Senator King.[30] This remark was made with full knowledge that the President contemplated the appointment of civilian members to the commission.

The only qualification of the President's authority as Commander in Chief to appoint civilian members would seem to be that he cannot exercise powers of compulsion over civilian members. If the President's military authority is to be cited the commission should be operating in the military realm.

Other examples of the use of civilians on commissions created pursuant to the President's military authority were the First and Second Philippine Commissions. The activities of these commissions ranged from advice and fact-finding to the enactment of legislation. When a question was raised as to the authority for creating such commissions, Elihu Root, then Secretary of War, answered that an "analysis of the military power" shows that "when exercised in territory under military occupation" it "includes the executive, judicial, and legislative authority." And inferentially, that in the exercise of that power the President might create any commission he wishes.[31]

(D) COMMISSIONS PURSUANT TO "EMERGENCY POWERS"

Just as important a source of presidential authority for the creation of commissions as the power stemming from his position as Commander in Chief, is the undefined yet increased presidential authority which springs into being in time of war or national emergency. The scope of this authority for the creation of commissions cannot be defined. The Supreme Court has said that "extraordinary conditions do not create or enlarge constitutional power."[32] But looking at emergency realistically, if it does not create power, the concept is certainly used to justify acts which in normal times would not be possible. The line of authority for the creation of the War Industries Board of the last war and the Office for Emergency Management of the present war are dim and difficult to trace. Each of the agencies received congressional sanction by indirection.[33] In time of emergency, however, the authority of the President to set up such bodies is not usually questioned, although Senator Taft in 1941 characterized the whole defense organization as "a kind of super-bureaucracy with no relation to the agencies set up by Congress." [34]

That the lines of legal authority sometimes grow dim is indicated by the legal memorandum which counsel for the Office of Price Administration prepared in justification of the agency and its powers. Authority is found, said part of a twenty-one page memorandum, in "the implied constitutional powers of the Chief Executive during a period of emergency, and the obligation of the President 'to take care that the laws be faithfully executed.'. . ." [35]

The President's use of war and emergency powers to create committees for advisory, fact-finding and executive purposes deserves a special study.

(E) AS CHIEF FOREIGN AGENT

A fifth source of presidential authority for the creation of commissions is found in the fact that the President is the chief agent of the United States in the field of foreign relations. Over the years the practice of appointing special agents, individual or as a group, has become accepted practice.[36] Such appointments are made without the advice and consent of the Senate and the expenses of the agents may be paid out of the President's contingent fund. The activities of executive agents in the field of foreign relations may range from secret assignments involving the sending of information to the President,[37] to more formal duties such as the Commission to Russia of 1917 to encourage Russia to remain in the democratic fold.[38]

Executive agents may go forth for fact-finding purposes such as when President Coolidge appointed Henry L. Stimson as special representative to investigate the situation in Nicaragua in 1927.[39] Or they may go forth as personal representatives of the President as in the cases of Colonel House and Harry Hopkins. "Confidants of Presidents," these two men did jobs which the Presidents themselves would have done had they been free. The same may be said of Justice Samuel I. Rosenman, frequently described as President Roosevelt's "fact-finder." [40]

It appears however that agents' activities are not necessarily proscribed by the field of "foreign relations." Agents or commissions may be sent to foreign countries to get facts and figures that may be used as background material for domestic policies. Thus President Hoover sent John J. Leary, former labor editor of the *New York World,* to investigate systems of public employment offices in Europe, and Lee Frankel of the Metropolitan Life Insurance Company to report on foreign systems of social insurance.[41] In 1936 President Roosevelt set up a Committee to Study Cooperatives in Some European Countries, and a Commission on Industrial Relations in Great Britain and Sweden.[42]

It is doubtful if authority for the creation of such commissions can be found in the President's authority in the field of foreign relations. The clearer line of authority would seem to come from the President's duty to recommend for congressional consideration such measures as he deems necessary and expedient.

(F) PURSUANT TO SPECIFIC CONGRESSIONAL GRANT

In the foregoing pages the President's authority to create commissions has been found in constitutional provisions which by implication and by interpretation have been used as authority for creating commissions. By far the largest number of commissions created by the President, however, are those authorized by Congress and appointed by the President. In this study commissions which are created by Congress for its own purposes, the members of which are appointed by the President, are of no particular concern. Thus the Interstate Commerce Commission, the Federal Trade Commission, and similar bodies are not treated as presidential commissions even though the members are appointed by the President. Commissions such as the National Commission on Law Observance and Enforcement for which appropriations were made by Congress at the request of President Hoover, however, are treated as presidential commissions.

The Wickersham Commission was the result of an idea which originated with the executive but before he appointed the commission, congressional consent to its creation in the form of an appropriation was obtained. Taft's Committee on Economy and Efficiency of 1910–1913 was similarly authorized by Congress as a result of a direct request from President Taft.[43] There is no question of the power of the President to create commissions under these circumstances.[44] He is acting under direct authority from Congress. He is also acting under limitations which Congress may impose and is not free to conduct investigations if he must rely on Congress for authority and appropriations. If Congress does not like the results of preliminary reports of such committees, it may cut off further appropriations for them. The preliminary report of the Wickersham Commission, for example, was severely criticized in Congress [45] and the difficulty which President Hoover had in getting additional funds for the commission [46] indicates too clearly how Congress may curtail the activities of a presidential commission if it does not like what the commission is doing. The principal conflict between President Hoover and the opposition in Congress in connection with the Wickersham Commission was with regard to the point of emphasis of the commission's investigation. President Hoover wanted an investigation of law enforcement as a whole. The opposition in Congress wanted an investigation of *prohibition* law enforcement. Both problems needed study. The point to be noted, however, is that when reference is made to the President's power to create commissions as a result of a specific grant of authority and appropriations from Congress, it is no real power because Congressional control is so great.

Although the President may appropriately create a commission with the consent of Congress where there is country-wide support for the investigation, and no strong lobbies in Congress to curtail the investigation, investigations brought about in this method are as much congressional as presidential. A President who is the leader of his party and who has the support of Congress, may get considerable congressional assistance for his commissions, but if a commission created by the President with congressional support were to make findings which reflected upon Congress, one may be sure that its appropriations would be short lived.[47]

(G) PURSUANT TO A GENERAL CONGRESSIONAL GRANT

A seventh source of authority for the creation of commissions by the President is pursuant to a general grant of power by the Congress. President Roosevelt, under the broad powers and extensive appropriations in the recovery and relief statutes of the 1930's was able to create and support numerous presidential commissions. An opinion of the Attorney General has given legal sanction to the appointment of commissions if they are authorized "in a general way by law." [48] The National Industrial Recovery Act contained one of the broadest delegations when it authorized the President "to establish such agencies . . . as he may find necessary" to effectuate the policy of the Act—a delegation broad enough to leave the President virtually unrestrained in the creation of commissions subject to his control.[49]

The commissions set up by the President under this act deserve a special study. They range in character from the Executive Council set up July 11, 1933,[50] to provide an orderly presentation of business to the President, and to coordinate interagency problems, and the National Emergency Council set up on November 17, 1933 [51] to make "more efficient and productive the work of the numerous field agencies of the government established for the purpose of carrying into effect" the National Industrial Recovery Act, to the Committee on Social Security [52] to "study problems relating to the economic security of individuals and to report to the President." [53] While the use of the National Industrial Recovery Act as authority for the creation of commissions ended with the declaration of the act's unconstitutionality, there was still need for a Committee of Industrial Analysis "to complete the summary of results and accomplishments of the National Recovery Administration." [54] This commission itself was the result of a broad delegation of power to the President to expend relief moneys.[55]

The Emergency Relief Appropriation Acts supplied authority for the creation of commissions as widely separated from the relief problem as the President's Committee on Administrative Management [56] and the President's Advisory Committee on Education. Commissions of this type had very little in common with Works Progress Administration projects—other than the same pay check symbols.

Another example of the use of a broad congressional grant for authority to create a presidential commission is found in The Reciprocal Trade Agreements Act of 1934 [57] which provided that the President must give persons interested in presenting their views before the negotiation of an agreement an opportunity to be heard by "such agency as the President may designate." It provided further that "the President shall seek information and advice with respect thereto from . . . such other sources as he may deem appropriate." The Committee for Reciprocity Information, authorized in effect by the first provision quoted above, was set up [58] to grant the hearings required by law. In addition to the Committee specifically authorized, however, the second provision quoted above led to the creation of an Interdepartmental Committee on Trade Agreements which was to be a policy-forming body.[59] And it may be assumed that the broad delegation of power might have been made the basis for the creation of other commercial policy commissions had the President desired. The extent to which a President will go in creating commissions for his own purposes under broad grants of power such as these cited is determined by the boldness of the Chief Executive. An aggressive President may use broad delegations of power and lump sum appropriations as authority for the appointment of almost any commission which he may desire. The only restraint upon the President is a nervous Congress or an obstinate Comptroller-General.

3

METHODS OF APPOINTING AND FINANCING PRESIDENTIAL COMMISSIONS

I. FINANCIAL LIMITATIONS ON PRESIDENTIAL COMMISSIONS

THE existence of any limitations upon the free use of commissions by the President is not a result of a lack of power to create them. The sources of power to create are plentiful. The limitations on the creation of commissions are traceable to lack of money to support them. Much needed investigations or fact-finding may be forestalled by purse string control which is an effective deterrent to the creation of commissions which the President may think necessary.

Section 8 of the Sundry Civil Act of 1909 is the statutory embodiment of congressional financial control of presidential commissions. Passed as a result of President Theodore Roosevelt's liberal creation of commissions, it remains in the statutes today as a warning to the Executive that Congress will not give financial support to commissions unauthorized by law. Section 8 reads:

> No part of the public moneys or of any appropriation made by Congress, shall be used for the payment of compensation or expenses of any commission, council, board, or other similar body, or any members thereof, or for expenses in connection with any work or the results of any work or action of any commission, council, board, or other similar body, unless the creation of the same shall be or shall have been authorized by law, nor shall there be employed by detail, hereafter or heretofore made, or otherwise, personal services from any executive department or other Government establishment in connection with any such commission, council, board, or other similar body.[1]

This provision is the only statutory attempt to interfere with the President's creation of commissions. It gives advance notice that no moneys will be made available except when the commission is congressionally authorized.[2] This epitomizes the purse-string control exercised by Congress over a President whom it feels is exceeding his power. This legislation seeks to prevent the assignment of public officials to work with commissions created by the President. Both purposes were clearly expressed at the time the section was passed. President Roosevelt had created, without congressional authority and in a short period of time, the Inland Waterways Commission, the National Conservation Commission,[3] the Country Life Commission,[4] and the Commission on Public Lands, as well as some less important bodies.[5] All of these commissions were voluntary but much of their personnel was made up of regular government employees. Objection was made that the material gathered "is dumped into the department, and the time of the employees is used for the purpose of working out . . . the information and data thus obtained." Congress refused to appropriate money for the tabulation and organization of information gathered by the Country Life Commission because some Congressmen thought the information was valueless and because others thought the Commission was not legally constituted.[6]

The effects of Section 8 are threefold. In the absence of congressional appropriation, it forces the President to rely on private resources for the support of commissions and in the presence of an appropriation it subjects the Executive to the leverage of a political body; secondly, the President is encouraged to seek methods of legal evasion of the terms of the act; and, finally, the act discourages the creation of presidential commissions which may be badly needed.

Some of the harmful consequences of reliance on private funds have been suggested. The legality of the President's use of private funds was discussed in 1930 when President Hoover requested an appropriation to continue the work of the Wickersham Commission. When the request was rejected by the Senate, Mr. Hoover commented: "I have no doubt that there are private citizens sufficiently anxious for the Nation to know the whole truth . . . that I shall be able to secure from sources the $100,000 necessary to carry this work forward to completion."[7] This statement aroused discussion in Congress where Representative La Guardia charged that such a procedure would violate the law which prevents outside compensation to officers of the government.[8] Representative Celler thought that if the President could use private funds for conducting an investigation, he could use them for any other purpose and Congress might be deprived of its purse string control over the Executive. Senator Wagner expressed the opinion that there was no legal obstacle to prevent the President from going to outside sources for contributions to continue the investigation.[9]

As with many other questions of presidential power, it is difficult to see what could be done to prevent the President from building up a war chest from private contributions for his own investigations if he so desired. Congressional action would have to go to the extreme of impeachment or resort to retaliatory action in other matters—cutting the executive office appropriation, for example.

Almost as basic as the question of the use of private funds for governmental purposes, is the question of the degree of control which Congress should be able to exercise over a presidential commission even when it was originally authorized by Congress. When money is appropriated for a presidential commission, Congress may be parsimonious in the amount appropriated and thus limit the scope of the commission's activities. The Committee on Departmental Methods (the Keep Committee) appointed by President Roosevelt in 1905 was limited in its effectiveness because of congressional penury. In 1906 $25,000 was requested by the President for salaries and compensation of persons outside the government who were working for the commission; $5,000 was made available. Taft's Commission on Economy and Efficiency suffered because of reduced appropriations. During the years of 1912–1913, the President requested $250,000 to continue the Commission, the chairman of the Commission estimated that $500,000 was needed for a good job. The Commission finally received $75,000 and was permitted to employ only three persons at salaries over $4,000 a year.[10] The scope of investigations into the business methods and practice of the executive departments, such as those undertaken by the commissions named above, would seem to be more properly determined by the head of the executive branch of government rather than by Congress, since the President is largely responsible for the efficiency of the executive departments.

The Sundry Civil Act has a tendency to encourage the President to seek ways to evade its strict terms. The Act prevents the President from using employees of the executive departments in connection with any board or commission not authorized by law. The Executive can, however, refer questions to employees of the executive departments when those matters are properly within the scope of their employment, and the employees can operate as a committee if they wish.[11] The Act apparently prevents government employees from rendering services to any board or commission which may exist outside the regular departments unless such services are authorized by act of Congress. This prevents collaboration between lay experts and government employees unless Congress consents, unless the government men contribute their spare time, or unless the collaboration is completely informal. Since the President can bring the lay men, as experts, into the department with which he wants them to work, however, he can circumvent the Act—unless the Comptroller-General sees a violation of its spirit. It has been the experience of some experts called to make special investigations for the President or for other executive officers to find that they could not be called "commissioners," but rather had to be classed as special investigators connected with some particular bureau or department. This is a device for avoiding the prohibition in the Act that public moneys should not be used for the expenses of "any commission, council, etc." unless the creation of the body shall have been authorized by law.[12]

It has been possible to avoid a too stringent application of Section 8 of the Sundry Civil Act by reading into existing laws an implied authority for the creation of a commission. The Attorney General has held that Section 8 "does not require a specific authorization of a commission by a law of the United States; it being sufficient if their appointment is authorized in a general way by law."[13] A board created pursuant to implied authority would be "authorized by law" within the meaning of this section.[14]

One Attorney General has gone so far as to indicate that a provision such as that in the Sundry Civil Act exceeds the power of Congress. Congress has an obligation, according to this view, to meet the expenses incurred by a presidential investigation undertaken pursuant to the executive's duty faithfully to execute the laws.[15] The question is academic, as there is no way of compelling Congress to do its duty—if duty it be.

While there are ways in which Section 8 can be circumvented,[16] it is not a healthy situation to have a statute on the books which calls for circumvention by an executive intent on doing a good job. Unless there is some important reason why presidential commissions should be hamstrung by such an act, it should be repealed. With the Comptroller-General sitting in judgment to see if the moneys appropriated by Congress are spent for the purposes for which they were provided, there would seem to be small likelihood that the President or any of his Cabinet members would run amuck in the creation of commissions unauthorized by law unless Congress itself continues to make broad grants of power to the President. Moreover, the broader question may be raised at this point as to whether the President should have the right to inaugurate investigations on his own without congressional consent evidenced by an appropriation. The repeal of Section 8 would not provide the President with funds to run his own investigations. He might find petty cash which might be used for special presidential commissions and he might find an occasional government employee who could better be put on some job of a research or investigative character. The repeal of Section 8 would not leave the President free to divert large sums for the use of his own commissions and boards, however, nor would it leave him great freedom to switch government employees to projects in which he may be interested.

Failure to repeal the provision means that an aggressive President will stretch the law to meet his needs, or ignore it by getting money from outside sources. The docile President will let this congressional control impair his effectiveness as Chief Executive.

2. TECHNIQUES IN CREATING COMMISSIONS

Distinguished from the *source* of presidential authority for the creation of commissions, are the *methods* which have been used to create them. These methods vary from the formality of an executive order to the informality of a telephone conversation. There is no hard and fast relationship between the source of the authority and the method of creation, though some fairly regular lines are discernible. If the President is exercising an authority directly or indirectly given to him by Congress, the commission is likely to be created by a formal executive order. Thus the Committee on Economic Security was set up by an executive order which cited the broad provisions of the National Industrial Recovery Act as authority for its creation.[17] The National Commission on Law Observance which had been specifically authorized by congressional appropriation [18] was, however, appointed by informal announcement of its membership.[19] If, on the other hand, the authority be that encompassed in the duty of "faithfully executing the laws," the President is likely to eschew formality in the creation of commissions and rely on letters and telephone or personal conversations in the formation of a committee.[20] It is by these informal methods that most presidential commissions are created.

The Library of Congress in a list of Federal Commissions, Committees and Boards compiled in 1929 says in its prefatory note that

A complete list of all the Federal agencies that in any respect resemble a commission and which fall within the period 1901–1929, whether those agencies were created by the legislative branch of the Government, or by the executive branch, is a perhaps unattainable ideal.[21]

A perusal of this list as well as supplementary materials from the Legislative Reference Service of the Library of Congress and the United States Information Office indicates the informality with which many committees are created by the President. Of many the only record is that of a press release announcing the creation of the commission, of others the only record is that of a telephone conversation with the White House. Comparatively few of the commissions under consideration were created by executive orders or formal proclamations. Many of the letters creating commissions do not become available until the report of the commission is published. Even then the letter may not be included and to have any knowledge of when, why, and by what authority some committees are created one must wait for the President's papers to become available. The creation of commissions by the President is not recorded in the Federal Register unless they are set up by executive, administrative, or military order or by proclamation.[22] It is possible that the President could treat their creation as having legal effect and so have letters and notices of their creation published in the Register, but thus far this has not been done.

It is in this informality in setting up presidential commissions that much of the difficulty of studying and evaluating them arises.

Looking at the total problem of the creation of presidential commissions, three points are worthy of note. First, is the haze which surrounds the undoubted authority of the President to create commissions for his own purposes; second, is the lack of a standardized procedure for organizing the commissions; and, third, is the practical limitation on the potential effectiveness of such commissions by reason of congressional purse-string control. Presidential commissions are enveloped in an informal, extra-legal atmosphere. Whether presidential commissions have prospered as a result of this environment, whether they would lose their *raison d'être* if given a more formal niche in our government are problems which, it is hoped, a more complete analysis of their past functions and characteristics will enable us to solve.

4

FACT-FINDING AND OPINION-GUIDING COMMISSIONS

B ROADLY, the functions of presidential commissions may be classified as *informative and administrative.*

Informative commissions—in general—secure pre-policy or pre-legislation facts. They may be organized with definite legislative ends in mind; they may be created for the purpose of spot-lighting some issue and crystallizing public opinion; they may be organized to study some controversial subject and to work out a generally acceptable answer or to reconcile some important clash of interests.

Another type of informative commission is that which is concerned with administrative investigations. This type has been included as a separate category because of its importance and because commissions of this type deal with one subject matter. Only such administrative investigating commissions as are concerned with the overhaul of administration, as distinguished from those concerned with some alleged wrong doing, are included under this classification. Commissions concerned with administrative wrong doing are treated as Boards of Inquiry.

Administrative commissions as the term is used herein are commissions concerned with the execution of policy. The President has created such commissions, first of all to act as agents in the execution of policy; second, to coordinate the execution of policy; third, to advise the President as to how he should act in the execution of some policy; and fourth, to act as troubleshooters, or even as inquisitors, to find out what may have gone wrong in the execution of policy.

This outline is far from definitive. The categories are not mutually exclusive nor are they adequate to take in every presidential commission. In many cases the placing of a commission in one category rather than another has been arbitrary. It is not always clear whether a commission is informative or administrative. It is a poor administrative committee which does not have policy considerations in mind. An administrative advisory commission will often find that it needs to recommend new legislation. A more detailed study with illustrations of each of the above categories will clarify the purposes for which presidential commissions have been created.

INFORMATIVE COMMISSIONS

In these days of complex economic relationships no one should question the wisdom of having facts before action,[1] although it may not always be possible to hold off action until all the facts are known. Commissions, if properly chosen, may supply an inordinate amount of fact drawn from experience and personal knowledge without the time lapse essential to careful research. Former President Hoover has suggested some of the values of commissions: they supply regional and individual experience; they serve to recruit new ideas; they distill the judgment of many minds; they secure agreement from conflicting sources; and they give assurance to the people of the correctness of conclusions of fact upon which action may be based.[2]

When speaking of fact-finding or informative commissions, however, care must be exercised because facts are elusive things and the question of "what is a fact?" is a problem in semantics as well as in philosophy. A "fact" found by a presidential commission is not necessarily, as Webster defines the term, "reality," "actuality," or "truth." Economic, political, or social "facts" are not facts in the same sense as scientific facts. This is because of the unpredictable human element which cannot be precisely determined in "facts" of an economic or political nature. It is a scientific fact that phosphorus exposed to the air will burn. It is predictable. It will burn every time. That is reality, actuality, or truth. Economic or political facts, however, cannot be regarded as true in the same sense; they must be qualified because of the human element. This qualification must always be kept in mind when speaking of fact-finding commissions concerned with political facts.

Despite the difficulty of knowing the degree of truth in political, economic, or social facts, they presumably are the basis of policy determinations in a democracy. In theory at least, policy determinations in a democracy should include the following steps: 1) obtain the facts; 2) make the facts available to the public; 3) discuss, debate and interpret the facts; and 4) decision by the majority will as to the policy to be pursued on the basis of the facts. Presidential commissions as informative or fact-finding bodies are concerned primarily with the first step in this process.

Since some facts may invariably indicate that a certain policy should be pursued, or, to put it differently, since some facts postulate certain action, the economic predilections of the fact-finders are important. They may find the "facts" which they know will demand the course of action to which the fact-finders' economic predilections commit them. Moreover, since facts found by presidential commissions may not necessarily be true in the scientific sense, and capable of proof, the fact-finders may be suspected of finding facts to suit their fancies.

It is undoubtedly true that fact-finders have their prejudices—just as judges do. However, even though almost every presidential appointment to the bench of the Supreme Court is subject to attack by some group opposed to what it believes are the economic predilections of the appointee, it is generally recognized that the Supreme Court may be independent or subservient, strong or weak. The analogy holds for presidential fact-finding commissions. They may be independent or subservient. Their stature as a governmental device depends upon the stature of the fact-finders selected by the President and upon the willingness of the President to make the facts they find available to the public.

Government would probably have kept up with science if the facts of each were capable of the same precise determination and evaluation. Accepting as true the observation that economic, political, and social facts are not as precise as scientific facts, the important problem which remains for democratic government is that of doing the best it can through new or old devices to obtain the political facts.

The success of presidential commissions as fact-finders will depend largely on the President. They will not achieve a reputation as fact-finders if the President requests "an impartial report in favor of" his pet projects, as one President is reported to have done upon occasion. Moreover, the position of the President as a political figure may appear to some to be such that he cannot select impartial fact-finders. The opposite may be the case, however, when one considers that the importance and prominence of the President make it difficult for him to select a body of fact-finders who are obviously unfit for the job either by reason of ability or preconceived ideas about the facts to be found.

It is believed that the following pages which discuss informative commissions will show that presidential commissions offer good possibilities of finding the "true" facts—"facts" as true as it is possible to obtain in the science of government.

(A) INFORMATIVE COMMISSIONS WITH DEFINITE LEGISLATIVE GOALS

In governments based upon the theory of the separation of powers, the job of finding facts which will serve as the basis for particular legislation is in theory, at least, one which should be undertaken by the legislative body.[3]

Actually, however, recent years have seen an increased use of commissions by presidents for this purpose. The executive departments and the President play an increasingly important role not only as originators of legislation, but as fact-finders. Special presidential messages to Congress which recommend legislation carry weight if they are buttressed by facts and figures supplied by a commission of recognized competence. Congress has recognized that some recommendations for legislation should proceed from executive agencies. Thus the Federal Trade Commission Act provides that the Commission shall "make annual and special reports to the Congress and . . . submit therewith recommendations for additional legislation."[4] Similar provisions are found with regard to the Interstate Commerce Commission,[5] the Federal Communications Commission,[6] the Securities and Exchange Commission,[7] and the Civil Aeronautics Authority.[8]

Marshall Dimock, writing on congressional investigating committees in 1929, pointed out that "congress has of recent years increasingly utilized temporary commissions, composed largely of technical experts, to investigate and report concerning some specific problem. . . ."[9] The last decade, however, has found Congress increasingly relying on investigations and reports prepared by presidential commissions.

During the period between March 4, 1929, and January, 1941, there were at least twenty-four committees or similar bodies created by the President to find facts upon which legislative recommendations could be based.[10] In contrast, from September 14, 1901, to March 4, 1929, a period of nearly twenty-eight years, there were only approximately ten such commissions.[11] Thus the last ten years have seen presidential commissions with definite legislative goals in mind created at least six times as frequently as prior to 1930.

These figures are based on commissions which were created without any authorization from Congress. It should be noted that Congress frequently authorizes the President to create commissions which are to report to Congress through the President. Such commissions show a reliance by Congress upon the President for facts, but they are instances where Congress determines the policy, i. e. that facts are needed, and imposes upon the Chief Executive the duty of getting those facts.[12] Commissions appointed by the President pursuant to congressional resolution will not be treated as presidential commissions *unless* the congressional authorization resulted from the insistence of the President.[13]

Ordinarily when the President appoints a commission to make a study which he hopes will lead to specific legislation, the job of promoting the forthcoming legislative proposal falls to the Executive. But occasionally Congress will approve of the activities of the commission and proceed to act as though the body had been congressionally authorized in the first instance. The Committee on the Conservation and Administration of the Public Domain is an example of a body appointed by the President in 1929 "to study the whole question of the public domain particularly the unreserved lands" [14] and whose report was transmitted to Congress at its request.[15] Until recent years, however, the reports of presidential commissions with legislative ends in mind have been more prone to gather dust than to serve as bases for legislation.

President Franklin D. Roosevelt was more successful in presenting and procuring the adoption of presidential proposals for legislation than his predecessors. At a time when Congress needed leadership in formulating legislation, the President supplied it.

A good example of a successful presidential commission with definite legislative ends in mind was the Committee on Economic Security.[16] This committee composed of government officials was appointed in 1934 pursuant to the general grant of power given the President in the National Industrial Recovery Act. It was instructed "to draw up a comprehensive program which will give protection to the individual from all the vicissitudes and hazards of modern life." [17]

The general way in which the Committee and the President proceeded to bring the desired legislation to the attention of Congress is well indicated in the following excerpt from the President's message of January 17, 1935, submitting the report of the Committee to Congress.

> In my annual message to you I promised to submit a definite program of action. This I do in the form of a report to me by a Committee on Economic Security, appointed by me for the purpose of surveying the field and of recommending the basis of legislation.
>
> I am gratified with the work of this Committee and of those who have helped it: the Technical Board on Economic Security drawn from various departments of the Government, the Advisory Council on Economic Security, consisting of informed and public-spirited private citizens and a number of other advisory groups. . . . All of those who participated in this notable task of planning this major legislative proposal are ready and willing, at any time, to consult with and assist in any way the appropriate Congressional committees and members, with respect to detailed aspects.[18]

The remarkable thing about this document is the way in which it shows the initiative taken by the President even though Congress was in a mood to adopt social security legislation. "I promised a program of action," "I appointed a Committee," "I thank the Committee." Submitting this "major legislative proposal," the administrative experts "are ready and willing . . . to consult with and assist . . . Congressional committees . . . with respect to detailed aspects." The Committee ceased to function when the President signed the Social Security Act [19] although it was revived on August 31, 1939, by a letter from the President to the Secretary of Labor.

It is small wonder that the public accepted the social program of the 1930's as Roosevelt's program, and not the work of Congress.

There have been other commissions that have done the same job preliminary to legislation.

The National Power Policy Commission created by letter from the President to the Secretary of Interior on July 5, 1934, and including membership from other government departments is of particular interest because according to the system of functional classification followed herein, it does not clearly fall within commissions with definite legislative goals or within the category of those serving spotlight or opinion-guiding purposes. It has been included as a fact-finding committee concerned with specific legislative policy because that is the first purpose for the creation of the committee as mentioned in the President's letter of creation. The Committee was to "consider what lines should be followed in" shaping legislation on the subject of holding companies.[20] Later in the letter, the President remarked: "The committee is to be advisory to the President." And still later, when the President's papers were edited, the purpose of the committee was described as that of coordinating "the Administration's policy with respect to the development of electric power for the benefit of domestic, rural, commercial and industrial consumers." In fact, the first report of the committee dealt with public utility holding companies and played a large part in the enactment of the Public Utility Holding Company Act of 1935.[21]

Another committee set up in a similar manner, i. e. by a letter to Chairman Ickes and to the other members of the official family, and which found facts which served as a basis for legislation, was the Committee to Recommend Legislation for the Bonneville and Other Power Projects of January 18, 1937.[22] This was an "informal" committee of men generally "familiar with the subject" to report in "a couple of weeks" on a "national power generating, transmitting and distributing policy" which would serve to supply uniformity in treatment of power developed at various government projects. When the recommendations were made they were transmitted to Congress [23] and in substance were enacted into law.[24] The National Power Policy Committee which today operates within the Department of Interior is a successor to the two bodies just described as well as to the National Defense Power Committee.[25]

A series of presidential commissions was created to deal with conditions arising out of the drought of 1935–1936. While touring the drought areas in the summer of 1936, President Roosevelt appointed the Great Plains Drought Area Committee "to carry on a study looking toward the most efficient utilization of the natural resources of the Great Plains Area" and to report to the President.[26] The preliminary report of this Committee recommended further detailed studies to determine what new federal legislation might be necessary to deal with the situation.[27] To help bring the general suggestions of the Great Plains Drought Area Committee to legislative fruition, the President appointed two new committees.

The first of these, the Crop Insurance Committee, made up of government officials was appointed September 19, 1936, in a letter from the President to the Secretary of Agriculture. The Committee was directed "to prepare a report and recommendations for legislation providing a plan of 'all risk' crop insurance." Final recommendations for legislation were to be formulated with the advice and assistance of national farm organization leaders so that the plans could be submitted to Congress with the approval and support of the representatives of the farmers.[28] The report of the Committee was transmitted to Congress with a presidential message on February 17, 1937.[29] The presidential message noted that the report "provides an adequate basis for legislation" and significantly "that because economic and social reforms of this character are essentially national in scope and in administration, the citizens of our nation believe that our form of government was never intended to prohibit their accomplishment." In February of 1938 an act providing for crop insurance was passed.[30]

At the same time as the creation of the Crop Insurance Committee, the President created another committee headed by Morris L. Cooke, Administrator of the Rural Electrification Administration, made up of government officials, the Committee to Recommend a Long Term Program for the Utilization of the Resources of the Great Plains Area, or more briefly, the Great Plains Committee. The committee was instructed to report to the President within three and one-half months "on a long term program for the efficient utilization of the resources of the Great Plains area," and "to include such recommendations for legislation" as may be deemed necessary.[31]

The report of the Great Plains Committee was transmitted to Congress in February, 1937.[32] Although the President felt as of May, 1941, that Congress had taken no specific action on the basis of the report,[33] it seems clear that the studies and the resulting report served at least as background material for the Conservation Act of 1937.[34] One need not be unduly critical of the legislative results, however, as the whole problem of the Great Plains Area is not susceptible of treatment by one legislative act. The recommendations of the Committee were general and the presidential message on the matter lacked the decisiveness and clarity so necessary to induce legislation.

The Special Committee on Farm Tenancy created by presidential letter to the Secretary of Agriculture, November 17, 1936 [35] represents a slightly different type of treatment of a problem similar to those of crop insurance and long range planning for the Great Plains area. In the letter of creation the President did not refer directly to the necessity of recommendations for remedial legislation, though such an inference can be drawn from the fact that he asked the Committee to report within less than two and one-half months. This Committee was made up jointly of governmental officials and lay experts who had "both an extensive knowledge of the problem and a sympathetic interest in its solution" and so in composition differed from the Great Plains Committee whose membership consisted of government officials. The President suggested that the Committee consult with Senator John H. Bankhead and Representative Marvin Jones who had been working on the problem.[36] The creation of this Committee by the President and the transmittal of its report to Congress on February 16, 1937,[37] did create, as the President wrote in his Papers: "widespread public interest in farm tenancy and in related problems." [38] The report was quoted in Congressional debate [39] and though it may be somewhat presumptuous to claim that "as a result of my (President Roosevelt's) message . . . legislation was passed to aid tenant farmers," there is no doubt but that the Bankhead-Jones Farm Tenant Act of 1937 [40] owes its existence in part, at least, to the work of the President's Committee. One other presidential commission may be briefly described although its activities did not lead as directly to legislation as the action of the foregoing committees and although it might with considerable reason be classified as a "mediation" commission.

The President's Committee to Submit Recommendations Upon the General Transportation Situation, or the Committee of Six, was appointed by the President on September 20, 1938 following a White House conference concerned with a proposed 15% wage reduction for railroad employees. The Committee of Six, equally divided between employer and employee representatives, was described by the President as an "informal committee to discuss the general problem of transportation with a view of bringing out a sufficiently broad plan that would be placed before Congress and the nation for study and possible adoption." [41] The Report rendered on December 23, 1938 recommended that subsidies to competitors of the railroads be curtailed, that there be tolls levied on the use of waterways, and that the taxes of railways be decreased.[42] The Report of this Committee was submitted to Congress by the President without comment. The Wheeler-Lea bill which was subsequently passed by Congress is in part based upon this report.[43] The *New York Times* attributed the origin of the bill to this Committee, but such an interpretation appears to be subject to question.[44] The Wheeler-Lea bill provides, among other things, that water carriers are to be brought under the regulation of the Interstate Commerce Commission so that the Committee's desire for equality of treatment of water and rail carriers is now more susceptible of achievement.

The President's appointment of the Committee of Six is interesting because it represents only one of a number of studies in the transportation field, all designed to do something in a legislative way for (or to) the railroads.

A very great deal of lack of coordination is evident when one looks at the transportation problem since 1933. President Roosevelt, in a letter of June 16, 1933 to the Secretary of Commerce, had appointed a Transportation Legislation Committee which functioned from the passage of the Emergency Railroad Transportation Act of 1933 until Coordinator Eastman was appointed.[45] During the period when Eastman was making his studies, Senator Wheeler was conducting his investigation of the transportation situation.

In early 1938 President Roosevelt asked Commissioners Splawn, Eastman, and Mahaffie "to present, somewhat hurriedly and informally, recommendations" dealing with the financial emergency faced by the railroads. The report of these commissioners accompanied by comments from eight other individuals or groups with whom the President had talked was sent to Congress on April 11, 1938 with a presidential message.[46] Several of the recommendations of this Committee were embodied in the Transportation Act of 1940 or made effective by existing governmental agencies.[47]

Next the Committee of Six was appointed, and finally on April 10, 1940, the President appointed Owen D. Young "to head a committee to make a long-range study of the nation's transportation problem." This body was to carry on the studies begun by Mr. Eastman as Federal Coordinator of Transportation.[48]

The presidential commissions which have thus far been considered as commissions created with definite legislative goals in mind have run almost the entire gamut of the important economic problems of the 1930's. Dealing with economic security, aspects of the farm problem, government ownership and operation of utilities, and the transportation problem, they illustrate rather well the role played by presidential commissions in the formulation of legislation. But these are the more formal commissions which have been created. Other committees of an interdepartmental character have been appointed to prepare legislation for submission to Congress.

An Interdepartmental Committee Re Federal Communications made a study of Federal communications and its findings were instrumental in the establishment of the Federal Communications Commission. The Committee was established by the Secretary of Commerce at the request of the President in the latter part of 1933 and made up of members invited to serve by the Secretary. The Report of the commission was transmitted to Congress.[49]

The Interdepartmental Committee on Civil Aviation Legislation and Regulations was similar in character to the above commission. A White House statement of February 2, 1934, approved a suggestion made by the Secretary of Commerce that a study be made which "would seek to ascertain to what extent coordination may be effected and greater efficiency attained in promoting and fostering aviation for military, commercial, air mail and private flying purposes." [50] In late 1937 the Committee was created by a letter from the President to Secretary Roper. Its purpose was to consider and to formulate a long-range civil aviation policy and program and to study all aviation legislation introduced at the 75th Congress. The report of this committee included a proposed bill which was introduced by Congressman Lea, Chairman of the House Interstate and Foreign Commerce Committee.[51] A similar bill was enacted into law as a part of the Civil Aeronautics Act of 1938 which set up the Civil Aeronautics Authority.[52]

There may be some question in the minds of strict constructionists as to whether the Executive should appoint commissions to find facts and recommend legislation. Objection cannot be so easily made to presidential recommendations when the legislation concerns some aspect of foreign affairs. The Cabinet Committee to Review the Nationality Laws of the United States, discussed heretofore, was instructed to review and recommend revisions in the nationality laws of the United States and to codify those laws into one comprehensive nationality law for submission to Congress. The report and the draft legislation transmitted by the President to Congress, served as the basis of the Nationality Act of 1940.

Another committee dealing with international affairs was the Interdepartmental Committee on Civil International Aviation created by the President on June 20, 1935. The President instructed the Secretary of State, the Secretary of the Treasury, the Postmaster General, and the Secretary of Commerce each to designate an official to serve on the committee. The Committee was instructed to make observations and to gather information pertaining to civil international aviation in all its phases and to submit such recommendations to the President as might seem to be called for. The Committee was disbanded on June 23, 1938 with the creation of the Civil Aeronautics Authority.

The Interdepartmental Board on the Great Lakes Project illustrates the use of a commission to find facts which were used by the President in an effort to get the consent of the Senate to the ratification of a treaty. Appointed by the President on September 14, 1933, the Board was instructed to investigate and to report on the economic and navigational aspects of the project. The chairman of the Board was Frank R. McNinch of the Federal Power Commission. The Board included representatives from the Departments of War, Commerce, and Agriculture, the Interstate Commerce Commission, and the New York Power Authority. President Roosevelt had long been interested in the St. Lawrence development and following the defeat of a congressional joint resolution which would have provided funds for part of the project, the President concluded that opponents of the St. Lawrence treaty "were going to stress the need for a comprehensive economic survey of the proposed undertaking." "I therefore decided," he wrote, "that I would have such a survey ready to be used in connection with the formal submission of the treaty to the Senate." [53] When the report of the Interdepartmental Board was rendered on January 10, 1934, it was summarized and sent to the Senate along with the Presidential message requesting the consent of the Senate to the ratification of the treaty which had been signed with Canada. While the proposed treaty was defeated by the Senate on March 14, 1934, the President's efforts to promote the project did not cease.[54]

In November, 1939 the St. Lawrence Waterway Survey was established as a result of informal discussions between the President and the Secretary of Commerce. The survey was created for the purpose of making a study and rendering a report on the economic advantages of establishing deep water transportation facilities between the Great Lakes and the sea port of Montreal. Allotments for the survey were made directly to the Department of Commerce.

The use of a commission to find facts to support the signing of the St. Lawrence Treaty was only one of many devices used by the President to obtain congressional consent for the project. This was one of President Roosevelt's most persistent efforts to get legislation. A detailed study of the pressures involved preliminary to undertaking this project might well be approached from the viewpoint of presidential pressure politics and the commissions which were established by the President might with justification be called "political commissions" rather than "legislative commissions." [55]

It should not be inferred from the committees described above that the use of committees by the President to secure facts for legislation which he wishes to recommend is a recent development. Indeed, looking back some years, one finds such important bodies as the Keep Committee and Taft's Commission on Economy and Efficiency which clearly had legislative ends in mind and achieved legislative results.

Two not so well-known presidential commissions appointed by President Theodore Roosevelt which had legislative goals in mind are described below.

In 1906 public complaint led to the appointment by the President of a Special Committee to Investigate the Conditions in the Stockyards of Chicago. A preliminary study by the Bureau of Animal Industry convinced the President that a more thorough investigation by men not connected with the Department of Agriculture was advisable. James Bronson Reynolds and Charles P. Neill, conducted a two and one-half week study and rendered a preliminary report which the President sent to Congress. The substance of the report's recommendation was that laws providing for federal inspection of meat food products entering into interstate commerce should be enacted.[56] Although it was not until 1921 that an effective Packer and Stockyards Act was passed [57] this presidential commission laid another faggot on the fire which finally produced enough heat to get congressional action.

Following two marine disasters in the early twentieth century, both of which were investigated by presidential commissions,[58] President Theodore Roosevelt created by Executive Order of May 12, 1908 a Commission on Revision of Laws Relating to Safety of Life at Sea.[59] The Commission consisting of five federal officers representing departments or bureaus concerned with marine problems was instructed "to examine the laws of the United States for the better security of the lives of passengers and crews with a view to their revisions, and to recommend to the President such changes as in their judgment the public interests seem to require." The report submitted in early 1909 by the Commission contained a draft bill providing for a Marine Inspection Service. The President commended to Congress the "systematic rearrangement and codification of existing law, together with such changes and amendments as past experience and consideration of present-day conditions seem to require." [60] Apparently no part of this draft was enacted into law.[61]

The most important fact revealed by this brief survey of presidential commissions with legislative purposes is their increased use in recent years, and the frequency with which their reports have been accepted by Congress as the basis for legislation.

There is little doubt that for some types of legislation the facts found by a presidential commission will be more complete and reliable than those found by a congressional body. Thus, if the prospective legislation concerns the operation of some of the executive departments, the executive is in a better position to supply information as to the needs of the departments—subject always to the scrutiny of Congress. The suggestion that Congress is perhaps not always the most efficient fact-finder is not new. Nelson McGeary has suggested that congressional investigations of a research character might be delegated to bodies outside of Congress.[62] One reason given by Dr. McGeary is that "legislators simply have too much to do." Another is that delegation may be good because "much can be said in favor of having the investigators detached from the body which is responsible for the inquiry and for the action resulting from the inquiry." Furthermore, congressional investigations are subject to electoral interruptions. And finally, research may be more efficient if the job is delegated to an agency which already has a staff or the nucleus for a staff.[63]

The principal danger in having presidential commissions find the facts upon which legislation may be based is that the reports of presidential commissions are not as likely to be accepted as the basis for legislation as are the reports prepared by congressional committees. Moreover, if the President is too insistent on having Congress follow the recommendations of a presidential commission, questions of congressional prerogative may overshadow the merits of the case.

The almost about-face in thinking which took place in the 1930's with regard to Congress as the originator of legislative fact-finding, is indicated by Roosevelt's statement during the banking crisis of 1933, with reference to his concept of the part the President should play in securing legislation. Commenting on emergency legislation and the necessity for a permanent program, the President suggested that perhaps "Congress should recess for I don't know how long a time but not for very long—for a matter of two or three weeks—to enable me to work out and draft more permanent legislation. . . ."[64] Apparently in 1933 no one thought this suggestion presumptuous.

It is suggested that the increased acceptance of responsibility by the President for legislation gives our government one of the characteristics of cabinet government. If the public and Congress expect executive leadership in the field of legislation, responsibility can more easily be fixed.

"We are unanimous in believing that the appointment of Royal Commissions is useful for the elucidation of difficult subjects which are attracting public attention but in regard to which information is not sufficiently accurate to form a preliminary to legislation." [65] Thus concluded a British Interdepartmental Committee whose Report suggests the second main purpose for which presidential commissions have been created; i. e. to engage in research which will serve to "spotlight" public opinion and to crystallize it.

The only difference between this type of commission and the "legislative commissions" previously treated is one of degree. Both are fact-finding and concerned with emerging legislative policy. These "spotlight" or "opinion-guiding" commissions, however, are only secondarily concerned with legislation. Their primary purpose is to lay the ground work in public discussion, to prepare the way for legislation which may later follow. [66] They are concerned with finding the facts merely for the sake of making the facts available to the public. The facts which they find may or may not suggest legislation. The primary purpose of legislative committees, on the other hand, is to find facts which serve to support particular legislation.

The drought committees described above illustrate the distinction. The first committee, the Drought Area Committee, had as its principal purpose the finding of facts which would bring the problem of the drought areas to the public's attention and crystallize opinion along the lines that something ought to be done. The Great Plains Committee and the Crop Insurance Committee concretely outlined what could and should be done. The two jobs might have been combined but, if time permits, it is probably better to use two steps: first, to show the public and Congress that there is a problem needing to be solved, and second, to show how the problem may be solved by offering a legislative solution. In these opinion-guiding commissions one finds the greatest similarity to British royal commissions. While British commissions are by no means limited to this narrow scope, their fame as a governmental device rests largely on their success in focusing public attention on problems of importance to the nation. In this function the American counterpart falls short.

In the past forty years, the most outstanding commissions in the United States whose principal functions were to focus public attention were the National Conservation Commission (1908), the Country Life Commission (1908), the Commission on Industrial Relations (1912), the Research Committee on Social Trends (1929), the National Commission on Law Observance and Enforcement (1929), and the Temporary National Economic Committee (1938). Three of these bodies were authorized by Congress and are included here as presidential commissions because the authorization came as a result of the request of the President.

The National Conservation Commission was one of a series of bodies created to deal with conservation. In March, 1907, President Roosevelt created the Inland Waterways Commission in response to numerous requests that a plan be devised for the river systems of the United States.[67] Headed by Congressman Theodore E. Burton and including five experts from the executive departments as well as two representatives and two senators, and operating without funds, this commission made a preliminary study and report which emphasized that the problem of dealing with inland waterways was intimately connected with conservation as a whole. Subsequently a Conference of Governors was called to meet with these experts and congressional representatives at the White House.[68] The Conference agreed that conservation was important and recommended the appointment of state commissioners of conservation.

President Theodore Roosevelt supplemented the work of the Conference by the appointment of the National Conservation Commission on June 8, 1908. In a letter to members, the President described his duty "to lay before the Federal Congress information as to the state of the Union in relation to the natural resources, and to recommend . . . measures" and ask that the Commission "inquire into and advise me as to the condition of our natural resources." [69] The assistance of the executive departments was made available to the Commission by executive order.[70] Membership of the Commission included senators, representatives, public officials, college professors, engineers, and other prominent persons.[71] The Commission held numerous meetings and arranged a Joint Conservation Congress which was attended by representatives of twenty-six state conservation commissions. The body operated wholly without funds and when early in 1909 the President transmitted the three volume report to Congress, asking for $50,000, he was accommodated not by an appropriation, but by an amendment to the Sundry Civil Act which denied him any funds and also sought to prevent the appointment in the future of such "unauthorized" commissions.

The value of the Conservation Commission is not found in specific legislation resulting from its studies; but rather in the part the Commission played in making the nation conservation conscious.

Many of the same difficulties in organizing and obtaining support were encountered by Roosevelt's Country Life Commission. Appointed by President

Theodore Roosevelt in a letter of August 10, 1908, the Commission, of which Professor L. H. Bailey was chairman, was asked to report on the means which are "now available for supplying the deficiencies which exist" in the country life of the United States. "My immediate purpose," wrote the President, "in appointing this commission is to secure from it such information and advice as will enable me to make recommendations to Congress." [72] The Commission was made up of lay experts who received no compensation for their services. They conducted some thirty public hearings and tabulated 120,000 answers to printed questionnaires. Their conclusions were of a general character. They encouraged extension work, proposed an inquiry into the use and control of streams, urged an investigation of the place of the middleman in our system, and suggested more financial assistance for the construction of highways to serve the farm population. They also recommended the adoption of a parcel post system and the inauguration of postal savings. The President asked Congress for an appropriation of $25,000 to enable the Commission "to digest the material it has collected," but the House refused to grant an appropriation on the ground first, that the information was worthless and second, that the Commission was illegally constituted.[73]

The difficulties encountered by President Theodore Roosevelt as a result of his liberal interpretation of "commission making" powers had a salutary effect on his successors.[74] President Taft receded from the prerogative theory of presidential powers and created commissions only when given authority and money by Congress.[75] Presidents Wilson, Harding and Coolidge eschewed the creation of commissions for opinion-guiding purposes and not until President Hoover's Research Committee on Social Trends do we find another important commission of this type created without congressional authorization. But in the interim two rather important presidential commissions were authorized by Congress upon the request of the President.

President Taft suggested in a message to Congress of February 2, 1912, that a Commission on Industrial Relations be authorized. The time was ripe, he thought, for a "searching inquiry into the subject of industrial relations." "One legitimate object of such an official investigation and report is to enlighten and inform public opinion, which of itself will often induce or compel the reform of unjust conditions. . . ." [76] A commission of nine was authorized to be appointed by the President with the advice and consent of the Senate and to include three employers and three representatives of labor.[77]

The membership was selected by President Wilson, Taft's nominees having failed of confirmation.

Congress made annual appropriations for the Industrial Commission [78] totaling $450,000, but supporters of the Commission continually faced a hostile barrage of questions when the matter of appropriations came up.[79]

The Report of the Commission on Industrial Relations as finally submitted was an excellent espousal of the points of view of labor and capital. There was no agreement, however, as to the causes of industrial unrest.[80] The Report of the Commission was printed and 100,000 copies were made available for distribution.[81] Aside from providing material for debating societies and scholars, however, it is doubtful if the Report had much effect. Mr. Jacobson concludes that the commission "was a convenient way of referring and delaying a matter on which it was hard and perhaps unwise, to lay down a general public policy.[82]

The second important commission of the opinion-guiding variety authorized by Congress at the instigation of the President during this period was the National Commission on Law Observance and Enforcement, better known as the Wickersham Commission.[83] The question to which an answer was sought was: to what extent, if any, prohibition was the cause of the alarming increase in criminal activity.[84] If the Commission, the President, the public, and Congress had agreed on the problem as set forth, the classification of this commission would be simple. But the fact that the commission was promised by candidate Hoover during the course of a political campaign, apparently as an attempt to corral both the wet and the dry vote [85] and the fact that prohibition was called an experiment noble in purpose by the candidate, created a reasonable doubt as to the bona fide quality of the fact-finding purpose.[86] This is not meant as a reflection on the membership of the Commission. Individually, they were above reproach. The membership consisted of eleven distinguished laymen [87] who concentrated not only on the problem of prohibition but also considered the whole problem of criminal law enforcement in the United States. Principal public attention was concentrated on the prohibition report. When the report was issued, the public was more befuddled than ever. President Hoover concluded that the Commission did not favor repeal. As far as the Commission itself was concerned, however, six out of the eleven members felt that there should be outright repeal or at least revision.[88] The Commission, so far as its prohibition report was concerned, was an unmitigated failure.[89]

The failure of the Wickersham Commission was a blow to the entire presidential commission idea. Its failure to agree in any material degree to a solution, the eleven different opinions in the report, the suspicion that the President had tampered with the results, the fact that the Commission had its genesis in the need for some political tight-rope walking, and finally the feeling that the report could be used to evade the repeal issue in 1932 [90]—all contributed to the disrepute of this presidential commission.

The failure of the Wickersham Commission as a presidential commission was not due to its membership and the quality of its work, but was due rather to the nature of the issue by which the members were confronted and to the fact that the President did not keep his hands off the Commission. In 1931 prohibition was an issue on the emotional level, not the intellectual.

Not so closely associated with the President as the Wickersham and Industrial Relations Commissions was the Temporary National Economic Committee.[91] In a message to Congress on April 29, 1938 President Roosevelt suggested a "thorough study of the concentration of economic power in American industry and the effect of that concentration upon the decline of competition." [92] In response to the message, Congress authorized the creation of a joint legislative-executive committee, the members of which were selected as follows: three from the Senate, three from the House, and six from executive departments or agencies as designated by their respective heads.[93] Membership thus was equally divided between the executive and legislative branches of government. The composition of the Committee was imposing, its hearings lengthy, its reports comprehensive (32 volumes of hearings, 44 monographs), but as to its value there may well be question.[94] More than 230,000 copies of its monographs and hearings have been circulated, and, according to the Superintendent of Documents, these reports lead all other government publications in sales.[95] Its reports are on reserve shelves in college libraries.[96] Some few of its recommendations have been enacted into legislation.[97]

How much of the information gathered by a committee such as this becomes consciously or unconsciously available to the voting public, is a matter for guess work. The purpose of opinion-guiding commissions, broadly conceived, is to educate the mass, to give the source of power in the democratic state the information on which to base its decisions. Within these volumes, ventured Senator O'Mahoney, "is to be found the substance of the reorganization for peace and democracy which must come after the war"; these volumes may well present "the last challenge for the establishment of an economic system which will protect the enterprise of the individual." [98]

One other important commission of this type created by the President upon his own authority was the President's Research Committee on Social Trends.[99] In announcing the creation of this expert lay body, President Hoover outlined the purpose as that of conducting "An extensive survey into the significant social changes in our national life over recent years. . . ." "The survey," he said, "will be a strictly scientific research, carried out by trained technicians. . . . It is believed that it will produce a body of systematic fact about social problems, hitherto inaccessible, that will be of fundamental and permanent value to all students and workers in the field of social science." [100] The funds were supplied by the Rockefeller Foundation and the report made available in book form by McGraw-Hill.[101] Much preliminary work was done by the Social Science Research Council.[102] When the report was given to the public in 1933, President Hoover remarked in the foreword that the "revolutionary" emphasis of the report was perhaps to be expected since the Committee had concentrated on the elements of instability.[103] He approved of the "scientific mood and . . . method, as correctives to undiscriminating emotional approach . . . in seeking for constructive remedies of great social problems" and approved also dealing with social problems as a whole.[104] President Hoover, however, seemed much more devoted to the appointment of expert commissions to find facts than disposed to accept those facts as basis for his own action. The Report of the Research Committee on Social Trends more nearly suggests a New Deal primer than a "scientific" guide for Mr. Hoover's social policies.

As such a "primer" the Report has undoubtedly had a wide influence in awakening the American people to the potentialities of their industrialized civilization.[105] The fact that the study was made under the auspices of the President may have impressed some uncritical readers. But so far as this Committee was to be a research device for turning up new facts, its advantage over a privately inaugurated study of the same scope is not apparent.

Several minor fact-finding commissions with the opinion-guiding purpose were created by President Franklin D. Roosevelt—though, in general, he was his own salesman of ideas as well as legislation. Illustrative are the Committee to Study Cooperative Enterprise in Europe (1936) [106] and the President's Commission on Industrial Relations in Great Britain and Sweden (1938).[107]

Both bodies were appointed without citation of statutory authority for their creation, apparently subsisted on funds made available through relief appropriations, and, except for one government employee consisted of private citizens. The two commissions made studies of the experiences of other countries with respect to cooperative and industrial relations. It was the hope of the President that the information thus gained would be "unbiased and authoritative" and serve to point the way toward American treatment of the same problems. The Committee to Study Cooperatives presented a report which was for the most part descriptive. Each of the members added his own comments on what he believed cooperative enterprise meant to America, in order that the one reading the report might have a "balanced and many-sided view that will help him in making up his own mind as to the place cooperative enterprise may fill in America." [108]

The Commission on Industrial Relations rendered unanimous reports on conditions in Great Britain and Sweden.[109] The reports established the fact, thought the Chief Executive, that "drastic legislative restriction on trade unions" was not desirable, and they seemed to promote public acceptance of the "efficacy of voluntary collective labor agreements as the basis of satisfactory and peaceful industrial relations." [110]

The effects of such reports are hard to estimate. The criterion of the successful opinion guiding commission is not whether legislation results; that is not the purpose. Success is measured by public awareness of the conclusions reached and stimulation which is traceable to the fact that the material was available.

President Hoover, faced by economic problems of an unprecedented character, resorted to committees and conferences to deal with problems which might better have been handled by specific legislative proposals—had his philosophy permitted it. A study of his commissions and the action taken on the basis of their findings, leads one to conclude, however, that many commissions were created only for the purpose of "showing activity" until such time as the "natural phenomenon" of the depression had run its course. President Hoover's activities in fighting the depression ranged from coordinating the publication of statements designed to bring a return of confidence [111] to the appointment of competent research bodies such as the Research Committee on Social Trends.

Early in the depression President Hoover announced the convening of a series of conferences of representatives of business and governmental agencies for the purpose of taking action which would maintain business progress.[112] This was not Mr. Hoover's first experience in combating depression by mobilizing the business interests which he thought were capable of action on their own. From September 26 to October 13, 1921, Mr. Hoover served as chairman of the President's Conference on Unemployment.[113] An outgrowth of the 1929 conferences was the National Business Survey Congress, called at the direction of President Hoover for December 5, 1929 for the purpose of suggesting means for the maintenance of wages and construction during the business depression.[114] Subsequently the President organized an Emergency Committee for Employment directed by Col. Arthur Woods and made up of Cabinet members "to submit plans continuing and strengthening the organization of Federal activities for employment during the winter." [115]

This Emergency Committee for Employment was not clearly a legislation committee as that designation has been used herein, since it was to advise the President on "plans continuing and strengthening the organization of Federal activities for employment during the winter." [116] Nor was it fact-finding or "spotlight" in character since it made no report to the public. In fact, President Hoover told the Senate that information and advice rendered by the Committee "represent that confidential relation of the President with Government officers which should be preserved." [117] It is difficult to see why any facts gathered by this Committee on a problem so important to the public should have been kept secret. Admittedly there may be times and situations where the President must ask that his recommendations be followed without query as to the information on which he bases his proposals. But secrecy as to the facts which back up unemployment relief proposals creates too much suspicion of a presidential plan imposed by one man's interpretation of the remedies called for by the facts.[118] The Emergency Committee was later succeeded by the President's Organization on Unemployment Relief, established August 19, 1931, of which Walter S. Gifford was chairman. The purpose of this body was "to cooperate with the public authorities and to mobilize the national, state and local agencies of every kind which will have charge of the activities arising out of unemployment in various parts of the Nation this winter." [119] A year later in requesting a special appropriation to continue the work of this organization, President Hoover described the body as "the only agency for national coordination and stimulation for the multitude of voluntary efforts and a clearing house for these thousands of organizations with suggestions and methods for the alleviation of unemployment distress. . . ." [120]

While the reports of these committees never directly became the basis of legislation, they did create the impression that the President was "doing something" about unemployment and business conditions. These bodies of course may be viewed as advisory in character as they undoubtedly were, but they also had the effect of focusing public attention on the problems. Moreover, they were bodies made up of men who themselves had power to act. It is possible that had business men as a group organized and carried out a concerted attack on the depression, government would not have found it necessary to extend its resources and impose its controls to the degree that was necessary in the 1930's.

It has been charged that many of the commissions appointed by Hoover were "political" in character, meaning that they were devices for avoiding taking a stand on controversial issues. There were numerous demands on the federal treasury for assistance to localities in meeting the problems arising out of unemployment. If one were convinced that the problem should be met locally, one device for leaving the problem in local hands without slamming the door of the federal treasury in the face of the applicants would be to appoint a committee to consider the problem. Prolonged committee consideration might put off federal doles until the "cyclical" business depression was again on its way up.[121]

The Citizens' Reconstruction Corporation organized by President Hoover Feb. 6, 1932 is an example of the use of the committee device to focus public attention on a problem without seeking any legislative action to solve it. It is also illustrative of an attempt to mobilize the strength of the "power-holding" classes to the end that they can accomplish reconstruction by their own power. In early February, 1932, President Hoover, in a press statement, appealed to citizens to stop hoarding money and said that he was "calling upon the heads of the leading civic organizations to meet with me . . . for the creation of a national organization" to prevent hoarding.[122] Colonel Frank Knox acted as chairman of the organization which exercised no coercive powers. It was nothing more nor less than a board of "shirt-fronts" designed to give authority to the claim that banks were safe, business was on the upswing, and money could again be safely invested. In March the President in a broadcast from the White House told the public that:

> The Citizen's Reconstruction Corporation . . . is seeking the support of every voluntary organization and every individual in the country to bring out of hoarding these great sums of money which have been withdrawn from the active channels of trade during the last ten months.[123]

By the time of the banking crisis of 1933 the Citizens' Reconstruction Corporation seems to have expired—as well it might.[124]

The activities of the President directed toward focusing the public's attention which have thus far been considered have been carried on by comparatively small groups of persons organized as committees. Many times presidential efforts to focus attention on a problem or to crystallize opinion take on the character of national conferences. The purposes of such conferences vary. Sometimes emphasis is on the coordination of similar though unrelated activities, sometimes emphasis is on drafting or suggesting legislation, and sometimes the purpose is undoubtedly political.

Good examples of the use of a national conference to focus public and professional attention are to be found in the series of White House Conferences on children held at ten year intervals for the past 40 years. Inaugurated by President Theodore Roosevelt in 1909, continued by President Wilson in 1919, they began to assume the character of an institution in 1930 when President Hoover appointed a committee headed by Ray Lyman Wilbur and including thirty-two other members to plan a White House Conference on Child Health and Protection.[125] The purpose of the Conference was "to determine the facts as to our present progress and our future needs in this great field and to make recommendations for such measures for more effective official and voluntary action and their coordination as will further develop the care and protection of children." [126] The costs of this Conference were met by $500,000 placed at the disposal of the President from private resources.[127]

The fourth in the series of conferences was organized at the suggestion of President Roosevelt in April, 1939. Indicating the new emphasis, the Conference was called the White House Conference on Children in a Democracy. The Conference was described as "a citizens' enterprise in which those representing many types of professional and civic interest . . . join together to consider the aims of our American civilization for the children in whose hands its future lies." [128] The recommendations of this Conference resulted in the establishment of the Child Welfare Committee by Secretary of Labor Frances Perkins on February 8, 1940 as a body to further the objectives of the Conference.

These Conferences are interesting from the viewpoint of presidential commissions because they illustrate the part the chief executive may take in focusing public or professional attention upon a particular problem. There is an aura cast around a conference called by the President that cannot be duplicated by any private organization. The willingness of a President to lend himself and the presidential office to worthwhile public projects is perhaps in part a political manoeuvre. It is more than that however. It is one of the "social" duties which is expected from all Presidents. Roosevelt's "Birthday Party" for the benefit of the victims of infantile paralysis is another example of how public support can be rallied around a worthwhile cause by the President. Red Cross appeals coming from the President, or the appointment of national committees for the furtherance of particular drives can also be included as presidential devices for spotlighting public attention. Other examples will occur to the reader.

Another example of a conference called to focus public attention on a particular problem with no expectation of legislative results was the Conference on Home Building and Ownership held in December 1932 after elaborate planning of more than a year. In August 1930 President Hoover appointed a Planning Commission headed by Robert P. Lamont and including thirty-two other members from all walks of life. The President outlined his purpose in these words:

> I have decided to undertake the organization of an adequate investigation and study on a nation-wide scale of the problems presented in home ownership and home building, with a view to the development of a better understanding of the questions involved and the hope of inspiring better organization and removal of influences which seriously limit the spread of home ownership, both town and country . . . it is not suggested that the results of the Conference will be recommendations for legislation but rather a coordination, stimulation and larger organization of the private agencies. . . .[129]

Funds for the entire research and activities of the Conference were supplied from private channels. When the Conference opened December 2, 1931 after some thirty committees had been engaged in collecting facts and making recommendations, President Hoover addressed it in part as follows:

> Like the solution of all practical problems, the facts first must be discovered; they must be assembled in their true perspective, and the conclusions to be drawn from them must be the inexorable march of logic. . . . The Conference represents a place in our mastery of forces that modern science and modern technology place at our disposal. It is not to set up government in the building of homes but to stimulate individual endeavor and make community conditions propitious.[130]

The success or failure of a conference as a governmental device for focusing the public's attention cannot be measured by recording legislation and noting new agencies which can be traced to the conference. Success is not measured by voluminous reports. More important than new agencies and new volumes is the inspiration and stimulus to individual delegates and the organizations they represent. The knowledge that the government recognizes a problem, the knowledge that other groups are dealing with the same problem—whether it be child welfare, home ownership, the prevention of accidents, crime, or wild life preservation—seems to reinvigorate each individual similarly concerned.[131] The conference also serves as a vehicle for the exchange of ideas, the dissemination of information, and the coordination of activities. Generally speaking, however, a conference is not very good as a fact-finding agency.

The most common conception of the way in which the President should

participate in legislation is that his concern should be with the general outlines and purposes of legislation, not with the details of legislation. So one
might expect that more presidential commissions would be for the purpose of
focusing public attention than for getting facts with specific legislative goals
in mind. This is not borne out by the facts, however. In the forty year period
from 1901 to 1941, there were approximately twenty-eight of the former type
created as contrasted with thirty-four of the "legislative" type.

It will be noted, however, that President Roosevelt exercised much
greater freedom than his predecessors in creating legislative commissions as
contrasted with those designed merely to focus attention. The decade from
1934 to 1944 was a period of intensified executive leadership. President
Roosevelt did not simply focus public attention on particular problems and then
leave action to Congress. He focused attention if necessary, had legislation
prepared under his guidance, and submitted the matter to Congress.

The failure of commissions such as the Wickersham and Industrial Relations Commissions to come up to the high standard of royal commissions is
not due wholly to the fact that no American commission device has the prestige and tradition of the royal commission. Rather, American commissions
designed to be opinion-guiding have frequently been less successful than
royal commissions because of the type of problem which the American executive has assigned to them. Some Presidents have expected their commissions
to do the impossible.

For example, the question of whether "to have or not to have prohibition,"
was not, in 1929–1930, a question capable of rational decision. Propaganda
had succeeded in fixing the convictions of most of the public. Instead of a
reasoned approach, most persons were rationalizing their preconceived beliefs. To expect any commission to examine such a question, to find indisputa-
ble facts, and to present conclusions upon which most reasonable men could
agree, was to expect the impossible.

The failure was in the creation of a commission in the mistaken belief that
an emotional controversy could be decided by "finding the facts." The only
chance of success for a prohibition commission in 1930 would have been to
recognize that there was no "right" answer upon which most men could
agree and for a commission to be appointed to search for a compromise solution. In the absence of compromise, one side or the other was bound to win
by counting votes. To have or not to have prohibition in 1930 was a matter
to be decided by votes, not by facts.

Felix Frankfurter has pointed out that in certain fields (public utility, for
example) agitation and advocacy have taken the place of solid judgment based

on understanding of complicated technical data. Agitation and advocacy, he wrote,

> are instruments of education, means for making effective the findings of knowledge and the lessons of experience. But the quiet, detached, laborious task of disentangling facts from fiction, of extracting reliable information from interested parties, of agreeing on what is proof and what surmise, must precede, if agitation is to feed on knowledge and reality, and to be equipped to reach the mind rather than to exploit feeling.[132]

The same general observations made regarding the Wickersham Commission are true with regard to the Industrial Commission except that the conflict between labor and capital is more significant. Facts cannot be found by parties to the class struggle which will assist in its rational solution with any greater ease than they could be found on the prohibition issue.

A body such as the Industrial Commission can only serve as a sounding board for the parties to the dispute. The success of such a commission cannot be measured by the facts it finds, but only by the hearing which each of the parties obtain for the "facts" which they present. In the case of labor this may mean in the long run a progressive but slow amelioration of its condition.

If there are to be presidential commissions to deal with *basic* social and economic controversies, on which most of the public is emotionally aroused, it must be recognized that they can't find "facts," they can only compromise.

This is not to say that there is no reason for the creation of presidential commissions of the fact-finding, opinion-guiding variety. There are many issues which the public recognizes as existent but upon which there are not enough facts available for the people to form a valid judgment. There are other issues of great importance to a small group of people—or of large importance but not widely recognized as such by the public at large. So far as presidential commissions find facts and spotlight these issues, they are of great value.

Before the appointment of a fact-finding commission designed to focus public opinion these warnings might well be observed. (1) The problem to be studied should not be one which is of such a nature that commission members are likely already to be emotionally committed on the issue involved. (2) The Commission should be of a non-partisan composition with regard to the problem. (3) The Commission should not be created for a political purpose if the prestige of presidential commissions is to be preserved, and (4) Insofar as the Commission agrees on the facts, the President should be willing to accept the statement of fact, although he may remain free to act or not to act.

The responsibility for the success or failure of presidential commissions in this field rests largely with the President. He must recognize the type of problem with which they can deal and realize that there are some issues upon which "facts" cannot be found by even the most competent of men. The best abilities and intentions will fail if based on faulty premises. Too frequently presidential commissions give evidence of having been created on the spur of the moment. From women's club to Congress, the American people appoint committees. Before any committee is appointed it is well to give pause and ask: what is this body expected to accomplish? and, is it reasonable to believe that this particular committee can accomplish this purpose?

The ideal opinion-guiding commission or conference would be one which produced new facts and put such facts, or not widely known facts, into a framework which would attract public attention. If a mere presentation of the facts does not point toward a solution of the problem, the commission should make its recommendations, becoming in a sense a body which would fit into the category of those with definite legislative goals in mind.

Presidential spotlight commissions so far as terms of reference, composition and staff might well be patterned on the experience of British royal commissions since the royal commissions have been used many times just for the purpose of spotlighting certain large social or economic problems. The principal commissions mentioned at the opening of this section have in general rendered complete reports and directed public attention to the problems concerned. The prestige which these commissions had a tendency to establish, however, has been to a large extent offset by a number of unimportant and poorly conceived and executed commissions. The remedy for this situation rests in the hands of the President.

(c) COMMISSIONS TO RECONCILE CONFLICTING INTERESTS

A third type of presidential commission essentially informative in character is that which seeks to reconcile conflicting interests. Democracy, it has been said, is based on the free exchange of ideas and implicit therein, upon the clash of interests.[133] Normally the clash of interests or ideas is resolved by the decisions of the legislative body or by the judiciary.

Occasionally, however, a clash of ideas or a conflict of interests cannot be settled by legislative or judicial determination. Yet the dispute may have assumed such a character that the public interest demands either a solution or a cessation of the conflict. The most common type of clash which in the public interest demands a solution is the labor dispute. In many labor disputes, the government does not interfere and a solution is left to the participants who may decide the clash by rational negotiation or by a test of force. In the event, however, that a large public interest becomes involved, whether it be by the size of the dispute, its protracted character, or its violence, the public interest may demand a solution. In the event that Congress is unable (or unwilling) to legislate a solution to a particular controversy as was done in the Adamson Act [134] or in the event that the courts cannot be called upon to settle the dispute, the President may appoint a presidential commission to deal with the matter.

The primary expectation is that the presidential commission will bring an end to the conflict. The technique used to accomplish this purpose depends upon the nature and circumstances of the clash. Thus any dispute which interferes with production in a war industry in wartime may of its very nature demand compulsory arbitration rather than a decision by more polite means.

In general, the commission may progressively try (1) to conciliate or compromise, (2) to arbitrate, (3) to set forth the opposing views and let the public choose sides, (4) to set forth the non-partisan facts, plus the commission's recommendation, and so bring public pressure to bear upon one of the disputants.

The success or failure of such "mediation" commissions has rested in the past not on their legal powers, for they were usually legally impotent, but rather on the prestige of the President and on the strength of the public demand for a settlement.

Labor disputes, which in time of peace might be allowed to run their course, assume such importance in a war period that they cannot be permitted. Congress might outlaw strikes in wartime but with an understandable reluctance has thus far refrained from doing so. This leaves the job of peaceful settlement either to the self-imposed restraint of the contestants, or to the President, backed by the public will and his war powers. Self-imposed restraint is not likely to be effective in a period of rising prices. Hence the job of preserving industrial peace in wartime is up to the President and his Department of Labor.

Although many presidential commissions have been created to deal with labor-management controversies, the specialized nature of these commissions is such that their treatment is not warranted in this study.

It is not only in the field of labor relations, however, that presidential commissions have been used to reconcile the conflict of interests.[135] The San Francisco Bridge Commission was organized at the suggestion of President Hoover in 1929 to deal with the disputed question as to whether a bridge should be constructed across San Francisco Bay. In announcing the appointment of federal representatives to the commission, Hoover explained that the body was organized "in order that we may have an exhaustive investigation with a view to a final determination which will be acceptable to all parties. . . ." [136] This commission tried and succeeded in arriving at a working arrangement whereby the admitted economic need of the bridge could be reconciled with the unavoidable interference with harbor and naval traffic.

Federal Prison Industries, Inc. was the outgrowth of a conference called by the President which sought to bring an end to the conflict of interest existing between private manufacturers, labor groups, and federal prison authorities. The private groups felt that the competition of prison labor was unfair, yet prison officials found it necessary to provide some kind of work for prisoners. A conference called by the President on March 7, 1934, between representatives of the Department of Justice and the American Federation of Labor to consider the problem led to agreement on legislation which served as the basis for setting up Federal Prison Industries, Inc.[137] The organization of Prison Industries indicates the prevalence of the idea of reconciling conflicting interests, for the act required that the board of directors include representatives of industry, labor, agriculture, retailers and consumers, and of the Department of Justice.[138]

Bodies which are concerned with reconciling conflicting interests may be selected with the idea of getting completely non-partisan representation or with the idea of having equal representation of the conflicting groups. The subject matter of the conflict seems to have no relation to the type of representation on the body.

Whether a board should be made up of bi-partisan or non-partisan persons should be conditioned by the function of the board. If the board is concerned with the *formulation* of policy to which the conflicting interests are expected to adhere, then the board should be bi-partisan in character. If, on the other hand, the board is concerned with the *execution* of a policy formulated by the conflicting groups then it should be non-partisan in character. The formulation of policy in the democratic state depends upon a compromise and a blending of interests. In order to have that compromise, all conflicting points of view should be represented. Thus the War Labor Conference Board which was to report on principles and policies which should govern the relations between workers and employers in war industries was made up of persons representing conflicting points of view. Similarly when the San Francisco Bridge Commission had to work out a policy for the construction of the bridge, local interests which knew the economic need of the bridge were represented, as were the War and Navy departments which were concerned with the maintenance of uninterrupted navigation. On the other hand, when a policy which represents a compromise is to be carried out, there should be no hint of partisan favor. When President Roosevelt set up the National Steel Labor Relations Board he was able to say: "This board consists of three impartial members, who will be thoroughly independent in their judgments." [139]

Commissions which are concerned with the settlement of controversy or bringing about a meeting of the minds frequently have stated or unstated functions co-equal with the conciliatory function. Thus the Commission on Handling Muscle Shoals the federal representatives of which were appointed by President Hoover in 1931 [140] included representatives from the Department of Agriculture, the War Department, and representatives from the states of Alabama and Tennessee. The Commission was created for the ostensible purpose of determining "a method for handling the Muscle Shoals plants. . . ." [141] It should be noted, however, that this joint federal-state commission was set up after the President had vetoed the Muscle Shoals bill which would have provided for government operation of the project.[142] The report of the Commission recommended a fifty-year lease to private interests for profitless operation. Thus while the Muscle Shoals Commission was concerned with bringing about a meeting of state and federal minds, it also functioned under the implied mandate that the solution presented should correspond with Mr. Hoover's ideas of private operation rather than with the will of Congress for government operation. This means that this Commission could be classified as advisory, i. e., advising the President and Congress along the lines of the advice the President wanted; or as political, i.e., an attempt by the President to use a commission and its unanimous report to foist the President's ideas on a Congress of a different mind.

In conclusion it may be said that the job of reconciling conflicting interests or bringing about a meeting of the minds is ultimately a function for Congress. It is Congress which should weigh the merits of conflicting points of view and determine the policy best suited to the public interest. Situations in which Congress has failed to act have been illustrated in the preceding pages. Sometimes the conflict is one into which politically conscious Congressmen are loathe to inject themselves—labor disputes, for example. Sometimes the conflict involves a dispute as to the facts, facts perhaps very difficult to ascertain—the rubber-gas dispute of 1942, for example. Again, the conflict may arise out of some conflict in the administration of a predetermined policy— for example, the construction of a bridge in a way which helps one group of interests and injures another interest.

In each of these cases and in others which will occur to the reader, the most appropriate method of achieving a satisfactory solution may be the appointment of a presidential commission. The sooner the idea is accepted that properly constituted presidential commissions have a very real value in bringing about an amicable settlement of many of these conflicts and that they do not constitute a threat to democracy, the more likely that our democratic forms will survive.

5

ADMINISTRATIVE COMMISSIONS

THE commissions described in the previous pages have been designated as informative commissions because they secure pre-policy or pre-legislation facts. The term is not a happy one because all commissions are presumably informative. The commissions treated in this section are concerned with the execution of policy as distinguished from preparation for the determination of policy. As has been suggested earlier, the commissions discussed in this section act as *agents* in the execution of policy, they *coordinate* the execution of policy, they *advise* the President how some policy should be carried out, and last, they act as trouble-shooters to investigate the process of administration.

I. EXECUTIVE AGENTS

Commissions are occasionally created by the President to carry on purely executive functions. They are set up to exercise some function which is peculiarly the President's own. They may govern in his name as Commander in Chief; they may be set up at the President's discretion to carry out some law; they may act as the President's agent in that portion of the foreign relations field which is his own. While these bodies may give advice, coordinate administrative activities or occasionally draft legislation, their principal function is to exercise some presidential power. They are more directly the agents of the President than other commissions which have been treated. They do things which the President himself might be expected to do if he had the time.

Executive commissions are most likely to be created in time of emergency to exercise the powers which the President finds necessary to use in time of stress. Some congressmen are awed by the complexities of a depression or war situation, others recognize the necessity of a unified authority and so legislation of a general policy-determining character is passed. Congress decides what amount of money is to be provided for the relief of unemployment or for the construction of defense instruments, and then appends a general grant of power to the President "to establish such agencies . . . as he may find necessary." [1]

Emergency calls for new activities on the part of government at the same time that regular functions must be carried on. The new activities may be given to the older agencies, impairing and interfering with the execution of their regular functions. Or they may be given to new agencies created by the President under a general grant of authority as cited above, or simply created by the President under authority inherent in his duty to see that the laws are faithfully executed. Moreover, during time of emergency there is more public demand that the President take action and less worry about the technicalities of authority. Just as the federal government finds its powers expanding at the expense of the states in times of emergency, so the President finds demands for his leadership increasing,—demands that make it impossible for the brain or body of one man to exercise the multifarious executive functions that are newly his. The limits of the President's power to appoint commissions to carry on executive functions cannot be defined, but a survey of its exercise may indicate to some extent the scope of the power.

In the last three major American crises, over-all executive agencies have been appointed to assist the President in the discharge of his duties. The War Industries Board of 1917–1918 was the principal executive agency for the coordination of industrial production and was the keystone of the American war effort. The Executive Council and the National Emergency Council of 1933, and its ramifications in the subsequent depression years, were less conspicuous and less successful presidential efforts to coordinate emergency recovery and relief programs. The Office for Emergency Management created in 1940 and its subdivisions "were to serve as extra eyes, hands, and brains for the President" [2] and to assist the President in the clearance of information with respect to measures necessitated by the threatened emergency. Each of these agencies was endowed with life by the President on tenuous statutory authority. The need for their creation was perceived by the Executive and Congress acquiesced in their organization.

The War Industries Board [3] originally created by the Council of National Defense,[4] was made an independent agency and responsible to the President by a letter to Bernard M. Baruch of March 4, 1918 which set forth the powers and duties of the Board.[5] The Board was given a more official status by an Executive Order of May 28, 1918,[6] issued pursuant to the authority conferred on the President to reorganize the executive agencies by the Overman Act.[7] This Executive Order "made it possible for the Board to draw on all the powers that Congress conferred on any executive branch" [8] and led to the board being characterized "as an agent of the President." [9]

In the final analysis there seems to be no question of the existence of authority to create the Board (although there was question as to the scope of the Board's authority).[10] Yet it is interesting to note that its *ad hoc* development resulted in an executive agency, not specifically authorized by Congress, but exercising powers almost dictatorial in character—powers delegated to the Board by the President.

The War Industries Board was not the only executive agency set up during World War I and directly under the control of the President. There were some nine other war administrations each of which reported to the President. The War Industries Board, however, was by far the most important as it served as the general coordinator and was responsible only to the President.

During the next great American emergency, untended until 1933, the National Emergency Council was the principal over-all executive agency for dealing with depression.[11] The functions of this body were never very clearly defined.

In July of 1933 the Executive Council was created by Executive Order "in order to provide for the more orderly presentation of Government business and to coordinate inter-agency problems of organization and the work of the new Government agencies."[12] The authority for its creation was found in the general grants of power in the National Industrial Recovery Act,[13] and the Federal Emergency Relief Act.[14] As a matter of fact, the composition of the Executive Council was hard to distinguish from the Cabinet except that it included the heads of the newer emergency agencies. Its functions were similar to those of the Cabinet, in that it was advisory and served to keep the President in touch with the emergency activities of the government.[15]

The National Emergency Council which later absorbed the Executive Council[16] was created by an Executive Order of November 17, 1933.[17] The original purpose for the creation of the National Emergency Council was to coordinate and make more efficient and productive the work of the numerous field agencies of the government which had been established to carry into effect the National Recovery Act, the Agricultural Adjustment Act, and the Federal Emergency Relief Act. It was expected that the Council would result in the elimination of many of the committees and agencies created in the early days of the emergency, and with that in mind several bodies in addition to the Executive Council were merged with it.[18] The mergers, however, seemed merely to confuse the functions of the Council. It functioned as a central informational bureau conveying information about the government to the public,[19] it helped to determine policy for the National Recovery Administration,[20] it made recommendations to the President with regard to relief, labor disputes, agricultural recovery, public works,[21] it engaged in the protection of consumers' interests,[22] it set up a committee to study a report regarding methods of increasing industrial employment by coordinating price and production policies,[23] it rendered reports on economic conditions in various regions of the United States,[24] and it set up a radio and film service to acquaint the public with government productions in those fields. This by no means delineates the activities of the National Emergency Council. It was an agency which might have become an additional right hand for the President, but instead became a welter of confused functions and duties, in which the most important duties of coordination and supervision were lost. The most that can be said for the National Emergency Council is that it was "a general coordinating and informational service" but insofar as it contemplated coordination, "it duplicated the functions of the Bureau of the Budget."[25] What remained of the Council was abolished and most of its functions transferred to the Executive Office of the President by Reorganization Plan II, July 1, 1939.[26]

The same Executive Order which eliminated the National Emergency Council as a separate agency and transferred its functions to the Office of Government Reports laid the ground work for the creation of the Office for Emergency Management—designed to serve as the over-all agency in time of crisis. Reorganization Plan II of September 8, 1939 provided in part that within the Executive Office of the President there should be "in the event of a national emergency, such office for emergency management as the President shall determine."[27] This plan, given tacit approval by the Congress pursuant to the Reorganization Act of 1939,[28] was the authority for an administrative order of May 25, 1940[29] which set up the Office for Emergency Management. In terms of the authority conferred upon the Office, it was to be a body to which the President could delegate much of his executive responsibility. It was to assist the President in the clearance of information, maintain liaison between the President and defense agencies which had been set up, and perform such other duties as the President might direct.[30] A subsequent order further defined the responsibilities of the Office, authorizing it "to advise and assist the President in the discharge of extraordinary responsibilities imposed upon him by any emergency arising out of war, the threat of war, imminence of war, flood, drought, or other condition threatening the public peace or safety."[31] In the words of the Office itself, it "and its future subdivisions were to serve as extra eyes, hands, and brains for the President. To it, he was able to delegate certain of his executive powers."[32] But the Office notes that it is to operate "under the direction and supervision of the President." Through the Office the President may coordinate, supervise, and direct the activities of public or private agencies. It is doubtful if the Office has fulfilled the expectations of the author of its descriptive brochure. After 1940 it was scarcely more than a reassuring gesture that there was unity amid disunity; its activities were largely of a house-keeping nature.

In time of emergency there is always an increase in the number of government agencies and there is no doubt of the need of the President to have additional executive agencies, peculiarly his own, to assist him in carrying on the immensely complicated executive functions of coordination and supervision. But there is little point in setting up such agencies unless they can exercise some of the President's powers upon their own initiative. They must be given power to make decisions without having to go to the President for every little matter. The principal reason for setting up such bodies is that without them there is too much executive detail for the President to handle and yet at the same time to avoid being a bottleneck. Executive decisions cannot be delayed in time of emergency because of the President's insistence on having every paper cross his desk.

One of the most elemental traits of the successful administrator is the ability to delegate responsibility. The most successful of the three executive agencies described above was the War Industries Board. Its success in turn can largely be ascribed to the willingness of President Wilson to turn over both problem and authority to deal with it to a man with executive capabilities the equal of his own. The fact that a man has been popularly elected chief executive is no indication that he is the best executive in the country—though such an expression of public confidence may make a man think he is. Both the National Emergency Council and the Office for Emergency Management were characterized by the lack of a responsible head. The difficulty is tersely and well described during the preparedness effort of 1941: "President is more and more immersed in over-all problems of strategy; is more and more unable to attend to executive detail. *Yet:* The whole defense program heads up to the White House, heads into the Executive Office, where even the biggest problems tend to get buried." [33]

If all that is wanted from an executive emergency agency is information and advice with reference to emergency activities, then headless and powerless emergency agencies such as the National Emergency Council and Office for Emergency Management will suffice. However, the problem is one of coordination, supervision, and the detailed execution of policy. The purpose of emergency agencies should be to clear the chief strategist's desk so he may have room to chart the broad lines of attack. Power must, therefore, be delegated to these emergency executive agencies and they must be headed by an administrator with full authority to accomplish the tasks which have been clearly assigned to him.

It is not only in time of emergency that the President appoints committees to help him in the performance of his executive functions. In the execution of normal peace-time laws the President is often given wide discretion to set up the agencies which shall execute the policy. A good illustration is found in the series of committees which developed in the course of the trade agreements program. Prior to the passage of the Trade Agreements Act,[34] the President created the Executive Committee on Commercial Policy by means of a letter to the Secretary of State.[35] This body, made up of representatives of all those departments and agencies concerned with import and export trade, was instructed to coordinate the commercial policy and the negotiation of commercial treaties and trade agreements. It continues today as the overall agency for the determination of commercial policy.[36]

After the passage of the Trade Agreements Act, the Executive Committee described above set up a special Committee on Trade Agreements [37] to be a policy-forming body in connection with foreign trade agreements and to arrange for studies country by country as the agreements progressed. This special committee was directly in charge of the committees set up to negotiate treaties with individual countries. Neither the Executive Committee nor the Committee on Trade Agreements was provided for by law. Their only authority for existence was the general grant of authority to the President to negotiate reciprocal trade agreements.

Subordinate to the Committee on Trade Agreements was the Committee on Reciprocity Information. The creation of this committee was authorized by the Trade Agreements Act in specific terms, section 4 providing that before any agreement was concluded, interested persons should have an opportunity to present views to the President or to such agency as the President might designate.[38] Thus of the three principal committees created to participate in the formulation and execution of commercial policy, only one had definite statutory authority.

So long as Congress had determined upon the reciprocal trade agreements program, few people would question the wisdom of the creation of the Executive Committee on Commercial Policy or the Committee on Trade Agreements. Both committees serve to bring more minds and more varied interests to bear on the execution of a policy with particularly wide ramifications. The conclusion of trade agreements is not the type of problem which is appropriately left to one man or to one department for execution. Even the opponents of the program should have been relieved to see that a matter so vital to their economic interests was not to be left to the discretion of one man.

Other types of executive commissions appointed by the President without regard to statutory authority are those created pursuant to his position as Commander in Chief of the armed forces of the United States. No legislation which Congress might pass could impair the President's power as Commander in Chief to order army men to serve on commissions.[39]

But the President's power as Commander in Chief is not confined to authority to assign men of the armed forces to special tasks. He has also assigned civilians, with their consent, to jobs related to the activities of the armed forces. Thus in 1927 President Coolidge requested Henry L. Stimson to go to Nicaragua as his special representative. There was no question of his appointment being confirmed by the Senate. He was to make observations and to report on the political conditions which were endangering American lives and property. The President instructed him to "straighten the matter out" if he had a chance.[40] As a result of arrangements concluded by Stimson, Brigadier General Frank R. McCoy was nominated by the President to head a commission to supervise the Nicaraguan presidential elections of 1929.[41] The actual appointment was made by the President of Nicaragua.[42]

This is a case where the conduct of foreign policy was so closely related to the use of the armed forces that it would be difficult, and probably of no great value, to determine whether the President was acting as chief agent in the conduct of foreign affairs or as Commander in Chief. In either case there would appear to have been adequate legal basis for his appointments.

The first and second Philippine Commissions show rather well the length to which the President can go under the inherent powers which he derives from the fact that he is Commander in Chief. The First Philippine Commission, known as the Schurman Commission, was appointed in early 1899 by President McKinley "in order to facilitate the most humane, pacific, and effective extension of authority through these Islands, and to secure, with the least possible delay, the benefits of a wise and generous protection of life and property of the inhabitants. . . ."[43] The body of six included four civilians and two representatives of the armed forces. The military government continued in operation during the time the commission was in the Islands, the commission serving more as an advisory body rather than as an executive. Jacob Gould Schurman, the chairman, conceived that the purpose of the commission was "to aid the Government in Washington in shaping that policy (of extending sovereignty)."[44] The four volume report made by the commission pointed out that duty bound the United States to remain in the Islands and suggested that a civilian government should be provided.[45] The Schurman Commission was to report through the Secretary of State and so gives the appearance of being a commission created by the President pursuant to his foreign relations power rather than his military power.

In accordance with the suggestion of the Schurman Commission's recommendations, the Second Philippine Commission (the Taft Commission) was appointed in 1900 to serve as the civil governing agency for the Islands. The military government continued to operate as the executive, and the Commission acted as the legislative authority. This was not an advisory body as the first commission had been, but was a civil agency with ample power to legislate for the Philippines.[46] Although it was made up entirely of civilians, authority for its creation was found in the military power of the President. Elihu Root, then Secretary of War, wrote:

> The question presented was how in the exercise of the President's military power under the Constitution to give the peaceful people of the Philippines the real benefit of civil government. The question was answered by an analysis of the military power, which, when exercised in territory under military occupation, includes the executive, judicial, and legislative authority. . . .[47]

The Taft Commission passed some 248 legislative acts during its first year.[48]

The action of the President in appointing the Commission was ratified by the passage of the Spooner Amendment [49] which, in addition, authorized the Commission to exercise the powers of government to the extent and in the manner and form set forth by the President's first instructions to the Commission of April 7, 1900. Henry Cabot Lodge in advocating the passage of the bill in the Senate supported the point of view that the creation of, as well as the powers exercised by the Commission properly proceeded from the executive branch. "The President, under the military power . . . could do all this bill provides. But it is well that he should have direct authorization of Congress. . . ." [50]

The First Philippine Commission was not an executive commission in the sense that that term is used in this discussion. It was a fact-finding, advisory commission designed to produce facts and recommendations upon which could be modeled a future Philippine policy. It was executive only in the sense that authority for its appointment was found in powers which are peculiarly the President's own. The Second Commission, however, was executive in the sense that it was engaged in executing a part of the President's military power. The President himself might have exercised the executive, legislative and judicial power in an area under military control. He could delegate power to exercise those functions to any person or group of persons he might choose. Although Congress gave its approval to the government which the President had set up, the legislation was not necessary. How far the President might go in continuing or extending his own particular brand of executive government to an area under military occupation is moot. Ex parte Milligan indicates a limit to the power of the military to suspend the writ of habeas corpus. But it gives no indication as to the outcome of a situation in which Congress might disapprove of the form of military government the President might set up, or in which Congress might disagree with the need of continued military occupation and government. Should such a matter ever come to a showdown, congressional weapons would be control over appropriations and the power of impeachment.

This by no means exhausts commissions which may be described as executive. The Isthmian Canal Commission of 1904 and as reconstituted in 1905 was created by act of Congress [51] to enable the President to construct the canal. The Commission, including representatives of army, navy, engineers and civilians, and appointed with the advice and consent of the Senate was placed in charge of the government of the Canal Zone and exercised all military, civil and judicial powers.[52] This Commission exercised substantially the same powers as the Second Philippine Commission, reporting through the Secretary of War. Although it was created pursuant to an act of Congress, the precedent of the Philippine Commission would indicate that it could have been created without congressional consent. The necessity of getting appropriations for the construction of the Canal was probably influential, however, in organizing the Commission under congressional authority rather than pursuant to the President's military power.

The Alaskan Engineering Commission of 1914, while not properly a presidential commission in the sense that it was created by the President was, nevertheless, executive in character. The Act of March 12, 1914 [53] authorized the President "to locate, construct, and operate railroads in the Territory of Alaska" and "to employ such officers, agents, or agencies . . . as may be necessary." A commission of three engineers was appointed to make preliminary surveys and they reported to the President through the Secretary of Interior.[54]

In 1917 at the request of the Kerensky government in Russia, a special commission of eminent railroad engineers was sent by President Wilson to Russia to help reconstruct that nation's transportation system.[55] John F. Stevens later became head of the inter-allied technical board which operated the railroad during the days of revolution.

The three foregoing commissions were active executive bodies in the sense that they directed technical jobs. They were executive in the same way that a foreman on a railway gang supervises the immediate job before him.

A different type of executive function was carried on by the Interdepartmental Radio Advisory Committee established in 1932.[56] This body was executive in the administrative sense. Its purpose was to draft executive orders which would allocate radio frequencies for government departments and to study the use of radio by the government.[57] Later this Committee became a part of the Defense Communications Board.[58]

Other executive committees were the Council for Industrial Progress and the Committee to Prevent Losses by Spring Floods. The Council for Industrial Progress was created by Executive Order in 1935 [59] to supervise, subject to the direction of the President, conferences of representatives of industry, labor, and consumers for consideration of the best means of accelerating industrial recovery.[60] The Committee to Prevent Losses by Spring Floods was created by a presidential memorandum of March 18, 1936, to determine and to carry out such plans as may be necessary on the part of the federal government to prevent loss of life, distress and destruction of property arising from the spring floods. These bodies were executive in that they "supervised" and "carried out" designated programs.

When the functions of the federal government increase, either as the result of recurrent emergencies or in the natural course of events, it is necessary to create instrumentalities for the execution of those functions. These instrumentalities may be created by Congress, or, as we have seen, they may be set up by the President. As the agencies increase, the job of the President becomes enormously complicated. Administrative assistants are appointed to help him do his job; men with a passion for anonymity, men who may ease his burden, but not men who can relieve the President of responsibility. Occasionally, and perhaps increasingly, it will become necessary for the President to delegate power and responsibility, if possible, to agents or agencies not within the regular departments. The Brandeis concept of bigness applies to government.

Occasions for such delegations have been described in this section. The one important conclusion is, that if executive power *per se* is to be delegated, it should be delegated to one man. If the delegation is to a commission, the responsibility for action must be lodged in one man. Commissions may be all right when their function is advisory or when a variety of points of view are necessary to the job before it.

It is not without reason that the President's Committee on Administrative Management reported that "for purposes of management, boards and commissions have turned out to be failures," [61] and added, "the conspicuously well-managed administrative units in the Government are almost without exception headed by single administrators."

2. ADVISORY COMMISSIONS

Many commissions appointed by the President are for the purpose of advising him with regard to specific acts or general policy.[62] The difficulty of distinguishing these so-called advisory commissions from those appointed with definite legislative ends in mind or for the purpose of crystallizing public opinion is readily apparent. The line of demarcation between them is one of degree. Commissions which recommend legislation and whose reports are sent on to the Congress for action have been treated as commissions with definite legislative goals. If, however, the commission in its report recommends action which the President can take without authority from Congress, it will be treated in this section as an advisory commission. Thus the President's Committee on Civil Service Improvement is treated as an advisory commission because the President was able to implement the report of the Committee by the issuance of an Executive Order. In most instances the order which establishes a commission indicates whether its primary function is to be advisory to the Congress or advisory to the President.

Presidential advisory commissions are created for two general purposes. They may give advice prior to the adoption of policy or they may give advice as to how a particular policy which has already been decided upon is to be executed. In both instances the wisdom of bringing a number of minds to bear in determining the policy or the method of its execution is scarcely subject to question if, once the method of execution has been decided upon, responsibility is fixed for the execution of the policy. Since the initial responsibility of execution rests upon the President and he is merely seeking advice as to how to do the job, the question of diffusion of responsibility is not likely to be present.

As we have noted at other points, the President does on occasion rely on the advice of one man either for policy advice or for advice as to the execution of policy. In 1905, for example, the President made Joseph L. Bristow a special commissioner to Panama for the purpose of "investigating and reporting upon certain questions, the answers to which deeply affect the policy properly to be pursued in the management by the Government of the Panama Railroad." [63] Such appointments can be made at any time and for any purpose by the President. For larger questions of policy, however, it is more appropriate to appoint a commission to make the investigation and the recommendations.

Such was the case when President Harding in 1921 appointed General Leonard Wood and W. Cameron Forbes to investigate the fitness of the Philippine Islands for independence.[64] It may be noted, however, that the finding of the commission that the Islands were unfit for independence may have been a foregone conclusion. Independence for the Philippines had become an issue in American politics. Nevertheless, the appointment of more than one man to find the facts and render advice seems wiser when the policy determination is important and the President is determined to get unbiased advice. Moreover, the President's hand is strengthened if he is able to point to the facts found and the recommendations made in support of the policy which he is pursuing.

A good example of a non-political, presidentially sponsored, advisory commission was the President's Aircraft Board (The Morrow Board) appointed in 1925. This Board was instructed "to make a study of the best means of developing and applying aircraft in national defense." Headed by Dwight Morrow, this body was above the reproach of partisan politics. The results of their study were made available to Congress although the board was essentially advisory to the President.

Although there is reason to believe that a good many of President Hoover's commissions were appointed for political purposes,[65] there is little doubt but that as a former engineer he was convinced of the necessity of seeking both facts and advice before he took action. He was probably more prone to getting advice which he later ignored, than his successor whose actions sometimes indicated haste and lack of preparation. One policy advisory committee appointed by Hoover was the Committee on the Conservation and Administration of the Public Domain, appointed in 1929.[66] This commission of twenty members was instructed to make a study of the entire question of the public domain particularly with reference to the question of conservation.[67] The President requested and was granted funds by Congress to carry out the study.[68] The report recommended in general terms that the public domain be turned over to the States.[69] Whether action would ever have been predicated on this report remains a matter of conjecture because party changes which were already under way by the time the report was made precluded action.[70]

A good example of a commission which advised the President on how policy should be executed was the President's Committee on Civil Service

Improvement (The Reed Committee). This Committee was created to advise the President the degree to which he should exercise powers granted to him by Congress to bring new categories of government employees within the merit system. In this case the President might have acted without advice, upon the advice of the Civil Service Commission, or, as he did, upon advice which he obtained from a chosen group of men representing both government and private interests—men in whom the President could have the greatest confidence.

Similar in that they advised the President how some of his powers should be executed were the Advisory Committee on Allotments, to recommend to the President the re-allotments of funds for projects under the Emergency Relief Appropriation Act of 1935, and the Flood Control Committee to advise on flood control projects.[71]

There is a third situation which gives rise to the creation of presidential advisory commissions. They are sometimes created to advise the President how some policy is actually working in practice. The creation of such a commission is not necessarily a prelude to change.

President Hoover's Commission to Study and Review United States Policies in Haiti is an example of an "after the policy is in execution" advisory commission used to determine how policies are being carried out. Before the appointment of the Commission the President requested authorization and an appropriation from Congress for the purpose of reviewing and studying American policy in Haiti in order that the United States might arrive at a more definite policy.[72] By the time the Commission was appointed the primary question for its consideration was that of how and when the United States was to withdraw from Haiti, and secondarily, what should be done in the meantime.[73]

Another commission used to determine how policy was being executed, without at the same time being an administrative investigating committee, was the National Recovery Review Board (The Darrow Board) created under authority of the National Industrial Recovery Act.[74] This Board, created because of congressional criticism, was to report to the President whether the National Industrial Recovery Act was designed to promote monopoly by the elimination of small enterprise and to recommend changes in the Act if that should prove necessary. Clarence Darrow, the chairman, was described as "foreman of a kind of governmental grand jury to tell the administration how the N.R.A. was working." [75]

These "after the policy is in execution" advisory commissions are just as essential to successful administration as are those created to assist in the initial determination of how policy is to be executed. It has been noted by implication that such commissions are similar in character to administrative investigating commissions discussed elsewhere. There is, however, a highly important distinction. In the case of the administrative investigations the thing under survey is the administrative process itself; in the case of these "after the policy is in execution" commissions, the thing under survey is the policy itself. Is the policy accomplishing the results which had been expected of it when established or have some unforeseen factors altered it?

It has been possible to point out only two commissions which could clearly be included within this category, important as "after the policy" studies would seem to be.[76] Too often the charge has been made that a policy which seemed good on paper was not working in actual practice the way it was expected to work—the results are not those which were contemplated. Yet if it was difficult to get the policy adopted in the first place it may become necessary from a face-saving point of view to insist on the retention of the policy. President Roosevelt with his "let's experiment" attitude in the early days of the New Deal plus the ease with which his measures were put through the Democratic Congress never to the knowledge of this writer voluntarily gave up an important policy to which he was committed.[77]

Even when a commission is appointed to see how a policy is working out in practice, there is danger, especially if the President has committed himself to the policy, that the commission may have been chosen to bring in the "right" answer. Or if it doesn't bring in the "right" answer the report may be "interpreted" or, from the viewpoint of publicity, ignored. President Hoover who was politically a prohibitionist, had to find approval for the noble experiment in the report of the Wickersham Commission. To have done otherwise, he thought, would have been politically inexpedient. He was probably wrong.

Of course there are occasions when commissions should be appointed to make an examination of the success or failure of important policies. On other occasions public reaction as evidenced in the press and in the Congress is a sufficient criterion of a policy. Moreover, periodic elections are in a sense "advisory bodies" serving to call a halt to policies which the public believes have been unsuccessful. Still advisory commissions may be necessary and when they are organized by the President it is clear that they must be made up of men whose integrity cannot be questioned and that the President must be honest in dealing with the findings of the commissions.

One of the best known and most important of advisory commissions created by the President within recent years was the Baruch Committee to investigate the rubber situation.[78] As a result of early Japanese successes in the war in the southwest Pacific area, the supply of raw rubber for the United States was cut off and it became necessary for the rubberized civilization of the United States to depend upon inadequate stock piles of raw rubber, reclaimed rubber, and synthetic rubber, for what might amount to the Nation's very existence. It was vital to the war effort for there to be not only conservation of existing rubber supplies but for the nation to settle upon a method for the manufacture of synthetic rubber. Most people in the United States recognized the importance of the problem but the possible solutions became so entangled in pressure conflicts, red tape, and emotions, that the public at large had no idea of a satisfactory approach to the solution of the problem. Apparently many governmental officials were in the same situation. No one was in a position to find the facts because, as columnist Arthur Krock pointed out:

> A fact-finding report by a Congressional group will not answer the [problem] . . . because of the controversy in Congress over WPB's alleged prejudice against synthetic rubber made from farm commodities. No survey by an existing government agency will meet it because of a rather widespread public impression that the rubber prospect has been deliberately exaggerated on the pessimistic side by executive groups in the hope of bringing home other war perils to the minds of the people.[79]

What was needed according to Mr. Krock was an investigation "by an outsider of known capacity . . . , a man who wants only to put the facts and the prospect before the people." "In the case of the rubber shortage, these facts are readily obtainable by a Presidential commissioner. There are a number of citizens, trained in weighing conflicting views on the factual scale, in whom the public would have confidence."[80]

In early June the President was reported to have requested Chief Justice Harlan F. Stone of the Supreme Court to make an independent inquiry into the rubber situation.[81] According to newspaper reports, the President had been counseled "to nominate some one in whom the public would have full confidence to get to the bottom of the whole rubber situation and report his findings so that a water-tight official policy could be based on them."[82] When Justice Stone declined to accept the offer, the President turned to Bernard M. Baruch who accepted the chairmanship of a committee consisting of Dr. Karl T. Compton, President of the Massachusetts Institute of Technology, and Dr. James B. Conant, President of Harvard University. The President instructed the committee to make "a quick but adequate survey of the entire rubber question."[83]

The report returned by the Committee pulled no punches. It was a "first-rate commission, and it . . . turned in a first-rate report" which was "candid and hard-hitting," [84] and which recommended nation-wide gasoline rationing for the purpose of conserving rubber. The President, even though the Report reflected to some extent on the administration, pronounced the Report "excellent" and agreed to act upon it at once.[85] The Report has been referred to constantly as a definitive statement on the rubber situation [86] and *The New York Times* declared that it was the type of fact-finding which should be undertaken more often with regard to problems of national importance.

> In its way even more important than the policy now to be put into effect with regard to rubber is the method of adopting that policy. What the President finally did in the case of rubber is a model of procedure that ought to be followed in solving every major problem raised by the war. . . . Because these men command the confidence of the country, the course they advocate also commands its confidence.[87]

The Baruch Committee has been cited as an example of a committee which was advisory to the President. In fact, of course, it was advisory to the public as well. Its success in either capacity was marked and suggests the wisdom of greater consideration being given to the more frequent use by government of the capacities of men of recognized ability, experience, and fairness. A more frequent use of their abilities, however, seems especially called for in times when pressure groups have strength enough to bend many congressmen and government officials to their will. It has often been noted that our governmental system does not make the best use of the experience of the outstanding men of our day. It was Plato who suggested that the best qualified guardians of the state would be the philosophers.[88] Although government by philosophers was not his method, perhaps this is a method by which such men may be used. Presidential commissions offer a device by which such men may be used.

3. COORDINATING COMMISSIONS

One of the most pressing concerns of the Chief Executive is to secure efficiency in the administration of the laws. This calls for a continuous survey of government activities to detect duplication or overlapping of functions. Occasionally disputes arise as to the jurisdiction of agencies and the President is called upon to resolve the conflicts. The coordination of government activities is one of the most important of the executive functions. As the scope of government activities increases and the duties of the President multiply, more frequent resort must be had to the appointment by the President of commissions and committees of coordination.

Coordination of activities may be accomplished in three ways, (1) by centralizing responsibility which induces coordination by force, or (2) by creating a committee representing equally the activities to be coordinated, which committee, if successful, induces coordination by cooperation, (3) by authorizing a committee of equals to render binding decisions by a majority vote which induces coordination by force. Coordination resulting from the centralization of responsibility has been treated in the chapter on executive commissions. In this section, the commissions treated are those which achieve coordination of activities by the cooperation of more or less co-equal authorities.

In attempting to classify coordinating commissions of this type several criteria may be used. In the first place these commissions might be classified according to the type of activity which is coordinated. Thus all coordinating committees dealing with welfare activities would be treated as one class. A second classification might be based upon the general relationship of the functions which were being coordinated. Thus coordination might be necessary in situations where functions overlap, duplicate, or conflict with each other, or where functions compliment each other or are parallel with each other at the same or different levels. A third classification, and the one which is used herein, is based upon the levels of activities coordinated or upon the units whose activities are coordinated. Breaking down coordinating committees and commissions in this way, it appears that the President has used such commissions in four principal ways: in the coordination of the activities of federal agencies, in the coordination of state and federal activities, in the coordination of public and private activities, and in the coordination of private activities.

By far the largest number of coordinating committees are created to prevent duplication and acting at cross-purposes among the federal agencies. This is true in normal times as well as in times of emergency. In normal times, however, the function of coordination does not loom as large in the public eye, and in normal times the job of coordination will be carried on by the executive offices acting through the Bureau of the Budget, by the Procurement Division of the Treasury Department, or by non-publicized intra or interdepartmental committees. In time of emergency, however, "emergency" agencies spring up by the score, "boondoggles" appear everywhere, and the problem of coordinating governmental activities becomes a political as well as an administrative problem. Then it is that coordinators come into their own. Thus while coordination is and should be a continuous function, it comes into prominence at time of crisis.

(A) COORDINATION OF FEDERAL ACTIVITIES

1. Auxiliary coordination

Continuous coordination is necessary with reference to the housekeeping activities of the federal agencies. Thus with regard to supply, inefficiency arises if one department needs new desks and buys them while another department has spare desks which it pays to store. Office supplies, disposal of waste material, mail room activities, mimeographing, etc., are common to all departments. Thus on a low housekeeping level regular procedures for coordinating such activities can be established. Coordination of many such activities have become formalized as a result of activities of the Bureau of the Budget.

Federal efforts to coordinate housekeeping functions by the use of presidential commissions have been rather spotty. Taft's Commission on Economy and Efficiency revealed the lack of coordination in many such activities. Coordination of these activities is a job for the Office of the President and one which he can accomplish to a considerable extent without authority from Congress. Early twentieth century efforts at coordinating supply were in the direction of getting departmental agreements on specifications for materials which were used by many departments. Many such agreements resulted from activities of interdepartmental committees.[89]

The most vigorous attempt to coordinate these auxiliary government functions by virtue of the President's authority was the creation of the Federal Coordinating Service in the Bureau of the Budget in 1921.[90] The Chief Coordinator, subject to the supervision of the Director of the Bureau of the Budget, was to handle "all questions of coordination arising through the application of the policies of the President and of the Congress to the routine business of the executive branch of the Government." [91] While the authority here conferred was broad enough to include the coordination of policy, the boards and committees which were appointed to bring about coordination were confined largely to auxiliary functions. In a series of Executive Orders, interdepartmental committees were set up for the accomplishment of a variety of auxiliary function coordinations. A Federal Purchasing Board composed of one representative from each department and independent establishment was set up to formulate policies and plans to coordinate the purchasing activities of the several departments and establishments. It sought to determine the advisability of centralizing purchases and utilizing surpluses.[92] An Office of Coordinator for Motor Transport in the District of Columbia, while not a commission, sought in the interests of efficiency and economy, to coordinate the activities of the executive departments in so far as they used motor vehicles.[93] A Federal Traffic Board was created "for the purpose of effecting economies and better business administration throughout the government service in the handling of passenger and freight shipments." The Board was to "prevent overlapping of service and duplication of effort in the conduct of the traffic business of the government.[94] The type of function which had formerly been handled by bodies such as the Paint Specification Board was taken care of by the creation of the Federal Specification Board. Suffice it to say that such matters as paint specifications, coordination of motor transport and similar matters occasionally come to the President's attention and it is necessary for him to take action such as that illustrated above.

Although in normal times the nation may not be particularly concerned about the problem of coordinating auxiliary functions and believes that the only result is inefficiency and not interference with basic policy, in time of emergency the failure to coordinate auxiliary activities may be so important that there may be interference with the execution of policy. One does not hear about the need for the most efficient utilization of manpower by the federal government (except from students of public administration) until the emergency is upon the nation. But if it is important to be efficient in the use of manpower in time of war, it is also to the advantage of the nation to be efficient in its utilization in time of peace. It is beyond the scope of this study, however, to deal with the coordination of activities which become essential in time of war.

2. *Policy Coordination*

As the scope of government activities increases and the nature of the problems faced by government becomes more complex, the need for coordinating the policies of governmental agencies becomes more important and more pressing. Modern government frequently must deal with subjects which cannot be compartmentalized. The day when foreign policy had little effect on farm prices, or farm prices little effect on foreign policy, is gone. The result is that the more important conflicts of policy between executive agencies work their way, frequently by way of the press, to the desk of the President where the decisions are made. Although many such decisions may be made without recourse to the appointment of a presidential commission, it will frequently be found that the policies apparently in conflict cannot be resolved by the simple expedient of choosing one or the other. Thus, the Department of Agriculture cannot be expected to give up irrigation projects because water taken for irrigation leaves none for navigation with which the Army engineers are concerned. Nor can the Army engineers be expected to permit irrigation projects to interfere with navigation. This is the type of policy conflict which may call for policy coordination by an interdepartmental committee [95] or which may lead to the creation of a presidential commission either for the purpose of coordinating the policies or for the purpose of conducting a fact-finding survey which may serve as a basis for a definitive decision between the conflicting policies.

At the same time as the problem of coordination of policy becomes more difficult because government activities are increasing and because the problems faced by government are becoming more complex, statutes, which might serve to some extent to define activities and thereby prevent conflicts of policy, are becoming more general and less particular. To some extent the tendency of statutes to be general rather than particular may be traced to the complexity of the problems with which the statutes attempt to deal. But part of the difficulty may be traced to Congress which ignores to a large extent the problem of assigning new functions. Thus Congress in recent years has assigned new functions to agencies which are independent of the existing executive departments, or, when new functions have been assigned to certain departments, Congress has made the assignments without giving enough attention to determining whether the assignment is within the scope of the activities of the particular department concerned.[96]

It seems obvious that the less statutory provision made for coordination, the more provision there must be for coordination by other devices. Thus the failure of Congress in some instances carefully to delineate the activities of new agencies has resulted in the use of presidential commissions to accomplish coordination which would have been avoided by proper statute drafting or which should have been coordinated within the governmental structure by the departments themselves.[97]

On the other hand some problems such as radio,[98] barriers to interstate commerce,[99] or certain aspects of government financial policy,[100] are of such a nature that they cut across departmental lines and require coordination not only of the activities of the independent agencies concerned but they require coordination which will lead to a definite affirmative policy. This is coordination for the purpose of evolving policy, not for the purpose of preventing conflicts.

In time of war, of course, the coordination of policy assumes more importance than coordination in peacetime. If there is failure to coordinate the policies of the War and Navy Departments in wartime, the result may be disastrous. Similar importance attaches in wartime to the coordination of private activities, as well as to government activities. Such agencies as the War Production Board, the War Manpower Commission, the Office of Price Administration, are in reality coordinating bodies for particular types of government and private activities which have importance during war.

No matter how effective Congress may be in clearly marking the limits of the proper activities of government agencies, however, there are bound to be many instances when policies determined upon independently by the agencies will come into conflict. Sometimes such conflicts will rage under cover for a long period of time, sometimes they will be stopped by the Bureau of the Budget, sometimes by the President. In those cases in which it is not clear which policy should prevail or in which it is clear that the policies must be merged, the appointment of a presidential commission may be the most effective step toward a satisfactory solution.

(B) COORDINATION OF FEDERAL-STATE ACTIVITIES

The President rarely creates commissions for the purpose of coordinating the activities of federal and state agencies. The coordination of activities, if it exists at all, is likely to take place on an informal basis among the agencies involved or by use of the device of financial grants to state agencies which are dependent upon their cooperation if the grants are to be continued (grants-in-aid).

In 1929 President Hoover appointed federal members to the California Water Resources Committee which considered engineering problems and policies with regard to the construction of the San Francisco Bay bridge as well as the development of irrigation, flood control, navigation and power in the State. The War Department, the Interior Department, and the Federal Power Commission were represented on the committee. In addition to engaging in research, this committee was to coordinate the activities of state and federal agencies concerned with the developments. California members sat on the committee and the State made an appropriation for its support. The federal agencies concerned contributed the staff and made information in their possession available to the Commission.[101]

Some state-federal coordination of activities comes about as a result of conferences called by the President. At a conference such as that on Children in a Democracy, the Department of Labor through its Children's Bureau sought to bring about some coordination of objective for private as well as state and federal agencies. The Governor's Conference called by President Roosevelt to meet two days after his first inauguration, however, seemed to be more of a political show than a coordinating conference. Although the agenda called for the discussion of "several problems which would require cooperation between the Federal and State Governments" results consisted for the most part of pledges of support and resolutions urging unity upon the country.[102]

In 1936 an Interdepartmental Drought Committee was appointed by the President to coordinate and accelerate the drought relief activities of the various state and federal agencies. This body was made up entirely of federal employees and states were left without representation.[103] Similar in non-representative composition was the Division of State and Local Cooperation in the Office of Emergency Management which was created during the "preparedness" period to keep state and local defense councils informed about the national defense program and tell them ways in which they might cooperate with the federal government.[104]

In this connection it may be remarked that coordination of federal and state activities by a committee having representation from only one level of government must accomplish its aim by reason of the good will or willingness of the unrepresented group to cooperate. If committees which are set up to coordinate activities of two different levels of government do not have representation from each of the levels, then they should have some method of forcing coordination of activities.

(c) COORDINATION OF PUBLIC AND PRIVATE ACTIVITIES

The President sometimes appoints commissions to coordinate the activities of public and private groups. Citizenship training has been a province open to federal, state, and private agencies. In 1923 the President created the Federal Council of Citizenship Training,[105] to make suggestions "as to how the Federal offices may cooperate to secure more effective citizenship training, both in their own work and in cooperation with all other public and private agencies throughout the country." While this body was made up entirely of federal representatives, its suggestions for improved methods of citizenship training were directed at public and private agencies.

During the depression President Hoover appointed a number of business and industrial committees to organize a concerted attack on the depression. Feeling as he did that recovery was not dependent upon government action alone, he called a national conference of these committees. The idea apparently was that these committees and the conference would "coördinate the mobilization of private and Governmental instrumentalities" to the end that a concerted attack might be made upon the depression.[106] Government action to combat the depression was kept at a minimum and most of the "coordination" was contributed by the private groups.

One other body coordinating public and private activities which might be mentioned is the President's Advisory Committee on Political Refugees. Created informally by invitation of the President, this committee representing the principal religious groups was "to coordinate the activities of private organizations in this country which deal with the problems of refugees from Germany and in forming a liaison between such organizations and the Government." [107] After the United States declared war, a War Refugee Board was established in the Department of State.

4. ADMINISTRATIVE STUDIES

Another type of presidential commission of which there have been enough established to warrant their treatment as a separate class are those created to investigate the process of administration. Here again some objection may be made that such investigations should be a job for Congress and that any attempt by the President to investigate his own administration is either dictatorship or whitewash. Moreover, presidentially sponsored administrative investigations look like a combination of the functions of prosecutor and jury.

Whether a presidential commission to investigate administration is a usurpation of a congressional function or an aid to the democratic process depends upon a more precise analysis of the purpose to the administrative investigation. Administrative investigations may be broken down into those of an inquisitorial character and those of a research character.[108] Inquisitorial investigations are those in which there is a search for wrong-doing or for inefficiency bordering upon misfeasance. Research investigations, on the other hand, do not look for wrong-doing and corruption but rather for inefficiency characterized by nonfeasance or malfeasance.

Mere description of the two general types of administrative investigating commissions indicates which is more properly the responsibility of Congress and which of the President. If the primary purpose of the commission is inquisitorial, the responsibility of the commission as a general matter should be to Congress. If the primary purpose is research with the aim of improving methods of administration, there are many advantages in having the job done by men with the executive point of view.

When the function of the investigation is to turn up alleged corruption and wrong-doing, it is very important that the investigators proceed with their job in a completely objective manner. A President who orders an inquisitorial investigation of one of the executive departments, no matter how objective the inquisition may be, is likely to be accused of partisanship. This is a result of the President's responsibility for the executive departments. The same accusation may of course be made when a congressional committee is investigating the executive if both executive and Congress are of the same political party. There is less chance of real foundation for the accusation, however, when the investigation is being conducted by a separate branch of government.

When, however, the function of the investigation is not inquisitorial but is devoted to the discovery of methods by which administration can be improved, it is most appropriately conducted by the executive.

Most presidential commissions engaged in the investigation of administration or administrative practices have been of the research type. The President is charged with the duty of seeing that the laws are faithfully executed. As the chief administrator he should also be concerned with seeing that the laws are efficiently executed. Insofar as inefficiency comes to light, it is a reflection on the President. Moreover, inefficiency in the executive branch may result in investigation by the legislative branch. Investigations designed to "tone up" the federal administrative service should be conducted under the guidance of the President, subject always to the congressional power to conduct its own investigation if the President should overlook inefficiency. As long as the President remains responsible to the people there is little reason to suspect the honesty of his attempts to improve administrative efficiency.

Weber has pointed out that logically "it is the legislature which . . . should from time to time institute such investigations as are necessary in order to assure itself that its agents are performing their duties in an efficient and economical manner." [109] This is good theory but as a recommendation it can only carry weight if it can be shown as a fact that legislative investigations of administration have been more thorough, and less subject to political pressures than executive controlled investigations. Weber himself indicates that legislative investigations are likely to be partisan affairs. It is difficult, he says, to secure "a thoroughly non-partisan and independent investigation if conducted under legislative auspices." [110] He might have added that congressmen are not easily convinced that such investigations should include any experts other than congressmen.[111] Yet one of the most important aspects of a successful investigation of administration is that it should be conducted by persons of "experience in reference to the matters inquired into by them" and also "in a position where they can make their criticisms and suggestions with the utmost independence and fearlessness." [112]

Investigations conducted under presidential auspices for the purpose of improving administration are likely to be more productive than similar investigations launched by Congress. The President is in a position where inefficiencies will come to his attention in the regular course of executive business. With the Bureau of the Budget in the Executive Office charged with authority "to assemble, correlate, revise, reduce, or increase the estimates of the several departments and establishments," [113] inefficient organization, divided responsibility, and excessive requests for appropriations should soon be apparent to the President. The President may also direct the Bureau to study the organization, activities, and methods of the executive agencies. Studies made by the Bureau may lead to suggested changes in administrative set-up or procedure. While the Bureau should not be charged with extensive investigations and large-scale reorganization plans because it does not represent the lay expert whose services are invaluable, and because its day-to-day functions are of full-time character, the Bureau's investigative functions do enable it to keep a finger on the pulse of administration and to detect conditions demanding major diagnosis. Congress, on the other hand, is not likely to be aware of the need for administrative reorganization until disorganization is in an advanced stage. Executive administrative investigations are like periodic medical examinations, they keep the administration healthy. Congressional administrative investigations, on the other hand, do not appear until administrative health is in a bad state.

The principal criticisms of research investigations conducted under the guidance of the Chief Executive are: (1) the danger that the investigators will be only reluctantly critical of the administration which created them. This danger can largely be avoided by selecting a personnel and staff of experienced men having no official connection with the government; [114] and (2) the difficulty of getting the recommendations of such commissions adopted by the Congress. This latter difficulty seemed so serious to Mr. Weber [115] that he suggested that legislative investigations of administration were the most desirable type of investigation. This difficulty, however, has been to a large extent mitigated by the experience of the last ten years. Not only was President Roosevelt able to get Congress to accept most of his important proposals, but the influence of the Executive in at least having his proposals for legislation given serious consideration has been on the constant increase.

While there have been a number of congressional inquiries of a research character [116] into the administrative departments, the more important studies in recent years have been conducted by committees appointed by and responsible to the President.[117] Though these committees have varied in composition and the sources of their support, they have all been concerned with an over-all survey of federal administrative practices.

One of the first presidential committees to investigate administration was the Committee on Departmental Methods, more commonly known as the Keep Committee.[118] Appointed by President Theodore Roosevelt in 1905 upon his own authority to investigate the business methods and practices of the executive departments, and to report plans for their improvement, the committee, headed by Assistant Secretary of the Treasury C. H. Keep, was made up entirely of governmental officials holding the ranks of assistant secretaries in the departments, or their equivalent. The official composition of this committee was in part due to the fact that no congressional appropriation for the committee had been made and it had to avail itself of the help of regular employees of the government. The President asked for an appropriation of $25,000 but was only given $5,000 "for salaries or compensation of persons not otherwise employed by the United States." [119] This was insufficient to pay for experts not in the employ of the government.[120] Eighteen reports were made by this committee on subjects relating to administrative activities. The reports were made to the President and he sent them to Congress if he believed that they merited congressional attention.[121] Some reforms were accomplished as a result of Executive Orders, but matters which were submitted to Congress were for the most part ignored. There was congressional opposition to the Committee largely because it was felt the President was acting without proper authority.[122]

The next important study of administration was made by the President's Commission on Economy and Efficiency requested by President Taft and authorized by congressional act in 1910.[123] The Sundry Civil Appropriation Act of 1911 [124] contained an appropriation of $100,000

> to enable the President to inquire into the methods of transacting the public business of the executive departments and other Government establishments and to recommend to Congress such legislation as may be necessary to carry into effect changes found to be desirable that cannot be accomplished by executive action alone.

This Commission functioned from 1910 to 1913 and during this period was voted annual appropriations by Congress totaling $260,000.[125] Except for the requirement that the Commission render its reports to Congress and for one specific request for an investigation of the Patent Office,[126] the President was free to direct the Commission to study any aspects of administration which the President desired to have studied. The President was also free to determine the character of the organization and its methods of operation.[127] The Commission, well balanced as between accountants and experts from official and private life, was headed by Dr. F. A. Cleveland, Director of the Bureau of Municipal Research of the City of New York.[128] The study made by the Commission has been described as "the most comprehensive and systematic investigation that has ever been made of the administrative branch of the national government." [129] Many of its 110 reports became the basis of subsequent legislative or executive changes in administrative organization.[130]

In the interval between Taft's Commission and President Franklin D. Roosevelt's Commission on Administrative Management of 1936 there were no very important presidentially inspired studies of administration made. A joint legislative-executive committee, the "Brown Committee" was authorized in 1920 by a Public Resolution which became law without the President's signature.[131] In 1921 the President was authorized to appoint a representative to cooperate with the joint committee.[132] The group made up of three representatives, three Senators, and headed by the President's appointee, Walter F. Brown, was instructed to propose departmental re-groupings to bring about similarity in departmental undertakings. The program submitted, though endorsed by Presidents Harding and Coolidge, was opposed by Cabinet members and other government officials and was never accepted. Most radical of the proposals submitted was one which would have consolidated the War and Navy departments.[133]

With the exception of some departmental and interdepartmental committees created by President Hoover concerned with specific aspects of administration, the next important over-all study of administration conducted by a presidential commission was the study made by the President's Committee on Administrative Management, appointed March 22, 1936.[134] The Committee was directed to examine the whole problem of administrative management in the executive branch and suggest, for the guidance of the President and Congress, "a comprehensive and balanced program for dealing with the overhead organization and management of the Executive Branch. . . ." [135] The Committee was made up of three lay experts in the field of public administration, Louis Brownlow, Chairman, Charles E. Merriam, and Luther Gulick. They selected a staff of 27, largely of teachers and scholars, which proceeded to Washington in the summer of 1936 to examine on the spot the federal administrative structure.

The President's Committee was not the first administrative investigating body in the field in 1936 since the Senate created a Select Committee to Investigate the Executive Agencies of the Government on February 24, 1936.[136] The creation of the Senate Committee undoubtedly prompted the President to create his Committee. Senator Harry F. Byrd acted as Chairman. Subsequent to the creation of the Byrd Committee and the President's Committee, the House of Representatives chose a committee at the suggestion of the President, chaired by James P. Buchanan, and the Senate selected a second committee chaired by Senator Robinson.[137] Thus during the summer of 1936, there were four different committees in Washington investigating the general subject of administration, three created by the President, or at his request, and one created by the Senate. For all practical purposes, however, attention can be confined to the President's Committee and the Byrd Committee, which, according to Mr. Brownlow agreed to divide the field for investigation between them.

The President's Committee was "to concern itself with the problem of administrative management from the over-all point of view." The Byrd Committee which was to make detailed studies of operating agencies selected the Brookings Institution to do the staff work.[138] The staffs of the two principal committees continued their work through the summer and fall of 1936 and in early 1937, the Report of the President's Committee was transmitted to the President and to Congress.[139] Senator Byrd submitted the Preliminary Report of the Select Committee to Investigate the Executive Agencies of the Government on August 19, 1937. Thereafter congressional hearings and debate centered largely on the findings and recommendations made by the two groups of experts. All might have gone smoothly had the experts agreed in their conclusions or had they been confined by their terms of reference to subject matter which did not overlap.

As a study of the reports will indicate, the lines of demarcation referred to above were substantially followed except on the important subject of financial administration. The President's Committee desired to see the Comptroller General shorn of his power of pre-audit, and the Byrd Committee recommended an increase in the power of the Comptroller General.[140]

Disagreement between administrative experts on such an important matter as the proper place of audit in a governmental system, is an indication either that there are two schools of expert thought on the matter, or that the experts may be induced to arrive at different conclusions because of different employers or for other reasons not stemming from a common source of good administrative practice. Lindsay Rogers has pertinently asked whether a clash of "expert" opinion could have been avoided if the experts had swapped employers before they began work.[141] Since the recommendations made relative to audit by each group of experts corresponded with what might be suspected as the wishes of the employers, it is suggested that the answers to Mr. Rogers' question would be "no." When "experts" are employed they are likely consciously or unconsciously to reflect to some extent the position of their employer so far as that position is known. This is regrettable but human. It is possible that a tradition may eventually be developed in the United States similar to that of the British royal commissions of whom it may in general be said that the membership holds fact, and policy recommendations stemming therefrom, in higher esteem than the reactions of their employer. Such a tradition can be developed only over a long period of time and by frequent examples of commissions finding facts and recommending policies which do not necessarily conform with the views of the employer. Such a tradition cannot be established if the "experts" make it a practice to consult their employer before they make the report as was apparently the case with the President's Committee.[142]

But to return from the tantalizing subject of "when is an expert not an expert," the principal point to be made relative to the reports of the Byrd Committee and the President's Committee is that when Congress and the President are operating in the same or closely related fields at the same time, it is not safe at our present stage of development in the use of administrative "experts," to permit two sets of experts to operate on the same subject under separate employers. There is too much danger that the result will be two sets of "expert" opinions. To avoid this danger it is important that the terms of reference be drawn in such a way that the committees' functions will not overlap. To fail to make a clear distinction between functions is likely to lead to a stalemate, to a loss of confidence on the part of the people in a governmental structure which enables experts to find opposite facts and form opposite opinions, and to ridicule of the experts.

The Report of the President's Committee which was submitted to Congress on January 12, 1937, was embodied in a bill which failed of passage in the third session of the 75th Congress largely because other issues had become involved including the President's proposal for the reorganization of the Supreme Court. Moreover, the President's insistence on a provision which would in effect have required a two-thirds vote for Congress to reject administrative reorganizations which the President might make under the act, gave the bill's opponents a peg upon which to hang trumped up charges that the bill would make the President a dictator.[143]

In 1939 the Reorganization Act was passed and many of the recommendations made in the Report of the President's Committee were embodied therein.[144]

It is beyond the scope of this study to analyze the Report of the President's Committee and to point out which recommendations became law and which failed of adoption. Suffice it to note that the Report led to the most thorough overhaul of the executive branch of government since the Budget and Accounting Act of 1921, which, like the Reorganization Act of 1939 owed its origin to a presidential commission, the Commission on Economy and Efficiency.

Although neither the Commission on Economy and Efficiency nor the President's Committee on Administrative Reorganization were as successful at getting their recommendations on the statute books as students of public administration might desire, it appears that the Committee on Administrative Reorganization had one important advantage over the Commission on Economy and Efficiency. That advantage lay principally in the fact that the Committee on Administrative Management operated without intermittent congressional control on its activities.

The Committee served as an adjunct of the National Emergency Council which provided the necessary office facilities and clerical personnel. The National Emergency Council was also the indirect source for the $100,000 made available for the committee from the Emergency Relief Appropriation Act of 1935. All but some $12,000 of the available money was spent.[145]

While the Committee on Administrative Management did not spend as much money as the Commission on Economy and Efficiency, it is interesting to compare the ease with which the respective investigations were launched and maintained. The $260,000 made available for Taft's commission came as a result of four separate congressional appropriations—all save one preceded by a presidential request. Before each appropriation was made, the Commission and its activities had to be justified before congressional committees.[146]

President Roosevelt, on the other hand, under the liberal terms of the Emergency Relief Appropriation Act of 1935 with its $4,000,000,000 was able to proceed unhampered by congressional restrictions. He neither asked congressional consent to organize the Committee nor accounted to Congress for its expenditures. As an act of executive grace he did ask the House and Senate to cooperate with him.[147]

While there are advantages in having the President able to inaugurate investigations of administration, when, as, and if he wishes, the necessity of congressional consent for important administrative changes must always condition the President's freedom.

In addition to the "over-all" administrative investigations just described, the President frequently appoints committees to make studies of some particular aspect of administration. Studies of this type are usually designed to remedy an abuse or a particular inefficiency, though other purposes may be present.

One such commission was the Dodge Commission appointed by President McKinley to investigate the conduct of the War Department in the war with Spain.[148] The Commission was administration-inspired although the source of the inspiration was the public's criticism of the conduct of the Spanish-American War, and the threat of a congressional investigation.[149] Secretary of War General R. A. Alger requested the President to appoint a committee with full power to investigate the War Department and its activities during the war. General Grenville M. Dodge headed the Commission. Nearly 500 witnesses were examined and criticisms of the War Department were publicly invited. Each of the bureaus in the Department was the subject of a study and report. Some few recommendations were made by the Commission, but in general, the conduct of the War Department was approved. Criticism of the Department as a whole was summed up in the words: "there was lacking in the general administration of the War Department . . . that complete grasp of the situation which was essential to the highest efficiency and discipline of the Army." [150] But this general criticism was dulled by the Commission's conclusion that "notwithstanding the haste with which the nation entered upon war with Spain, . . . the people of the United States should ever be proud of its soldiers" who put an end to Spanish colonial power in less than three months.[151]

While some of the recommendations made by the Commission may have resulted in changes in internal policy, no recommendation was important enough or basic enough to warrant legislation. If no important recommendations were made, one may properly ask what was the purpose of the Commission and wherein lay its value?

Galloway has suggested that the Commission was created in order to forestall a congressional investigation into the conduct of the war.[152] It is possible, of course, that the Secretary of War really wanted an investigation of the War Department which would result in suggestions as to methods for improving its organization and procedure, but that is doubtful. It is the exception rather than the rule for a man to ask that he or the organization operated under his direction be investigated.

In contrast to the Dodge Commission, the Commission on Naval Reorganization, appointed by President Roosevelt in a letter dated January 27, 1909, partook more of the nature of a "research" study than of an "inquisition." Roosevelt asked for two general reports on the naval organization. "First, as to the fundamental principles of an organization that will insure an efficient preparation for war in time of peace . . . , Second, specific recommendations as to changes in the present organization that will accomplish this result. . . ." [153] The Commission was composed of five retired rear-admirals, two ex-Secretaries of the Navy, and an ex-member of the House of Representatives who had been an active champion of the Navy. The most important suggestions made by the Commission led to centralization of responsibility and a reduction but not elimination of certain of the autonomous powers of the bureaus within the department.

The Attorney General's Committee on Administrative Procedure is another example of the President's use of a committee of the research character to investigate a technical aspect of administration. The Committee was appointed by Attorney General Murphy on February 23, 1939, pursuant to a letter from President Roosevelt. Disregarding the political reason for the creation of this committee, i. e. the Walter-Logan bill,[154] the Attorney General's order stated that

> the function of such committee shall be the investigation and consideration of the existing administrative practices and procedures of the several executive departments, independent establishments, and commissions, and the formulation of conclusions and recommendations for such action . . . as may appear appropriate.[155]

The Committee was headed by Dean Acheson and included ten specialists in the field of administrative law. The Director of the study was Walter Gellhorn who, with a staff of lawyer-investigators, undertook detailed studies of some 48 federal agencies engaged in administrative rule-making and the adjudication of private rights. The report was nearly two years in preparation, but when finished it was the most complete study of the field of administrative procedure made up to that time.

Although a draft bill was appended to the Final Report, it appeared that the principal value of the study would not be in having Congress adopt such a bill, but rather it appeared that the study would serve as a handbook of recommended procedures for administrative agencies.[156] Suggestions were made for improving procedure in many of the existing agencies, but most such suggestions were capable of being carried out by the agencies themselves.

The creation of an Office of Federal Administrative Procedure which was to be largely advisory in character was recommended but it appears doubtful if such a body will be created in the near future.

The Committee on Administrative Procedure was created without congressional authorization and its expenses were borne by the Department of Justice. Its creation would not appear to violate the Sundry Civil Act of 1909, however, since the study concerns the administration of justice and so would fall within the scope of the activities of an existing department.[157]

It is not likely that the report of the Committee will lead to legislation in the near future. The report will serve, however, as a warning to some agencies to alter their procedure. It should also serve as a guide to the President and Congress in the creation of the mushroom agencies attendant upon the war, but its effect in time of emergency is doubtful. In time of peace, emphasis in the democratic-capitalist society is upon the protection of private rights from the action of government. This is not true in time of war.

No student can question the contribution of the Committee's report to our knowledge of administrative proceedings in the federal government. Nor can one question the need for such a study. Whether the study was conducted under the proper auspices raises a political question. As has been mentioned earlier, any research study of administration by administration will be subject to the charge of politics. But when the study needs cooperation of members of the administration, the best procedure seems to be an administration-sponsored study. When a study is made by men within the agency, or within the administration, one would not expect it to be either objective or constructive. However, when the study is made by "outside experts" brought temporarily within the government employ, there is likely to be cooperation as well as objectivity and constructive suggestions—although the charge of politics is not avoided.

Somewhat similar in function to the Attorney General's Committee on Administrative Procedure was the President's Committee on Civil Service Improvement (The Reed Committee). This Committee was established January 31, 1939 and charged with the duty of making "a comprehensive study of methods of recruiting, testing, selecting, promoting, transferring, removing and reinstating personnel" for technical positions which the Civil Service Commission did not deem it practicable to fill by competitive examination.[158] The Committee was headed by Justice Reed and included three government and three lay officials, all with wide experience in the field of administration and personnel. The body was appointed as a prelude to bringing more of the high technical positions under competitive examination. The report which was over two years in preparation, recommended that professional, scientific, and higher administrative and investigative positions be brought within the merit system. There was a difference of opinion among the committee members with regard to bringing lawyers within the classified service.[159]

The report of the Committee was transmitted to Congress for its information, accompanied by a presidential message suggesting that the report should "help in devising effective means for enlarging the scope and extending the area of this type of civil service." There was no request for legislation and the Report was apparently sent to Congress solely for its information. Acting upon the recommendations of the majority of the Committee, President Roosevelt signed an Executive Order on April 23, 1941 which brought some 125,000 new positions within the classified service.

The Reed Committee is an excellent example of the effective use of a research committee by the President. With authority to bring new positions within the Civil Service [160] the President nevertheless delayed action [161] until the Committee had an opportunity to make a thorough study and report. Then the substance of the report was carried into effect by the President's order.

All of the "research studies" of administration, general or particular, show a number of similarities. Each of those mentioned, has been presidentially inspired. All, with the exception of the Keep Committee and the Brown Committee, included a number of lay experts. All rendered reports to the President which were advisory in character. The President was free to accept or reject their recommendations. Where legislation was necessary, as in the case of the report of the President's Committee on Administrative Management, the President had to fight for it. The mere transmission of a report to Congress without any presidential pressure, is an effective way to bury it. The report is forgotten by the legislators, although its information and ideas may not die.

What is the value of these presidentially-inspired research investigations? One need but point to the Budget and Accounting Act of 1921 which got a large part of its start from Taft's Commission on Economy and Efficiency—or to the many minor changes in the ensuing twenty years which had their origin in that Commission's suggestions.

More recently one can turn to the report of the President's Committee on Administrative Management and the Spring, 1941 copy of the Government Manual to see the impact of the Report on the federal government. True, the Committee's recommendation for new government departments was not accepted by Congress, but the President did receive power to set up new "agencies" which look and act very much like departments. It is worthy of note that most changes which demanded legislation were rejected by the Congress. For example, the elimination of the function of pre-audit in the Office of Comptroller-General, the creation of a one-man Civil Service Administration, or the creation of the new departments. But once the President had been given a limited power to consolidate and reorganize, he was guided to a very large extent by the Committee's report.

In conclusion, it may be said that the use of the presidential commission for the purpose of a research investigation of administration appears to be a governmental device which should be used more often. Since the President is the man responsible for effective administration, he needs a regularized method for discovering inefficiencies. This does not encroach upon the power of Congress because a recognition of the value and the use by the President of such commissions takes nothing away from Congress. It can still investigate if it wishes to do so. A wider acceptance of the idea that it is the province of the President to keep administration modern and up to date would go a long way toward improving the effectiveness of the executive branch of government.

For too long the idea has been generally accepted that the executive branch can get along without reorganizational changes until it begins to creak and groan. Instead, reorganization of administration should be a constant process. To some extent the Bureau of the Budget serves that purpose, but it tends to be immersed in administrative detail, which although important, leaves administration on the grand scale unattended. It is believed that this job can best be done by presidential commissions such as those described in the previous pages.

6

BOARDS OF INQUIRY

THE distinction between commissions created to study administration and those which, for want of a better name, are described here as boards of inquiry has already been drawn. The essential distinction is that the commissions described as engaged in administrative studies are bodies seeking to improve administration as such. They may be created as a result of charges that government is expensive, its methods antiquated, or that red tape is rampant. Boards of inquiry on the other hand are bodies looking for wrongdoing. They are trying to pin guilt on someone or some organization. They are usually created as the result of an obvious failure of government or a disaster for which the public demands a complete explanation. The distinction is a rough one at best but it serves to draw a necessary line between types of administrative investigations most appropriately undertaken by the Executive and those most appropriately undertaken by the Congress. As indicated heretofore, it is believed that administrative studies are most thorough and successful if undertaken under the auspices of the Executive, but that investigations which seek to uncover wrongdoing are most appropriately undertaken under the auspices of Congress.

One of the principal characteristics of the American form of government is that, in the eyes of the people, the President is so closely associated with the policy of each of the executive departments that a failure in any one of them is attributed to the President. Postmen encounter individuals who blame slow postal service on the President. Attacks on bureaucrats are none too subtle attacks on the President. Presidential responsibility for the activities of the executive departments means that an investigation under presidential auspices of shortcomings in any executive office cannot be undertaken without fear of charges that the President is not acting in good faith. The attitude is illustrated by a 1942 news item concerning a proposed investigation of charges made against the Navy's Bureau of Ships relating to the planning and production of invasion boats. The news item reported from the Secretary of the Navy had "decided to call in a man from outside the department and instruct him to investigate" in order "to avoid a 'self-investigation,' which might lead to talk of 'whitewash.' " [1]

Unfortunately, the public's suspicion of self-investigation is not always groundless. One such investigation was that of the Committee to Investigate the Charges of the Navy League which was created by President Hoover in 1931. The President of the Navy League, William Howard Gardiner, had charged that President Hoover was bending his efforts "to reduce and starve the United States Navy." President Hoover selected a committee of five, including three members of the Navy League and two members of the cabinet, to demonstrate the "untruths and distortions of fact" present in the charges of the Navy League's President. President Hoover added that he expected Mr. Gardiner to apologize for his statement.[2] The Committee held secret meetings, heard no witnesses, and a few days later submitted a 10,000 word report which "acquitted" the President of the United States.[3] The Committee attracted party comment, and the opposition claimed that it was designed to "whitewash" the President and was a "hand-picked," "judge-jury-prosecutor" committee. Although this committee was investigating policy rather than administration, it illustrates rather well the abuse to which presidential commissions may be subject. Such commissions if they are to establish a reputation as a governmental device, must not be used as a personal device to rationalize a particular policy or administrative practice. If attacks on presidential policy or administrative practice become unbearable to the President and, in his opinion, necessitate defensive action, the commission which he selects must be so outstanding and fair in its procedure, so correct and exhaustive of the facts, that no unbiased person could question the integrity of the commission's conclusions. These are difficult conditions to meet and in fact, they are so difficult as to indicate that boards of inquiry should as a general rule be chosen by some method which leaves no room for the charge of self-investigation.

Several other administratively sponsored "inquistorial" investigations might be mentioned in which there is some question of the commission's objectivity. On September 12, 1903, President Theodore Roosevelt appointed a Commission to Investigate the Conditions of the Immigration Station at Ellis Island. The Commission was appointed as a result of charges by the *New Yorker Staats-Zeitung* that enforcement of deportation orders was working excessive hardships, that the buildings on Ellis Island were crowded and vermin infested, and that the administration at the Island was harsh.[4] The Report of the Commission of Five was submitted two months later after hearings and a spot investigation. While the Report commended the Commissioner of Immigration at Ellis Island, thus avoiding any reflection on the President, a number of recommendations for improving conditions at the Island were made. For the most part the defects pointed out in the Report were attributed to failure on the part of Congress to provide adequate facilities for handling the large number of aliens who were being received.[5]

Another example was the Special Commission to Investigate Conditions of Labor and Housing of Government Employees on the Isthmus of Panama, appointed April 25, 1908, by President Roosevelt as a result of public criticism of the conditions at the project. The commissioners produced an objective Report and concluded that workers thought they were "being treated right." The Report contained an indictment, however, of housing conditions, disability compensation and vacation furloughs, as well as criticism of the administrative set-up of the Isthmian Canal Commission. President Theodore Roosevelt followed some of the Commission's recommendations with regard to the organization of the Isthmian Commission and asked that Congress provide more adequate compensation for canal employees who might be injured in the course of their work.

The President's Commission of the United States on the Investigation of the General Slocum Disaster, appointed June 21, 1904, had a more tangible effect upon the Steamboat Inspection Service than do most presidential inquisitorial investigations of the administration. The Commission was made up of high government officials and instructed "to make a thorough and exhaustive investigation of the disaster." [6] Among the members was the Supervising Inspector-General of the Steamboat Inspection Service. The report of this Commission, submitted on October 8, 1904, made a number of recommendations and touched off a series of legislative reforms.[7] But above all, it placed much of the responsibility for the disaster upon officers of the Steamboat-Inspection Service and the President ordered the dismissal of all officers concerned.[8]

Here was an instance where a presidentially inaugurated investigation which touched upon the administration and hence might conceivably have reflected upon the President was vigorously pressed. It may be noted, however, that there are some failures of administration or some cases of maladministration which are so obvious that for the President to do less than inaugurate a vigorous investigation would leave him open to serious criticism. The lesser of two dangers in such cases of administrative failure is to let in the light, rather than to try to hide the facts.

The most spectacular example in recent years of a presidential board of inquiry, cited here by reason of its importance was the Roberts Commission "to ascertain and report the facts relating to the attack . . . upon the Territory of Hawaii. . . ." [9]

Although the President as Commander in Chief has authority to appoint military commissions, it would not appear that he was acting in that capacity in setting up the Roberts Commission, Justice Robert was a civilian and the President's authority over retired officers, who made up most of the rest of the Commission, is severely limited. [10]

The President has statutory authority to constitute "a court of inquiry to examine into the nature of any transaction of or accusation or imputation against any officer or soldier. . . ." [11] The findings of any such inquiry are only advisory, thus differing from a court-martial which may punish. [12] A court of inquiry, however, is not effective for an investigation as important as that of Pearl Harbor. The court does not have power to compel the attendance of civilian witnesses, [13] and must be made up of officers, active or retired. [14] Therefore, the President did not use his statutory authority to create a court of inquiry to investigate the Pearl Harbor disaster.

The expenses of the Roberts Commission were met out of a fund of $100,000,000 made available in 1941 as an Emergency Fund for the President "to provide for emergencies affecting the national security and defense. . . ." [15] Had this money not been available, it is conceivable that the President might have had to designate the investigation as a "relief project," rely upon a court of inquiry, [16] stretch the words of some other appropriation act to cover this unexpected expense, [17] ask Congress for a special authorization, or give up the idea of a presidential investigation.

The Roberts Commission was instructed to find facts and advise the President. It could punish no one. "The purposes of the required inquiry are to provide bases for sound decisions. . . ." [18] The Executive Order could not, and did not try to give the commission powers of compulsion. Congress remedied this defect by an act which authorized the Commission to summon witnesses and to examine them under oath. [19] In the absence of such powers, the Commission might have encountered recalcitrant witnesses and if there had been perjury it might have gone unpunished.

The Roberts Commission is not an example tending to show the need of a statutory method for creating presidential commissions. Pearl Harbor united the country so that the investigation was easily launched. Money was available and compulsory powers were willingly given. But by the time the report was made, voices were heard suggesting a congressional investigation. [20]

The cry will always be raised that presidential commissions to investigate any of the executive departments will be "whitewash" commissions just as objection will always be made that congressional committees of investigation are not as interested in the facts as in politics.

The distinction between the type of investigation which can appropriately be conducted by the Executive and that which can be conducted by Congress is illustrated by the efforts made by the Executive and Congress to investigate the sinking of the submarine S-4 which was rammed and sunk by a Coast Guard vessel in 1927 with a heavy loss of life. The tragedy attracted a great deal of attention because it was believed that not all of the men aboard the sunken craft were dead and there was hope that some of them might be rescued. Rescue efforts failed, however, and there was a widespread feeling that bungling in the rescue operations had in part been responsible. An explanation was required.

Two principal questions were raised by the incident. First, who was to blame for the initial accident and who was to blame for the subsequent failure to rescue the men? Or, as it was remarked in the Senate: "whether the Navy was at fault or not at fault, and if it was at fault where does the blame lie?" In other words, the question of *blame*.[21] Second, do safety devices exist which might have been used to rescue the men or which might have prevented the accident but which, for some reason, were not available, possibly because inventive genius had not been given opportunity, possibly because Congress had not appropriated enough money, or possibly because not enough consideration had been given to the problem? In other words, the question of *safety devices*. The nation was interested in the answer to each of these questions and accurate answers were necessary to avoid, in so far as possible, similar tragedies in the future.

A letter addressed to President Coolidge by Secretary of Navy Wilbur on January 4, 1928, suggested the desirability of the creation of a commission of experts "to consider the development of safety devices for our submarines." This letter was sent to Congress accompanied by a draft resolution authorizing the President to appoint a commission composed of five members, of whom three were to be selected from civil life and two to be retired officers of the Navy.[22] The Secretary of the Navy conceded in his letter to the President that the President could appoint such a committee without congressional authority if he so wished and that such a body could perform a valuable service. The Secretary suggested, however, that a comprehensive investigation would not be possible without congressional authority.

When the Senate took up the draft resolution there was general concurrence in the proposition that the President could appoint such a commission on his own authority.[23] The Senate, however, wanted senatorial representa-

tion on the commission and the resolution failed on that point.[24] Another factor which contributed to the defeat of the resolution was the feeling by members of Congress that they did not want to give up their right to conduct their
own independent investigation. Although authorization for the creation of
a presidential commission would not necessarily have meant that Congress
could not have had its own investigation if it believed that the presidential
commission had not done an adequate job, the effect upon the public of two
governmental investigations perhaps reaching opposite conclusions, unfortunately not a rare situation, was not to be courted. Senator Robinson of Arkansas went so far as to voice his fear that:

> I should think it would be very bad policy for the Congress to authorize an
> investigation of this particular subject by two different committees, for the
> simple reason that in all probability the findings of the two committees
> would be different. Imagine what would be the situation of the country if
> the President were authorized by Congress to appoint an investigating com-
> mission and the Congress proceeded to appoint another investigating com-
> mission . . . , and the two commissions found the facts to be different and
> made different recommendations.[25]

Such a danger could have been avoided if a breakdown of the subject needing investigation into the two principal questions of *blame* and *safety devices,*
as suggested above, had been made. In that case it would have been proper
for the presidential commission to have investigated the subject of safety devices, going carefully into the subject, considering what science had to offer,
etc. This commission might even have found that Congress had not supplied
enough money for scientific research for safety devices for submarines—a fact
which it is doubtful if any congressional committee would find. On the other
hand, a congressional committee to investigate the cause of, and to fix the
blame for, the accident and to uncover any bungling in the rescue operations
would not have been charged with an attempt to protect the Navy Department from criticism as might have been the charge against any presidentially
sponsored commission trying to fix the blame.

As the investigation of this unfortunate incident developed, it turned out
substantially as suggested in the preceding paragraph, although it was apparently not consciously so planned. A Senate resolution authorized the Senate
Committee on Naval Affairs to make a "full and complete investigation of
the sinking of the S-4" . . . "and the rescue and salvage operations carried
on by the United States Navy subsequent thereto. . . ."[26] A sub-committee
of three senators conducted the hearings and made certain recommendations

with regard to the posting of lookouts. The report absolved the Navy of any blame in salvage operations, stating that everything humanly possible was done to save the lives of the men on the S-4.[27] So far as the question of safety devices was concerned, the sub-committee in general approved the report and recommendations made by a Naval Board of Inquiry [28] which was appointed by the Secretary of the Navy consisting of experts from civil and military life headed by the President of the Massachusetts Institute of Technology. On the basis of the conclusions of the Navy Board, the congressional committee concluded that "a more liberal policy" should be "adopted toward supplying funds that are necessary for the installation of safety and salvage apparatus in submarines." [29]

It is probably not desirable that there be any hard and fast rule as to the type of investigation which should be conducted by Congress as distinguished from the type of investigation which should be conducted by the President. But if the subject to be investigated indicates that some person in the executive branch of the government is likely to be found at fault, the investigation should probably be conducted by Congress. If, on the other hand, the subject to be investigated involves study and careful research, it should be conducted by men with the requisite technical skill and this is the type of man best chosen by the President and not by Congress. In other words, as has been said before, searches for wrongdoing are most likely to be productive of valuable findings if they are conducted by Congress, whereas research studies are most likely to be productive if undertaken under presidential auspices.

The above observation does not apply with the same force to commissions of inquiry or investigation created to investigate conditions existing outside of the government structure as it does to commissions investigating conditions within the government. The point is emphasized by contrasting commissions representative of the two types. The Special Committee to Investigate the Conditions in the Stockyards at Chicago was a presidentially appointed body to investigate certain conditions existing outside of the government. Instead of turning up corruption among governmental officials it turned up corrupt practices among private meat dealers. Instead of finding the executive branch of government at fault, it found that Congress had not properly legislated to protect the interest of the consuming public. The subject under investigation was one which Congress itself might well have avoided because of the "persuasive" arguments which powerful vested interest pressure groups might bring to bear upon Congress. It was the type of investigation particularly adapted to a presidential commission because the President's responsibility tends to be to the whole country while that of individual congressmen tends to be to organized groups which will remember how the congressman voted on issues of interest to the organization. Thus in theory, at least, the President should be above the influence of powerful minorities.

In conclusion it may be noted that this chapter has suggested nothing unusual in pointing out that investigations, brought about as the result of allegations or imputations of wrongdoing by persons or agencies in the executive branch, should be conducted under congressional rather than presidential auspices. The idea has long been current that this is one of the traditional functions of Congress and one which it most efficiently performs.[30] The suggestion has been offered, however, that some investigations of the activities of the executive branch, if undertaken by Congress, must be conducted with the greatest of care and discrimination—an investigation such as that of Pearl Harbor, for example. Moreover, there are some types of facts which may best be uncovered by a presidential commission rather than a congressional body. Examples of this type are found in the separately treated category of administrative investigations,[31] and searches for highly technical facts such as those involved in a search for safety devices for submarines. No clear line can be drawn to indicate where the congressional investigation should end and the presidential investigation begin. Where the line is to be drawn will depend in each case upon the caliber of the men chosen for the task.

The President, it should be noted, has no statutory authority to conduct a full dress investigation of the executive departments such as the authority vested in the Governor of New York State by the Moreland Act. The absence of such authority undoubtedly deters the President from undertaking some needed investigations and tends to leave the initiative for investigations of the executive departments to Congress. Congress would not give up its power to conduct an independent investigation if it were to authorize the President to create his own investigating commissions and the President would not therefore gain a power which could be used to forestall Congress. The principal advantage of such a grant to the President would be that it would enable him to put an end to situations which, if they were to remain without attention, might in time require congressional investigation. To grant the President authority to conduct his own investigations might be likened to giving him a small fire extinguisher which if conveniently placed and properly used will put out small fires before they can become raging conflagrations demanding the full attention of the fire fighting services.

7

PROCEDURE OF PRESIDENTIAL COMMISSIONS

As has been seen, presidential commissions have been created for a wide variety of purposes and the procedures which they have used have been nearly as varied as the problems they have considered. They have ranged from fact-gathering bodies such as the Baruch Rubber Commission which held its initial meeting on a park bench across the street from the White House, to the Roberts Commission on Pearl Harbor, endowed with power to compel testimony and swear witnesses. This diversity in procedure is characteristic of presidential commissions and indicative that they are still in their formative period.

The flexibility in the creation of and the procedure of presidential commissions are characteristics which make them of especial value as government devices. They have developed spontaneously to meet the need of the President or the public for facts or advice which are not readily obtainable from any existing source. In a sense they grow out of the inadequacies in the executive departments or in Congress, or, in some instances, they develop because of the unusual nature of the problem to be met.

Any attempt to say how a presidential commission normally conducts itself, is impossible because they have not shown any tendency to follow a set pattern. It has been observed by students of legal history that the common law courts of England became so involved in rules of procedure (in their attempt to find facts) that it was impossible to rely upon them in dealing with new situations which might cause a case to fall outside the established procedures. Courts of equity developed to meet this need and for generations equity provided the flexibility of procedure which was necessary to find the facts and render judgment in private as well as public disputes. In time, the courts of equity became as inflexible in their procedures as the older common law courts. Equity courts and equitable procedures have now been supplemented by the creation of regulatory commissions which provide the flexibility necessary in compromising some types of private conflicts or in providing continuous public regulation. Now the regulatory commissions are finding themselves faced with more and more inflexible procedures. Presidential commissions may in time provide the fact-finding flexibility which every generation of government has needed.

In the use of presidential commissions for fact-finding purposes, one of the most important questions is whether they have compulsive powers. Presidential commissions have compulsive powers only to the extent that such authority can be found in a congressional grant.[1]

The American people have inherited such a fear of the Star Chamber, expressed in the decisions of the courts, that even Congress frequently encounters constitutional difficulties when it seeks to delegate compulsive powers to executive agencies.[2] Presidential commissions created by the President on his own authority and for his own purposes must get along without compulsive powers unless the Congress sees fit to confer such powers upon them. It might be possible to argue that the President has an inherent power to set up commissions and to compel the testimony of witnesses by following the reasoning in *In re Neagle* [3] to the effect that the President is charged with the duty of faithfully executing the laws and pursuant to that broad constitutional grant he has an implied power to give compulsive powers to commissions which he may create in the course of faithfully executing the laws.[4] The trend toward executive government must go much farther than it has thus far before any court would accept such reasoning.[5]

If the President is not able to grant compulsive powers to his commissions, does it mean that they are impotent? To answer this question one must inquire into the general purpose for which presidential commissions are created. As has been noted heretofore, most presidential commissions can be placed in a general fact-finding category. Assuming this is the principal reason for the creation of such commissions, the question becomes the simple one of whether it is necessary for presidential commissions to have compulsive powers to get facts in situations in which they are generally used for fact-finding. If the facts which are sought are facts which may show wrongdoing—a wrongdoing which may result in someone's punishment, an individual wrong as contrasted with a public wrong, then compulsive powers are necessary. But this is not the type of fact generally sought by presidential commissions. Generally presidential commissions are looking not for wrongdoing by an individual, but for some more general facts or trends. To get these more general facts it is not necessary to compel witnesses to attend hearings or to present evidence. The prestige of presidential commissions is sufficient to bring parties before it without compulsion and, when there is no danger of personal prejudice, witnesses will talk.

To put the case more concretely, the Roberts Commission to investigate the attack on Pearl Harbor needed compulsive powers because someone was bound to be hurt by their findings. The Wickersham Commission, on the other hand, or President Theodore Roosevelt's Country Life Commission did not need compulsive powers to get people to appear before them and talk.

It is not meant to argue here that the President has absolutely no need for compulsive powers for any commission he may create on his own authority. There are economic situations which the President may wish to investigate and in the investigation of which it might be necessary for his commissions to have compulsive powers to do a good job. However, he does not need such powers for general fact-finding commissions—the type which he most frequently appoints.

The general failure to give presidential commissions compulsive powers causes them to be less formal in their procedure and to resort not so much to adversary proceedings to get their facts as to research and quiet appraisal of facts thus obtained. It will generally be observed that compulsive powers are associated with adversary proceedings and it is doubtful if such proceedings are the type most likely to get the type of facts in which presidential commissions are most frequently interested.

It may be argued that adversary proceedings have developed over a long period of years and that time has proven the efficacy of such proceedings and therefore that adversary proceedings and the rules of procedure which have developed with them are essential to effective fact-finding. It must be remembered, however, that adversary proceedings and the rules of evidence devised to control them were developed to assist an inexpert body of jurors in finding the facts. They were not developed for the benefit of expert fact-finders.[6]

It will be recalled that in the chapter on the classification of commissions, informative, or general fact-finding commissions, were divided into (a) those with definite legislative goals in mind, (b) those designed to spotlight public opinion, (c) those designed to reconcile conflicting interests, and (d) those engaged in administrative studies. In none of these cases is it necessary that the commission have compulsive powers or engage in adversary proceedings to find the facts. The same is true with regard to what have heretofore been called administrative commissions (a) acting as executive agents, (b) commissions to coordinate administrative activities, and (c) advisory commissions. The only exception to the statement that presidential commissions need not have compulsive powers would be in the case of commissions which have been described herein as boards of inquiry.

It may be noted here that the Moreland Act of New York State makes provision for the use of compulsive powers. The Moreland Commissioners, however, are generally looking for wrongdoing in which case compulsive powers are necessary. Moreover, a commission created by a State Governor does not have the prestige of a presidential commission and it is likely therefore to need compulsive powers to bring witnesses before it even for general fact-finding purposes. This is not the case with regard to presidential commissions except when they act as boards of inquiry.

In those instances when a presidential commission needs compulsive powers, the facts to be obtained will be so important or so controversial that Congress can be relied upon to grant the necessary powers or conduct a thorough investigation of its own. This conclusion is essentially in agreement with the findings of the British Departmental Committee on the Procedure of Royal Commissions of which Lord Balfour was chairman.[7] The Balfour Committee pointed out that although the power to send for persons and papers is usually given in the warrant establishing the commission, this cannot be enforced unless there is an act of Parliament confirming the power. Normally, concluded the Committee, such powers are not needed and there should be no blanket grant of such powers.[8]

There are two points, however, in the proceedings of every presidential commission where informality may be a danger. These danger points are at the time of the creation of the commission and again when its activities cease.

It is highly desirable that the commission have its objectives clearly defined, and that a plan or procedure for the particular committee be set up. If the objectives of the commission are not clearly defined or the bounds of its activities are not clearly indicated by its warrant, it has no business proceeding further. This point seems so clear that it should not be necessary to mention it. There have been many instances in the past, however, when commissions in every walk of life have not been able to see the forest because of the trees. The Balfour Royal Commission made this point by concluding that a fact-finding body should be created by a warrant of unambiguous terms and that the commission itself should narrow and clarify its aims.[9]

Once the objectives of the commission have been clearly established, the members must plan the procedure to be followed in arriving at the objectives. The procedures followed will vary with the objectives. The important thing is not the procedure followed but the fact that the commission has a clear idea of what it is doing at any particular moment and why, and that it know what the next step is to be.[10]

The other point at which there should be no informality in the activities of a presidential commission is in the preparation of a report. Great weight will be attached to a unanimous report of a reputable presidential commission. Every effort should be made by such a commission to indicate to the President and to the public the matters upon which there is unanimous agreement. These conclusions deserve to be put in writing and to be made accessible. There may be occasions when the objective of a presidential commission will best be achieved by inviting each member of the commission to write an essay on how he or she feels about the matter.[11] One of the principal advantages of a commission as a fact-finder over a single individual, however, is that the conclusions reached by a commission ostensibly represent the product of several minds stimulated by the exchange of ideas. The failure of a commission to reach agreement or any conclusions is likely to be conclusive evidence of the commission's failure. It is especially important therefore that presidential commissions formalize their conclusions.

With the increased frequency with which presidential commissions are created, it has been suggested that a permanent secretariat for presidential commissions should be created. The thought is that this would be a continuing body staffed to meet the needs of all presidential commissions and in general designed not only to make commissions easier to create but to assist commissions in their functions.[12] It is evident, however, that such a body would carry with it a formalization of procedure which would inevitably limit the freedom of the commissions operating under its aegis. If presidential commissions have functioned effectively when their procedures have been informal, then any change which tends to make the procedure formal should be eschewed until its necessity is proved beyond a reasonable doubt. As soon as the procedure of a government institution becomes too formalized, it faces the danger of being unable effectively to cope with a wide variety of new situations. The basic philosophy of presidential commissions is and must continue to be a philosophy of adaptability because in a large sense the President is a court of last resort for almost all important problems of a public nature.

So long as presidential commissions cannot hurt an individual, so long as their findings are subject to public scrutiny and debate before they are used as a basis for positive action, so long as the appointing power remains subject to popular control, the informality of a commission's procedures can be criticized only on the basis that such informality renders the commission inefficient and not on the basis that informality makes them dangerous.

8

THE FUTURE OF PRESIDENTIAL COMMISSIONS

IN present day government presidential commissions are important. One need only to call attention to the complexities that are begotten as the size and scope of government activities increase, or refer to the clash of interests which induce the participants to lose sight of all save the facts and policies which their own group wishes to prevail, in order to realize the imperative necessity for unbiased fact and for policy in the public interest.[1]

If some agency within our government were able to supply facts on an impartial basis, the need for a full development of presidential commissions would not be so necessary. There is no such agency within our government, however, where impartial facts can be found or where there is "a device whereby the regular, persisting governmental organism taps the surrounding substance of impartial, informed opinion in the body politic, and gains the guidance and strength which continued attempt at self-sufficiency could never give." [2] There is within the American government no fact-finding agency with the prestige or reliability of British royal commissions. The device which today would seem most nearly to fit the need is that of the presidential commission.

In 1937 A. Mervyn Davies, describing the success of British royal commissions, listed eight essential features to the successful operation of commissions of inquiry.[3] Against each of these features, one may compare the points made in the preceding chapters with regard to presidential commissions. (1) Prestige from the royal warrant; (2) sense of public duty on the part of the members and the fact that they receive no pay; (3) creation only when there is a public demand or clear need for them; (4) commissions of a representative character, in some cases impartial, in others, expert, but generally representative of the main interests concerned; (5) proper constitution of commissions with terms carefully stated; (6) granting of wide powers in connection with committee's own procedures, type of hearings, etc.; (7) selection of a good chairman; and (8) ability of the commission to crown its efforts by having its recommendations adopted. A ninth feature might be added; i. e., the experience and ability of the secretary upon whom so much depends and to whom credit is rarely given.[4]

The only commissions in the United States which can hope to have each of these features—features essential to good fact-finding—are those created by the President. This is not to say that all presidential commissions have such features, but a conscientious and careful President can see that each commission he appoints has them. The only other possibility of combining such features in a commission would be in a joint legislative executive body such as the Temporary National Economic Committee, but in general such bodies are too bulky and clumsy in operation to be of much value.

In 1926 Ernst Freund wrote that the problem of fact-finding is "one that only the legislative can handle adequately."[5] It is doubtful if this is true today. As indicated above, congressional committees are not as likely to have the essential features listed by Davies largely because they are political bodies and as such do not have the prestige, the sense of public duty, and the other features necessary to successful fact-finding. Under some circumstances they may be good fact-finders. But they are always suspect. They may be good devices to stir up discussion. But too often congressional committees and their hearings take on the nature of adversary proceedings. The committeemen don't want *the* facts, they want *their* facts.[6] The present war illustrates the difficulty. One week a sub-committee of the House Military Affairs Committee released a report which commended the efforts of the dollar-a-year men in Washington.[7] The next week the Truman Committee of the Senate said that many dollar-a-year men were "unable to divorce themselves from their subconscious gravitation to their own industries."[8] Can both have the facts? Or do neither have the facts? Or is the answer entirely one of opinion? And if the answer be entirely one of opinion is the question of such a nature that there is no consensus among rational and intelligent men?

The most logical conclusion to draw would seem to be that congressional committees are not reliable fact-finders with regard to the value of dollar-a-year men in wartime Washington. If not that, then this particular question is one which can be answered only at the emotional level.[9]

There are other illustrations that can be suggested which point to the general ineffectiveness of congressional committees in the fact-finding realm. For example, would the public have had confidence in the facts found by a congressional committee with regard to the wartime rubber shortage in the United States? To individual committeemen there may be considerations as important as the unearthing of fact. Someone has remarked that every statesman has to be a politician because only by election is he put in the position where he can be a statesman. So with the congressman on a fact-finding committee. He cannot find facts which will unseat him, or which he *believes* will unseat him. For that reason it is possible that he should not be asked to find facts.

The difficulties encountered by the congressman in finding facts because of the position he occupies with regard to public pressure politics is not the only reason he finds it hard to be a successful fact-finder. Another factor is the complexity of the facts which he may be expected to find. Referring to the difficulty of finding an answer to the wartime rubber problem of the United States, the *New York Times* remarked editorially:

> The issues presented are much too technical for Congress to understand without help, involving as they do the intricacies of petroleum chemistry, the merits of half a dozen promising but untried processes and the pressing need of high-grade steel, copper and other essential structural materials.[10]

This statement applies not only to finding the facts about rubber, but to many other problems confronted by modern society.[11] Perhaps Congress will in time resort more to specialists of its own.

One way to successful fact-finding in many cases, however, may be through the President. Presidential commissions have developed to the point where they can take over many of the fact-finding functions formerly undertaken by Congress. And this they may tend to do unless Congress recognizes the importance of expert advice and economic facts as contrasted with political facts.

The foregoing pages have indicated that to some extent presidential commissions have already replaced congressional committees. It has happened because too many congressmen respond more quickly to coherent demands of pressure groups than to less coherent and less well-formulated pleas on behalf of the community at large.

In an article entitled "The Great Fact-Finding Farce," a criticism of the Wickersham Commission, Lillian Symes made the point rather well when she wrote: "One does not expect the National Industrial Conference Board . . . to discover that the factory workers of New York State are grossly underpaid. . . ." Government investigations, she suggests, are no less unbiased and "to expect a fact finding committee appointed by Herbert Hoover to report back in favor of a federal 'dole' would be as naive as to expect a committee appointed by Al Smith . . . to find the Noble Experiment a howling success."[12] Miss Symes not only makes the point that presidential commissions may be packed, but she suggests that they are used as a sop to the public when politics so demands. "The fact finding investigation is becoming increasingly popular as a safety valve for public indignation, a short circuit for possibly dangerous discontent," she writes.[13]

No one would deny that presidential commissions may be used for both of these purposes and have been used for such purposes. Congressional fact-finders are subject to the same criticisms—perhaps even more so than presidential commissions. The fact that, as Miss Symes suggests, "The man in the street did not need a commission (whether presidential or congressional) to tell him—after nineteen months work at a cost of half a million dollars that prohibition does not prohibit . . . ," [14] does not mean that there are no problems in existence upon which the public does not have the facts or the emotions necessary to make a decision. Rather, the facts which do become available to the public are likely to be the facts disseminated by groups with an axe to grind. Moreover, the facts are likely to be distributed by media such as the motion picture or the radio which tend to arouse the emotions more than the intellect. This is true, unfortunately, at a time when the situations and decisions which confront democratic society are more complicated and difficult of factual determination and careful solution than ever before.

To find the facts in these new situations and on the basis of the facts to make decisions between conflicting points of view are among the most important problems of the day. However, there are in our society high minded, honest and intelligent individuals who can approach a difficult problem without prejudice and with controlled emotions. It is believed that these men can find facts and present them to the public in the same way that a scientist can observe and report.[15] Moreover, their judgment on and beyond the facts deserves to be made available to the public. At the present time the most likely way to enlist the assistance of these men is through the device of the presidential commission.

The reason why, as a practical matter, it would be impossible to persuade Congress to give up its fact-finding activity is that once the accurate facts are on the record, the nature of the action necessary is likely to be obvious. Once it is clear for example that the rubber stock pile is low, that rubber reclamation has certain quantitative limits, that new sources can be measured, and the Army demand for rubber is inflexible, the need of conservation is readily apparent. The question which remains is one of policy—how to conserve rubber. Shall it be by the rationing of gasoline, by making cars which travel more than a specified mileage subject to heavy penalty, by public education, or by some other device? These are the questions which Congress should answer.

It is not the contention of this study that no fact-finding functions should remain in Congress. They must remain in order that there may be a check upon the executive and upon the veracity of the facts found by presidential commissions. But many of the fact situations of the modern world upon which legislative action must be predicated are so complicated that a political body cannot hope to find the real facts. For that reason they must delegate this responsibility to someone else—either representative of the Congress or representative of the executive. Since the executive is responsible to both Congress and the people and since the President has developed the presidential commission device, it is suggested that Congress should recognize the good that can come from its further development, not hinder that development, and if necessary, encourage it. Encouragement may come by giving the President a comparatively free hand to find facts when and where he thinks the search should be made or for Congress to order the executive to find facts in certain fields in which Congress contemplates action.

Once the facts have been found by a presidential commission, it will be possible for Congress through its committees to subject those facts to the scrutiny of cross examination and debate. If the facts stand up from such scrutiny, there remains for the Congress the most important job of all, that of determining the policy to be adopted with reference to the known factual situation.

NOTES

CHAPTER I

1. Fritz Morstein Marx, "Commissions of Inquiry in Germany," *American Political Science Review*, vol. 30, Dec., 1936, p. 1134.

2. William Starr Myers, *The State Papers and Other Public Writings of Herbert Hoover*, 2v. (Garden City, N.Y.: Doubleday, Doran and Co., Inc., 1934), p. 197.

George B. Galloway in the only other study of Presidential Commissions which the writer has found, commented that commissions probably "will increase not only in number but also in scope with the increasing centralization of political processes and the expanding functions of government. Pressed with a thousand problems, Congress and the President may rely more and more for information and advice upon fact-finding commissions and advisory councils."

Presidential Commissions, Editorial Research Reports, vol. 1, No. 20, May 28, 1931, at p. 364, also at p. 356.

See also, W. F. Willoughby, *Principles of Public Administration*. (Washington: The Brookings Institution, 1927), p. 171.

3. No effort is made to draw a technical distinction between these terms inasmuch as the terms are usually indiscriminately used in practice. The Brookings Institution in its report for the Byrd Committee used the term "board" to refer to "any body of a collective composition, whether called board, commission, committee, authority or something else." *Preliminary Report of the Select Committee to Investigate the Executive Agencies of the Government*. Pursuant to Sen. Res. No. 217, 75th Cong., 1st sess., Senate Report No. 1275, Aug. 16, 1937, p. 19. The term committee technically refers to a sub-division of a larger body, while a commission is an independent group. For a definition of committee see McConachie, G., *Congressional Committees*, N.Y. 1898.

4. Quoted in Bent, Silas, "Mr. Hoover's Sins of Commissions," *Scribner's Magazine*, vol. 90, p. 9, July, 1931, at p. 14.

5. Bent, Silas, *ibid.*, p. 9.

6. President Franklin D. Roosevelt has referred to the effectiveness of British royal commissions but expressed doubt of the efficacy of a similar device in this country. "The royal commission makes a report to the Parliament and the thing goes through almost automatically, without fuss or feathers." But in the United States we lack the proper "temperament." Excerpt from confidential press conference remarks of April 21, 1938, N.Y. *Times*, Nov. 30, 1941. *Public Papers and Addresses of Franklin D. Roosevelt*, vol. 1938 at p. 288.

7. Myers, *The State Papers and Other Public Writings of Herbert Hoover, op. cit.*, vol. I, pp. 312, 313. For a list see U.S. Congress, Senate, *Federal Commissions, Committees and Boards*, Senate Doc. 174, 71st Cong., 2nd sess., 1930.

8. W. S. Myers and W. H. Newton, *The Hoover Administration*. (N.Y.: C. Scribner's Sons, 1936), p. 492.

9. The difficulty of rendering a completely accurate statement of the number of commissions, committees and similar bodies is readily apparent when one considers what

is to be included in the list. Should single commissioners be included when appointed by the President? When appointed by a Cabinet member? Should departmental committees be included? Bureau committees? Independent commissions set up by Congressional act? Special Congressional investigating committees? The figures above represent, as nearly as possible, (a) bodies appointed by the President, (b) special committees and independent commissions set up by Congress, and (c) in some cases the more important committees created by Cabinet officers.

10. In 1900 a magazine editorial remarked on the cost of congressional and executive commissions. While the Executive needs help in finding facts "the reports of their commissioners are seldom accepted as conclusive, either by legislators or the people at large." *The Nation,* vol. 70, No. 1814, p. 255, April, 1900.

11. Frankfurter, Felix, *The Public and Its Government,* pp. 162–163.

12. Dimock, Marshall E., *Modern Politics and Administration,* pp. 149–150.

13. Willoughby, W. F., *Principles of Legislative Organization and Administration.* (Washington: Brookings Institution, 1934), pp. 586–587.

14. Webb, Sidney and Beatrice, *Methods of Social Study.* (New York: Longmans, Green and Co., 1932), p. 45.

Smith, J. Toulmin, *Government by Commissions, Illegal and Pernicious.* (London: S. Sweet, 1849.)

15. For a comparison with British Royal Commissions see: Gosnell, Harold F., "British Royal Commissions of Inquiry," *Political Science Quarterly,* vol. 49, p. 84, March, 1934. "Royal commissions have certain advantages over American governmental and private bodies of inquiry. They have back of them a long and in the main successful history. They enjoy some of the aloofness and prestige which attach to the institution of the monarchy. They can rely upon the efficient services of the secretaries recruited from the higher branches of the civil service. They can look forward to possible cabinet support for their recommendations. In the United States, governmental investigations, whether executive or legislative, tend to be partisan and the rivalry between the executive and legislative branches of the government has defeated many proposals," p. 118.

16. Clokie, H. M., and Robinson, J. W., *Royal Commissions of Inquiry.* (Stanford: Stanford University Press, 1937), p. 21.

17. *31 U.S.C. 673; 35 Stat. at L. 1027,* Sec. 8, Sundry Civil Act of March 4, 1909.

18. Helm, William P., *Washington Swindle Sheet.* (New York: Albert and Charles Boni, 1932), p. 198.

19. 72nd Cong., 1st sess., Congressional Record, House, Feb. 18, 1932, v. 75, Pt. 4, at pp. 4256–4258. Of 38 commissions appointed by President Hoover, "seven received some appropriation for their work, the others were voluntary or supported by public institutions." Myers, William Starr, and Newton, Walter H., *The Hoover Administration, op. cit.,* p. 492.

20. Bent, Silas, *Mr. Hoover's Sins of Commissions, op. cit.,* p. 14.

21. New York Laws of 1907, Ch. 539.

22. Address before the Gridiron Club, Dec. 14, 1929. Myers, *The State Papers and Other Public Writings of Herbert Hoover, op. cit.,* vol. I, p. 190.

23. Weber, Gustavus A., *Organized Efforts for the Improvement of Methods of Administration in the United States.* (New York: D. Appleton & Co., 1919), p. 44.

CHAPTER II

1. Commissions authorized by Congress, the members of which are appointed by the President, are not within the scope of this study. Thus, regulatory bodies such as the

Interstate Commerce Commission are not viewed as "presidential commissions" in the sense that that term is herein used.

2. Constitution. Article II, Section III.

3. In re Neagle, 135 U.S. 1 (1890).

4. Caleb Cushing in his defense of Tyler's authority to create a commission to investigate the custom-houses cited a number of earlier presidential commissions. (See *Congressional Globe,* vol. 11, pp. 481–482, May 9, 1842.) President Van Buren sent a commission to Europe to investigate the postoffice establishments and get information on which the President could act, and also sent an agent to get information on the armies of Europe. Jackson appointed two commissioners to investigate the Naval Department. Even the "Father of our Country" sent a commission "unauthorized by law" to deal with the rebellious elements of Western Pennsylvania; "the report of the commissioners marks their firmness and abilities . . . and" shows "that the means of conciliation have been exhausted." (Washington's Sixth Annual Address to the Congress, Aug. 7, 1794, *The Addresses and Messages of the Presidents of the United States.*) (N.Y.: McLean and Taylor, 1839.) For more detail on Jackson's appointments, see: House Report No. 194, 24th Cong., 2d sess.

5. *Congressional Globe,* vol. 11, p. 214, 27th Cong., 2d sess.

6. Richardson, James D., *A Compilation of the Messages and Papers of the Presidents, 1789–1908.* (Washington: Bureau of National Literature and Art, 1909), vol. 4, pp. 99–100.

7. President Tyler to George Poindexter, Feb. 11, 1842. Printed in *Congressional Globe,* vol. 11, p. 476, May 4, 1842.

8. Statement of Mr. Tawney of Minnesota upon introduction of amendment to Sundry Civil Act of March 4, 1909. *Congressional Record,* 60th Cong., 2d sess., Feb. 25, 1909, p. 3119. But see Mr. Parker at p. 3120.

9. Sundry Civil Act of 1909. Section 8, 35 Stat. 1027; 31 U.S.C. 673.

10. See Roosevelt, T., *Autobiography.*

11. Quoted in Galloway, George B., "Presidential Commissions," *Editorial Research Reports,* vol. 20, p. 358, 1931.

This remark was made with reference to a commission to Haiti which concerned foreign affairs, a field in which the President is less subject to control.

The Deficiency Act of 1913, 77 Stat. at L. 813, March 4, 1913 provided in part: "Hereafter the executive shall not extend or accept any invitation to participate in any international congress, conference or like event without first having specific authority of law to do so." This is an unconstitutional infringement of a presidential power in the opinion of Graham H. Stuart, *American Diplomatic and Consular Practice.* (N.Y.: D. Appleton-Century Co.), pp. 48–49. United States v. Curtiss-Wright Export Corporation, 299 U.S. 304, 57 Sup. Ct. 216 (1936) in its broad outline would seem to support this view.

12. Silas Bent, "Mr. Hoover's Sin of Commissions," *op. cit.,* Congressional debate in 1928 on a resolution making an appropriation for investigating the sinking of the submarine S4 generally conceded the right of the President to appoint his own commissions. While there was general concurrence on the President's authority to appoint such a body, there was confusion as to the source of the authority. See *Congressional Record,* 70th Cong., 1st sess., vol. 69, Jan. 2, 1928.

Senator Swanson: "The President appointed the (Morrow Aircraft Board) without any authority of the Congress. He could appoint a commission in this case without any authority of Congress," p. 1773.

Senator Robinson of Arkansas: ". . . as Commander in Chief of the Army and Navy . . . the President of the United States already has plenary power to make any investigation on this subject he chooses," and although "he cannot incur any debts or obligations without authorization by Congress," p. 1774, "I would vote him any reasonable amount that might be necessary," p. 1776.

Senator Pittman: The President "can have any investigation he wants. I would be willing to vote . . . $100,000 if he asks for it," p. 1777.

Senator King: "I have no doubt that the Commander in Chief has full authority to make such an investigation as he sees fit," p. 1778.

Despite the general agreement on the President's authority, the resolution was lost because the House and Senate could not agree to the scope of the investigation.

13. *N.Y. Times,* December 2, 1941.

14. Corwin, Edward S., *The President: Office and Powers.* (New York; New York University Press, 1940), p. 67.

15. Corwin, *ibid.,* cites Title II of the National Industrial Recovery Act of June 16, 1933, authorizing the President to "establish such agencies . . . to appoint without regard to the civil service laws, such officers and employees . . . as he may find necessary." 40 U.S.C. 401. On appointing power in general see Corwin, pp. 65–76.

16. *Congressional Globe,* vol. 11, p. 482, May 9, 1842.

17. As early as 1842 Henry Clay could say that "the practice of investigating abuses, or supposed malpractices" by presidential commissions "had grown into use long since in the Executive Department, and no doubt in this instance (custom-houses investigation) mere precedent had been followed." (*Congressional Globe,* vol. 11, p. 231, Feb. 14, 1842.)

18. Executive Order No. 6115, April 25, 1933. See the Report of the Committee and the President's message transmitting the Report to Congress; House Committee Print, Committee on Immigration and Naturalization, 76th Congress, 1st sess. (U.S. Govt. Printing Office, June 13, 1938.)

19. Public No. 853, Ch. 876, 76th Congress, 3rd sess.

20. Card file: U.S. Information Service; U.S. Government Manual, March, 1941.

Other Cabinet committees included the *Cabinet Committee to Investigate Conditions in the Cotton Textile Industry,* April 26, 1935.

21. Article II, Section 2 of the Constitution of the United States of America.

22. 10 U.S.C., Secs. 495, 576, 577.

23. 10 U.S.C., Sec. 990.

24. 10 U.S.C., Sec. 540, gives the President power to detail men of the Army, Navy and Marine Corps to assist South American countries in military matters if they request such help.

25. Corwin, *President: Office and Powers, op. cit.,* pp. 344–345.

26. *Cong. Record,* 77th Cong., 1st sess., Senate, Oct. 23, 1941, p. 8413.

27. *New York Times,* July 3, 1927, p. 6, col. 5.

Federal Commissions, Committees and Boards, Senate Doc. No. 174, 71st Cong., 2d sess. (Wash.: U.S. Govt. Print. Off., 1930). Compiled under direction of William Adams Slade, Chief Bibliographer, Library of Congress. Hereafter referred to as Senate Doc. 174, 71st Cong., 2d sess. See p. 121.

28. See Professor Corwin's disappointment "that the President's Committee on Administrative Management failed" to consider the question of the value of the Comptroller General's present powers and independent position as a defense of Congress' control of the purse and of the check which this provides against the executive. Corwin, *The President, op. cit.,* p. 108.

29. *Infra,* p. 89.

30. *Congressional Record,* 70th Cong., 1st sess., vol. 69, p. 1778.

31. *Infra,* p. 60.

32. Schechter Poultry Corp. v. United States (1935), 295 U.S. 495; 55 Sup. Ct. 837.

33. *Infra*, p. 55.

34. *New York Times*, April 19, 1941.

35. *New York Times*, May 30, 1941. The repeated reliance on the "faithfully executed" clause as a source of presidential authority is perhaps justification for branding it the President's elastic clause.

"Of all the important administrative agencies established during the recent war to carry on some phase of war activity, very few were expressly created by statute. Congress thus apparently recognized the importance of entrusting the details of war administration to the President. On the other hand, several war agencies, such as the Committee on Public Information and the War Industries Board, were created by the President without authority of statute, but by virtue of his powers as Chief Executive and Commander-in-Chief." Berdahl, *War Powers of the Executive in the United States, op. cit.*, p. 117.

The Committee on Public Information was created as a result of a joint letter from Secretaries Lansing (State), Baker, (War), Daniels (Navy) to the President: "It is our opinion that the two functions—censorship and publicity—can be joined in honesty and with profit, and we recommend the creation of the Committee on Public Information. . . . We believe you have the undoubted authority . . . without waiting for further legislation . . ." Berdahl, *op. cit.*, p. 197 from Official Bulletin, May 10, 1917.

"All this was done on the sole authority of the President, the committee even operating for a considerable time on the executive budget, but later securing some appropriation from Congress." Berdahl, p. 199 (*N.Y. Times*, Nov. 1, 1919 for statement by George Creel).

36. See Wriston, Henry M., *Executive Agents in American Foreign Relations*. (Baltimore: The Johns Hopkins Press, 1929), pp. 106–204.

37. *Ibid.*, p. 693 et ff.

38. *Ibid.*, p. 199.

39. Stimson, Henry L., *American Policy in Nicaragua*. (N.Y.: Chas. Scribner's Sons, 1927), p. 42.

40. *New York Times*, August 28, 1942, p. 1.

41. Galloway, George B., "Presidential Commissions," *Editorial Research Reports*, vol. I, No. 20, May 28, 1931, p. 361.

42. *Infra*; also Henry M. Wriston, *Presidential Special Agents in Diplomacy, op. cit.*, p. 819 et ff.

43. See Sundry Civil Act of 1911, June 25, 1910; See also: Weber, Gustavus, *Organized Efforts for the Improvement of Administration, op. cit.*, p. 84.

44. Ex-President Theodore Roosevelt thought the President had power to create commissions for purpose of advice without any statutory authorization from Congress. He was critically cynical of President Taft's request for congressional authorization for the Committee on Economy and Efficiency. "My successor," wrote Roosevelt, "acknowledged the right (of Congress to control the creation of commissions), upheld the view of the politicians . . . and abandoned the commissions to the lasting detriment of the people as a whole." Roosevelt, Theodore, *Autobiography, op. cit.*, p. 369.

45. Principal criticism of the preliminary report was that it indicated very little time had been devoted to the "thorough inquiry into the problem of the enforcement of prohibition" for which a $250,000 appropriation had been made. (See especially the comments of Senator Glass, *Congressional Record*, 71st Congress, 2d sess., June 26, 1930, vol. 72, p. 11813 ff.)

46. *Infra*, p. 39.

47. Senator Walsh made this rather disturbing suggestion to the Senate while it was considering an appropriation for investigating the sinking of the submarine S4: "Has it occurred to you that the investigation conducted by the proposed commission may be an investigation of ourselves, that this commission might properly find that the Congress . . . has failed to give the Navy sufficient money . . . for rescuing human lives . . ."

Congressional Record, 70th Cong., 1st sess., Jan. 20, 1928, vol. 69, pp. 1793–1794. Charges of this type were presented to the Morrow Aircraft Board and some congressional rancor was evident. See statement of Mr. Madden in House debate on Urgent Deficiency Bill, 1926, Cong. Record, 69th Cong., 1st sess., Feb. 2, 1926, vol. 67, p. 3169.

48. 27 Opinions of the Attorney General, 308.

49. See Public Law No. 67, 1933; June 16, 1933, c. 90, Title I, Sec. 2, 48 Stat. 195; 15 U.S.C. 702.

50. Executive Order No. 6202A.

51. Executive Order No. 6433A.

52. Executive Order No. 6757, June 29, 1934.

53. Executive Order No. 6757, June 29, 1934.

54. Executive Order No. 7323, March 26, 1936.

55. See Emergency Relief Appropriation Act of 1935, Act of April 8, 1935, c. 48, 49 Stat. 115.

The Emergency Relief Appropriation Act of 1935 carried very broad powers for the President. It appropriated $4,000,000,000 to be used in the discretion and under the direction of the President "to provide relief, work relief and to increase employment. . . ."

Section 3 provided that the President in carrying out the act may "accept and utilize such voluntary and uncompensated services, appoint without regard to the provisions of the civil service laws such officers and employees, and utilize such Federal officers and employees . . . as may be necessary, prescribe their authorities, duties, responsibilities and tenure, and, without regard to the Classification Act of 1923 . . . , fix the compensation of any officers and employees so appointed."

Broadest of the delegations for the purpose of setting up bodies which can be classed as presidential commissions was that contained in Section 4 providing, "In carrying out the provisions of this joint resolution the President is authorized to establish and prescribe the duties and functions of necessary agencies within the government."

56. *Infra.* p. 80.

57. 19 U.S.C. 1001, see Sec. 1354, June 12, 1934, c. 474, Sec. 4, 48 Stat. 945.

58. Executive Order No. 6750, June 27, 1934.

59. *Infra,* p. 59.

CHAPTER III

1. March 4, 1909, c. 299, Sec. 8, 35 Stat. 1027; 31 U.S.C. 673.

2. But see supra p. 15 for an opinion of the Attorney General who "interpreted" this provision of the Sundry Civil Act to permit the President to appoint commissions "if their appointment is authorized in a general way by law."

3. *Infra,* p. 37.

4. *Infra,* p. 38.

5. Senate Doc. 174, 71st Cong., 2d sess., *op. cit.,* pp. 13–30.

6. See debate *Congressional Record,* 60th Cong., 2d sess., vol. 43, pp. 3659–3664.

7. Myers, *Hoover's State Papers, op. cit.,* v. I, p. 344, Statement of June 27, 1930.

8. 31 U.S.C. 655.

But the point has been made that members of commissions not paid from government funds are not "officers," their appointment need not be confirmed by the Senate.

9. See *N.Y. Times,* June 29, 1930, 1:7.

Also, Helm, William P., *Washington Swindle Sheet.* (N.Y.: Albert and Charles Boni, 1932), pp. 196–198.

10. Jacobson, Walter O., *A Study of President Taft's Commission on Economy and Efficiency.* (N.Y.: Columbia University, Master's Essay, unpublished), pp. 45–46.

11. 27 Opinions of Attorney General 406.

12. The Independent Offices Appropriations Act, after providing for the Office of President, reads: "employees of the executive departments and other establishments of the executive branch of government may be detailed from time to time to the Office of the President . . . for such temporary assistance as may be deemed necessary." (See Act of 1936, 49 Stat. 6, Feb. 2, 1935.) Thus the President has some freedom in calling men from the departments and having them do special jobs for him.

13. 27 Opinions of the Attorney General 308 (1919).

14. 27 Opinions of the Attorney General 459 (1919).

15. 6 Opinions of the Attorney General 28; 4 O.A.G. 248 (1843).

Corwin, Edward G., *The President: Office and Powers, op. cit.,* p. 126.

16. As has been indicated earlier, the restrictive character of the Sundry Civil Act has been largely by-passed in recent years by the provisions in emergency legislation which give the President power to create new agencies if their purposes can be fitted into the concepts of "relief" or "emergency."

Financial support for some presidential commissions has been found in the use of the President's emergency fund. Too liberal a use of this fund by the President, however, may result in congressional restrictions in its use. Thus a fear on the part of Congress that the executive might rescue the National Resources Planning Board and the Farm Security Administration, denied funds by Congress, led the Senate Committee to ban the use of the emergency fund "for any of the functions of any agency of the Government for which appropriations have been duly made by the Congress, or for functions for which estimates have been submitted by the Budget and for which Congress has failed to make appropriations." (*Washington Post,* June 3, 1943, editorial.)

17. Executive Order No. 6757, June 29, 1934.

18. 45 Stat. 1613.

19. *U.S. Daily News,* May 21, 1929, p. 1.

20. When there is no specific statutory authorization for the creation of a commission, the President may resort to the device of starting the executive order with the words: "By authority of the powers vested in me by the Constitution of the United States and the laws passed pursuant thereto, I hereby appoint . . ." a form used as introduction for many executive orders.

21. *Federal Commissions, Committees, and Boards,* Sept. 14, 1901, March 4, 1929. Sen. Doc. 174, 71st Cong., 2d sess., U.S. Govt. Printing Office: 1930.

22. 44 U.S.C. 305.

CHAPTER IV

1. President Hoover wrote in 1929: "The truth . . . is hard to discover; it must be distilled through the common judgment of skilled men and women from accurately and patiently collected facts and knowledge of forces before the extraction of the essence

of wisdom. . . . The President himself cannot pretend to know or to have the time for detailed investigation into every one of the hundreds of subjects in a great people. But the fine minds of our citizens are available and can be utilized for the search." Myers, *Hoover's State Papers, op. cit.,* vol. I, p. 197.

2. Address before the Gridiron Club, Dec. 14, 1929. *Ibid.,* p. 190.

3. Freund, Ernst, *Standards of American Legislation,* Chicago, The University of Chicago Press (1926). See also, Dimock, Marshall E., *Congressional Investigating Committees.* (Baltimore: Johns Hopkins Press, 1929), pp. 82–83.

4. 15 U.S.C. 46.

5. 29 U.S.C. 21.

6. 47 U.S.C. 154.

7. 15 U.S.C. 78w.

8. 49 U.S.C. 426.

In some instances statutes requesting administrative bodies to recommend legislation have gone so far as to authorize them to make independent investigations. 7 U.S.C. 12 provides in part: ". . . and in order to provide information for the use of Congress, the Secretary of Agriculture may make such investigations as he may deem necessary to ascertain the facts regarding the operations of boards of trade. . . ." (See Lilienthal, 39 H.L.R. 694.)

9. Dimock, Marshall E., *Congressional Investigating Committees, op. cit.,* pp. 83–84, citing as examples the Panama Canal Commission, 1901; the Commission on Industrial Relations, 1916; the Muscle Shoals Commission, 1925.

10. Listed here are presidential commissions with definite legislative ends in mind which were created from 1929 to 1941 and which are not described in the body of this study.

Committee on Coordination of Veterans Service appointed by letter May 23, 1929. Interdepartmental in character. Led to establishment of Veterans Administration, see Library of Congress, Legislative Reference Service, File Commissions, Federal JF533B, 211442, p. 3; also Congressional Record, 72nd Cong., 1st sess., vol. 75, pt. 4, p. 4355.

Special Committee for the Study of Education in Haiti appointed by the Secretary of State, June 4, 1930 and made up of prominent educators to make a study with a view to improving the system of education. Library of Congress, *ibid.,* p. 8; *Cong. Rec., ibid.,* p. 4356.

National Drought Committee announced August 19, 1930 to coordinate Federal, State and other activities and to recommend a national program. Led to Red Cross action and appropriation for agricultural relief. Library of Congress, *ibid.; Cong. Rec., ibid.,* p. 4355; *U.S. Daily,* Aug. 20, 1930, vol. V, p. 1919.

Commission on Handling Muscle Shoals appointed July 14, 1931, *U.S. Daily,* July 15, 1931, vol. VI, pp. 11, 117.

Investigation into Bankruptcy Laws made by Departments of Justice and Commerce at the direction of President Hoover. Myers, *Hoover's State Papers, op. cit.,* v. II, pp. 126–127, Feb. 26, 1932.

Committee to Consider Tonnage Tax (War Department) established by a memorandum from the President to the Secretaries of War and Navy, No. 11, 1933. Card file, U.S. Information Service.

President's Special Committee on Wildlife Restoration appointed by the President December, 1933, to make a study of the entire range of wildlife restoration possibilities. Many of its recommendations have been translated into action or legislation. Card file U.S. Information Service. Submitted Feb. 8, 1934, published by Dept. of Agriculture.

Up-stream Engineering Conference Organizing Committee appointed by Presidential letter to Secretary of Agriculture, June 16, 1936. *Roosevelt's State Papers, op. cit.,* v. 1937, pp. 193–196; Senate Documents Nos. 167, 198, 74th Cong. 2d sess.

11. Listed *infra,* footnote 61.

12. Examples of commissions with legislative goals in mind created by the President at the request of Congress: The United States Commission to Revise and Codify the Criminal and Penal Laws. A provision in the Sundry Civil Act of 1899 authorized the President to constitute the commission with the advice and consent of the Senate. (See Report, May 15, 1901, Wash.: Government Printing Office, 57th Cong., 1st sess., Sen. Doc. No. 68.)

National Coast Defense Board appointed Jan. 31, 1905. Report Feb. 1, 1906, Senate Doc. No. 248, 59th Cong., 1st sess. The American Samoan Commission created by the President pursuant to Public Res. No. 89, 70th Cong., approved Feb. 20, 1929 and including two Senators, two Congressmen, and two Island chiefs to "recommend to Congress such legislation concerning the Islands of eastern Samoa as they shall deem necessary or proper."

See Report, U.S. Govt. Print. Off., 1931.

President's Committee on Waterflow appointed to supply Congress with "a comprehensive plan for the improvement and development of the rivers of the United States" as requested by the Norris-Watson Senate resolution of Feb. 2, 1934. See Preliminary Report "Development of the Rivers of the United States" and Message from the President transmitting the Report. House Doc. No. 395, June 4, 1934, 73d Cong. 2d sess.

The Advisory Committee on Fiscal Relations Study appointed by the President in fulfillment of the congressional appropriation of "Not to exceed $50,000 . . . for expenditure under direction of the President, for making an independent study of the fiscal relations between the United States and the District of Columbia and enabling him to report to Congress . . ." Appropriation Act for 1937, Pub. No. 762, 74th Cong. approved, June 23, 1936. See Report (U.S. Govt. Print. Off., 1937).

13. See, for example, Taft's Commission on Economy and Efficiency, or the Wickersham Commission.

14. *U.S. Daily,* vol. 25, p. 1; *Myers, Hoover's State Papers, op. cit.,* vol. I, pp. 109–111.

15. Report of the Committee. Transmitted to the President . . . in pursuance of the Act of April 10, 1930 (Wash.: Govt. Print. Off., 1931).

16. For a more detailed study of this Committee, see Reynolds, Mary Trackett, *Interdepartmental Committees in the National Administration.* (N.Y.: Columbia Univ. Press, 1939), p. 30 et ff.

17. Executive Order No. 6757, June 29, 1934; *Roosevelt's State Papers, op. cit.,* vol. III, p. 321; and for summary of work of Committee, vol. IV, p. 47 et ff.

18. *Roosevelt's State Papers, op. cit.,* vol. 4, p. 43 et ff.

19. August 14, 1935, c. 531, 49 Stat. 620.

20. See *Roosevelt's State Papers, op. cit.,* v. III, pp. 339–340.

21. Aug. 26, 1935, c. 687, 49 Stat. 838.

See President's message to Congress transmitting the Report. *Roosevelt's State Papers, op. cit.,* v. 4, p. 98, March 12, 1935, House Doc. No. 137, 74th Cong., 1st sess.

22. See *Roosevelt's State Papers,* v. V, pp. 686–687. It is not clear whether this was a new committee or simply a reconstituted Power Policy Commission. The President seemed to treat it as a new committee.

23. *Roosevelt's State Papers, op. cit.,* v. 1937, p. 93.

24. Public No. 329, 75th Cong., 50 Stat. 731.

25. See *U.S. Govt. Manual*, March, 1941, p. 284.

26. *Roosevelt's State Papers, op. cit.*, v. V., pp. 264–269, July 22, 1936.

27. See *The Future of the Great Plains*, Preliminary Report of Aug. 27, 1936; also *Roosevelt's State Papers*, vol. V, p. 305.

28. *Ibid.*, pp. 366–368.

29. House Document No. 150, 75th Cong., 1st sess.

30. Federal Crop Insurance Act of 1938, 7 U.S.C. 1501. See *N.Y. Times*, Feb. 15, 1938, for summary of law.

31. See *Roosevelt's State Papers, op. cit.*, vol. V, pp. 369–370.

32. House Doc., No. 144, 75th Cong., 1st sess.

33. *Roosevelt's State Papers, op. cit.*, vol. 1937, Note p. 74.

34. 16 U.S.C. 590 r., 50 Stat. 869.

35. *Roosevelt's State Papers, op. cit.*, vol. 1939, pp. 590–593.

36. This is one of the few concessions made to Congressmen in committees appointed by President Roosevelt. Since President Wilson omitted Senators from the delegation to Versailles, the belief has been current that a certain amount of appeasement of congressional pride is essential if the President wants full cooperation from Congress.

37. House Doc. No. 149, 75th Cong., 1st sess.

38. *Roosevelt's State Papers, op. cit.* vol. 1936, pp. 590–593.

39. *Congressional Record*, vol. 81, part 6, pp. 6670, 6757 et ff.

40. July 22, 1937, c. 517, 7 U.S.C. 1000, 50 Stat. 522.

41. *N.Y. Times*, Sept. 21, 1938. 14:1.

42. *N.Y. Times*, Dec. 24, 1938, 1:8—Report of the Committee Appointed Sept. 20, 1938 by the President to Submit Recommendations Upon the General Transportation Situation. Available from the Association of American Railroads.

43. Transportation Act of 1940, 54 Stat. 898.

44. See *N.Y. Times*, Sept. 10, 1940, 33:6; See also Wheeler's adverse comment on the Report, *N.Y. Times*, Dec. 24, 1938, 1:8.

45. *Roosevelt's State Papers, op. cit.*, vol. II, p. 153. Oral direction of the President to the Secretary of Commerce in 1934 set up a *Committee on Railroad Fixed Charges* to conduct studies of the railroad indebtedness problem. Card file, U.S. Information Service.

46. House Doc. No. 583, 75th Cong., 3rd sess.

47. *Roosevelt's State Papers, op. cit.*, vol. 1938, pp. 208–213.

48. *N.Y. Times*, May 10, 1940, 39:6.

49. "A Study of Communications by an Interdepartmental Committee," transmitted to Congress. Senate Doc. No. 144, 73rd Cong., 2nd sess., Jan. 23, 1934.

See also, Presidential recommendation to Congress based on the findings of this committee. *Roosevelt's State Papers, op. cit.*, vol. III, p. 107, Feb. 26, 1934.

50. *Roosevelt's State Papers, op. cit.*, vol. III, p. 76.

51. See Hearings before Committee on Foreign and Inter-State Commerce, House of Representatives, 75th Cong., 3rd sess.

52. Public No. 706, 75th Congress, approved, June 23, 1938 (52 Stat. 977).

53. *Roosevelt's State Papers, op. cit.*, vol. 3, at p. 34.

54. *Roosevelt's State Papers, op. cit.*, vol. 5, p. 117 et ff. for message to the Great Lakes–St. Lawrence Seaway and Power Conference, March 11, 1936 and a note which sketches the President's activities in support of the project.

55. Another less relevant example of a presidential commission operating in the foreign relations field was the *Joint Preparatory Committee on Philippine Affairs* created April 14, 1937 pursuant to an arrangement between the Presidents of the United States and the Philippine Islands. The purpose of the committee, headed by Francis B. Sayre

and, subsequently, J. V. A. MacMurray, and including twelve others, was to study trade relations between the United States and the Philippines and to recommend a program for the adjustment of the Philippine national economy to meet its approaching freedom. While this committee was not directly concerned with legislation in the United States and while authority for its creation by the President was contained in the Hawes-Cutting Act, it represents a slight variation upon the theme of presidential participation in suggesting legislation in the field of foreign affairs. (See "Report of Joint Preparatory Committee on Philippine Affairs," Dept. of State Pub. No. 1216, Conference Series 36, 3 vols.)

56. *Congressional Record,* vol. 40, part 8, pp. 7800–7802; 59th Cong., 1st sess. House Doc. No. 873.

57. Packers and Stockyards Act, 42 Stat. 159.

58. Commission of the United States on the Investigation of the General Slocum Disaster, *N.Y. Tribune,* June 22, 1904, Report Oct. 8, 1904, Govt. Print. Off.; *Investigation of the Steamboat Inspection Service,* Senate Doc. No. 174, 71st Cong., 2d sess., *op. cit.,* p. 9; *Commission on the Valencia Disaster,* Feb. 7, 1906, *ibid. cit.,* pp. 14–15.

59. Executive Order No. 794.

60. Sen. Doc. No. 701, 60th Cong., 2d sess., serial No. 5408, Feb. 8, 1909.

61. Other presidential commissions with definite legislative purposes in mind created from 1900 to 1929 include:

Commission on Naturalization appointed by Executive Order of March 1, 1905 to investigate the subject of naturalization, to report to the President and, to prepare a draft of a proposed naturalization law. Members from State, Justice, and Labor departments. (Report Nov. 8, 1905.)

Inland Waterways Commission originally created by letter of President Roosevelt of March 14, 1907, and instructed to prepare and report a comprehensive plan for the improvement and control of the river systems of the United States. (Preliminary Report, Feb. 3, 1908, Sen. Doc. No. 325, 60th Cong., 1st sess.)

Committee on Grades and Salaries created by Executive Order dated June 11, 1907 "to prepare clear and consistent tables of estimates for positions and salaries in conformity with the schedule and recommendations of the committee on department methods of Jan. 4, 1907." Interdepartmental membership.

Special Mission of Investigation to the Philippine Islands appointed by letters from President Harding to the Secretary of War and from the Secretary to the members dated March 20 and 23, 1921, respectively. Not clearly a "legislative purpose" commission. Instructed to render judgment between conflicting views in re freedom for the Islands. "Political character" since it was to disprove President Wilson's claim that the Islands were fit for independence. (Report of the Special Mission to the Secretary of War, House Doc. No. 325, 67th Cong., 2d sess., serial No. 8105.)

Interdepartmental Committee on Oil Pollution of Navigable Waters. Appointed at the suggestion of the Secretary of Commerce, as a result of a joint resolution of Congress, approved by the President, July 1, 1922, which requested the President to call a conference of maritime nations with a view to the adoption of effective means for the prevention of pollution of navigable waters. Senate Doc. No. 174, 71st Cong., 2d sess., *op. cit.,* p. 96.

Merchant Marine Policy Committee appointed by President Coolidge, March 12, 1924, to study and make recommendations affecting the American merchant marine.

Agricultural Conference on Agricultural Legislation appointed by President Coolidge, Nov. 7, 1924. *N.Y. Times,* Nov. 8, 1924, 2:1; Preliminary Report, Sen. Doc. No. 190, 68th Cong., 2d sess.

Muscle Shoals Inquiry appointed by President Coolidge, March 26, 1925, to report on the most practical methods and specific purposes for use of the Muscle Shoals facilities. Report, House Doc. No. 119, 69th Cong., 1st sess., serial No. 8565.

62. McGeary, M. Nelson, *The Development of Congressional Investigative Power.* (N.Y.: Columbia University Press, 1940), p. 116.

It may be noted that on occasion President F. D. Roosevelt has "delegated" requests for congressional investigations instead of vice versa as suggested by McGeary. A message to Congress of March 14, 1938 recommended "study by a joint committee of the forest land problem of the United States." Pursuant thereto Congress established a *Joint Committee on Forestry* (52 Stat. 1452) which concluded that the problem of forest regulation was primarily a job for the states subject to federal standards. (*Roosevelt's State Papers*, vol. 1938, pp. 144–150.) Not able to accept this conclusion, the President continued via the National Resources Planning Board, to press upon the Congress the necessity of the federal government assuming primary responsibility. (State Papers, *op. cit.*, vol. 1940, pp. 36–37.)

63. McGeary, *op. cit.*, pp. 117–120.

64. First Press Conference, March 8, 1933, *Roosevelt's State Papers, op. cit.*, vol. III, at p. 33.

65. Report of the Departmental Committee on the Procedure of Royal Commissions, Lord Balfour, chairman. Appointed by His Majesty's Secretary of State for the Home Department, April 19, 1909. *Parliamentary Papers* (Cd 5235), p. 6.

66. The commissions dealt with in this section are not all clearly "spotlight" bodies. Some deal with matters about which the general public shows little or no interest. They elucidate subjects about which there is not enough known to form a preliminary to legislation. They are "pre-legislation" advisory bodies as distinguished from "post-legislation" advisory bodies.

67. See Preliminary Report of the Inland Waterways Commission, Senate Doc. No. 325, 60th Cong., 1st sess. (serial No. 5250). See also Roosevelt's *Autobiography, op. cit.*, pp. 380–384.

68. Proceedings of a Conference of Governors in the White House, Wash., D.C., May 13–15, 1908. House Doc. No. 1425, 60th Cong., 2d sess., serial No. 5538, pp. V–XII.

69. Report of the National Conservation Commission, Feb. 9, 1909, Sen. Doc. No. 676, 60th Cong., 2d sess., 3 vols., serial nos. 5397, 5398, 5399, at p. 115.

70. Executive Order 809, June 8, 1908.

71. For organization see Report, *ibid.*, vol. 1, pp. 115–120.

72. See Report of the Country Life Commission, 60th Cong., 2d sess., Senate Doc. No. 705, Govt. Print. Off., 1909.

73. *Cong. Record*, 60th Cong., 2d sess., vol. 43, part 4, Debate, pp. 3659–3664.

Similar in character and purpose was the President's Homes Commission appointed by letter on May 4, 1907, and instructed "to ascertain and consider the results of the best efforts of public enterprise and private philanthropy to improve the homes and better the lives of the industrial classes in . . . cities"; Reports Relating to Affairs in the District of Columbia, Senate Doc. No. 599, 60th Cong., 2d sess., serial no. 5394; also doc. no. 644, Jan. 8, 1909. The Report underwent attack in Congress as being absurd, *Cong. Record*, 60th Cong., 2d sess., vol. 43, part 4, p. 3664, and a resolution was introduced suggesting that it be "excluded from the mails as obscene literature unfit for circulation." *Cong. Rec., op. cit.*, p. 3210.

74. Several bills were introduced in the 62nd Congress, 1st sess., providing for a congressional investigation of Presidential commissions. For example, Senate Bill 1376 "To provide for a commission to investigate commissions and to make recommenda-

tions. . . ." House Res. No. 100 "For appointment of special committee to investigate certain commissions, boards, etc." None of the measures came out of committee.

75. Roosevelt, Theodore, *Theodore Roosevelt, An Autobiography.* (N.Y.: The Macmillan Co., 1914), pp. 381–384.

76. Message to Congress, Feb. 2, 1912, Cong. Record, 62nd Cong., 2d sess., vol. 48, part 2, p. 1661.

For background for creation see Jacobson, Walter O., *op. cit.,* pp. 79 et ff.

77. Act of August 23, 1912 (37 Stat. 415–416).

78. 38 Stat. 312; 38 Stat. 628.

79. *Cong. Rec.,* 63rd Cong., 2d sess., vol. 51, part 10, pp. 10343–10347; part 12, pp. 11681–11685.

80. Final Report, Sen. Doc. No. 415, 64th Cong., 1st sess., serial no. 6929, pp. 29–68.

81. April 28, 1916, 39 Stat. 59.

82. Jacobson, *op. cit.,* p. 80.

See also, "Fiasco of Industrial Commission," *Nation,* vol. 101, Aug. 26, 1915, p. 251.

In 1919 the First Industrial Conference met in Washington "for the purpose of reaching, if possible, some common ground of agreement and action with regard to the future conduct of industry." Called by President Wilson, the conference had representatives of employers, employees, and of the general public. The conference did not bring "capital and labor into close cooperation" and disbanded when the employer group voted against a resolution expressing the proposition that wage earners had a right to organize and bargain collectively. Dept of Labor, Office of the Secretary, Proceedings of the First Industrial Conference. Govt. Print. Off., 1920.

83. The Urgent Deficiency Appropriation Act of March 4, 1929, 45 Stat. 1613, appropriating $250,000 "For the purpose of a thorough inquiry into the problem of the enforcement of prohibition . . . to be expended under authority and by direction of the President . . . , who shall report the results of such investigation to Congress, together with his recommendations with respect thereto. . . ."

84. *The Nation,* Jan. 22, 1930, vol. 130, No. 3368, p. 89.

85. *Outlook and Independent,* Feb. 5, 1930, vol. 154, p. 218, where the politics of the commission's creation are outlined. William J. Donovan has been credited with the idea.

86. *Cong. Rec.,* 71st Cong., 1st sess., vol. 71, part 3, pp. 2406–2407. See Jacobson, *op. cit.,* pp. 83–84.

87. Myers, *Hoover's State Papers, op. cit.,* vol. I, pp. 14–15.

88. Enforcement of the Prohibition Laws, House Doc. No. 722, 71st Cong., 3d sess., serial no. 9361.

See for Press reaction, the *Literary Digest,* Jan. 31, 1931, vol. 108, pp. 5–7.

89. The other reports of the Commission were of a technical character and only attracted the attention of specialists. See "Reports of the National Commission on Law Observance and Enforcement," 30 *Michigan Law Review* 1 (Nov., 1931).

90. See *Outlook and Independent,* Feb. 4, 1931, vol. 157, p. 171: "the Capitol firmly believes that Mr. Hoover intervened to block a recommendation for revision of the Eighteenth Amendment."

91. While the stimulus for creating the Committee came from the President, after its organization Senator O'Mahoney, the chairman, was in charge. See the letter from President Roosevelt "hoping" the Committee would "assume the task of analyzing the financial machine in its relation to the creation of more needed wealth." *Roosevelt's State Papers, op. cit.,* vol. 1939, pp. 338–340. For official summary of organization and work of the Committee see: "Final Report and Recommendations of the T.N.E.C.," Senate Doc. No. 35, 77th Cong., 1st sess., March 31, 1941, pp. 691 et ff.

92. *Roosevelt's State Papers,* vol. 1938, at p. 315.

93. Pub. Res. No. 113, 75th Cong., 52 Stat. 705; *Roosevelt's State Papers, op. cit.,* vol. 1938, p. 320 et ff. It is suggested that it might be productive to explore the advantages and disadvantages of commissions of mixed congressional, executive, and lay composition, such as the T.N.E.C. and the National Conservation Commission. A commission with a mixed membership undoubtedly has advantages from the point of view of obtaining funds from Congress and of having its findings viewed with less suspicion by Congress. Disadvantages might come from a tendency to use such a commission as a sounding board rather than for the purpose of finding facts.

94. Final Report, March 31, 1941, Sen. Doc. No. 35, 77th Cong., 1st sess.

95. *Cong. Record,* 77th Cong., 1st sess., vol. 87, part 3, p. 2699 et ff. for comment on submission of Report to the Senate. For the Executive Secretary's evaluation of the Committee's work, see Final Report, *op. cit.,* pp. 727–729.

96. For a preliminary report on sales of T.N.E.C. monographs see *Cong. Record,* 76th Cong., 3d sess., vol. 88, part 12, pp. 13830–13831.

97. Patent recommendations adopted, Public Acts Nos. 286, 287, 288, 341 and 358, 76th Cong., 1st sess.

98. *Cong. Record, op. cit.,* pp. 2698, 2701.

99. But see the President's Conference on Unemployment of 1921 "to consider relief for four to five million unemployed resulting from the business slump." Under the chairmanship of Herbert Hoover a number of committees were appointed. A conservative approach to the economic difficulties of the decade was presented in the study *Recent Economic Changes in the United States,* Report of the Committee on Recent Economic Changes of the President's Conference on Unemployment, Herbert Hoover, Chairman. Including the reports of a special staff of the National Bureau of Economic Research, 2 vols. (N.Y. and London: McGraw-Hill Book Co., Inc., 1929). For a comparative study of the results of this Committee and the Social Research Committee, see Bigelow, Karl W. "Recent Social Trends," *The Quarterly Journal of Economics,* Nov., 1933, vol. 48, pp. 150–170.

100. Myers, *Hoover's State Papers, op. cit.,* vol. I, pp. 195 et ff. contains list of members.

101. *Recent Social Trends in the United States.* (New York: McGraw-Hill Book Company, 1933.)

102. See Myers, *Hoover's State Papers, op. cit.,* vol. II, pp. 559–560.

103. *Recent Social Trends, op. cit.*
See *The New Republic,* Jan. 11, 1933, vol. 73, pp. 228–230, for editorial comment; also at pp. 231–235 for a brief discussion of the report by George Soulé.

104. Myers, *Hoover's State Papers,* vol. II, p. 560, Press Statement of Jan. 2, 1933.

105. Stuart Chase seized upon the Report as source material for some portions of his *The Economy of Abundance,* the title of which is scarcely suggestive of President Hoover's approach. (N.Y.: The Macmillan Co., 1934.)

106. A committee of six, headed by Jacob Baker, Assistant Works Projects Administration Administrator, was appointed June 23, 1936. *Roosevelt's State Papers, op. cit.,* vol. V, pp. 226–228, the President referred to Marquis Child's *Sweden, The Middle Way* and suggested that it had influenced his desire to have cooperatives studied.

107. Letters to nine members, June 21, 1938, *Roosevelt's State Papers, op. cit.,* vol. 1938, pp. 383–384. See for brief note "Monthly Catalogue United States Public Documents," May, 1937, p. 527.
Similar in character was the *Agricultural Commission to Europe* appointed by the Secretary of Agriculture in August, 1918. The committee was instructed "to ascertain

conditions of European agriculture as they had a bearing upon agriculture in the United States . . ." Leland and Mereness, "Introduction to the American Official Sources, etc.," p. 185.

108. *Report of the Inquiry on Cooperative Enterprise in Europe,* 1937, U.S. Govt. Print. Off., p. 5.

109. *Report of Commission on Industrial Relations in Great Britain,* 1938. Labor Dept., U. S. Govt. Print. Off. *Report of Commission on Industrial Relations in Sweden,* 1938, Labor Dept., U.S. Govt. Print. Off.

See President's comments on the Reports, *Roosevelt's State Papers, op. cit.,* vol. 1938, pp. 507–508; 528–529.

110. *Roosevelt's State Papers, op. cit.,* vol. 1938, p. 508.

111. See Beard, Charles A. and Mary R., *America in Midpassage* (N.Y.: The Macmillan Co., 1939, 2 vols.), vol. I, p. 86 et ff.

112. Myers, *Hoover's State Papers, op. cit.,* vol. I, pp. 133–134.

113. Report of the President's Conference on Unemployment, Herbert Hoover, Chairman, Sept. 26 to Oct. 13, 1921, Wash., Govt. Print. Off.

114. *Commercial and Financial Chronicle,* Dec. 7, 1929, p. 3576; Dec. 14, p. 3736.

115. Announced Oct. 17, 1930, Myers, *Hoover's State Papers, op. cit.,* vol. I, p. 401, 402; *U.S. Daily,* Oct. 20, 1930, vol. V, p. 2540.

116. *Hoover's State Papers, op. cit.,* vol. I, p. 401.

117. *Ibid.,* p. 471.

118. *Washington Daily News,* editorial, "Why the Mystery?" Dec. 17, 1930.

119. *Hoover's State Papers, op. cit.,* vol. I, pp. 609–810.

120. *Ibid.,* vol. II, pp. 220–221. Message to Congress, July 5, 1932.

121. See the Beards, *America in Midpassage, op. cit.,* vol. I, pp. 92–93.

122. *Hoover's State Papers, op. cit.,* vol. II, p. 108, Press Statement, Feb. 3, 1932.

123. *U.S. Daily,* Feb. 6, 1932, p. 1 for organization.

124. Other commissions which might have been included within the spotlight category if space and importance warranted, are:

Joint Committee to Study the Gold Situation appointed by the Secretary of Interior, July, 1918. Sen. Doc. No. 174, 71st Cong., 2 sess. p. 72.

President's Committee on Outdoor Recreation appointed April 14, 1924, which in turn led to the National Conference on Outdoor Recreation held in May, 1924. See in Doc. 174, 71st Cong., 2d sess., pp. 103–104.

National Committee on Wood Utilization established by direction of the President in 1925 to bring about wiser and more efficient use of forest products. See *U.S. Govt. Manual,* March, 1941 ed., p. 638.

National Timber Conservation Board created by presidential memo, Dec., 1930. Card file, U.S. Information Office, *U.S. Daily,* Dec. 6, 1930, vol. 5, p. 3047.

Deposit Liquidation Board created Oct. 15, 1933 to stimulate and encourage liquidating agents of closed banks to borrow from the R.F.C. Card file, U.S. Information Office.

Board of Inquiry for the Cotton Textile Industry, created by Executive Order No. 6840, Sept. 5, 1934, and to report not later than Oct. 1, 1934, through the Secretary of Labor to the President. Abolished by Executive Order No. 6858, Sept. 26, 1934.

Cabinet Committee to Investigate Conditions in the Cotton Textile Industry, appointed by the President, April 26, 1935. Report, Sen. Doc. No. 126, 74th Cong., 1st sess.

Advisory Committee on Education (President's Committee on Vocational Education) established by President's letter Sept. 19, 1936, to study the need for an expanded program of federal aid for vocational education. Report to the President, Feb. 18, 1938.

Federal Interdepartmental Safety Council created by President's letter to Secretary of

Labor, March 10, 1937, to reduce injuries among government employees. (Executive Order 8071, March 21, 1939.)

President's Commission to Investigate University of Puerto Rico to recommend and outline a procedure to make this an Inter-American University. Created by President, April, 1939, on suggestion of the Secretary of the Interior. See *"Report of the President's Commission on an Inter-American University in Puerto Rico,* Aug. 23, 1939.

Interdepartmental Committee on Handicrafts created by presidential letter to James Young, Chairman, Feb. 8, 1940, to promote the general production and distribution of handicrafts. (Card file, U.S. Information Service.)

Committee to Investigate Complaints of Discrimination Against Negroes in Defense Industries created by Executive Order of June 25, 1941.

125. *Commercial and Financial Chronicle,* Aug. 17, 1929, p. 1065.

126. *Hoover's State Papers, op. cit.,* vol. I, pp. 73–74.

127. *White House Conference, 1930, addresses and abstracts of committee reports.* (N.Y.: The Century Co., 1931.) The Conference set up a number of committees such as the Committee on the Medical Care of Children, the Committee on Public Health Organization, the Committee on Family and Parent Education, the Committee on Vocational Guidance and Child Labor, the Committee on Youth Outside and Home and School, the Committee on Socially Handicapped. These committees rendered reports most of which were published by the Century Company.

128. See *Conference on Children in a Democracy, Papers and Discussions at the Initial Session held April 26, 1939,* Children's Bureau, Labor (Wash., U.S. Govt. Print. Off.).. The Conference on Children in a Democracy held two sessions, one in April, 1939 and the second in January, 1940. In the interim special committees were preparing reports to be submitted to the final conference. The second conference adopted a general report and authorized the preparation of a more elaborate final report. *"Children in a Democracy," general report adopted by the White House Conference on Children in a Democracy,* Jan. 19, 1940 (Wash., D.C., U.S. Govt. Print. Office).

129. *Hoover's State Papers, op. cit.,* vol. I, pp. 362–364.

130. *Ibid.,* vol. II, pp. 36–40.

131. Other examples of spotlight conferences are:

Hoover's Conferences of Business and Governmental Agencies on Maintaining Business Progress, Press statement, Nov. 15, 1929, *Hoover's State Papers, op. cit.,* vol. I, pp. 133–134, also pp. 135–136. These preliminary conferences were followed by the National Business Survey Congress (Conference on Maintenance of Wages and Construction during Business Depression); see *Commercial and Financial Chronicle,* Dec. 7, 1929, p. 3576; Dec. 14, p. 3736.

Conference on Crime called by the Attorney-General to meet in Washington, Dec. 10, 1934, "to center national interest on the breadth of the crime problem and on constructive measures to deal with it." *Roosevelt's State Papers,* vol. III, p. 495, also at p. 242 et ff.

National Conference on Street and Highway Safety, the third of which was called by President Hoover in 1930; see *Hoover's State Papers,* vol. I, p. 266, also pp. 300–302.

The Accident Prevention Conference created as the result of a letter from President Roosevelt to Secretary of Commerce Roper, Nov. 20, 1935. For brief report see Congressional Record, 75th Cong., 1st sess., vol. 81, p. 3788.

North American Wildlife Conference called to meet in Washington in 1936 to encourage "new cooperation between public and private interests and between Canada, Mexico, and this country. . . ." See *Roosevelt's State Papers,* vol. IV, pp. 500–501, vol. 5, p. 77, also Senate Doc. No. 168, Jan. 30, 1936, 74th Cong., 2d sess., Serial No. 10,015.

132. Felix Frankfurter, *The Public and Its Government*. (New Haven: Yale University Press, 1930), p. 153.

133. See Herring, Pendleton, *The Politics of Democracy*. (N.Y.: W. W. Norton & Co., 1940.)

134. 39 Stat. 721, Sept. 3, 1916.

135. No attempt is made to trace the development of the National Labor Relations Board, which, in its early stages had many of the characteristics of a presidential commission. See, for example, the National Steel Labor Relations Board, *Roosevelt's State Papers, op. cit.*, vol. 3, p. 310, and also Public. Res. 44, 73rd Cong., June 19, 1934, 15 U.S.C. 702 (a) which authorized the President to establish boards to investigate the facts in labor disputes arising under Section 7 (a) of the National Industry Recovery Act.

136. *Hoover's State Papers, op. cit.*, vol. I, p. 90, Press Conference Statement of Aug. 13, 1929.

137. *Roosevelt's State Papers, op. cit.*, vol. III, p. 495 et ff., 18 U.S.C. 7441.

138. June 23, 1934, c. 736, 1, 48 Stat. 1211.

139. *Roosevelt's State Papers, op. cit.*, vol. III, p. 310.

140. See *U.S. Daily*, July 15, 1931, vol. 6, pp. 11, 117.

141. *Hoover's State Papers*, vol. I, p. 598, Statement of July 14, 1931; See *N.Y. Times*, July 15, 1931, 14:2 for list of members representing the States.

142. *N.Y. Times*, March 4, 1931, 1:1.

CHAPTER V

1. See, for example, Public No. 67, 1933, June 16, 1933. 15 U.S.C. 702.

2. *Office for Emergency Management; Functions and Administration*. (Washington: Govt. Print. Off., April, 1941), p. 3.

3. The following description is based largely on Kester, Randall B., The War Industries Board, 1917–1918; A Study in Industrial Mobilization. 34 *American Political Science Review* 655, August, 1940, pp. 657–661; 675–677.

4. 39 Stat. 649 (1916).

5. Baruch, *American Industry in the War* (Final Report of the War Industries Board, 1921), p. 25.

6. Executive Order No. 2868.

7. 40 Stat. 556 (1918).

8. Kester, *op. cit.*, p. 676.

9. Kester, *op. cit.*, p. 682, United States v. Kraus, 33 F (2d) 406 (C.C.A. 7th, 1929).

10. Kester, *op. cit.*, p. 683.

11. For a brief description of the National Emergency Council see *Preliminary Report of the Select Committee to Investigate the Executive Agencies of the Government*. U.S. Congress, Senate, pp. 122–124.

12. Executive Order No. 6202-A, July 11, 1933.

13. Public No. 67, 73rd Congress.

14. Public No. 5, 73rd Cong.

15. See *Report of the Executive Secretary of the Executive Council to the President*, August 25, 1934. U.S. Govt. Print. Off., 1934, being a summary of reports and statistical material of various government departments and agencies "for the purpose of summarizing their objectives and accomplishments in the national program of economic recovery and reconstruction."

16. Executive Order No. 6889-A, October 29, 1934. *Roosevelt's State Papers*, vol. III, p. 441.

17. Executive Order No. 6433-A.

18. The Industrial Emergency Committee created by Executive Order No. 6770, June 30, 1934, to make recommendations to the President on problems of relief, public works, labor disputes, and industrial recovery, was merged with the N.E.C. by Executive Order 6889-A, October 29, 1934; also the Special Industrial Recovery Board, Ex. Order 6513, Dec. 19, 1933.

19. *Roosevelt's State Papers,* vol. II, p. 514, White House Statement of Dec. 6, 1933.

20. Executive Order 6513, Dec. 19, 1933.

21. Executive Orders 6770, June 30, 1934, 6889-A, October 29, 1934.

22. See *United States Government Manual,* March, 1941, p. 629.

23. Card file, Office of Government Reports, on Committee to Study Report of the Secretary of Agriculture Made to the Executive Council, October 2, 1934. Regarding Means to Increase Industrial Employment by Coordination of Price and Production Policies in Industries of Vertical Series, Housing, Automobiles, etc.

24. See for example, Report on the Economic Conditions of the South, Prepared for the President by the N.E.C., July 25, 1938.

25. *Preliminary Report of the Select Committee to Investigate the Executive Agencies of Government, op. cit.,* p. 123.

26. Part 3, section 301.

27. See 53 Stat. 1431.

28. Public Law 19, 76th Cong., effective July 1, 1939, 53 Stat. 561.

29. *Federal Register,* June 4, 1940.

30. *Ibid.,* Administrative Order of May 25, 1940.

31. *Ibid.,* Administrative Order of January 7, 1941.

32. *Office for Emergency Management; Functions and Administration.* (Washington, U.S. Govt. Print. Off., April, 1941), p. 3.

33. *United States News,* July 11, 1941, p. 6.
See also report of the sub-committee of the House Military Affairs Committee in which it notes that "the Administration has been too prone, when difficult problems arose, to dispose of them easily by creating another board, only to add to the confusion of the assortment of agencies we now have."

34. Public Act 316, 73rd Cong.

35. *Roosevelt's State Papers,* vol. II, p. 466, Nov. 11, 1933.

36. Executive Order No. 6656, March 27, 1934; Executive Order No. 7260, December 31, 1935; see also *United States Government Manual,* March, 1941, p. 179.

37. Letter from Secretary of State, June 23, 1934, Card file, U.S. Information Service.

38. Executive Order No. 6750, June 27, 1934.

39. For example, An American Military Mission to Armenia was organized in 1919 under authority of the President to investigate and report on political, military, geographical, administrative, economic, and other considerations included in possible American interests and responsibilities in Armenia, Russian Transcaucasia, and Syria. Sen. Doc. 174, 71st Cong., 2d sess., p. 80.

40. Henry L. Stimson, *American Policy in Nicaragua.* (New York: Chas. Scribner's Sons, 1927), pp. 42–43.

41. *N.Y. Times,* July 3, 1927, p. 6.

42. Harold Norman Denny, *Dollars for Bullets.* (New York: The Dial Press, 1929), pp. 354–381.

43. From the President's letter of instructions, *Report of the Philippine Commission to the President,* January 31, 1900. (Washington: Govt. Print. Off., 1900), vol. I, pp. 185–186.

44. "Philippine Affairs, a Retrospect and Outlook." An Address by Jacob Gould Schurman, President of the First Philippine Commission, before Members of Cornell University. Cited in George A. Malcolm, *The Government of the Philippine Islands.* (Rochester, N.Y., 1916, The Lawyers Co-operative Publishing Co.), pp. 205–206.

45. Report, *op. cit.,* p. 121.

46. For President's instructions to the Commission, see Annual Report of the War Department for the fiscal year ended June 30, 1901. (Washington; Govt. Print. Off., 1901), vol. I, part 10, pp. 5–10.

47. Malcolm, *op. cit.,* p. 215. See Ex Parte Milligan, 71 U.S. 2 (1866).

48. See Message from the President transmitting Reports of the Taft-Philippine Commission, (Wash., Govt. Print. Off., 1901.)

49. 31 Stat. at L. 895.

50. Quoted in Malcolm, *op. cit.,* p. 224.

51. June 28, 1903, 32 Stat. 481–484.

52. Act of April 28, 1904, 33 Stat. 429.
Also Executive Orders of May 9, 1904, April 1 and 3, 1905.

53. 38 Stat. 305.

54. *Congressional Directory,* 63d Cong., 3d sess., 2d ed., p. 333.

55. *N.Y. Times,* May 4, 1917, p. 7.

56. Established by the President and the Secretary of Commerce, April 24, 1932; Executive Order 6742-A, Dec. 2, 1933.

57. U.S. Information Service, card file.

58. *U.S. Govt. Manual,* March, 1941, p. 81.

59. Sept. 26, 1935, Executive Order No. 7193.

60. Card File, U.S. Information Service. Council now abolished and its records are with the N.R.A. records in the Dept. of Commerce.

61. The President's Committee on Administrative Management, *Administrative Management in the Government of the U.S.* (Wash., U.S. Govt. Print. Off., 1937), pp. 31–33; See contra, Charles S. Hyneman, "Administrative Reorganization," *The Journal of Politics* (Feb., 1939), vol. 1, pp. 62–65.

62. It is recognized that most advice upon which the President predicates action comes from the executive departments. No effort is made herein to set forth the criteria which might aid the President in determining whether to rely on the advice of an existing agency or to turn to a body created especially for the purpose.

63. *Report of Joseph L. Bristow . . . to the Secretary of War,* June 24, 1905. (Washington, 1905), p. 95; Sen. Doc. 174, 71st Cong., 2d sess., p. 10.

64. "Between these conflicting views (independence or continued tutelage) you are to render judgment." *Report of the Special Mission of Investigation to the Philippine Islands to the Secretary of War.* (Wash., Govt. Print. Off., 1921), p. 7.

65. Commission to Investigate Charges of the Navy League for example.

66. *United States Daily,* vol. 25, p. 1; *Congressional Directory,* January, 1932, p. 350.

67. *Hoover's State Papers,* vol. I, pp. 109–111.

68. Act of April 10, 1930.

69. *Report of U.S. Committee on the Conservation and Administration of the Public Domain.* Transmitted to the President . . . in pursuance of the Act of April 10, 1930. (Wash., Govt. Print. Off., 1931.)

70. A similar commission was the United States Advisory Committee on Employment Statistics, to advise on methods of setting up statistics of employment and unemployment. See Report, May, 1931. (Wash., Govt. Print. Off.), House Doc. 814, 71st Cong., 3d sess., The Social Science Research Council gave assistance with staff, facilities, and money.

(Other commissions which might be placed in the policy advisory classification include: Advisory Council for the Government of the Virgin Islands, created by President's letter to Secretary of the Interior, Feb. 23, 1934. *Roosevelt's State Papers,* v. III, pp. 101–102; the Business Advisory Council, *ibid.,* vol. V, p. 589, v IV, p. 156; the Committee to Investigate Debts Contracted by Government Employees, and to advise how they may be collected, no date, card file, U.S. Information Office; the Interdepartmental Committee on Merchant Marine Policy to recommend a policy for the U.S. Merchant marine to the President; the Interdepartmental Committee to study International Broadcasting, first meeting Feb. 21, 1938, report confidential and never published, card file, U.S. Information Office. Mention has been made elsewhere of the President's Committee to Submit Recommendations Upon the General Transportation Situation.)

The President is not the only executive officer who uses advisory commissions. They are established by executive departments, agencies and officials for a wide variety of purposes.

In connection with the war, there have been a number of advisory committees created. Once an agency or committee is set up to execute some general policy, there is a tendency to set up advisory bodies. A glance at the Office of Emergency Management in 1942 indicated that in the Division of Purchases there was an Advisory Committee as well as a Food Procurement Advisory Committee, the latter body being made up entirely of lay representatives; the Priorities Board had advisory representatives; the Coordinator of Health, Welfare, and Related Activities was authorized with the approval of the President, to appoint such advisory committees and sub-committees as he might find necessary in carrying out his coordinating functions; and finally, most of the agencies had a number of "consultant" positions in the higher brackets. (See *Office for Emergency Management, Functions and Administration, op. cit.,* pp. 18, 20, 23, 46, 55.)

This is by no means an exhaustive list of the policy advisory committees. Many of the departments and newer agencies have set up their own advisory groups. Thus the Secretary of State in 1938 created a General Advisory Committee of the Division of Cultural Relations and the President authorized traveling expenses for the group. Membership included Dr. Stephen P. Duggan and other officers of scientific and cultural organizations. (Nov. 8, 1938, card file, U.S. Information Office.)

In the same year the Interdepartmental Committee on Cooperation with the American Republics was created as the result of an oral conversation between the Under Secretary of State and the President. The committee was to examine the subject of cooperation with the other American Republics and draft for the President's consideration a concrete program designed to bring about better relations. The Committee was made up of representatives of 13 departments and agencies with the Under Secretary of State acting as chairman. (Appointed May, 1938, Report of the Interdepartmental Committee on Cooperation with the American Republics, Together with the Program of Cooperation Endorsed by the Committee, House Doc. 251, 76th Cong., 1st sess.; also State Department Press Release, December 3, 1938.)

In early 1940, the Secretary of State set up an Advisory Committee on Problems of Foreign Relations, with membership selected from the Department of State. (U.S. Information Service, card file.) This committee was instructed to gather data on the immediate and long-range results of the war and the way in which problems likely to arise could be handled.

Secretary of Agriculture Wallace, at the request of the President in 1939 set up the Agricultural Advisory Council composed of representatives of the farmers, laborers, goods distributors and the general public, to assist in the formulation of policies to deal with the situation brought about by the outbreak of war in Europe. (U.S. Information Service, card file; U.S. Government Manual, March, 1941, pp. 109–110.)

The Secretary of Labor announced a National Committee on Conservation of Man Power in June, 1940, to cooperate with the national defense program and to assist the Labor Department in providing essential information about industrial accident and health exposures and to advise what could be done to control or eliminate them. (Information, Office of Secretary, Labor Department.) The Labor Department also created a Federal Committee on Apprenticeship to advise on policy in connection with training apprentices, and a Labor Advisory Committee to the Women's Bureau on Standards for the Employment of Women. (U.S. Government Manual, March, 1941, pp. 127–128.) Sidney Hillman, Labor representative in the Office of Production Management appointed a Labor Policy Advisory Committee. (July, 1940, U.S. Information Service, card file.) The Secretaries of War and Navy, not to be outdone, created a Construction Advisory Committee of civilians to stimulate construction and to advise the Army and Navy Munitions Control Board in the formulation and review of national defense plans. (July 22, 1940, *ibid.*)

Another advisory board set up during this period was the War Resources Board created by the chairman of the Joint Army and Navy Munitions Board with the approval of the President. This board was to act as a civilian advisory body to the Army-Navy Board on policies pertaining to the mobilization of the country's economic resources. The report of the Board, terminated by the President, November 24, 1939, was never made public. (U.S. Government Manual, *op. cit.*, p. 646; *N.Y. Times*, Aug. 10, 1939, 1:4; Nov. 4, 3:7; Nov. 25, 2:6.)

Of the ten different advisory bodies mentioned in the preceding paragraphs, all but two (the Advisory Committee on Problems of Foreign Relations and the Interdepartmental Committee on Cooperation with the American Republics) were made up of non-governmental personnel. The value of such composition seems twofold: first, outside minds are brought to bear on problems the execution of which is left to the government, and second, the creation of such bodies helps bring about cooperation between private and public activities. The use of contacts outside the government for advice serves to keep government administration from getting too far away from the public.

The increased use of advisory committees by the President and the executive Departments is significant. It indicates that the problems of policy up for decision are more complex than heretofore. They call for analysis by more than one mind with more than one approach. The creation of such advisory bodies in time of emergency indicates that there has been a recognition that unity without resort to force, demands policy which is the product of thought and deliberation by several men, not by one.

71. Advisory Committee on Allotments (E.O. 7034, May 6, 1935) membership of government officials; Flood Control Committee, Conference held Aug. 10, 1936 (An informal committee, card file, U.S. Information Service). Also included might be the Advisory Committee on Veterans Preference, Nov. 12, 1930 (Legislative Reference Service, No. 211442, p. 11, White House List, Jan., 1932); the Committee on Utilization of Abandoned Army Posts, May 12, 1931 (Legis. Ref. Serv., No. 211442, p. 13, White House List, January, 1932); the Advisory Council (N.I.R.A.) Executive Order N. 7075, June 15, 1935; and the Advisory Committee on Selective Service, Sept. 21, 1940, to coordinate plans on selective service. (35 A.P.S.R. 82, Feb., 1941.)

72. *Hoover's State Papers,* vol. I, p. 140.

73. *Ibid.,* p. 209; see also vol. II, p. 72 for comment.

74. Executive Order No. 6632, March 7, 1934; abolished, E.O. No. 6771, June 30, 1934.

75. Irving Stone, *Clarence Darrow for the Defense.* (Garden City, Doubleday, Doran & Co., 1941)), pp. 507–514.

76. Other commissions such as the Commission on Law Observance and Enforcement might, of course, be included.

77. In spite of the President's "horse and buggy" characterization of the Supreme Court decision in the N.R.A. case, many people have believed that the President was glad to be rid of the Blue Eagle.

78. See Digest of Report, *N.Y. Times,* September 11, 1942, p. 15. Although outside the 1900–1940 period dealt with in this study, the Baruch Commission is treated because it was a commission which attracted wide attention. Moreover it illustrates rather well the use of the commission device in a situation where the facts are clouded by emotion and politics.

79. *N.Y. Times,* May 29, 1942.

80. *Ibid.*

81. *N.Y. Times,* July 7, 1942, p. 1.

82. *Ibid.*

83. *N.Y. Times,* Aug. 7, 1942; Arthur Krock, *ibid.,* also Mark Sullivan, "The Baruch Committee," *Wash. Post,* Aug. 18, 1942.

84. *N.Y. Times,* editorial, Sept. 12, 1942.

85. *Ibid.* See also Arthur Krock, *N.Y. Times,* Sept. 11, 1942.

86. *Washington Post,* editorial, March 26, 1943, p. 10; Indianapolis News, October 16, 1943, editorial, p. 6.

87. *N.Y. Times,* September 12, 1942, editorial.

88. Plato, *The Republic,* Bk. VI. See also Lord Bryce and his comments in *The American Commonwealth.*

89. See for example the *Unification of Portland Cement Specifications; Preliminary Statement Relative to the Present Status of the Efforts of the Departmental Committee to Secure Agreement upon a Single Uniform Specification for Portland Cement.* (Wash., 1912), Sen. Doc. 174, *op. cit.,* p. 39; also the Interdepartmental Committee on Paint Standardization, pp. 76–77; The Committee on Standardization of Petroleum Specifications, p. 74.

90. Executive Order promulgated in Bureau of Budget Circular No. 15, July 27, 1921.

91. *Congressional Directory,* January, 1930, pp. 450–451.

92. Executive Order promulgated in Bureau of Budget Circular No. 25, August 25, 1921; *Cong. Dir.,* Jan., 1930, p. 451, Sen. Doc. 174, *op. cit.,* p. 90.

93. B. of B. Circular No. 35, Sept. 23, 1921; *Cong. Dir.,* January, 1930, p. 451.

94. Created by Executive Order promulgated in Bureau of the Budget Circular No. 41, October 10, 1921; *Cong. Dir., op. cit.,* p. 451.

95. Reynolds, Mary Trackett, *Interdepartmental Committees in the National Administration, op. cit.*

96. *Report of the President's Committee on Administrative Management,* submitted to the President and to the Congress in accordance with Public Law No. 739, 74th Cong., 2d sess. (Govt. Print. Off., 1937), p. 31 et ff. This report points out that in 1937 there were "over 100 separately organized establishments and agencies presumably reporting to the President," p. 32.

97. See for example, the Interdepartmental Committee on Alaska, created in 1920 by President Wilson "to coordinate and bring together facts and suggestions touching on matters affecting Alaska, and to make recommendations for definite action to the department charged with the particular function, to the end that duplication may be avoided and effi-

ciency secured." *N.Y. Times,* December 5, 1920, 18:4. Also, Interdepartmental Committee on Alaska created in 1934 by President Roosevelt for substantially same purpose (U.S. Information Service Card File). Also, Interdepartmental Committee on Philippine Affairs created by memorandum from President to Secretary of State, January 3, 1935 (Information and Records in Office of Philippine Affairs, Dept. of State). Puerto Rican Rehabilitation Committee created by oral direction of the President in July, 1934, to correlate and coordinate activities of certain government agencies (Card File, U.S. Information Service).

98. The Secretary of Commerce created an Interdepartmental Board on Coastal Communications in 1916, and in 1922 an Interdepartmental Radio Advisory Committee. Senate Doc. 174, *op. cit.,* pp. 57 and 94.

99. An Interdepartmental Committee on Interstate Trade Barriers to study and unify government activities for combatting inroads to the free flow of commerce between the States was created in 1939 by the Secretary of Commerce. (U.S. Inf. Serv. Card File.)

100. For example: The Special Committee on Government Borrowing established by the President in 1933 to coordinate all government borrowing. (Created July 25, 1933. U.S. Information Service Card File.) An Interdepartmental Loan Committee to coordinate federal lending activities. (*Roosevelt's State Papers, op. cit.,* v. 1934, p. 450.) A Committee to Coordinate Activities Affecting the Banks (U.S. Information Service, card file, Aug. 2, 1933, abolished January 24, 1935). The President's Fiscal Advisory Committee (Economic Board) to canvass and knit together the Government's fiscal and monetary policies in relation to the nation's production needs and national income. (U.S. Information Service, card file, November 19, 1938.)

101. *Hoover's State Papers, op. cit.,* vol. I, p. 90.

102. *Roosevelt's State Papers, op. cit.,* vol. II, pp. 18–20.

103. *Ibid.,* vol. V, p. 265.

104. *Office for Emergency Management, op. cit.,* p. 52.

105. E.O. 3773, January 12, 1923, Sen. Doc. 174, *op. cit.,* p. 97.

106. *Hoover's State Papers,* v. II, pp. 266–274.

107. U.S. Information Service, card file; also *PM,* Dec. 13, 1940, p. 5.

108. McGeary, *op. cit.,* pp. 121–122.

109. Weber, Gustavus, *Organized Efforts for Improvement of Administration, op. cit.,* p. 20.

110. Weber, *op. cit.,* p. 21.

111. The Joint Commission on Executive Departments, Organization, etc. (Dockery-Cockrell Commission), 1893–1895. See Weber, *op. cit.,* pp. 66–74.

112. *Ibid.,* p. 19.

113. 42 Stat. 20.

114. See Weber, *op. cit.,* pp. 18–19.

115. *Ibid.,* pp. 20–21.

116. See list in Weber, *op. cit.,* pp. 45–56; see also the brief historical account presented by John J. Cochran of Missouri, *Congressional Record,* 75th Cong., 1st sess., House, v. 81, Pt. 10, pp. 2455–2462, August 16, 1937.

117. Weber, *op. cit.,* p. 19: Most of the official economy and efficiency committees have been under the auspices of the executive. "Though their establishment was authorized and the funds for their support were voted by the legislature, provision was in most cases made that their personnel should be selected by the Chief Executive and that they should work under the general direction of and report to that officer."

118. *Ibid.,* p. 74.

119. 34 Stat. 635.

120. See *American Monthly Review of Reviews,* April, 1903, p. 411.

121. See 60th Cong., 2d sess., Doc. 714, for report by the Keep Committee on the Documentary Historical Publications of the United States, with draft of proposed bill providing for the creation of a permanent commission on national historical publications. Reference to other reports published as Congressional documents will be found in Weber, *op. cit.*, p. 74 et ff.

122. Holcombe, A. N., "Governmental Efficiency," *Annals of the American Academy of Political and Social Science*, XLV, p. 242.

123. See Jacobson, Walter Otto—*A Study of President Taft's Commission on Economy and Efficiency.* Master's Thesis, Columbia University, New York City, June, 1941.

124. 36 Stat. 703.

125. Sundry Civil Act, June 25, 1910 ($100,000); *ibid.*, March 4, 1911 ($75,000); *ibid.*, Aug. 24, 1912 ($75,000); plus a joint resolution of Aug. 21, 1912 (36 Stat. 1363–1364; 37 Stat. 417) appropriating $10,000 to investigate the administration of the Patent Office.

126. 37 Stat. 643.

127. Weber, *op. cit.*, pp. 84–85.

128. See Names of the Members of the Commission on Economy and Efficiency, Jan. 25, 1912, 62d Cong., 2d sess., Sen. Doc. 294, Serial No. 6180 (Washington; Govt. Print. Off., 1912). Also Jacobson, *op. cit.*, p. 39 et ff.

Evaluation of the Reports submitted by the commission as to reorganization results and action upon the reports; See 62d Cong., 2d sess., House Doc. 670 (Govt. Print. Off., 1912).

129. Weber, *op. cit.*, p. 84.

130. For list of reports see Weber, *op. cit.*, p. 94 et ff. See also Jacobson, *op. cit.*, p. 72, where he summarizes the action on the reports. Also, Economy Commission, Circular 31, Message of the President, Reports of Committee on Economy and Efficiency, Jan. 8, 1913, 62nd Cong., 3rd sess., House Doc. No. 1252, Serial No. 6470. (Wash., Govt. Print. Off., 1913), pp. 21–36.

"The principal immediate value of the investigation," says Jacobson, "was to reveal hitherto unexplored phases of government activity" (p. 72). The long-range value of the study was that the material gathered became groundwork upon which to build governmental reforms.

131. Public Resolution No. 54, 66th Cong., Dec. 17, 1920. See also President Wilson's letter to the Senate stating that after the Resolution became law without his signature, the document had been lost. *Cong. Record*, v. 60, pp. 1086, 1218, 66th Cong., 3d sess.

132. Public Resolution, 67th Cong., May 5, 1921.

133. See Report of the Joint Committee on Reorganization, House Document 356, 68th Cong., 1st sess. (Wash., Govt. Print. Off., 1924.)

134. White House Statement, March 22, 1936. *Roosevelt's State Papers, op. cit.*, v. V., p. 144.

135. See Message transmitting the report to Congress, *Ibid.*, v. V., p. 668; *The President's Committee on Administrative Management. Report of the Committee with Studies of the Administrative Management in the Federal Government*, (U.S. Govt. Print. Off., Wash., 1937, p. III).

136. Senate Resolution 217, 74th Congress.

137. For organization background see: Statement of Louis Brownlow in *Hearings before the Joint Committee on Government Organization: Congress of the United States.* (Govt. Print. Off., Wash., 1937), p. 1 et ff.; also, introductory pages of *Preliminary Report of the Select Committee to Investigate the Executive Agencies of the Government* (the Byrd Committee), Senate Report 1275, 75th Cong., 1st sess., August 19, 1937; and

for criticism see Lindsay Rogers, "Reorganization: Post Mortem Notes" *Political Science Quarterly*, v. LIII, No. 2, June, 1938, p. 161 et ff.

138. Hearings before Joint Committee, *op. cit.*, pp. 1, 2.

139. In accordance with Public Law No. 739, 74th Cong., 2d sess.

140. See *Hearings before Select Committee on Government Organization*, 75th Cong., 1st sess., p. 424 et ff. which shows the sharp conflict between the President's "experts" and Senator Byrd's "experts."

141. Lindsay Rogers, "Reorganization: Post Mortem Notes," *op. cit.*, p. 167.

142. See *Hearings before the Joint Committee on Government Organization, op. cit.*, p. 12, where the Chairman of the President's Committee appeared to be evasive in answering the question: " 'Was this report rewritten to conform to the wishes of the Administration?' Mr. Brownlow: 'The President, in his message to the Congress made a statement about the report. We were appointed. We did not see the President. . . . We had no communication with the President of the United States whatsoever from the time this thing began until it was practically in its completed form. We had two or three conversations with him. One immediately before he went to Buenos Aires and three or four after the work was done.' Representative Gifford: 'The question I am asking, do you consider that this has the approval of the administration?' Mr. Brownlow: 'I do not want to undertake to speak for the President. . . .' "

143. For discussion, see Lindsay Rogers, *op. cit.*, p. 165 et ff.

144. 53 Stat. 561; 5 U.S.C. 133, April 3, 1939.

145. See Treasury Department, *Combined Statement of the Receipts and Expenditures, Balances, etc. of the United States,* annual. (Govt. Print. Office, 1936), p. 492; 1937, p. 497; 1938, p. 561.

146. But see the statement of John J. Cochran of Missouri in which he says $130,000 was the full amount. *Cong. Rec.,* 75th Cong., 1st sess., vol. 81, pt. 10, p. 2460. See for example the Statement of the Secretary to the President concerning the President's Inquiry in re Economy and Efficiency before the Subcommittee of House Committee on Appropriations in charge of Sundry Civil Appro. Bill for 1912, Feb. 6, 1911 (Wash., Govt. Print. Off.). Among other things, Mr. Norton was asked: "Are there no men in the Government service qualified to do any of the work?" "How long will it take and how much will it cost?" "What has been the line of the investigation thus far, in a general way?" Questions were raised as to the salaries to be paid experts, and in the Sundry Civil Act of August 24, 1912, it was specifically provided that "not exceeding three persons may be employed . . . at rates . . . exceeding $4,000 per annum."

147. See *Roosevelt's Papers,* vol. 1936, pp. 144 et ff.

148. See *Report of the Commission Appointed by the President to Investigate the Conduct of the War Department in the War with Spain* (Wash., Govt. Print. Off., 1899).

149. Resolutions were offered in both the House and Senate. See *Cong. Record,* 55th Cong., 3rd sess., pp. 16, 637, 678, 687.

150. *Report of Commission to Investigate the Conduct of the War Department, op. cit.,* p. 12.

151. *Ibid.,* p. 129.

152. See *8 Encyclopedia of Social Sciences,* 251, Public Opinion.

153. From the reports of the Commission, Senate Doc. No. 740, 743, 60th Cong., 2d Sess. (#5409.)

154. H. R. 6324 (76th Cong., 1st sess.), introduced May 15, 1939 (*Cong. Rec.* v. 84, pt. 5, p. 5561), by Mr. Walter became the basis of the Walter-Logan bill, but Senate Bill 916 introduced by Senator Logan on January 24, 1939 "to establish a United States

Court of Appeals for Administration" (*Cong. Rec.* v. 84, pt. 1, p. 668, 76th Cong., 1st sess.), was undoubtedly the move forcing the President to create the Attorney General's Committee on Administrative Procedure. The American Bar Association had submitted recommendations for rather extensive, and some feared, suicidal, changes in administrative procedure with regard to rule-making, notice and hearing, and particularly court review of administrative findings. The Walter-Logan bill which sought to enact these recommendations into law was opposed by the President and subsequently vetoed by him on Dec. 18, 1940. See *Cong. Rec.,* vol. 86, pt. 12, p. 13942, 76th Cong., 2d sess. At the time the President vetoed the Walter-Logan bill, the Attorney General's Committee had not yet reported but the fact of its existence was used by the President in justifying his veto.

155. See Final Report of the *Attorney General's Committee on Administrative Procedure* (Wash., Govt. Print. Off., 1941, p. 252).

156. See Frankfurter in *Columbia Law Review,* 1941, April.

157. 27 Opinions of the Attorney General 406.

See Walter Gellhorn, *Federal Administrative Proceedings* (Baltimore: The Johns Hopkins Press, 1941).

158. Executive Order 8044, Jan. 31, 1939. This Committee should be distinguished from Hoover's Council of Personnel Administration established April 25, 1931 (Executive Order 5612), and Roosevelt's Council of the same name established June 24, 1938 (Executive Order 7916). The latter two bodies were made up for the most part of representatives of the personnel offices of the various departments and establishments and served as advisory bodies to the Civil Service Commission and the President. They were authorized by the Civil Service Act (5 U.S.C. 631), which provided that the President might employ "suitable persons to conduct . . . inquiries" into the qualifications of candidates for civil service positions.

159. See *N.Y. Times,* Feb. 25, 1941; *N.Y. Herald Tribune,* February 25, 1941.

160. Executive Order 7916, June 24, 1938, 5 U.S.C., 631, and the subsequently passed Ramspeck Act passed in 1940 (54 Stat. 1211).

161. Executive Order 8044, Jan. 31, 1939.

CHAPTER VI

1. *N.Y. Times,* Aug. 28, 1942, p. 14.

2. See *N.Y. Times,* Nov. 8 and 26, 1931. There is no indication that Mr. Gardiner ever publicly apologized for his statement.

3. For editorial comment see *Literary Digest,* Nov. 14, 1931; Nov. 21, 1931; and *Outlook Magazine,* Nov. 11, 1931. The Committee found "that in its entirety Mr. Gardiner's statement contains many inaccuracies, false assertions and erroneous conclusions, and that his assumption as to the President's attitude toward the Navy is wholly unwarranted." Report of the U.S. President's Committee to Examine and Report on the Statement of the Navy League, Oct. 28, 1931, released to press Nov. 7, 1931.

4. 11 *Charities Magazine* 324.

5. 12 *ibid* 223. The Report of the Commission was rendered to the Department of Commerce and Labor. For full report see: *New Yorker Staats-Zeitung,* April 30, 1904.

6. *N.Y. Tribune,* June 22, 1904.

7. See Short, Lloyd M., *Steamboat Inspection Service.* Institute for Government Research. Monograph N. 8. (N.Y.: D. Appleton & Co., 1922), p. 18 et ff.

8. Another commission within the Department of Commerce and Labor to Investigate

the Steamboat Inspection Service was created, as well as a separate board of retired naval officers, both reporting to the President through the Secretary of Commerce and Labor. (Sen. Doc. 174, *op. cit.,* p. 9.) Subsequently, on May 12, 1908, President Roosevelt created the Commission on Revision of Laws Relating to Safety of Life at Sea.

9. Executive Order No. 8983, Dec. 18, 1941, *Federal Register,* vol. 6, #247, Dec. 20, 1941, p. 6569

"Pursuant to the authority in me vested by the Constitution of the United States, I hereby appoint as a commission to ascertain and report the facts relating to the attack made by Japanese armed forces upon the Territory of Hawaii on Dec. 7, 1941, the following:

Associate Justice Owen J. Roberts, U.S. Sup. Ct., Chairman.
Admiral William H. Standley, U.S. Navy, Retired.
Rear Admiral Joseph M. Reeves, U.S. Navy, Retired.
Major General Frank R. McCoy, U.S. Army, Retired.
Brigadier General Joseph T. McNamey, U.S. Army.

"The purposes of the required inquiry and report are to provide bases for sound decisions whether any derelictions of duty or errors of judgment on the part of the United States Army or Navy personnel contributed to such successes as were achieved by the enemy on the occasion mentioned, and if so, what these derelictions or errors were, and who were responsible therefore.

"The Commission will convene at the call of its Chairman at Washington, D.C., will thereafter proceed with its professional and clerical assistants to Honolulu, Territory of Hawaii, and any other places it may deem necessary to visit for the completion of its inquiry. It will then return to Washington, D.C., and submit its report directly to the President of the United States.

"The Commission is empowered to prescribe its own procedure, to employ such professional and clerical assistants as it may deem necessary, to fix the compensation and allowances of such assistants, to incur all necessary expenses for services and supplies, and to direct such travel of members and employees at public expense as it may deem necessary in the accomplishment of its mission. Each of the members of the Commission and each of its professional assistants, including civilian advisers and any Army, Navy and Marine Corps officers so employed, detailed or assigned shall receive payment for his actual and necessary expenses for transportation, and in addition and in lieu of all other allowances for expenses while absent from the place of his residence or station in connection with the business of the Commission, a per diem allowance of twenty-five dollars. All of the expenses of the Commission shall be paid by Army disbursing officers from allocations to be made to the War Department for that purpose from the Emergency Fund for the President.

"All executive officers and agencies of the United States are directed to furnish the Commission such facilities, services, and cooperation as it may request of them from time to time."

White House   (Signed) Franklin D. Roosevelt

See Report of the Roberts Commission, *N.Y. Times,* January 25, 1942.

10. 10 U.S.C., Sec. 990,991. There have been cases where the President's position as Commander in Chief has been urged as authority for commissions made up in whole or in part of civilians. Elihu Root believed that the First and Second Philippine Commissions were so authorized. (See Malcolm, George A., *"The Government of the Philippine Islands,"* The Lawyers Co-operative Pub. Co., Rochester, N.Y., 1916, p. 215.)

See also the remarks of Senator King, *Cong. Record,* 70th Congress, 1st sess., vol. 69, p. 1778, referring to a presidential investigation of the sinking of the submarine S4 to be made up in part of civilians. "I have no doubt that the Commander in Chief has full authority to make such an investigation as he sees fit."

11. 10 U.S.C.A. 1569. For Navy see 34 U.S.C.A. 1200, Sec. 55 et ff.

12. 8 O.A.G. 335, 1857.

13. 10 O.A.G. 501, 1890.

14. 10 U.S.C.A. 991, 1570; 34 U.S.C.A. 1200, art 55, 56.

15. Public Law, 28, 77th Cong., 1st sess., April 5, 1941. Independent Offices Appropriations Act, 1942. This was in addition to an Emergency Fund of $100,000,000 in the Military Appropriation Act of 1941.

A further sum of $100,000,000 was appropriated by the Third Supplemental National Defense Appropriation Act, 1942, "To enable the President, through appropriate agencies of the Government, to provide for emergencies affecting the national security and defense and for each and every purpose connected therewith, and to make all necessary expenditures incidental thereto, for any purpose for which Congress has previously made appropriation or authorization and without regard to the provisions of law regulating the expenditure of Government funds. . . ."

The terms of these emergency defense grants are so broad as to leave the President free to spend the money in any way he wishes.

16. Naval Appropriation Act, 1942, Pub. Law 48, 77th Cong., 1st sess., Ch. 86, May 6, 1941, see Miscellaneous Expenses.

17. See the appropriation for the Office for Emergency Management, for example. Second Deficiency Appropriations Act, 1941, Public Law 150, 77th Cong., 1st sess., Ch. 273, July 3, 1941.

18. Executive Order, supra, note 9.

19. Public Law 370—77th Cong., Approved Dec. 23, 1941, providing in part: "The Commission or any member of the commission or any agent or agency designated by the commission for such purpose may administer oaths and affirmations, examine witnesses, and receive evidence. . . . (b) In case of contumacy or refusal to obey a subpoena . . . any district court of the U.S. . . . within the jurisdiction of which said person guilty of contumacy is found . . . shall have jurisdiction to issue . . . an order requiring such person to appear . . . and any failure to obey such order of the court may be punished by said court as a contempt thereof."

20. *New York Times,* January 27, 1942.

21. U.S. 70th Cong., 1st sess., Jan. 20, 1928, *Cong. Rec.,* v. 69, pt. 2, p. 1769.

22. *Ibid.,* Jan. 4, 1928, v. 69, p. 973.

23. Supra p. 12.

24. 70th Cong., 1st sess., *Cong. Rec.,* v. 69, pt. 2, pp. 1773, 1774, 1776, 1777, 1778. Senate refusal to accept compromise res., pp. 5354–5355.

25. *Ibid.,* pp. 1774–1775.

26. 70th Cong., 2d sess., Sen. Rpt. 1988, v. A, serial no. 8978.

27. *Ibid.,* p. 9.

28. *Ibid.,* p. 13.

29. *Ibid.,* p. 18.

30. McGeary, *op. cit.*

31. *Ibid.*

CHAPTER VII

1. This chapter does not discuss the problem of the fact-finding of administrative-agencies set up by Congress or set up by the President on a clear mandate from Con-

gress. Discussion of the compulsive powers of such bodies is beyond the scope of this study.

See Lilienthal, David E., "The Power of Governmental Agencies to Compel Testimony." 39 *Harvard Law Review* 694, April, 1926; Hart, James, *An Introduction to Administrative Law*, with selected Cases (N.Y.: F. S. Crofts and Co., 1940), pp. 214–216.

2. See Jones v. Securities Exchange Commission, 298 U.S. 1 (1936). The dissent of Cardozo J. reads in part as follows: "A commission which is without coercive powers, which cannot arrest or amerce or imprison though a crime has been uncovered, or even punish for contempt, but can only inquire and report, the propriety of every question in the course of the inquiry being subject to the supervision of the ordinary courts of justice, is likened with denunciatory fervor to the Star Chamber of the Stuarts. Historians may find hyperbole in the sanguinary simile."

In Ellis v. I.C.C., 237 U.S. 434 (1915), at p. 445, Justice Holmes said that the I.C.C. may not engage in "a fishing expedition into the affairs of a stranger for the chance, that something discreditable might turn up."

3. 135 U.S. 1 (1890).

4. Dimock, *Congressional Investigating Committees, op. cit.*, pointing out that the legal basis of congressional investigative power "is found in the implied powers of the Constitution, whereas the rights of (administrative) commissions are strictly circumscribed by statute," pp. 151–152.

5. But see W. Harrison Moore, "Executive Commissions of Inquiry," 13 *Columbia Law Review* 500, at p. 520 where he says: "The conclusion submitted from the foregoing inquiry is that there is no rule of law which attaches illegality in any definite sense to the mere issuance of a commission of inquiry by the Crown, or to the act of investigation in pursuance of such a commission. The distinction between public matters of lawful inquiry and private matters which are not to be inquired of (Clough v. Leahy, 4 S.R. [N.S.W. 401], 1904) . . . seems really material only as founding a claim in the former case to exercise powers of compulsion which, as a result of common law powers, are now abandoned and may be treated as obsolete."

6. Miller, Urban R., "Application of the Rules of Evidence to Fact-Finding Boards," 17 *Chicago-Kent Law Review* 145 (March, 1939).

7. *Parliamentary Papers,* CD 5235, Report of the Departmental Committee on the Procedure of Royal Commissions, Lord Balfour Chairman. Appointed by His Majesty's Secretary of State for the Home Dept., April 19, 1909.

8. But see Australian practice. The Royal Commission Act of 1912 gives wide discretion to the executive "to appoint commissions to inquire and report upon any matter relating to or connected with the peace, order and good government of the Commonwealth or any public purpose or power of the Commonwealth." Broad powers of compulsion are given to the executive. See W. Harrison Moore, "Executive Commissions of Inquiry," 13 *Columbia Law Review* 500. The Balfour Committee reached the conclusion that set rules of procedure to which all Royal Commissions should adhere should not be set down because the "commissions are so variable and the difficulties so difficult to foresee." It was found desirable, however, to "lay down . . . certain general principles." Cd 5235, *op. cit.*

9. Cd 5235, *op. cit.*

10. Marx, Fritz Morstein, in 30 *American Political Science Review* 1134, December, 1939, writing with reference to German commissions of inquiry, states: "If German experience with commissions of inquiry offers any lessons at all, they appear to be these: First, the investigating process depends for its success on a regularized procedure which combines a reasonable measure of flexibility with consistency in the pursuit of

clearly defined objectives. . . . Second, the commission should be in a position to feel free from any obligations toward the appointing agency as well as toward the witnesses. . . . Third, the size of the committee should be kept within narrow bounds. . . . And fourth, the findings of the commission should include the full record of evidence assembled," p. 1143.

11. The Committee to Study Cooperatives in Europe, for example.

12. W. Harrison Moore, 13 *C.L.R.,* 500, pp. 504–505, discusses a formalized version of such a body which was created in Australia:

"In Australia one of the latest acts of the Commonwealth Parliament constitutes a permanent body which, in addition to its administrative and judicial functions, is charged with the duty of investigating from time to time all matters which in its opinion ought to be investigated affecting production of and trade in commodities, the encouragement and improvement of Australian industries, external trade, the tariff, prices, profits, wages and social and industrial conditions, labor employment and unemployment, foreign bounties, population, immigration and such other matters as may be referred for investigation. The commission has full power to send for persons and documents. It serves to call attention to the fact that inquiry and publicity are regarded as powerful weapons in coping with some of the most characteristic of modern social difficulties."

CHAPTER VIII

1. Fritz Morstein Marx in an article in the *American Political Science Review* (vol. 30, p. 1134) on German commissions of inquiry pointed out that from 1872 until the war Germany used "commissions of inquiry only as a last resort whenever the resourceful ministerial staffs felt in need of special piloting on the uncharted seas of modern industrial development. . . . Officially organized investigations were confined in Germany to the role of devices of crisis government" (p. 1140).

2. This statement was used to describe in part the function of British Royal Commissions. *A Finding List of British Royal Commission Reports,* 1860–1935, Preface by Arthur Harrison Cole; (Cambridge: Harvard U. Press, 1935), at p. 5.

3. A. Mervyn Davies, "Brains in Government—Commissions to Find the Facts," *Forum,* May, 1937, V. 97, p. 310.

4. Arthur Macmahon and John D. Millett have stressed the importance of the trained administrator. (Macmahon and Millett, *Federal Administrators,* N.Y., Columbia Univ. Press, 1939.) A similar study of presidential commission secretaries might be very productive.

5. Ernst Freund, *Standards of American Legislation, op. cit.* (1926).

6. See Arthur Krock, *N.Y. Times,* May 29, 1942, where with reference to the necessity of gasoline rationing to conserve rubber, Senator La Follette was reported to see the ruin of Midwest farm production and the tourist business if those areas were subject to rationing.

7. *Washington Evening Star,* June 18, 1942, p. 1.

8. *N.Y. Times,* June 19, 1942, p. 1.

9. George Galloway, associated with the Twentieth Century Fund has severely indicted Congress along lines which indicate that Congress is no longer an effective factfinder. Speaking before a 1943 session of the American Political Science Association, he answered the question of "What's Wrong with Congress?" by listing the following as defects: (1) "The Committee system is 'obsolete, duplicative and dispersive; inefficient for peacetime purposes and quite unequal to the requirements of wartime.' (2) Congress

has failed 'to equip itself adequately with unbiased sources of information.' (3) . . . , (4) Congress has no protection against pressure groups. . . ." *Washington Post,* January 30, 1943. The principal points to be noted for the purposes of this study are that Congress does not have unbiased sources of information and has no protection from pressure groups. If these defects are well founded, it is hard to see how there can be effective reliance on facts found by Congress.

10. *N.Y. Times,* July 25, 1942, editorial.

11. Thus the Senate Truman Committee in April, 1943, worried about the manpower situation in the United States called for "a scientific determination of the number of men who can be usefully employed in the armed forces." It was not suggested that Congress undertake such a survey. (Frank R. Kent, *The Evening Star,* Washington, April 30, 1943.)

12. Lillian Symes, "The Great Fact-Finding Farce," *Harpers Magazine,* February, 1932, v. 164, pp. 354, 356, 368.

13. *Ibid.,* pp. 355–356.

14. *Ibid.,* p. 366.

15. Columnist Arthur Krock, in discussing the appointment of Mr. Baruch to investigate the rubber shortage pointed out that a man who is to find facts for the public must be one "with unique qualifications. His 'experience in business and production' must be well-known to the public and of high caliber. His patriotism must be established to the point where the public, as well as officials, would accept whatever he signed as factual. . . . His detachment from the executive branch of government must be as definite as his sympathetic knowledge of the ordinary American economy." (*New York Times,* August 7, 1942.)

Mark Sullivan in discussing the report of the Baruch Committee asked if it would not be possible for the President to "find a small group of men who would act as sponsors for all sorts of steps, including orders, requests and announcements made to the public? Men whose names would carry conviction that the step is based on necessity only and is not unnecessarily in the interest of any political party, or ideology, or section or group." (*Washington Post,* September 16, 1942.)

Each of the above journalists has approached the basic problem from a different point of view, but the problem is the same—that of finding and reporting facts to the public— facts which the public can believe have been found by men dedicated to truth and to the public interest.

The foregoing pages have shown that presidential commissions can achieve this end, or that they can fail miserably. But it is within the competence of the President to raise commissions consistently to that level.

INDEX OF PRESIDENTIAL COMMISSIONS

THE
MYTH OF
PRVATE
EQUITY

AN INSIDE LOOK AT WALL STREET'S
TRANSFORMATIVE INVESTMENTS

JEFFREY C. HOOKE

Columbia University Press
Publishers Since 1893
New York   Chichester, West Sussex
cup.columbia.edu

Library of Congress Cataloging-in-Publication Data
Names: Hooke, Jeffrey C., author.
Title: The myth of private equity : an inside look at Wall Street's
transformative investments / Jeffrey C. Hooke.
Description: New York : Columbia University Press, [2021] | Includes
bibliographical references and index.
Identifiers: LCCN 2021004497 (print) | LCCN 2021004498 (ebook) |
ISBN 9780231198820 (hardback) | ISBN 9780231552820 (ebook)
Subjects: LCSH: Private equity—United States. | Finance—United States.
Classification: LCC HG4751 .H66 2021 (print) | LCC HG4751 (ebook) |
DDC 332.6—dc23
LC record available at https://lccn.loc.gov/2021004497
LC ebook record available at https://lccn.loc.gov/2021004498

Columbia University Press books are printed on permanent
and durable acid-free paper.
Printed in the United States of America

Cover design: Noah Arlow
Cover image: iStockPhoto

Myth: A widely held but false belief or idea
Oxford English Dictionary

Transformative: Causing a major change in something,
often in a way that makes it better
Cambridge Dictionary of American English

Finance does not mean speculating—although speculation,
when it does not degenerate into gambling, has a proper and
legitimate place in the scheme of things economic. Finance most
emphatically does not mean fleecing the public, nor fattening
parasitically off the industry and commerce of the country.
Otto Kahn, *High Finance* (1915)

Contents

The Myth of Private Equity

1

A Day in the Life

IT IS A TUESDAY morning in Baltimore. The sun is shining, and the weather is crisp. With a mild breeze, the flags adorning official buildings flutter gently. The city's crowded streets beckon the stream of commuters into the downtown core. At the traffic circle formed by the city's Battle Monument, a striking marble sculpture dedicated to war casualties, a young Caucasian woman walks uneasily between the lines of the cars waiting at the stop light. Disheveled, with a ragged army jacket and stringy blond hair, she asks drivers for spare change. Her gnarled, weather-beaten hands hold a makeshift cardboard sign that reads, "Veteran, will work for food."

A block away, at the corner of Baltimore and Calvert Streets is the SunTrust tower, an imposing office building that houses many corporate and government tenants. Occupying the fourteenth floor is the headquarters of the Maryland State Pension Fund, which manages over $50 billion in assets on behalf of several hundred thousand beneficiaries (see figure 1.1).

FIGURE 1.1 Baltimore skyline

As 9:00 A.M. approaches, pension fund employees traverse the well-appointed marble lobby and flash their ID cards for the guards manning the security desk. A small crowd gathers near the elevators. Conversations, while polite, are short. Most employees endure long commutes and are in no mood to talk. A popular address for pension employees seems to be Towson, a thriving jurisdiction just north of the city.

A Board Meeting

Upstairs, the Maryland state treasurer, Nancy Kopp, gets ready to chair the fund's regularly scheduled board of trustees meeting. At seventy-six, Kopp is a petite woman, with an affable personality and a quick smile. Well dressed, her reserved appearance and low-key style do not translate easily into Hollywood central casting's image of a financial titan. She is intelligent, having degrees from both Wellesley College and the University of Chicago, and she completed the coursework and preliminary exams for a PhD in political philosophy.

Kopp came to the treasurer's office in 2002, following seven terms—or twenty-eight years—as a Maryland state legislator representing Montgomery County, an affluent suburb of Washington, D.C. "She was a star in the House of Delegates, because she understood the budget like nobody else," says state attorney general Brian Frosh.[1] This quality provided the impetus for Kopp to get elected by her legislative colleagues to the treasurer's post for five consecutive four-year terms.

With a total of forty-six years tenure as an elected official, Kopp is a stalwart supporter of the Democratic Party, which executes an iron control over most facets of Maryland government policy through the party's veto-proof majority in both the lower and upper legislative chambers. Critics say that she is generally well intentioned, but now, after many years, she meanders through the job, making sure Democratic Party officials are happy, while not rocking any boats.

Over her eighteen years in office as treasurer, she supervised a remarkable upsurge in activity at the pension fund. During this time, the number of plan members rose from 320,000 to over 405,000, and assets increased from $27 billion to $54 billion.

The fund acts as a giant piggybank for state retirees. Current employees contribute a portion of their monthly paycheck to the fund, and taxpayers supplement these amounts with an annual billion-dollar payment. Supplementing these two sources of cash is the fund's investment income. From this combined pool of money is deducted the allowances dedicated to retirees. People assume the state guarantees all pensions, but this belief is not enshrined in the statutes, so proper fund management is paramount (see figure 1.2).

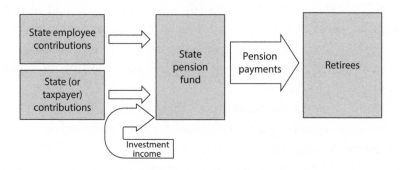

FIGURE 1.2 Maryland state retirement system—illustration of cash flows

Yet the safety of retiree pensions declined over the last two decades, as the system fell from a 95 percent funding ratio at the beginning of Kopp's tenure to 72 percent in 2020, indicating a $20 billion shortfall. Eventually, this deficit must be made up in the future, either through increased taxes, higher employee contributions, lower employee benefits, or more investment profits. In fact, the $20 billion deficit exceeded the state's regular debt obligations several times over. Thus, in the abstract, the pension fund's health is a key concern to state employees and retirees.

Sitting near Kopp is Peter Franchot, the state comptroller and vice chair of the pension fund board. At seventy-two, Franchot is a well-built six-footer. His hair is blond and streaked with grey. A handsome individual, he smiles often, and displays a sunny disposition. Elected to his fourth term as the state's chief financial officer in 2016, Franchot looks the part of a solid, stable, professional politician, with a courtly demeanor, ubiquitous blue suit, and red tie.

Despite his title, Franchot has no formal finance training. A lifelong Democratic functionary, he graduated from Northeastern University Law School and served as a Capitol Hill staffer in Washington, D.C. At forty, he got himself elected to Maryland's part-time state legislature, representing Takoma Park, a staunchly liberal, and slightly quirky, town that touts itself as Maryland's only "nuclear free zone." He served for five terms (twenty years) while working as a business consultant for commercial firms dealing with local governments. His predecessors, William Donald Schaefer and Louis Goldstein, were also experienced Democratic politicians with law degrees and minimal finance backgrounds.

Many insiders consider Franchot to be the consummate political animal, weighing policy decisions solely on the political calculus of his own career advancement. "Any Franchot decision that intersects with the actual merits is a total coincidence," explains one Democratic officeholder.[2] Sticking with the status quo or following the pension fund tactics of more prominent states is the premeditated decision, rather than asking his staffers to study the Maryland pension fund in a deliberate manner.

Franchot's decisions on fund investments impact hundreds of thousands of Marylanders and hundreds of millions of tax dollars, but in trustee meetings, he appears disinterested. He stays mostly quiet. The time that he should spend on poring over reams of financial data is, instead, frittered away on political-campaign-style gatherings in small Maryland towns, such as Sudlersville (population 497) where his appearance might headline a local news story. Here, before a semi-starstruck audience, he pumps up his voter base and name identification by giving his stump speech and handing out "Franchot coins" to attendees. These round metal medallions are campaign props that provide the local residents a tangible monetary connection to the comptroller's office, the function of which is not well understood by many voters.

Franchot's campaign contributor reports are dominated by a motley collection of liquor firms, government contractors, and real estate developers. Many of these same entities participate in industries that the comptroller's office is supposed to regulate. Despite his influence at the pension fund, financial firms and financial executives are far down the contributor list. This reality may reflect federal regulations that curtail earlier pay-to-play schemes, whereby money managers donated to state political campaigns to secure contracts from state pension funds. The inability to extract campaign contributions from money managers might explain Franchot's indifference to the pension fund's investment policy.

Following in the comptroller's footsteps, many Maryland politicians have already concluded that the pension fund, while large and fiscally important, is an obscure topic to most voters. Instituting reforms requires heavy efforts to educate and then convince their colleagues, the press, and their constituents. So why bother? Ultimately, the collective sentiment among the political class is that voters will not provide the reformers with much credit anyway. Furthermore, promoting change at the pension fund, or making waves, might piss off Wall Street, which has collected billions in fees from the fund. Wall Street is a fertile source of contributions for those elected officials seeking higher office. Antagonizing Wall Street is a futile endeavor, as many politicians have discovered.

Legislative hearings regarding pension fund investments are drab, perfunctory affairs. The annual performance review features both the treasurer and the pension's chief investment officer providing a summary of the fund's total return for the preceding fiscal year. The two officials begin by reeling off assorted financial jargon that unnecessarily exceeds an educated layperson's comprehension. Both individuals then close by saying that the fund beat its internal benchmarks for the past year, and that, essentially, there is nothing for the legislature to worry about. Nothing is said about the fund's lackluster investment performance. For years, its returns have placed in the bottom 10 percent of its peer group, and the fund (and virtually every other state pension fund) has failed to beat a simple, passive blended mutual fund, such as those run by low-cost operators like Vanguard Group. During the hearing, legislators pose few, if any, questions on the subject, and they quickly revert to less important fiscal matters, such as a $980,000 bond for a local firehouse.

The blended mutual fund in this context is the Vanguard Balanced Index Fund, which mirrors a popular benchmark by maintaining a portfolio comprised of 60 percent U.S. stock index and 40 percent bond index. This mixture is a popular, independent, and objective tool, and institutions, like the pension fund, frequently use it to gauge their own investment performance. If their results are better than the 60–40 index for a given year, they claim success. Many mutual funds attract investors by copying the index and charging low fees for passive management (see figure 1.3).

The legislature has a broad oversight role with respect to the pension fund's investment activities, but it has little power to interfere directly in decisions, like which stocks to buy or sell. For such matters, the fund's professional civil-service staff selects a small army of outside money managers to pick and choose investment opportunities. Neither the legislature nor the executive branch has specific inputs into this process.

The fund staff negotiates payment for the outside managers, and such payments are off budget. In political speak, *off budget* means the payments do not appear anywhere as operating expenses in the state budget nor do such payments require legislative approval. The staff answers only to the board of trustees, a mix of political appointees and members designated by statute. This governance arrangement depoliticizes the pension fund in

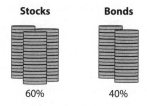

FIGURE 1.3 Popular investment benchmark—60–40 index

a certain way, since politicians cannot easily steer pension fund contracts to friends or send pension money to pet projects. But the fund's seeming independence comes at the cost of accountability. Being hands-off, the legislature and executive branch do not say much about pension investments. Thus, they believe they cannot be held responsible for investment losses, should they become a campaign issue. Indeed, when I interviewed a member of Governor Hogan's administration about the situation in March 2020, he pointed to Treasurer Kopp as the reason for the substandard performance, implying that the executive had minimal power to interfere. On the other hand, the fund's independence suggests that the staff and trustees have little to fear when things go wrong.

Years earlier, the legislature formed a special Joint Committee on Pensions to be comprised of fourteen legislators. The objective was for the committee to provide more supervision from the legislature. Today, the committee has little weight. Most members are inexperienced freshmen, and only one, state senator Andrew Serafini, has practical finance expertise.

Eight years into the treasurer's tenure, and two years into Franchot's first term, disaster struck. The 2008 financial crisis caused a stock market collapse. The pension plan's assets, comprised primarily of publicly-traded stocks and bonds, fell in value by 20 percent, or $8 billion over twelve months. The unfunded liability ballooned to $15 billion. As one means to cut the deficit, governor Martin O'Malley, a Democrat, pushed through legislation that mandated small benefit reductions and a modest increase in employee contributions. But the pension fund managers had to do their part. One option was to stay the course with the current portfolio of mostly publicly traded stocks and bonds and to wait for an economic recovery. The second option was to commit more money to complex, more opaque, and harder-to-sell alternative investments, like private equity funds and hedge funds. The alternative managers promised the impossible—not only higher returns than their publicly traded counterparts but

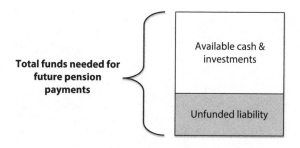

FIGURE 1.4 Unfunded pension liability

also less risk. Thus, this second option proved attractive to the trustees, since the better projected returns meant less real-time cash injections into the fund. In a decision they lived to regret, the trustees swallowed the alternative sales pitch hook, line, and sinker (see figure 1.4).

Maryland mimicked the strategy of several prominent state funds that, in turn, copied the tactics, to a lesser degree, of David Swensen, the almost legendary manager of Yale University's (see figure 1.5) endowment fund. After leaving Wall Street for Yale in 1985, Swensen persuaded the endowment to drop traditional stocks and bonds in favor of alternatives, and the results proved highly favorable for two decades. But managers at other institutions found duplicating Swensen's success to be elusive, a point that Swensen himself, and numerous business colleagues, were quick to acknowledge.

Within a few years, the Maryland pension fund invested billions in such alternative vehicles, and their purported returns, at least on paper, seemed higher than the traditional investments.[3] However, Maryland's portfolio return remained significantly below the fifty-state average, and the state's unfunded liability stayed stubbornly high.[4]

Despite the mixed results, the new policy showered Wall Street with retiree dollars, and Maryland's outside manager fees

FIGURE 1.5 Yale University

quintupled, to roughly $500 million by 2020. Money that could have gone to union retirees was instead directed into the pockets of alternative asset partners. Some of the cash found its way into purchases of Park Avenue penthouses, Southampton mansions, and luxury Mercedes automobiles. Other dollars supported expensive vacations to London, Paris, and the Orient. None of the money ended up in the bank accounts of state retirees.

Such is the situation today. As the treasurer and the comptroller host the meeting, their fellow trustees are seated at a large conference table. The room is utilitarian, with few amenities. A sizeable number of staffers and visitors attend, so standing room only is the rule of the day. At the center of the table, opposite from Treasurer Kopp, sits Andrew Palmer, the chief investment officer, and several of his lieutenants. In general, the board meeting is an unsatisfying forum, as the trustees tend to remain blandly quiet, Palmer and his team dominate the discussion. As is the case in

FIGURE 1.6 Board meeting

many large organizations, the staff provide direction to the board, rather than vice versa (see figure 1.6 for a board meeting image).

Today's board consists of fourteen trustees. They serve for four years and their terms of office are staggered, so that approximately one-third are elected annually. Five are elected by the unionized state employees, and six are appointed by the governor. Three ex-officio trustees are appointed by statute: the state treasurer, the state comptroller, and the secretary of management and budget. By tradition, the state treasurer and state comptroller serve as chairman and vice chairman, respectively. A trustee post is a prestigious position in the Maryland financial community, as well as in broader investment circles (see figure 1.7).

The board and its governance are designed to balance several interests. The union representatives ensure that the ultimate beneficiaries—state employees—have a voice. These union representatives begin their careers as state employees, working in jobs such as prison guards, police officers, and schoolteachers, before

11

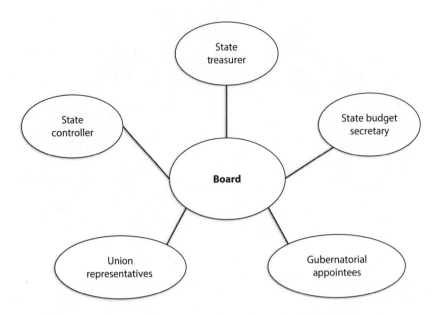

FIGURE 1.7 Composition of State of Maryland Pension Plan Board of Trustees

turning to union politics. As a group, they are intelligent, but they have little practical finance experience. The governor's picks are high-ranking business executives with financial knowledge, and some supported his campaign. For example, trustee Eric Brotman gave $1,000 to Governor Hogan's Inaugural Committee. These individuals relay the executive's policy point of view. The ex-officio members speak to separate interests. The legislature votes in the treasurer, the citizens elect the comptroller, and the governor appoints the budget secretary. Despite their titles, as noted earlier, neither the treasurer nor the comptroller has a formal finance background. The board is a self-governing body with a mix of expertise, and its investment decisions and management budgets are walled off from overt legislative interference.

Assisting the board's decision making are three unpaid public advisors who are selected for three-year terms based on their professional investment experience. Michael Barry is the chief investment officer of the Georgetown University endowment, which suffered a slight 1 percent loss in its latest fiscal year, even as the stock market rose.[5] Stephen Kitsoulis administers investments for the $23 billion portfolio of the Howard Hughes Medical Institute. Monte Tarbox is the investment head of the $14 billion International Brotherhood of Electrical Workers retirement fund. Cross criticism is unlikely. The advisors usually echo the staff's recommendations. Large institutions tend to copy one another and follow the conventional wisdom at any given time. This tradition reminds one of the old saying, "The middle of the herd is a nice, safe place to be on Wall Street."

Both the union and ex-officio trustees speak little at the meeting, a custom one union official relayed to me in February 2018 as resulting from the fact, "they lack expertise, and they don't want to be embarrassed by asking the staff what sounds like a stupid question." Still, the absence of professional knowledge among these trustees is not the only reason for the staff's domination of the board. The gubernatorial appointees know the subject matter in general; and thus, they have the capacity to ask the staff insightful questions. Nonetheless, except for Brotman and Linda Herman, the appointees provide little leadership and remain silent. Brotman has a financing planning practice in suburban Baltimore. Herman serves as the chief investment officer of the $2 billion, retirement plan of Montgomery County, an affluent subdivision located in the Washington, D.C., suburbs.

Whether the board spends much time on its duties is debatable. Little is said about either the consistently poor returns or the costly outside money-management fees. Staff proposals are approved with minimal discussion, and accepted beliefs about how to run an institutional portfolio are rarely questioned. The board sees no incentive to "make waves" by questioning accepted wisdom—like whether the Yale model works—even if such an action produces a public good. Outside faultfinders, or the occasional unfavorable newspaper article, have zero impact on their behavior, as the board long ago developed a rhinoceros hide against criticism. The trustees are passive figureheads, listening to what staffers tell them to do. Inertia is the modus operandi.

The board's indifference to the $20 billion unfunded pension shortfall is not surprising. Trimming benefits is unpopular, and kicking the car down the road is politically expedient. No one mentions the Detroit or the Puerto Rico municipal bankruptcies and the resultant retiree benefit reductions. The drastic step taken by one of the largest musician pension plans in the United States—for instance, "cutting retirement benefits that had been already earned by thousands of musicians—in order to keep the plan from running out of money"—is not in the trustees' mindset.[6] The customary viewpoint is that today's cash-strapped state pension funds will receive unlimited taxpayer lifelines in the future.

Among other matters, today's agenda includes approving a $100 million commitment to the $12 billion Green Equity Investors VIII leveraged buyout (LBO) fund.[7] The agenda ignores LBOs and their job-killing behavior. The agenda fails to mention that Maryland's investment return for calendar year 2019 was 3 percent below the average of similar funds and 5 percent below the benchmark 60–40 index. Nor does the agenda point out that for the last ten years, Maryland returns fell in the bottom 10 percent of its peer group, implying an opportunity, or lost income, cost to the state of $4 billion. The agenda does not say that this shortfall contributed to an increase in unfunded liabilities, which restricts benefit enhancements for state workers.[8]

Over this ten-year period, the retirement plan gorged on private equity funds, paying huge fees to Wall Street managers who promised, yet failed to deliver, superior performance by picking investment winners. Indeed, independent academic studies show that since 2006, private equity funds underperformed relevant public indices, a fact that is easily eclipsed by the Wall Street marketing machine. Unfortunately, the exact amount of fees will never be known since the board has never requested a full accounting. Nevertheless, a reasonable estimate for the last fiscal year is $300 million in private equity (PE) fees, based on comparisons with the few peer plans that release such data. No one asks if this money would have been better spent on helping poor people, like the homeless veteran mentioned at the beginning chapter. Of the various pages in the agenda, not one indicates that Maryland, like several states, passed laws to keep private equity fee arrangements secret. In fact, the industry's influence is so pervasive that the Government Accounting Standards Board (GASB) allows states to ignore most private equity fees altogether for record keeping purposes. Meanwhile, the Financial Accounting Standards Board, a sister agency to the GASB, endorses an unusual provision that permits state plans to price their hard-to-sell private equity investments as if the funds traded publicly, like Amazon or Exxon stocks. Nothing is said about Warren Buffett's recommendation of low-cost index funds for institutional investors. He indicates that "$100 billion has been wasted on bad investment advice the last decade."[9]

No trustee points out that the state relies on Green's previous fund VII performance to justify this new investment and that neither the state nor its investment consultant has independently verified the prior fund's posted results, which are totally dependent on the future sale prices of existing acquisitions. Indeed, since its 2016 inception, the prior Green fund VII has spent $7 billion on deals and has yet to sell a single investment. The new Green fund VIII commits the state to a ten-year "no-cut" obligation, the length of which is far superior to a premium professional athlete's contract, and to pay a minimum of $15 million in fees, a full 15 percent of the state's dollar obligation.[10] This $15 million is paid whether the fund makes a profit or not. Similarly, the state's investment consultant receives more compensation when recommending private equity funds instead of low-cost index funds. Such a misalignment of incentives is missing in today's agenda.

Based on such meager information, the board approved the $100 million commitment to the Green Equity Investors VIII leveraged buyout fund.

2

The Private Equity Industry

MAY 20, 1983 WAS a pivotal day on Wall Street. On that day almost forty years ago, Gibson Greetings, the third largest greeting card manufacturer and a business whose incorporation dated back to 1895, completed its initial public offering (IPO) at $25.25 per share. The IPO was one of several that month, valuing the business at $290 million, but Gibson Greetings was far from a routine IPO. It was the first leveraged buyout (LBO) to garner extensive media attention, owing to the fantastical profits achieved by its backers, the no-money-down nature of their commitment, and their remarkably short holding period.

Just sixteen months earlier, an investment group headed by William Simon, a former U.S. treasury secretary, bought the company for $80 million. In a feat of financial legerdemain, they borrowed $79 million (or 99 percent) of the purchase price, indicating a down payment of $1 million, a mere 1 percent of the buy-in. The new owners personally guaranteed none of the new Gibson debt, so the lenders took on substantial risk. Buffeted by a rising stock market and the sizeable borrowing, the IPO turned Simon's

$330,000 original investment into a $70 million windfall, providing an amazing 200× return. Thus, the PE playbook was on full display: put up little of your own money, take almost no risk, and let the lenders sort out potential problems.

A few buyouts predated the Gibson deal, but the IPO's visible wealth creation set tongues wagging in the financial community. Before long, a crop of imitators joined the few existing buyout shops, and previously conservative lenders, to boost profits, loosened their purse strings to support similar debt-laden deals. The buyout business experienced a meteoric rise, and multiple billion-dollar U.S. companies fell like dominoes into the portfolios of PE funds. By December 1988, just five years after the Gibson deal, this intensifying phenomenon reached its crescendo, with the $25 billion buyout ($51 billion today, adjusted for inflation) of RJR Nabisco, a massive tobacco and food conglomerate with a bevy of iconic brand names, such as Camel cigarettes and Oreo cookies. After a frenzied six-week auction for the business, involving the crème de la crème of American investment banking, the eventual buyer, PE firm Kohlberg Kravis Roberts & Co. (KKR), borrowed $22 billion to close the deal, or 87 percent of the purchase price (see figure 2.1).

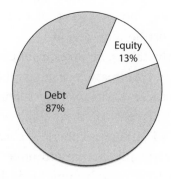

FIGURE 2.1 RJR leveraged buyout

With its huge dollars and palace intrigues, the RJR deal became notorious, and the transaction inspired a best-selling book and a TV movie. One undue excess was the management team's arrogance and cupidity. In plain sight, the team attempted to steal the company, initially bidding, in partnership with the Wall Street firm Shearson Lehman Hutton, a price of only $17 billion. This low-ball offer represented a steep 30 percent discount to KKR's final purchase price, and management's actions turned conventional corporate governance on its head.

Of the $3 billion of in-deal equity, KKR's $1.5 billion cash contribution came from a new $5 billion PE fund it managed. In that fund, KKR invested just $50 million, or 1 percent, of the total commitment. News reports exclaimed that for a mere $15 million (1 percent × $1.5 billion),[1] KKR's managers controlled one of the largest companies on earth, but the reality was even more astounding. KKR paid itself a fee of over $100 million to arrange the deal, so its "going in" down payment, in fact, was negative.

This first buyout boom represented more than simple corporate machinations. It was an underpinning for the 1980s culture of greed, a profoundly troubling time in America, when prominent businesspeople compiled wealth and defined success by the shuffling of assets instead of the development of new and innovative products. Part of the trend was laid bare by the cinema classic *Wall Street*. The protagonist, financier Gordon Gekko, made millions acquiring companies, selling their assets piecemeal, and firing hundreds of employees. The rewards of these tactics were evident from a perusal of the *Forbes* 400, a list of America's richest people, increasingly populated by financial players. As set forth later in this chapter, the buyout boom arose not out of serendipity but from a confluence of conditions that promoted the technique.

Before reviewing these phenomena, a study of financial vocabulary is helpful. An annex to this chapter covers the basic terms such as *conventional investments, risk, indexes,* and *diversification.*

Here the chapter reviews the definitions of *private equity*, *alternative investments*, and *institutional investors*.

Private Equity

The PE industry, the subject of this book, refers to investment funds that do one of the following:

- Buy the common shares of companies that are not publicly traded on a stock exchange.
- Buy publicly traded firms and transform them into closely held firms.

As noted, PE principally invests in mature companies, well beyond the startup phase, and participants see a close connection between the underlying assets of PE funds (particularly leveraged buyout funds) and those of a broad stock market index. As a result, the most utilized comparator for investment performance is the S&P 500 index. Many LBO investors adjust index comparisons for the higher debt loads of leveraged buyouts, relative to public companies, and the consequent greater risk.

The buyout industry's marketing thrust is that it provides better returns than its comparator, the S&P 500, while at the same time, offering lower risk. This alleged attribute is the attraction for major investors, like the State of Maryland pension plan. This oft repeated assertion—high returns, low risk—flies in the face of sixty-five years of financial market theory, which postulates that investments with superior performance have historically had greater risks than those with inferior returns. The marketing thrust also contradicts common sense and the time-honored maxim, "No risk, no reward."

Nonetheless, investors, industry observers, and business media have ignored this incongruity, as well as dismissing recent fact-based evidence. This arrangement builds support for the narrative that PE managers have a secret sauce that enables them to defy financial gravity and earn premium returns.

The PE industry is mostly comprised of three sectors:

- Leveraged buyouts
- Growth capital
- Venture capital

The three sectors are quite different from one another, and investors tend to segment the results of each sector in financial reporting.

Leveraged Buyouts

Leveraged buyouts (LBOs) represent about 65 percent of the PE business, and they are the focus of this book. In a leveraged buyout, a PE fund acquires all the common stock of an entire company. The PE-LBO fund managers (sometimes called general partners) are Wall Street types who know how to close deals, but they do not know how a normal business works on a day-to-day basis. Having no operating experience and yet controlling the company, they appoint executives who know how to run a manufacturing or service business, and these executives direct the new acquisition's operations.

The PE-LBO fund finances most of the purchase price by having the company borrow money, and the new creditors look to the company's future earnings and, to some extent, its collateral value for eventual repayment. Neither the LBO fund nor the PE managers guarantee the debt. The debt portion of the deal accounts for roughly 70 percent of the purchase price, and the PE fund commits to a 30 percent cash equity investment, although these percentages fluctuate with market conditions and individual company characteristics. The debt-to-equity ratio of an LBO is perhaps two times higher than that of a similar publicly traded firm. The general idea behind buyouts is that the increased leverage promotes a better equity return than that of a more conservatively indebted business. Besides higher leverage, the PE-LBO industry touts several other factors that supposedly boost returns, such as giving executives above-average incentives, so they work smarter, but leverage is the key. Figure 2.2 compares capital structures of a buyout and a typical public company.

LBOs are friendly deals, not the hostile takeovers portrayed in Hollywood movies. The PE-LBO fund managers need a cordial relationship with the target's executives since these individuals will be charged with running the business. The fund managers (i.e., those individuals working at the buyout fund) and the executives therefore must cooperate to further a buyout endeavor.

To convince lenders to supply most of the purchase price, buyout funds search for acquisition targets that fit a certain profile, which is set forth below.

LBO Target Profile

- *Low-tech business,* so the lenders are not exposed to a target's products becoming obsolete.

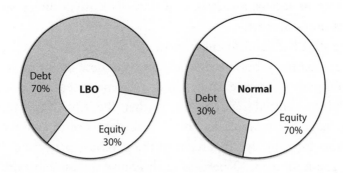

FIGURE 2.2 Capital structure comparison

- *Low debt,* so the LBO fund can attach more debt to the business.
- *Positive growing earnings,* so the lender has the confidence of future earnings for loan repayment. Thus, distressed firms in need of a lot of improvements are ineligible.
- *No financial-oriented business or regulated utility,* as many of these businesses involve government supervision of their leverage ratios and owner cash dividends.
- *Moderate exposure to the business cycle,* and no commodity-oriented businesses, like oil companies or mining companies, because their earnings pattern is highly cyclical, leading to a heightened possibility of default in a downturn.
- *Available at a reasonable price.* LBOs purchased at low value ratios, like a low price-earnings ratio or a low price to book ratio, tend to provide the best returns. To illustrate, the prime performing funds in recent times did most of their acquisitions in 2008 and 2009, when corporate valuations hit bottom (see figure 2.3).[2]

My early research conducted with Ted Barnhill, and later work with Ken Yook, examine LBOs of publicly traded companies between 1985 and 2012. The study showed that over 90 percent of public buyouts fit this profile.[3] Related work by L'Her, et al. and Dan Rasmussen, respectively, echoed such findings.[4] Prominent deals meeting the profile were RJR Nabisco, Hospital Corp. of America, Harrah's Entertainment, and Toys "R" Us.

About 20 percent of publicly traded companies fit this profile, so investors, if they want, can reproduce a buyout fund through purchasing public stocks. In fact, a few industry observers and academics, including myself, created stock indexes that mimic parts of the profile, and the back-dated performance of such LBO indexes compares favorably to actual LBO funds.[5] Verdad Capital, a small money manager, operates the only index fund adhering to such principles, and the fund amount is comparatively tiny,

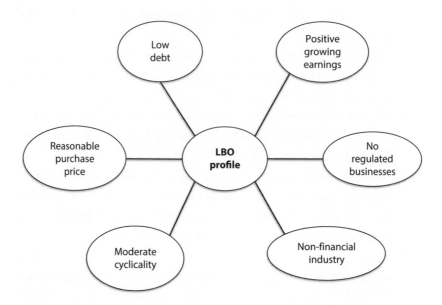

FIGURE 2.3 LBO profile

totaling only $140 million. Remarking on institutional investors' reluctance to embrace this buyout replication concept, one consultant whispered to me, "Endowment managers can't justify their big salaries if they devote money to replication indexes!" By way of demonstration, Neal Triplett, chief investment officer of Duke University's endowment, which owns $ 1.2 billion in PE, earned $3.5 million in compensation in 2018 despite the endowment's returns not beating standard index benchmarks.[6]

Growth Capital

Growth capital is another alternative asset category. A fund specializing in growth capital makes minority equity investments in reasonably mature companies. These companies need money to expand, but they are not ready to complete an initial public offering (IPO) to raise capital, so they choose the private route. To illustrate, video conference firm Zoom closed several rounds of growth capital prior to its 2019 IPO. A "minority position" means the fund's position is less than a 50 percent interest in the company's stock, and therefore the fund does not call the shots in managing the business—unlike the LBO situation, where the fund has a controlling stake. Like LBOs, purveyors of growth capital funds claim that they beat the stock market's returns. The growth capital category comprises about 15 percent of the PE business.

Venture Capital

Venture capital (VC) refers to an equity investment in a young company. Despite the apocryphal stories surrounding the VC industry and its successes, like Apple Inc., most firms backed by VC funds already have moved out of the founder's garage, have a functioning business, and have advanced beyond the startup phase. The companies have products and revenues, but many lack positive earnings. Their business models are not 100 percent proven. People often associate venture capital (VC) solely with high-tech firms, but VC funds participate in a broad variety of industries. For example, Good Buy Gear markets children's clothes and toys, and it raised $8 million in VC in 2020.[7] Independent studies indicate that VC investments, on average, do not outperform the stock market. No matter. As Wall Street likes to say, "Sell the sizzle, not the steak." VC accounts for about 15 percent of the PE universe, according to database provider Preqin.

For ease of reading, this book makes buyout funds synonymous with private equity.

Other Alternative Investments

LBOs, growth capital, and VC are nonconventional, or alternative, investments. They are not publicly traded stocks or bonds. Other popular alternative categories are hedge funds, real estate funds, and physical commodity funds.

Hedge Funds

Non-Wall-Streeters frequently confuse hedge funds with buyout funds, but the two categories are quite different. Like a buyout fund, a hedge fund pools capital from institutions and wealthy individuals. However, hedge funds primarily invest in publicly traded securities and related derivative instruments, such as options, swaps, and futures. Few of their commitments are to privately-held companies.

The *hedge* derives from the strategy of the original hedge funds, which employed a long/short equities model. Under their model, the fund buys a certain number of common stocks that it thinks will increase in price. At the same time, the fund short sells stocks it thinks will fall in price. With this combination of positions, the fund is immunized from a stock market crash (although the model also limits upside gain); and, hence, the fund investors "hedge" their bets. If the fund managers make the proper stock selections, the hedge fund makes money in both up and down markets. Wall Street refers to this stance as market neutral.

After getting burned in repeated stock market crashes, big institutional investors, like state pension plans and university endowments, have long searched for assets whose values move in a direction that is opposite to that of the stock market. Hedge funds pledged to fulfill that need. Such funds grew rapidly in the 2000s, but their modern strategies veer wildly from the original model goal of being market neutral. Nowadays there are over a dozen classifications of hedge funds, ranging from the long/short model, which still has adherents, to the macro style, which gives the fund manager discretion to go long, short, or neutral on stocks, bonds, and other instruments on a global basis. Because of these many strategies, hedge fund returns are difficult, as a group, to benchmark. Given the mix of public equity–oriented investments and public fixed-income securities in many hedge fund portfolios, a 60–40 index is a good comparator for a diversified collection of hedge funds.

Hedge fund managers, like buyout fund executives, cultivate an aura of mystery and expertise, suggesting that they also have a magical elixir that delivers premium results. The facts tend to speak otherwise. For example, the State of New Jersey pension plan invested in over eighty hedge funds covering a wide style range during the last five years. A 60–40 index handily beat the hedge fund returns.[8]

As of this writing, the amount of money managed by hedge funds is comparable to combined total for buyouts, growth capital, and venture capital.

Thousands of hedge funds operate today, and they often function in a herd fashion, jockeying for the same investment holdings. With competition so fierce, one Washington lawyer who works with the asset class told me, "The business has degenerated into a fierce scramble for inside information," because traditional research analysis does not furnish enough of an edge for a typical hedge fund (see figure 2.4).

Private Real Estate Investing

Because of the contractual nature of rental payments, commercial real estate earned a reputation as stock-market-crash resistant.

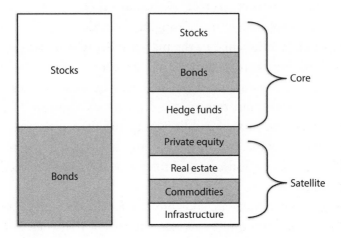

FIGURE 2.4 Traditional portfolio vs. modern institutional portfolio

Accordingly, in the 1980s institutions increased their buying of funds that aimed at commercial real estate properties. While providing an income stream divorced from stocks, real estate returns entail a cyclical component, and the asset class is not a panacea for stock market volatility, as real estate values can collapse in a recession.

Commodity Funds

Some investments are set up to take possession of physical commodities, such as gold, oil, and timber. Investors can purchase the common stocks of companies that produce such items, but the premise is that a specialized fund, instead of an operating business, provides a better exposure to the commodity itself. Investors opt for these funds to attain the perceived benefits of (1) diversification, (2) inflation protection, and (3) contra-stock-market returns.

Institutional Investors

As set forth in this book, an institutional investor is a large entity with ample cash to place in a group of assets, which the institution administers in a professional manner. Examples of such institutions include pension funds, mutual funds, sovereign wealth funds, foundations, university endowments, insurance companies, PE funds, and hedge funds.

On Wall Street, an individual investor, like myself, is referred to as a retail investor. Retail investors participate in the financial markets through individual brokerage accounts, mutual funds, and 401K accounts.

Many institutions are fiduciaries. A fiduciary manages investment assets on behalf of others. For example, a union pension plan manages assets for the union members who are retired or who will eventually retire. A fiduciary owes its beneficiaries the duties of good faith and trust, and it should act in a prudent manner when managing assets.

With this vocabulary in place, we now turn to the history of the leveraged buyout business.

LBOs' Fortuitous History

For decades, fiduciaries took their duties to mean that the assets under their care should be invested principally in high-quality bonds to provide steady income and to minimize the possibility of a loss of principal. A small portion of the portfolio was dedicated to blue-chip stocks that paid a regular cash dividend.

At first glance, it seems odd that a fiduciary investor, in those early days of PE, considered a leveraged buyout fund to be a suitable investment. First, the fund itself was a blind pool, so investors committed money without advance knowledge of the fund's acquisitions. Historically, Wall Street considered blind pools to be speculative ventures. For LBO blind pools, managers provided investors with a general statement regarding likely assets and objectives, but the fiduciary institutions relied almost totally on the managers' reputations, since the LBO business model and track record were thin. Second, the buyout premise was to load up acquisitions with debt, which, on its surface, sounded risky. Thirdly, the fund required investors to sign a ten-year, no-cut contract with the manager, who thus earned a ten-year stream of fees, whether the fund ever made a profit. For these reasons, many sizeable investors rejected buyout funds as being too dicey.

Given the drawbacks, what factors led fiduciaries eventually into the LBO business? The next section covers the important developments that furthered their interest.

Greater Acceptance of Modern Portfolio Theory

Modern portfolio theory (MPT) is a complex, mathematical framework that big investors use to divide their portfolios into stocks, bonds, and other assets. They hope to maximize future returns and moderate risks. MPT measures risk by examining the historical performance of the portfolio's assets, but it is not fortune telling, since the future income of assets routinely deviates from the past. At the time of MPT's introduction in 1952, institutional portfolios predominantly consisted of publicly traded stocks and bonds.

Just as Graham and Dodd's seminal *Security Analysis* book helped elevate stock picking into a respectable profession, MPT's gradual acceptance among institutions provided a scientific veneer to the nascent portfolio management and investment consulting businesses. Complementing the rise were the money-center banks and brokerage houses, which welcomed MPT. Its institutional acceptance meant that the ensuing portfolio turnover became a huge source of revenue for sales and trading desks. By the early 1980s, large institutions, including fiduciaries, consistently applied MPT to their asset management methods.

Money manager Ken Solow describes the now commonplace strategy for constructing institutional-quality portfolios. Through MPT, portfolios devolve into separate "core" and "satellite" portions. The MPT core portfolio is the part of the portfolio invested in traditional assets, such as publicly traded stocks and bonds. Satellite holdings are nontraditional assets, like private equity, hedge funds, real estate, and commodities. All satellite holdings have the same objective, "outperforming traditional investments in the core portfolio while, at the same time, having presumably low correlation to the core portfolio."[9]

When I first heard of this strategy fifteen years ago, I likened it to a wealthy individual having (1) a basic savings account, with the bulk of his or her retirement in safe stocks and bonds; and (2) a smaller portion of his or her savings set aside as "play money," with which to gamble on riskier, untested offerings. The play money is more interesting to analyze and more fun to watch, as the related securities gyrate in valuation, but the investors need a greater degree of sophistication in order to prepare for adverse outcomes. Little did I know that major players, such as the Ford Foundation, would make alternatives the bulk of their portfolios, thereby shunning the older portfolio approaches.

Loosening Regulations for LBOs

Federal and state regulators assisted MPT and LBO activity by loosening regulations designed to enforce a conservative approach that reduced the likelihood of institutional insolvency. In their book, Harvard's Lerner, Leamon, and Hardymon point to the liberalization of the federal government's "prudent man" rule in 1979.[10] Earlier, pension plans interpreted the prudent man rule as prohibiting alternative assets, which carried a high-risk perception, but the federal government loosening opened the door. And, as the Pew Foundation explains, the states followed suit, "Before the early 1980s, many public retirement plans were bound by strict regulations limiting their investment options. State plans, for example, were previously limited in their investment options by restrictive 'legal lists' that were also used to regulate insurance and saving banks, for which safety was the principal concern. But these restrictions were gradually relaxed in states in the 1980s and 1990s, allowing pension plans much more latitude to invest in a broad variety of financial instruments."[11] This change promoted a long-term shift in state pension plans away from conservative bonds and into equities and alternatives.

Junk Bond Expansion Boosts Buyouts

Prior to the 1980s, junk bonds were fallen angels—the bonds of once investment-grade companies that experienced hard times. Junk bonds were risky, with high default rates. Financier Michael Milken and investment bank Drexel Burnham Lambert popularized the use of newly issued junk bonds to finance the fledgling buyout industry, thus providing a new source of ready money for such transactions.

The liberalization of regulations supported the junk bond phenomenon. Heretofore, conservative institutions, such as pension funds, savings and loans, and life insurance companies, avoided these securities. With the new rules, they took flyers on low-rated bonds in a search for more income. The changes cost the federal government dearly when hundreds of savings and loans failed in the late 1980s, and the government had to make good on over $100 billion in deposit guarantees.

Favorable Tax and Legal Treatment for LBOs

As the LBO industry grew, investors became aware of the favorable tax treatment accorded to it. Sizable interest charges on debt were tax deductible, most of the buyout purchase prices were tax depreciable, and capital gains tax rates were historically low. In one buyout deal I worked on, a $300 million retailing company with $18 million in annual cash flow paid no income taxes. Effectively, the federal taxpayer was an unknowing supporter of such deals.

Furthermore, despite PE's pattern of owning multiple LBOs under the same fund umbrella, PE lawyers maintained the fictional position that the portfolio companies did not operate under common oversight, and that they were totally independent. As such, when Apollo portfolio company Harrah's Entertainment, a major casino operator, went bankrupt, Harrah's creditors were unable to seek resources from sister portfolio company, Smart & Final, to remedy a repayment problem at Harrah's. In legal circles, this separation was called the "corporate veil." Gordon Brough described this principle well in his book, *Private Limited Companies: Formation and Management* (see figure 2.5).[12]

Perfect LBO Storm in the 1980s

As these developments coalesced in the early 1980s, they formed a perfect storm for LBO expansion, culminating in the massive RJR buyout. America's corporate leaders realized PE was a force in industry by this time, but in the early 1990s activity slowed. Several headline bankruptcies, the prospect of poor returns on several large deals (like RJR), and the 1989 stock market crash, caused in part by a failed United Airlines buyout bid, cast a pall over the business for several years.

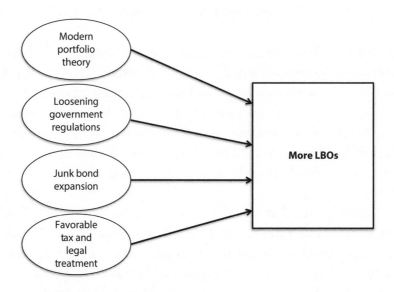

FIGURE 2.5 Developments promoting buyouts

Additional negativity arose from the $6 billion Safeway super-market chain deal. The buyout was the subject of a Pulitzer Prize–winning article by *Wall Street Journal* reporter Susan Faludi. "She examined the human costs of finance," according to the Pulitzer committee.[13] After closing the deal, the Safeway LBO owners laid off sixty-three thousand workers and cut the wages of the remaining rank and file. Amidst the suffering, the funds and top Safeway executives made big profits. The impact on low-level employees seemed patently unfair, and Faludi's article shone a hostile light on the buyout industry. A few observers pondered the social policy surrounding such ruthless capitalism, but the soul searching was short lived. Wall Street has few deep thinkers, and the Safeway experience was quickly forgotten. LBO activity rebounded in the mid and late 1990s. Incredibly, over one hundred new LBO funds opened yearly during this time, as PE executive Guy Fraser-Sampson noted in his book, *Private Equity as an Asset Class*.[14]

The main result of the industry's navel gazing was the successful rebranding of debt laden takeovers into *private equity*, a term that conveys a softer image and a more constructive tone than *leveraged buyout*.

The 2000 dot-com blowup and 2001 recession saw a hiatus, which disappeared when the economy recovered a few years later. Activity spiraled upward, as institutional investors, spooked by the S&P's 49 percent plunge during 2002, turned partly to buyout funds for the prospect of higher returns and stock market downside protection. When measured against 2002, the 2007 deal volume showed a 500 percent increase, but the 2008 crisis abruptly ended the upward climb. Transaction numbers dropped precipitously during the ensuing recession (see figure 2.6).

The 2008–2009 downturn did not last long, and investors (and lenders) poured money into buyouts after a couple of years, ignoring the bankruptcy filings of two of the largest deals—the $45 billion Energy Holdings and the $31 billion Harrah's transactions. LBO fundraising totals climbed to record heights during the last four years, 2017–2020, and multiple managers closed megafunds, each with more than $10 billion in institutional commitments. Apollo's 2018 fund, for example, had $25 billion in commitments.

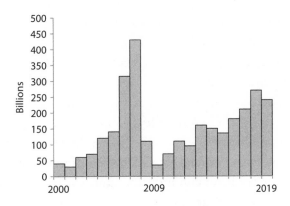

FIGURE 2.6 U.S. buyout volume. Source: Preqin

The Evolution of LBOs

During the industry's first two decades, LBOs morphed into three categories, as Bruce Wasserstein, legendary M&A banker, explains.[15]

The classic LBO: The classic LBO structure was a device to buy the maximum assets with the most debt borrowed and the least amount of equity cash invested by the buyout fund manager.

The breakup LBO: This structure featured a high debt level, but the company was not expected to repay debt solely from operations. Selling parts of the business was necessary to pay down loans.

The strategic LBO: An LBO fund buys a moderate-sized company and then expands the business by grafting onto it multiple smaller competitors. The larger company then becomes an attractive acquisition target or IPO candidate.

As the buyout business prospered, funds differentiated themselves by focusing on one of the above categories. Others avoided sameness through either a size focus or an industry focus. This tactic made sense as investors, over time, surmised that a certain level of specialization brought the fund managers deeper experience in lessons learned as well as economies of scale in portfolio oversight.

Over time, investors decided that certain skills applied to size, and they placed LBO funds into three buckets or market segments.

Large market: Deals greater than $500 million

Middle market: $100 million to $500 million

Small market: Below $100 million

For example, Stone Goff Partners invests in companies with between $3 million and $10 million in operating earnings, suggesting a deal size under $100 million. Platinum Equity's 2018 fund backs companies with up to $45 million in earnings, suggesting a maximum deal size of $500 million. Investors conclude that specific skill sets are crucial for success in different-size companies.

Most LBO funds remain industry agnostic, but a minority have an industry focus, reflecting an untested view that such focus brings better returns. A prominent example is Vista Equity Partners, which closed a $10 billion fund in 2019 for enterprise software takeovers. Another example is TSG Partners, which manages $9 billion in funds concentrating on businesses with well-known consumer brands, like Vitamin Water.

With over seven hundred LBO fund groups now in operation, the industry has plenty of room for a variety of styles, and it occupies a solid position in American commerce.[16] LBO funds collectively control over seven thousand companies, including many established firms, such as PetSmart and Staples.

The number of Americans directly employed by LBO firms totals several million, and equity invested by U.S. buyout funds stands at close to $1 trillion. This equity supports assets under the industry's supervision that are two to three times this number. Buyout fund commitments are present in 90 percent of the largest state and municipal pension plans, according to the American Investment Council, and many university endowments and nonprofit foundations participate in buyouts.

This lofty economic status has transferred into the nation's political, cultural, and educational spheres. PE executives hold high elected office and occupy important appointive posts. For example, under the Trump administration, former fund executives served as chairman of the Federal Reserve Board and U.S. secretary of commerce. As of this writing, Biden administration officials with former connections to the PE industry include the White House Chief of Staff, Secretary of State, Secretary of Defense, National Economic Council head, Comptroller of the Currency, Secretary of Commerce, Special Envoy on Climate, and Coordinator of the Covid Task Force. Fund managers serve on the boards of our most prestigious institutions, such as Harvard University, the Ford Foundation, the Brookings Institution, the Metropolitan Opera, and the Mayo Clinic.

Attaining this elevated position in American society has not been accomplished without some controversy. As the embodiment of unfettered capitalism—with a reputation for unflinching layoffs and relentless profit drives—LBO funds have earned the ire of progressive politicians, like Senator Elizabeth Warren, who object to the bankruptcies and job layoffs spawned by many buyout deals. They want to change the rules by which the funds freely operate. Headline bankruptcies provide fodder for left-of-center writers, such as Nicolas Shaxson, who describes Alden Global Capital Partners in the following manner: "The financial firm that has bought up local newspapers and stripped them bare. A PE firm like Alden can load up a company with debt, pay the proceeds to itself, crush the company and walk away rich."[17]Alden, run by ex-Wall Streeter Randall Smith, owns the *Denver Post, Saint Paul Pioneer Press*, and other newspapers, amid accusations of bleeding the papers dry while laying off reporters and other staff.

My experience and research indicate that LBO funds do not make most of their profits in this manner but glaring examples to the contrary, like the Tribune Company, Lyondell Chemicals, and Toys "R" Us buyouts, provide good story lines. These deals featured rounds of layoffs, bankruptcies, and lawsuits, even as the fund managers extracted huge fees.

On the other side of the coin fall the promoters' arguments, which stipulate that the buyout industry does the following:

- Makes its portfolio companies more efficient, and thus LBOs are a positive for the U.S. economy, which is a position advanced by several academic researchers.
- Creates new jobs for American workers, which is a less defensible argument.
- Provides favorable investment returns for the investors that participate in LBO funds, particularly the pension funds supporting American workers. This assertion is a favorite theme of the industry's lobbyists, and it frames the buyout industry's public response to the occasional protest regarding the mediocre returns and the high fees.

Stephen Pagliuca, cochairman of Bain Capital, one of the larger buyout fund groups, summed up this narrative in a January 2020 CNBC interview by saying, "Private equity is a great thing for America." The three television anchors, including *New York Times* reporter and best-selling author Andrew Ross Sorkin, stood mute, enabling this questionable comment to go unchallenged.[18] Pagliuca's net worth is $450 million, so PE worked for him but not so well for some of his investors. The substandard performance of recent Bain buyout funds was problematic, and the bankruptcies of two of Bain's largest deals—the $24 billion iHeart Media buyout and the $7 billion Toys "R" Us takeover, resulted in massive layoffs.[19]

One might chalk up CNBC's reluctance to mention these facts by citing the likelihood of access journalism, whereby interviewers avoid tough questions that might embarrass a high-powered guest in order to preserve access to the guest and similar individuals. A more cynical interpretation draws upon Noam Chomsky's media analysis, which suggests that the status quo is the objective viewpoint for career-concerned journalists (and their employers).[20] In this explication, Mr. Pagliuca's statement was (and is) the status quo, so it need not be challenged.

For years, academic researchers and other PE observers backed the industry's stipulations; however, in recent times, there has been pushback, with several published papers refuting the industry's claims. Given the secretive nature of the industry's operations, collecting accurate data for an objective analysis on certain aspects, like PE's contribution to job growth, presented a challenge. Conclusions were sometimes hard to verify, and the information shortage provided an opening for buyout promoters to advance legitimate counterarguments.

An undeniable beneficiary of the buyout boom is the owner of a midsize, low-tech firm. As long-time investment banker Phil Erard indicates, "Earlier, if a business was not in a fashionable sector, not an IPO candidate, the owners were left with the option of either selling to a competitor pretty cheap, or leaving the business to the family."[21] Nowadays, this sort of firm is an ideal LBO candidate, and decent low-tech companies receive fair offers when the owners decide to sell. Another beneficiary is a cash-strapped state government. By investing in PE, the state employee pension plan is able to forecast higher future returns (with no guarantees) than a conventional portfolio, and the plan's actuary will bless the forecast. Even though the returns may not be realized, the actuary gives the government the legitimacy to devote less cash to current plan contributions and to assert plan solvency. This tactic frees up monies for other state budget items.

What is not widely understood is the chasm between the vast wealth accrued by PE managers (sometimes called general partners) through money management fees and moderate returns provided to LBO fund investors (called limited partners). The disparity in returns—many fund managers have become mega wealthy—is a subject considered off-limits in the industry and one that outside critics have an uphill battle in publicizing.

One of many poster children for the critics is Steven Klinsky, the principal general partner of New Mountain Capital.[22] He built a $3 billion net worth by supervising just $15 billion in investor commitments and by putting up just a fraction of these commitments with his own money. Only one of his six funds, a 2007 vintage, doubled investors' money over its ten-year life, and the largest fund, a $6 billion vehicle started in 2017, performed worse than the stock market. Interestingly, in January 2021 New Mountain closed a new $9 billion fund.

Annex to Chapter 2

This annex to chapter 2 introduces basic investment concepts for some and a refresher course for others.

Conventional Investments

People refer to publicly traded stocks and bonds as "conventional investments." *Conventional* in this sense refers to the fact that large institutions and wealthy individuals—at least up to the 1980s—dedicated the bulk of their portfolios to such investments.

Publicly Traded Stocks

A publicly traded stock represents an ownership interest in a profit-seeking corporation. Anyone with a brokerage account can buy or sell publicly traded stocks. To protect investors, federal and state governments, as well as the exchanges where the stocks are traded, have many rules and regulations. Key regulations surround the voluminous information that listed companies must provide investors and the requirement for audited financial statements. In this way, an investor who studies this information knows what kind of company they are purchasing into. Furthermore, the exchanges provide an ongoing forum for investors to buy and sell stock in a quick and orderly manner. Investors refer to this attribute as "liquidity." Examples of companies with publicly traded stock are Apple, Exxon, and J. P. Morgan.

In the United States, roughly four thousand companies issue public stock that trade actively. The top five hundred companies represent 80 percent of market value. Another ten thousand or so stocks trade infrequently in an over-the-counter setting rather than a formal stock exchange.

The annual rate-of-return of a common stock encompasses two elements:

(1) The change in price over the year
(2) A cash dividend, if any

When you combine (1) and (2), you have the stock's total return. For example, a stock begins the year with a $20 price, and it pays a $1 annual cash dividend. At the end of the year, the stock price rises to $22 per share, which indicates a 10 percent price gain ($22 − $20) / $20 = 10 percent gain). The dividend provides a 5 percent yield ($1/$20 = 5%). The total return is thus 15 percent (i.e., 10% price gain + 5% dividend = 15% total return). Over long periods, the broad stock market has a compounded annual return of 10 percent, depending on what period is measured.

For comparative purposes, Wall Street expresses stock prices in terms of value ratios. The most widely used indicator of stock prices is the price earnings ratio (P/E), which compares a stock price (the *P*) with the company's underlying earnings (the *E*). A high P/E suggests a valuable growing business. At this writing, the stock market P/E was 22× (see figure 2.7).

Publicly Traded Bonds

A bond is a "fixed income instrument that represents a loan made by an investor to a borrower (typically corporate or governmental)."[23] Bond details include the end date when the principal of the loan is to be repaid and the terms for interest payments made by the borrower. A bond is a legal contract, and a bondholder

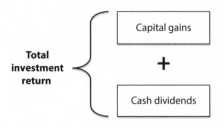

FIGURE 2.7 Total investment return

can seek legal remedies if payments are not forthcoming, such as placing the borrower in bankruptcy.

Public bond issuers must comply with legal information disclosure requirements and make various reports available over the internet. Investors can thus research the issuer's activities. Except for bonds of sizeable issuers, such as the U.S. government, bonds tend to be less liquid than many publicly traded stocks. If a bond issuer encounters financial problems, bondholders have a prior claim on the issuer's assets compared to stockholders. The bondholder's potential return is mostly fixed—for instance, the interest rate, while in theory, a stockholder's return is potentially unlimited, since the stock can climb upward for a long time. Amazon went for $60 per share in 2000 to over $3,000 per share in 2020 (see figure 2.8).

The total return of a bond includes both (1) the price change and (2) the interest payment. Bond prices are inversely coordinated with interest rates: when rates go up, bond prices fall, and vice versa. However, bond prices are less volatile than stock prices.

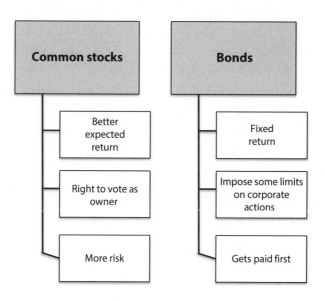

FIGURE 2.8 Common stocks and bonds

Many publicly traded bonds have ratings assigned by one or more of the leading credit rating agencies: Standard and Poor's, Moody's, and Fitch Ratings. The higher-quality bonds, with a low perceived threat of default, receive an investment-grade rating. Noninvestment grade or junk bonds carry a greater risk of default, whereby the holder can lose a substantial part of the bond's face value. By virtue of its high debt load, an LBO is a junk rated bond issuer. The grading scale for Standard and Poor's appears in table 2.1.

Owing to the sizeable amount of government issuance, the bond market is several times larger in value than the stock market. Over the last fifty years, the bond market has generated a compound annual return of 5 percent compared to the stock market's 10 percent.

A junk bond may yield 3 percent to 4 percent per year more than an investment-grade bond due to the junk bond's higher default or bankruptcy risk. Investors want to be paid for the extra risk. The net return premium after bankruptcy losses is around 1 percent.

Table 2.1
Bond credit ratings

Investment grade "low risk"
AAA
AA
A
BBB
Noninvestment grade "junk"
BB
B
CCC
CC
C
D

Risk

What is risk? Everyone talks about it, but what does *risk* mean? In personal terms, risk is a situation that exposes you to the threat of danger. In financial terms, most people see risk as the possibility of an investment losing value. In money management circles, risk is not just losing your principal, it is also the likelihood that an investment's future outcome is significantly different than the outcome that you expected when you bought the investment. For example, you expected a yield of 5 percent in year one and 5 percent in year two. Instead, the investment provided 3 percent in year one and 6 percent in year two. This is not strictly a loss but more variation than you anticipated. Added uncertainty implies more risk, which most people do not like.

One risk that most people recognize is default risk, whereby a company's stock becomes worthless, or its bonds fall in value from the 100 percent issuance price. Lehman Brothers, a former employer of mine, is a good example. The stock traded as high as $65 in the year before bankruptcy and then fell to zero. After bankruptcy, Lehman's bonds traded down to 35 cents on the dollar.

Besides the risk of a big loss, there is the risk of the investment return fluctuating widely from your expectation of a smooth upward glide. For example, you purchase a portfolio of common stocks, with the expectation of an annual return of plus 7 percent over several years. In the first year, the stock market falls, and the portfolio's total return (price change plus dividends) is minus 5 percent, not plus 7 percent. Subsequent year returns are plus 8 percent, plus 16 percent, minus 1 percent, and plus 13 percent. Instead of having a smooth, upward slope of 7 percent each year, your portfolio rises in fits and starts, exposing you not only to the possibility of an absolute loss but also to a loss relative to competing investments, such as bonds or real estate (see figure 2.9).

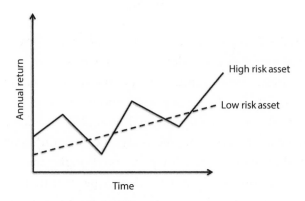

FIGURE 2.9 Risky asset shows volatility

The differences between the average portfolio return—7 percent yearly in this example—and the differing returns in each year, such as minus 1 percent or plus 8 percent, is called risk. Finance uses several statistical tools to measure risk, and the tools carry mathematical names such as *standard deviation* and *beta*. From the investor's point of view, an investment with more risk, less smoothing, or greater uncertainty should offer a higher return than a predictable asset. This is the reason why junk bonds show greater yields than investment-grade securities.

Over the course of many years, the markets have shown that investments with the higher risk (i.e., more return fluctuation from their average return) provide a greater profit than those with less risk. The profit difference is not linear and changes with the time selected. Moreover, future risk is ultimately measured in financial markets by examining an investment's past performance, and these historical markers are far from accurate prognosticators.

The graph in figure 2.10 compares the risks and returns of a few popular asset classes.

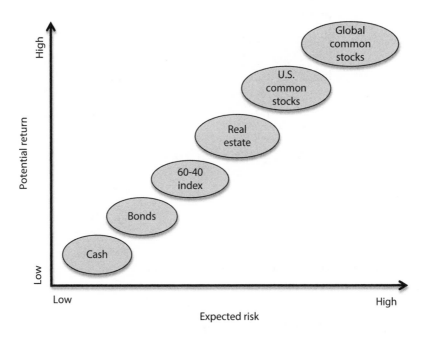

FIGURE 2.10 Asset class: risk return chart

Indexes

A stock market index is a hypothetical basket of common stocks, which represents a designated segment of the stock market. Investors use the total return performance of the index as a benchmark from which they compare the returns of their own portfolios. The most popular stock index is the Standard & Poor's 500 (S&P 500) index, which contains five hundred of the largest (by market value) U.S. stocks and represents a broad section of the U.S. economy. A typical refrain of an equity portfolio manager (who specializes in large company stocks) might be, "I beat the S&P 500 by 1 percent this year!" Complementing the S&P 500 index are dozens of other stock indexes that investors use as measurement devices.

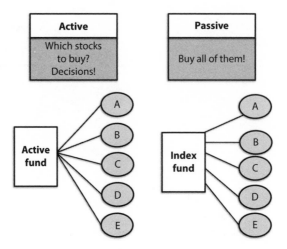

FIGURE 2.11 Active vs. passive equity management

Many mutual funds and exchange traded funds (ETFs) offer investment vehicles that mimic an index. The largest such fund is the Vanguard 500 Index Fund, which mimics the S&P 500. Because the mutual fund manager or ETF manager does not actively select index stocks, such vehicles are considered passive investments, and their operating expenses and their fees are low compared to an actively managed portfolio where the manager must analyze companies and then pick and choose stocks (see figure 2.11).

Leveraged buyout funds invest in mature-type companies. Such companies are, in many respects, like numerous publicly traded firms. Accordingly, buyout participants frequently compare their rate-of-return performance to the S&P 500 index.

Like equity investors, bond buyers use a variety of bond indices to measure relative performance. The Bloomberg Barclays U.S. Aggregate Bond Index is a common benchmark.

For institutional investors (or individuals) who are willing to absorb a moderate amount of risk, a traditional yardstick (as noted in chapter 1) is the 60–40 index. "It's the gold standard for

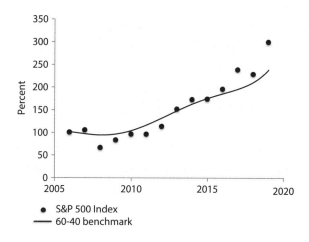

FIGURE 2.12 S&P 500 index vs. 60–40 benchmark

institutions," one consultant told me. This hypothetical basket of publicly traded securities is comprised of, in market value terms, 60 percent S&P 500 index and 40 percent U.S. Aggregate Bond Index. This allocation enables 60–40 index holders to enjoy part of an equity market upside, with downside protection from stock market corrections because of the bond holdings.

For example, in the 2009 market crash, the S&P 500 fell 37 percent, while the 60–40 dropped 14 percent. Conversely, during the 2019 stock market run-up, the S&P 500 climbed 31 percent, when the 60–40 rose just 20 percent (see figure 2.12).

Diversification

In plain English, investment diversification means "don't put all your eggs in one basket." Diversification enables an investor to avoid serious loss when one asset class, or one particular asset, collapses in value. Diversification is attained by allocating a port-folio among several classes, such as stocks, bonds, and real estate.

Diversification is enhanced further by multiple distinct individual assets within a class. For example, within a stock portfolio, achieve diversification by buying thirty stocks of companies involved with thirty different industries.

Because of the similarity of buyout funds' underlying assets to publicly traded stocks, one might argue that the funds are not a true diversification away from the stock market. The counter argument is twofold: (1) PE offers investors additional corporate opportunities in unlisted firms; and (2) PE has a supposed history of smoother returns than the stock market.

3

How Does the Private Equity Industry Work?

IT IS A DARK SUNDAY NIGHT in suburban Stamford, Connecticut, a leafy New York suburb thirty minutes form the nation's financial capital by commuter train. In a low-slung office complex surrounded by empty, windswept parking lots, a solitary light burns in a fourth-floor conference room. Inside is Ray Miller, vice president of Lambeth Equity Fund III, and he is hunched over a table hard at work. Fund III specializes in U.S. LBOs, like its predecessors, Fund I and Fund II, and Fund III targets firms with purchase prices between $100 million and $300 million. With $500 million in equity commitments from its institutional partners, Lambeth engages in a constant battle for new acquisitions, and Ray is on the front lines. Many buyout groups have acquisition criteria like Lambeth, and the competition for deals is cutthroat. "You've got a hundred funds and a dozen strategic buyers chasing the same companies," explains Ray. "It's crazy."

Worried about losing potential targets and stalling his career, Ray puts in the extra time. Tonight he proofreads the email blasts that Lambeth's digital marketer sends out to various contact lists. Different messages go out to different audiences—family-owned businesses, medium-sized investment banks, and corporate law firms. For example, the investment bank email blast says: "Lambeth equity is seeking infrastructure service businesses with revenue greater than $100 million and earnings greater than $15 million." He reviews his weekly schedule, which includes long hours, emailing, calling, and texting bankers, deal finders, and business owners. Ray looks for a connection that gives Lambeth an edge in uncovering a transaction. Like many of his PE colleagues, Ray has a sterling pedigree: Ivy League undergraduate degree, Wharton MBA, and Wall Street experience. His salary and bonus are attractive, but he has not yet reached the partner role—those fortunate few who share in Lambeth's lucrative management fees. That position is a few years away, if he has the fortitude and luck to stick it out. "You have to produce, and you have to produce in the short run," he points out.

At times, Ray has second thoughts about his career choice. Before taking the job, he came to believe LBOs presented a constructive intellectual challenge with defined tasks—analyzing a company's capabilities, its profit-making potential, and its markets, and then gauging its ability to grow and to service debt in the light of future competitors and economic conditions. The buyout industry's sizeable assets once indicated to Ray that fund managers such as Lambeth had a magic elixir that improved businesses, but the reality turned out to be far different—an LBO fund was, in effect, a marketing marathon in the acquisition search process, with the dire hope that Lambeth could close two or three deals per year, keep investor returns in the plus column, spend all of Fund III's money, and plan for a new Fund IV before anyone was the wiser.

Ray Miller is a fictional character, but knock on the door of any buyout fund, and you will find individuals like him. They are young, ambitious people striving to make the pitiless climb to the top of the PE ladder—where one attains the rank of general partner and the wealth that goes with it.

The LBO Fund Business—How Does It Work?

From the fund manager's perspective, the leveraged buyout business involves six distinct phases.

- Fund formation, raising money
- Searching for companies to buy
- Valuing the deals
- Holding investments and trying to improve them
- Finding the right time to sell
- Starting a new fund, raising money again

Figure 3.1 illustrates a typical timeline. Note that the phases overlap. For example, the fund sells certain firms in its portfolio at the same that it labors to improve others.

Fund Formation, Raising Money

A new fund is a blind pool, set up as a legal partnership. Upon formation, the new fund has no portfolio companies nor does it have agreements to buy businesses in the immediate future. The fund's offering prospectus presents investors (i.e., limited partners) with vague assurances that the fund intends to:

- Acquire control of firms that fit the LBO profile and meet preset size criteria.
- Improve portfolio firms' management, operations, and growth.
- Pay reasonable prices for deals.
- Sell investments at opportune times.

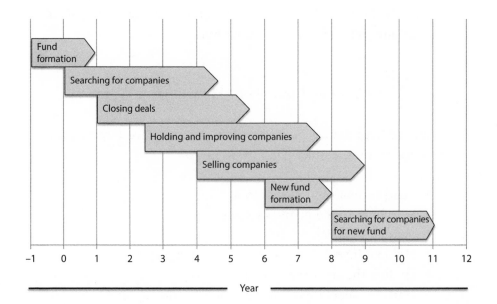

FIGURE 3.1 Buyout fund timeline

In a perfect world, "private equity investors are looking for diversification away from public stock markets, as well as a higher return," says Ady Adefris, chief operating officer of Ion Pacific Funds.[1] How do the investors select one blind pool versus another to heighten the chances of achieving these two objectives?

HISTORICAL TRACK RECORD

To start the fund selection process, the institutional investor examines the historical track record of a fund management team. If the team's first two funds, Fund I and Fund II, performed well compared to other LBO funds, investors conclude that a new Fund III as a good chance of outperforming its peer group, so the investors sign on to Fund III.

"Performing well" in PE circles meant that Funds I and II earned returns in the top quartile (or top 25 percent) of the many similar funds investing over similar time periods. What was special about the top quartile? Those were the buyout funds that produced returns that were meaningfully higher than the stock market. Amazingly, given the flood of money into the asset class, LBO funds in the bottom three quartiles (or bottom 75 percent) provided returns equal to or inferior to the stock market, particularly in the last twenty years.[2] That is why a common institutional money manager saying is, "I only invest in top quartile funds" (see figure 3.2).

Few institutional investors took the trouble to read independent studies regarding the flaws in this historical-track-record-based methodology. Over the last ten years, several researchers examined the likelihood of a top-quartile LBO fund repeating its superior performance in a subsequent fund.[3] The results were dismal according to the most recent study by McKinsey & Company, the well-known management consulting firm. "The story is worse for top quartile funds," says McKinsey. "From 1995 to 1999,

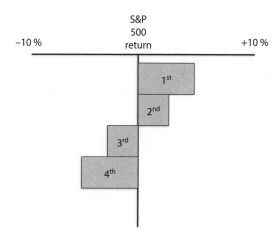

FIGURE 3.2 Approximate LBO fund annualized returns by quartile vs. S&P 500

an average 31 percent of top-quartile funds were followed by similar successors, but by 2010–2013, this average had fallen to only 12 percent."[4] In other words, an LBO fund lacked the ability to replicate its previous success, a fact that was first identified fifteen years ago.[5] Rather than picking an LBO fund manager based on past performance, an institutional investor could have earned more money by throwing darts blindfolded at a list of buyout managers (i.e., general partners) and making choices accordingly (see figure 3.3).

A study in the prestigious *Journal of Financial Economics* (2017), covering 865 buyout funds, says it best, "Private equity has, therefore, largely conformed to the pattern of other asset classes in which past performance is a poor predictor of the future."[6] That being said, I can't count the number of times people in the LBO business have told me variations on the following:

FIGURE 3.3 Monkey throwing darts to select buyout fund

"Past performance is indicative of future performance," "achieving top quartile returns is not random," "we only invest in top quartile funds," and "our successful LBO acquisition process carries over from fund to fund."

Interestingly, in contrast, top quartile venture capital funds, the LBO industry's smaller cousin, exhibit a consistency in results from prior fund to successor fund.

BORROWING A TRACK RECORD: SPINOUT FUND

An institutional investor that uses the historical-track-record approach for selecting an outside manager is a good potential customer for an established fund seeking new money, but how is a prospective new buyout team supposed to break into the business? The team has no track record, so how does it persuade an institutional investor to say yes to an untested manager? To alleviate such concerns, the new team borrows the track record of the team's former employer—namely, an already established fund manager—and convinces possible institutional partners that the team members learned the ropes at their previous jobs and, therefore, they are ready to apply this knowledge to the institutions' benefit. The PE industry refers to this practice as a spinout. "These spinout GPs (managers) are really doing the same thing they've been doing for years," says Eric Zoller, investment banker at Sixpoint Partners.[7] Examples of spinout LBO firms abound, such as Mid Ocean Partners (from Deutsche Bank PE), NMS Capital (Goldman Sachs Merchant Banking), Diversis Capital (Gores PE), and Equistone Partners (Barclays Bank). Essentially, the methodology for choosing a spinout fund is a variation on the historical-track-record technique, because the investor ultimately decides on the basis of past performance (see figure 3.4).

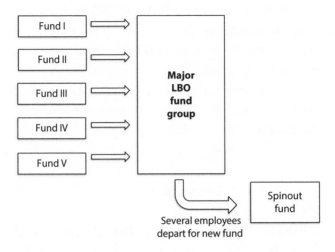

FIGURE 3.4 LBO fund spinout

BRAND-NAME APPROACH

Suppose an institution is reluctant to rely heavily on the historical-track-record technique for selecting a buyout fund manager. In this case, the institution can then use the brand-name approach. Here is the institution's step-by-step rationale for selecting a brand-name fund manager:

- What if the institution invests in fund with a little-known manager and something goes wrong?
- Won't the investment executives at the institution get blamed for the poor outcome even if their fund selection process had a semiscientific logic?
- Isn't it a better career move for the institutional executives to simply choose a well-known fund manager that everyone has heard of? A brand name, so to speak . . . like Blackstone or Goldman Sachs?
- That way, if the LBO investments blow up and the returns are lousy, the institutional executives have plausible deniability.

- They can say, "We invested with Goldman Sachs (or a similar brand name), which is totally blue chip. How did we know they'd screw things up?"
- Everyone else invested with them, and our private equity consultant recommended them!

The brand-name approach is thus career protection, reminiscent of the saying, "No one ever got fired for buying IBM." This IBM saying refers to the only safe bet. As Duena Blomstrom, CEO of PeopleNotTech said, "This was to shield an organization's employees from repercussions if anything had gone wrong, as IBM presumably had the strongest reputation for not allowing that to happen."[8] The financial market equivalent of the safe bet is the following expression: "The middle of the herd is a nice safe place on Wall Street." If many other institutions pile into a brand-name fund, and the fund fails to beat the stock market, the institutional executives avoid accountability.

Despite having prominent positions, favorable buyout reputations, and tens of billions of dollars under management, the brand-name fund managers as a group barely outperformed a random grouping of obscure funds, as Ken Yook and I discovered in our study, "The Relative Performance of Large Buyout Fund Groups," published in *The Journal of Private Equity*.[9] We surveyed eighteen of the largest buyout managers with multiple funds under management, and we found that investors do not pay a lot of attention to these managers' quartile rankings. After a few completed funds, the large managers had a blank check from the institutional investor community. For example, Providence Equity Partners raised $5 billion in 2013 after two failed funds with multiple bankruptcies.[10] Kohlberg Kravis & Roberts (KKR) bombed in its 2006 and 2008 funds, scoring in the third quartile both times. Such performance is a death knell for lesser-known brands, but KKR had little trouble raising an $8 billion fund in 2013. Similarly, another famous name,

Bain Capital, had two problematic funds in succession, Bain IX and Bain X, yet the successor, Bain XI, raised $7 billion. Acknowledging these shortcomings, while still recommending another Bain commitment, the Pennsylvania state pension plan glossed over the damaging facts with imprecise wording, "Bain has spent much time and effort enhancing the Firm's investment decision process."[11]

Noting the seeming irony of brand-name managers getting rewarded for poor results, an institutional consultant told me in April 2020, "Having a large LBO firm with a track record takes you a long way. You have an established investor base that simply repeats." A good example of this phenomenon is the Washington state pension fund, which committed over $6 billion to KKR funds over the last thirty-five years, despite the firm's inconsistent track record.

In all cases of new funds, the institutions expect the fund manager to provide a 3 percent match to the institutions' equity commitment, and statistics show half of the managers above this number and half below. An approximate average is 5 percent, according to *Pension & Investments* magazine.[12] Thus, if the new fund has a $500 million size, the managers pledge a minimum of $25 million of their own cash (5% × $500 million = $25 million) as the fund closes acquisitions. The PE industry and its acolytes make a brouhaha over of this arrangement, trumpeting that the match aligns the interests of both the managers and the institutions. In fact, the $25 million is a fraction of the $75 million in guaranteed management fees, monitoring fees, and transaction fees that the managers receive from a $500 million fund over its ten-year life. Even a 10 percent manager outlay falls short of the guarantees. It thus becomes obvious that managers have zero skin in the game and, therefore, zero risk in a new fund. Neither PE textbooks, media articles, nor state retirement plans mention this salient fact. And the institutions pay the $75 million in fees whether the fund makes a profit or not.

Searching for LBO Deals After the Fund Closing

Once the new buyout fund has been established, the manager's fortunes are assured for the next ten years. This by itself is a major accomplishment. The next challenge for the managers is finding companies to buy. Within the LBO profile, the basic parameters of the acquisition targets are already set—size, geography, and industry—so it is up to the manager to generate a steady stream of investment opportunities for the fund to evaluate. This is what Wall Streeters call "deal flow."

For most fund managers, producing deal flow is not difficult. Successor funds develop deal flow from their predecessor fund's built-in relationships. For spinouts, managers carry their contacts and reputations from their old jobs to the new fund, so the transition from old to new deal flow is seamless. Nonetheless, the mathematics of sifting through LBO opportunities are daunting. "A good rule of thumb is that you have to look at 100 possible deals in order to close one transaction," says Andrew Gunther, managing director at Darby Private Equity.[13] In other words, a fund manager must kiss a lot of frogs before finding a prince.

Fund managers develop deal flow through three channels:

- New business calls
- Referrals
- Investment banks advising sellers

NEW BUSINESS CALLS

A successful buyout fund has an active outreach program. Waiting by the phone does not produce enough viable leads to sustain a successful operation. On the one hand is a direct mail and a direct email effort. Using rented contact lists, as well as in-house proprietary lists, the fund sends out a regular stream of communications to private companies, investment bankers, industry consultants law firms, accounting firms, and other sources. The mailings advertise deal closings and remind people about the fund's acquisition criteria. Many companies are not officially for sale. From time to time, such regular and repeated contracts prompt a response regarding a possible acquisition. More important is an organized person-to-person connection program. Fund executives maintain an active new business-calling regimen, and, like the fictional Ray Miller, pad their schedules full of personal emails, direct phone calls, and onsite meetings with many of the individuals on the contact lists. This doorbell-ringing, as the trade calls it, is very productive. It enables the deal source to place a fund name to a face, and it gives the fund executive a chance to explain his or her acquisition criteria in some detail. Focus Investment Bank, a middle-market M&A firm at which I am a senior advisor, receives several such visits per week. Fund executives tell me that, during a typical day trip away from their office, they conduct five or six new business calls.

Supplementing their out-of-town travel destinations is their attendance at conferences related to the PE industry. Besides the occasional LBO focus, the conferences cover the M&A process, the use of PE in a family wealth office, the availability of PE for growing enterprises, and associated other matters. The attendees are a source of M&A referrals as well as possible investors. By speaking at a conference or renting a booth where attendees can talk with employees and learn more about a PE fund, the buyout executives heighten their employer's profile in a positive manner.

To expand the marketing effort further, some funds hire niche investment banks and small finder firms to solicit acquisition interest from private companies meeting the fund's acquisition criteria. A fund pays a monthly fee in addition to a success fee for such services. At the same time, the heads of the fund's portfolio firms keep an eye out for potential acquisition add-on targets in their respective industries. Trade shows, conferences, chance airport meetings, and similar contacts result in transactions.

REFERRALS

Senior fund managers usually have fifteen years or more in the business. Over time, they build relationships with many individuals who refer deal ideas or deal opportunities. These referring individuals work as corporate lawyers, accountants, commercial bankers, corporate executives, business consultants, hedge fund managers, business appraisers, and entrepreneurs. In many cases, the referral is at best a half-baked concept, and the fund manager goes down a rabbit hole by following up. For example, the following scenario is typical: A buyout fund manager gets a lead from a lawyer about a family firm ready to sell. Through the lawyer, he contacts the company and studies relevant information. He travels to the company and meets with the family. He follows up with calls and emails, seeking more information and extolling the benefits of working with his fund. He has the fund's junior analysts model the company and prepare a valuation estimate. After three months of this back and forth, the family decides it is not ready to sell, and the manager's efforts have been wasted. Nonetheless, spending time on fanciful ideas is part of the business, and currying favor with those referral sources, even when confronted with long-shot proposals, is a necessary evil. Indeed, fund managers derive most of their acquisitions through the referral route.

INVESTMENT BANKS ADVISING SELLERS

Statistics show that a high proportion of companies that are in a sell mode hire an investment banker to assist in the M&A process. Such selling companies fall into several categories:

- Entrepreneur-owned firm
- Family-owned business
- Portfolio company of a PE fund

- Division of a large private firm
- Division of a publicly traded company
- Publicly traded company

The owners' reasons for selling are many and varied. An entrepreneur may want to move on and start another operation. A second-generation family business may lack children that want to carry on the business. Buyout funds are also in the selling mix because their investors want the funds to dispose of their portfolio companies prior to the end of the fund's contractual life. Large corporations frequently operate several divisions that are distinct businesses, unrelated to one another. From time to time, corporate management decides the time is right to sell a division and allocate the cash proceeds to another project. In other situations, a large publicly traded company agrees to a takeover for strategic reasons or accepts an attractive offer for its shareholders' benefit.

Whatever the reason for selling, the future acquisition candidate's first step is often retaining an investment banker to administer the long and arduous marketing process. After some due diligence, the banker prepares an information memorandum (info memo) that describes the seller's businesses, operations, and financial results. Next, the banker compiles a list of potentially interested buyers. For a medium-sized U.S. company, this buyer list typically includes fifty to one hundred prospects. If the seller fits the LBO profile, the list contains fifty or more LBO funds that acquire companies like the seller. Through this M&A identification process, a buyout fund receives several inquiries per week from investment bankers regarding the fund's interest in acquiring the bank's sell-side client.

THE SIFTING PROCESS

The efforts devoted to new business, referrals, and investment bankers produce many leads that must be run down and studied, and that is an important part of the job of midlevel employees like the aforementioned Ray Miller. Most leads are rejected out of hand with little investigation—reading some documents, making a phone call, or holding a brief meeting. Perhaps 15 percent to 20 percent of the deal flow requires an additional time commitment—and thus a weekly stream of ten or fifteen ideas results in one or two opportunities that involve significant follow-up on the fund's part. Data requests and seller onsite meetings allow the fund manager to separate the wheat from the chaff by determining if the seller's business, management team, and asking price fit with the fund's objectives and debt financing sources. Over the course of a year, the fund makes fifteen offers, of which two or three result in new portfolio investments (see figure 3.5 for an illustration of the sifting process).

Unfortunately, for the fund manager, finding deals that are both doable and economical is not quite the iterative exercise I just described. If a fund wants to pay top dollar for acquisitions, it can deplete its investors' money very quickly. Most funds, however, take a measured approach, hoping to close two to three deals per year. Following the first three to four years of a fund's

FIGURE 3.5 Buyout fund sifting process

life, it is then fully invested, with a total of ten to twelve companies in the portfolio. After a couple investments have been sold at a profit, the managers are ready to raise a new fund. The goal is for the manager to operate multiple funds, whereby the manager can realize economies of scale quickly (see figure 3.6).

During those first few years of a fund's life, the managers (i.e., the general partners) hit dry spells when their buyout offers are topped by competitors or when they simply cannot find suitable targets. Pressure builds to spend money, as the investors want to see transactions alongside the fees they are paying. "The walls start

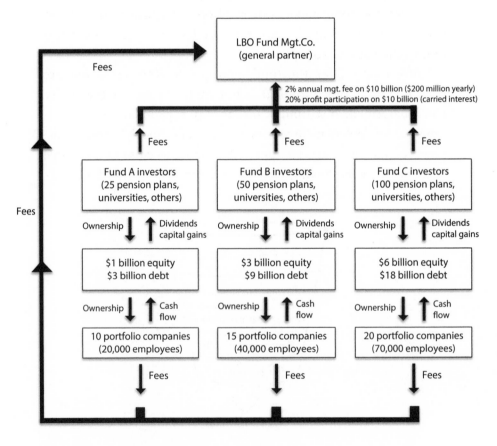

FIGURE 3.6 LBO fund manager economics

to close in," said one PE executive. "The LPs [limited partners; i.e., institutions] start complaining: 'Why aren't you writing checks?' " Inevitably, the fund manager succumbs to the strain and begins to make compromises. The fund pays a higher price, or it absorbs more risk than that it suggested in its charter. The fund reduces its selectivity. "It's like dating," explained one fund manager. "If you get too picky, you'll never have a guy to go out with."

Valuing an LBO Target

After a few exchanges with the target company or its investment banker (if it has one), the fund manager has enough information to develop a reasonable offer price. The valuation methodology relies heavily on comparable companies analysis, whereby the fund examines the value placed on similar businesses in the public equity or M&A markets. Such information is widely available in free and fee-based databases. The M&A appraisal process is similar to the real estate model, whereby the worth of a four-bedroom house in Montclair, New Jersey, for example, is established by the pricing of four-bedroom homes in the same neighborhood. If the median sale during the previous twelve months was $1 million, then that number is the baseline value of the subject house. The appraiser adjusts this figure for specific qualitative and quantitative attributes, such as the subject house having a bigger yard, fewer bathrooms, or more square feet than its comparables. Lacking the uniformity of real estate attributes, the corporate appraiser measures a target's worth by reviewing comparable target pricing expressed as a multiple (or ratio) of the target's earnings before interest, taxes, depreciation, and amortization (EBITDA). EBITDA is a common accounting term that roughly equates to a company's cash flow from operations.

The numerator in the ratio is the target's enterprise value (EV), which is the target's equity pricing, plus its existing debt, minus its cash-on-hand. Since LBOs by definition must have positive EBITDA in order to repay acquisition debt, the EV/EBITDA ratio is ubiquitous in buyout discussions and trumps the other valuation ratios you might see in financial reports, such as the price/earnings ratio, price/book ratio and EV/revenue ratio. For illustration, an acquisition target has $10 million in annual EBITDA, no debt, and no cash. Comparable public firms trade at a median value of 7× EV/EBITDA and comparable M&A deals are priced at a median 9× EBITDA. The fund manager might start the negotiations at 8× EBITDA (or $80 million), knowing the seller will likely have the same information on similar deals. The seller's response (or its investment banker's rejoinder) might be, "But the M&A comps were at 9×. How does 9× EBITDA strike you?" Beginning with a low-ball price, like 6× EBITDA, is unproductive for the fund manager, because the seller moves on to more realistic buyers—an occurrence experienced by many prospective homebuyers in the real estate market. "Any U.S. company with more than $2 million in EBITDA is pretty well shopped," said one executive. "You cannot find any bargains."

Prior to the pandemic, LBO profile firms sold for the following ratios set forth in figure 3.7.

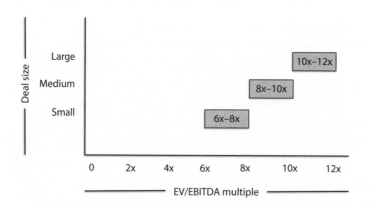

FIGURE 3.7 Buyout funding pricing of target companies, 2016–2019

Holding, Ownership, and Sale Phase

Once an offer has been accepted, the LBO fund performs an exhaustive due diligence on the target, raises the acquisition debt, finalizes the legal documentation, and plans the target's postclosing operations. After closing begins the "hold and improve phase" indicates Mike Gaffney, a former buyout executive and founder of the consulting firm Bancroft Group.[14] Over the next five years, the fund hopes to expand the targets' revenue, increase profit margins, pay down part of the acquisition debt, and ready the company for sale to another buyer. A schematic of the cash flow cycle appears as figure 3.8.

Unlike many venture-capital-backed businesses that lose money, an LBO target is already profitable and has been in-the-black for many years; otherwise, the lending community does not touch the deal. The fund manager suggests operational changes at the

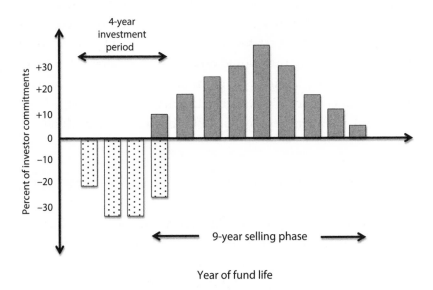

FIGURE 3.8 Annual cash flows of typical buyout funds with a twelve-year life and 150 percent payout

target, but these do not produce seismic shifts. Rather, the best the fund can hope for are marginal improvements to boost earnings and add-on acquisitions to push revenue growth.

PE advocates like to say that buyout funds take underperforming companies and then improve them, as this *Harvard Business Review* article states: "The fundamental reason behind private equity's growth and high rates of return is something that has received little attention, perhaps because it's so obvious: the firms' standard practice of buying businesses and then, after steering them through a transition of rapid performance improvement, selling them."[15] But this statement is an exaggeration. LBO candidates, for the most part, are not underperforming. They have a history of profitable operation.

The basic math shows the LBO cannot spend much on renovating a portfolio company's operations. For example, a new $80 million buyout with $10 million in annual operating cash flow might have $7 million in annual debt service payments. At most, this leaves a scant $3 million for the capital expenses necessary to reengineer the business, hardly enough to promote the massive improvement forecast for portfolio firms in PE promotional materials. "Anything that would take more than a trivial amount of capital and have a longer payout time doesn't generally fit with a private equity model," says Steve Dennis, founder of Sage Consulting and a former executive of LBO retailer Neiman Marcus.[16]

Comparing the LBO Process to Stock Picking

Finding, studying, and closing a buyout transaction is a laborious endeavor that requires a high level of analytical skill and financial expertise. Boiled down to its particulars, the fund manager's selection process bears a strong resemblance to a mutual fund manager's picking of public stocks. Both managers claim to use a systematic form of analysis to decide which opportunity (acquisition target or publicly traded stock, respectively) will provide a good rate of return. They discard many possibilities along the way toward making a purchase decision on one investment. For example, a mutual fund manager specializing in midsized firms may have one thousand stocks to choose from in their designated category. After subjecting this large number of stocks to systematic analysis, he or she may pick fifty in constructing a portfolio.

In contrast, an LBO manager faces a different magnitude of purchase options compared to the mutual fund stock picker. To start, in the United States an average year sees ten thousand to fifteen thousand M&A deals, and an equivalent number of near transactions. Perhaps 20 percent of these deals meet the LBO profile, so the initial selection grouping is large, numbering several thousand possibilities. With size, industry, and geographical preferences, the LBO fund manager narrows the list to a couple hundred, from which it must choose two or three each year.

Admittedly, by purchasing 100 percent control, the buyout manager directs the portfolio company's operations. This control element is far more hands-on when set against the mutual fund manager's relatively small and therefore passive ownership position of a few percentage points. Nonetheless, I liken an LBO fund, with ten to twelve deals, to a high-conviction mutual fund, where the stock picker concentrates their top fifteen choices. My belief is that the LBO control, or directional, factor is of minimal value in the scheme of things (see figure 3.9).

Closing

The investment returns of LBO funds have a random quality. It is likely the methodical approach outlined herein has been largely abandoned by most managers, given the 2000s proliferation of funds, the onslaught of competition for available deals, and the favorable economics (to the manager) of seeding multiple funds

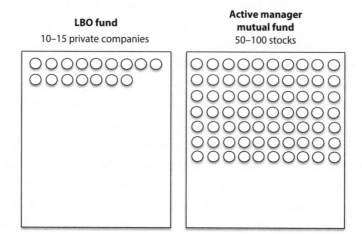

FIGURE 3.9 LBO fund vs. mutual fund

as quickly as possible. Institutional investors desire careful, studied deliberation from an LBO manager prior to the fund's purchase of a company. However, what the investors get instead is a fund implementing a spray-and-pray tactic, whereby the manager doesn't quite know what works, so it makes ten or twelve bets and counts on a few bringing home the bacon. How else do you explain the Green Equity Investors Fund VII, which bought forty companies in a mere two years? How selective can that acquisition process be? An examination of returns sheds light on the industry's effectiveness.

4

The Poor Investment Results

THE LBO INDUSTRY'S marketing linchpin—its reason for being—
is that it supposedly provides a higher rate of return than public
equities. The commentary of Mario Giannini, CEO of global advisory firm Hamilton Lane, is not unusual, "Private equity has outperformed every asset class, and it has done it for a long time."[1]
However, this assertion does not square with the facts.

The industry must perpetuate the story line of higher returns to
stay in business. Otherwise, why would a rational person invest
in an LBO fund versus a public stock portfolio? The former has
a ten-year lock-up, expensive fees, and obscure mark-to-market
practices. Because the funds' investments are not publicly traded
on a stock exchange, an investor is never quite sure how the fund
is doing until perhaps 90 percent of the underlying deals are sold.
A public stock, on the other hand, has instant liquidity—the investor can sell at any time at the indicated price per share. Moreover,
a public index fund charges a tiny fraction of buyout fund fees, so
more of the money is put to work in an index fund.

Over the last ten years, industry observers published several independent studies in this regard. In early 2020, Bain & Company (not affiliated with Bain Capital), one of America's top management consulting firms, published a study that showed PE funds underperforming the broad stock market over the previous ten years.[2] Three executives with AQR Capital Management, the $140 billion global asset manager, echoed these conclusions in the *Journal of Alternative Investments*.[3] Finance professors from prestigious schools, such as University of Virginia and Oxford University, presented similar finds, noting that in several cases the return shortfall extends back to 2006, while generally conceding that pre-2006 returns provided a premium to public markets.[4] In 2018 and 2019, the State of Oregon pension plan, the first major institution to participate in LBOs (dating back to the 1980s) reviewed its PE performance and found matching outcomes.[5]

In fairness, I should mention a countervailing argument advanced by two finance professors, Gregory Brown and Steven Kaplan, in a 2019 paper titled, "Have Private Equity Returns Really Declined?"[6] The professors indicate that the buyout industry outperformed the Morgan Stanley Capital International All Country World Index (MSCI ACWI). The MSCI ACWI is a popular benchmark for global-oriented equity portfolios, but it is not a suitable comparator for U.S.-based companies. It is well-known that the S&P 500, a U.S. centric measure, is a better comparator for U.S. buyouts, which explains the S&P 500's common usage for assessments rather than the MSCI ACWI. It is also known that the MSCI ACWI profits fell way short of the S&P 500 over the period, which makes the Brown and Kaplan paper at best a false positive and at worst quite misleading. Their PE defense was little more than an effort to shift the goalposts. Interestingly, the industry offered no in-depth rebuttal to the underperformance research. Why bother? Buyout funds raised tens of billions despite the new information coming to light.

1980s and 1990s

The 1980s and 1990s set the principal basis for the industry's ongoing claims of hyper performance in the 2000s. However, the results in the 1980s were based on a slim data set representing a small grouping of funds. Several funds did very well, but the 1980s' performance was overshadowed by the mediocre profits of the RJR buyout. By way of example, Oregon's early 1980s (1981–1986) capital commitments achieved a median annual return of 26 percent, but the later (1987–1989) commitments, which included RJR, produced just 9 percent.[7] The 1990s, on the other hand, were the industry's golden years, with demonstrable earnings above those of the stock market.

Early 2000s

The early 2000s showed promise, but cracks appeared in the armor. In a prescient November 2001 research report, Goldman Sachs had this to say: "The available data suggests that average returns in private equity may not outperform the long-term average of the public equity markets . . . that approximately 15 percent–20 percent of managers have final internal rates of return (IRR) that are zero or negative."[8] Goldman pretty much proved its own thesis, as just one of its three LBO funds raised after that date beat the S&P 500. Post-2005 returns for the industry are outshone by the stock market whenever you examine the returns in a critical manner.

In other words, depending on the years chosen, the foundation for a trillion-dollar industry's marketing fanfare rests on the narrow shoulders of a ten- to twelve-year performance span, which is now over fifteen years old, or several lifetimes in financial circles. And this measurement is done against public market returns with no bonus provided to the buyout investor for their ten-year contractual period of illiquidity. If one adds the requisite 3 percent premium, as recommended by many experts, for the PE investor's inability to sell, the LBO industry's justification for existing is tenuous indeed.

Why hasn't this dearth of positive results been more highly publicized? For close to two decades, most of the business media has followed a self-imposed blackout on research undermining the LBO industry's performance claims. In February 2020, Jonathan Ford of the *Financial Times* was the first representative of a major media outlet to report on the return inadequacy,[9] followed by a second article from Dan Primack, business editor at Axios.com.[10] There was minimal follow-up after the two articles, and the notion quickly fizzled out.

A business editor's reluctance to authorize a story on buyout returns is understandable. An investigation into returns means navigating a labyrinth of compelling statistics, complex finance terms, and questionable value propositions. Sorting through the data is difficult for a trained practitioner, and the challenge for a business reporter, without deep quantitative skills, becomes quite formidable. Over the years, I helped multiple reporters wade through an intimidating blizzard of numbers and assumptions associated with institutional investment accounting. In one journalistic example with the *Houston Chronicle*, a financial report for just one year of a prominent endowment, the Texas Permanent School Fund, totaled 152 pages of dense verbiage, numbers, and charts written in a mind-numbing, lawyer-like style.[11] Data on portfolio composition, returns by time period, and fixed fees were scattered through the document and sometimes buried in obscure footnotes. Reporters' questions posed to the endowment trustees received scant replies or halfhearted answers. For four months, three reporters scoured the financial report and those for prior years, representing a major resource commitment by their employer. Most media outlets refuse to dedicate such resources to institutional investment returns.

Unsold Buyout Fund Assets

To begin, I should point out an interesting fact that rarely comes to light. About 56 percent of all deals bought by PE funds since 2006 have not been sold to follow-on buyers. The statistic for post-2009 PE transactions? Sixty-eight percent are not sold to a buyer, and the PE fund still owns the acquisition. This situation is a far cry from the industry's stated goal of selling an investment after a three- to five-year holding period. Yes, these terrific deals—that have supposedly spawned great returns—either do not have buyers or have no takers at reasonable prices. The returns displayed by investors, therefore, are in large part derived from the guesstimates of what the fund managers think they can sell the deals for. To illustrate, in 2013 the State of Oregon committed $1.5 billion to several LBO funds. Over the next five years, the funds invested the full amount. By 2020, the posted annualized return on the funds was an impressive 15.3 percent, but only $756 million of the return had been paid in cash to the state. The remaining profits, $1,533 million, or two thirds of the total, consisted of unsold portfolio gains (see figure 4.1).

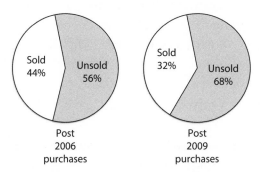

FIGURE 4.1 Unsold portfolio companies as a percent of total portfolio.
Source: Cambridge Associates

By way of definition, an unsold portfolio gain is when the fund invests in the equity of a portfolio company for $100 million. Five years later, the fund appraises its equity position at $150 million. The implied gain is $50 million ($150 million – $100 million = $50 million), although the profit remains unrealized and may just be a twinkle in the eye of the fund manager.

The long holding period situation is reflective of a general maxim in the merger and acquisition (M&A) business—"Buying is easy, selling is hard." The competition for transactions over the last ten years pushed funds into purchases they might not have made twenty years ago. "Many of these deals should never have been done in the first place," says Dan Ilsevitch, who has been an operating executive under three PE owners.[12] Ultimately, many of today's buyout funds will need to extend their contractual ten-year lives to allow the additional time required to sell their portfolio businesses.

The portfolio value guesstimates, although published widely in aggregate terms, are not verified well by third parties at the fund level. This guesstimating not only blemishes current return calculations, but it also taints older analyses that promote the industry. Both measurement sets have (or had) a heavy reliance on in-house fund appraisals of portfolio companies, which I liken to an eight-year-old grading his own homework. If you take the cynical view that fund managers view their portfolios through rose-colored glasses, then current return calculations are overly optimistic. A true assessment can only occur after a fund sells all its assets.

Data Services Only Capture 60 Percent of Buyout Funds

Five data services act as arbiters of the buyout industry's aggregate performance—Preqin, Pitchbook, Cambridge Associates, Burgiss, and Thomson Reuters. These data services derive information from the buyout managers, certain limited partners, and Freedom of Information Act filings with state and municipal pension plans. Participation by buyout fund managers is voluntary, and many choose not to disclose their results to the data services. Using the means at their disposal, the data services capture about 60 percent of the buyout funds, which leaves 40 percent of the funds as nonreporting. Simply put, the aggregate performance results publicized by the industry, the data services, and other observers have a significant gap.

The question becomes: Do the 40 percent nonreporting funds do better than the average fund, or worse? Because of the secretive nature of the industry, this question is difficult to answer. Many funds may conclude that reporting results to a data service publicly has no benefit; a top performer may already have an established investor base and may not need the recognition, for example, of a superior Pitchbook ranking. It is also conceivable that mediocre performers may want to maintain confidentiality to preserve their ability to massage their performance. The public scrutiny implicit in reporting information to a database hinders the mediocre funds' desired presentation of results to outsiders. Without reporting results to Preqin, for instance, the mediocre performer can tally up its own statistics and say, "Yes, we are in the top quartile for funds."

The danger for outside investors of the self-reporting by fund managers is self-evident. Consider the Bernie Madoff scandal as one illustration. Madoff's claimed returns were very favorable compared to benchmarks, but no third party verified the returns for many years.

Furthermore, the aggregate results for buyout funds make no adjustment for survivorship bias. Funds that close or stop reporting are not included in the return results generated by the PE data services on which many investors rely. A reasoned conclusion is that such funds are underperformers, which indicates an upward slant to published returns, although the precise impact of survivorship bias is impossible to discern.

One-Year Returns

The industry's year-to-year records, as opposed to long-term gains, also pose questions. The Preqin data service is a good illustration. Preqin determines single-year industry performance (dividends plus alleged capital gains) by gathering data from hundreds of funds. Over the last sixteen years for which Preqin has information, the cumulative return for buyouts, assuming each of the sixteen-year single returns was accurate, was a multiplier of over seven times. This number suggests that an investor in a representative set of LBO funds has a compound annual IRR of 17 percent. At this IRR, a $1,000 investment at January 1, 2004, becomes over $10,000 in 2019, but that result is much higher than fund cumulative track records over the period. The results thus look suspect, throwing the entire horizon reporting system into question (see table 4.1).

Buyout Returns and Lines of Credit

The use of credit lines is a financial engineering gimmick that allows a buyout fund to juice up its returns. It artificially shortens the holding period of a portfolio company for the purposes of the IRR calculation, a statistic presented to large database services. How did the gimmick originate? As buyout funds grew, the funds themselves attained the ability to borrow on their own earnings power. With their own balance sheets, they supplemented their financial strength with a pledge (to the lending bank) of anticipated institutional capital commitments. Initially, the funds used the credit lines to bridge short-term finance needs so they could reduce the frequency of calling investors for money—for example, having a cash call once every three months instead of monthly.[13] Over time, the practice morphed into gaming returns. The funds began to buy companies well in advance of investor pay-ins.

Table 4.1
U.S. buyout horizon returns—one-year periods

1 year to Dec. 2004	29%
1 year to Dec. 2005	38%
1 year to Dec. 2006	31%
1 year to Dec. 2007	25%
1 year to Dec. 2008	–30%
1 year to Dec. 2009	15%
1 year to Dec. 2010	21%
1 year to Dec. 2011	9%
1 year to Dec. 2012	15%
1 year to Dec. 2013	20%
1 year to Dec. 2014	15%
1 year to Dec. 2015	15%
1 year to Dec. 2016	13%
1 year to Dec. 2017	21%
1 year to Dec. 2018	13%
1 year to Dec. 2019	20%
Cumulative Return	**991%**
Compound Annual Return	*17%*

Source: Preqin, Cambridge Associates.
Note: This book uses statistics generated from paywalled private equity databases, such as Preqin, Pitchbook, and Cambridge Associates. The statistics are not static, and, depending on the statistic, the statistic may change over time, as the databases input new information. The book provides statistics at the latest available time as of the writing of the book. The statistics cannot be specifically referenced by author, article, title, or web link.
Note: The IRRs do not adjust for credit-line usage, investor cash waiting in the bank, vintage year shifting by funds, 40 percent of nonreporting funds, or alleged LBO price-fixing. The IRRs assume accurate valuation of unsold investments.

The database services did not develop a means to track credit line usage and the resultant impact of returns.

With credit line money, a buyout fund purchases a company in March, for example. However, it requests the needed equity money from its investors in September, a six-month delay. If the fund sells the business for a profit three years later, the fund's IRR on that particular investment is several points higher with the credit line than without the credit line. It is a statistical sleight of hand, like increasing a baseball player's batting average from 0.260 to 0.290 by eliminating every third strikeout.

Enhancing the IRR with a credit line on a single deal seems trivial, but if a fund expands the practice to multiple transactions (and if its overall portfolio is doing well), the credit line helps the fund eclipse the customary 8 percent IRR hurdle rate. This accomplishment allows the fund managers to participate in fund profits (i.e., a carried interest). Credit-line-using funds also gain an advantage in the all-important quartile rankings vis-à-vis their peers that do not use lines. The result is a race to the bottom as funds increasingly resort to credit lines (see figure 4.2).

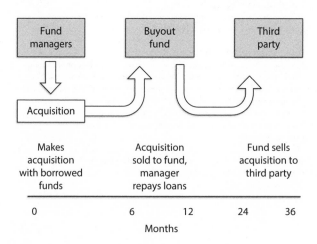

FIGURE 4.2 Illustration of credit line use

Speaking to a somewhat different practice, famous investor Warren Buffett commented at Berkshire Hathaway's May 2019 annual meeting about PE firms elevating performance. Some firms include money that is sitting in treasury bills waiting to be deployed when charging management fees, but they exclude it when calculating so-called IRR. "It's not as good as it looks," Buffett said.[14]

Top-Quartile Rankings

PE funds that fall into the top quartile (or top 25 percent) of their peer group, in terms of performance, are the funds that provide investors with the preponderance of returns over and above the stock market. This is a well-known fact; and thus, buyout funds clamor for the opportunity to register in the top quartile. Such placement ensures a successful money-raising round for a successor fund (see table 4.2).

The proliferation of funds purporting to be top-quartile performers prompted several academics to examine the classification process. They published articles with titles, such as "Are Too Many Private Equity Funds Top Quartile?" and "Top Quartile Status Doesn't Tell Us Much." What they found was a lack of reliable data and a lack of standardization of measurement in the industry. By choosing the data set that serves them best (Preqin, Pitchbook, Thomson Reuters, Burgiss, or Cambridge Associates),

Table 4.2
Quartile buyout fund rankings and comparative returns

1st	Significant premium to S&P 500
2nd	Modest premium to S&P 500
3rd	Modest deficit to S&P 500
4th	Significant loss to S&P 500

and by shifting into or out of an adjacent start-date definition, up to 77 percent of funds (instead of 25 percent) can assert top-quartile status.[15] Garrison Keillor's fictional Lake Wobegon, "where all the children are above average," has a true-to-life parallel in the LBO industry.

Remarking on the confused quartile rankings, the board member of one foundation told me, "Everybody can spin data on quartile rankings. I'm fascinated that there isn't more rigorous info out there." The trade association for limited partners (i.e., investors) in the PE class, the Institutional Limited Partners Association (ILPA), encourages a more rigorous ranking procedure, but the ILPA has no power to enforce its recommendations.

LBO Performance By the Numbers

Recognizing the limitations of the available data, this chapter now turns to numerical measurement of LBO fund performance. Due to the illiquid nature of the assets and the fund manager's ability to time cash flows in and out of a fund, a consensus on the best measurement technique is difficult to reach. Academics, industry participants, and data services use six or seven tools. The most popular are the IRR, the Kaplan-Schoar Public Market Equivalent (KS-PME), and the total value to paid-in (TVPI).

IRR

The IRR measures the annualized percentage return of a fund. For a layperson, a comparator is a bond yield, which appears in many newspapers and business websites. If a bond's yield is 5 percent, for example, that is the discount rate at which the future cash flows are equal to the bond's current price. Similarly, to calculate an LBO fund's IRR, you first plot the fund's historical cash payments on a timeline, and then you determine what percentage discount rate makes the future payments equal to the initial investments. The IRR determination assumes that unsold investments have the value assigned to them by the fund manager and that they are sold on the calculation's final date.

The attraction of the IRR for LBO funds is that it is easy to contrast IRRs between asset classes, like bonds, stocks, PE, and real estate. The disadvantage, from the investor's point of view, is that the IRR has the potential for manipulation. A fund manager can deliberately push asset sales to the front of the timeline, which has the effect of artificially increasing the IRR—possibly at the expense of overall cash profits during the fund's life. Some researchers have hinted that PE funds sometimes sell winners early to demonstrate future profits and to tee up marketing campaigns for their successor funds (see figure 4.3).

Another criticism of the IRR is that the calculation presumes that early cash distributions are reinvested by the investor at the same IRR. If the IRR is unduly high because of some early distributions, then many argue that the entire calculation is inflated—particularly for a long-lived asset such as a PE fund. Apollo's Leon Black says that since a 1990 inception, Apollo's buyout funds

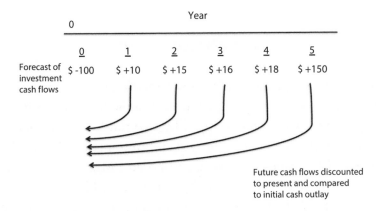

FIGURE 4.3 Discounted cash flow illustration

Table 4.3
Internal rates of returns—annualized (%)
U.S. buyouts versus the S&P 500
Years ending June 30, 2020

	Years			
	1	*3*	*5*	*10*
Buyouts	(0.5) %	9.9 %	11.8 %	13.9 %
S&P 500	7.5	10.7	10.8	14.0
Public market premium	8.0	0.8	(1.0)	0.1

Source: Pitchbook

Note: The buyout IRRs do not adjust for credit-line usage, investor cash waiting in the bank at low interest rates, vintage year shifting, 40% nonreporting funds, or alleged LBO price-fixing. The PE IRRs assume accurate valuation of unsold investments and provide no IRR penalty for the illiquidity of PE funds. June 30, 2020 PE results became available January 5, 2021.

have a net-to-investor of IRR of 24 percent.[16] The strict calculation is probably accurate, but, by appearances, this claim sounds misleading, since an original investor of $1 million in 1990 would therefore have a 2020 payoff of $1.3 billion.

Set forth in table 4.3 are LBO fund IRRs and public stock market IRRs as of June 30, 2020, reflecting the latest PE results available in early 2021.

Kaplan-Schoar PME

Public market equivalent (PME) is a metric used to compare private equity performance to public stock indices.[17] The KS-PME is an ingenious invention developed by two finance professors, Steven Kaplan (University of Chicago) and Antoinette Scholar (MIT). The KS-PME refines two earlier proposed PMEs, and it resolves some of the IRR's limitations by discounting PE cash flows by the stock market index value. Simply put, the stock market has a discounted value of 1.0, so a PE fund with a KS-PME score of more than 1.0 provides a better return than the stock market. For example, a 1.1 score over a ten-year fund life indicates that the fund earned 10 percent more than if the money was placed in the S&P 500 index. The calculation tracks PE funds by vintage year—namely, the year in which the fund began investing money. The main problem with the KS-PME is that it ignores the timing of cash flows, so the early payments, which investors tend to prefer, do not receive their proper recognition, although it has other flaws as well.

Industry participants usually benchmark LBO returns against the S&P 500, which is considered representative of the broad U.S. stock market. As a buyout fund comparator, the S&P 500 has several flaws. One, it encompasses exceptionally large companies, when LBOs are smaller in size. Two, its results are skewed by well-performing high-tech companies. Three, most S&P 500 firms do not fit the LBO profile. Four, the KS-PME excludes an LBO fund penalty (or an IRR premium) for the fact that an investor's money is tied up for ten years. For comparison purposes, the more circumspect members of the institutional community impose a 3 percent annual premium to the S&P 500 returns to account for illiquidity, which removes any hint of perceived buyout-to-S&P 500 favorability. Various observers have developed PMEs that adjust for these factors, including myself, but they have not attained the acceptance of the KS-PME. Even with the KS-PME measurement system working in the industry's favor, the buyout results are less than stellar (see table 4.4).

Total Value to Paid-in

A third important metric is the total value to paid in (TVPI). "Total value" is the sum of (1) the amount of cash distributed to investors plus (2) the estimated value of the unsold companies at the measurement date. The total value (1 + 2 = 3) is divided by the

Table 4.4
LBO funds and KS-PME result scores

Vintage year	KS-PME score
2005	1.2
2006	1.1
2007	1.1
2008	1.0
2009	1.2
2010	1.2
2011	1.3
2012	1.3
2013	1.3
2014	1.3
2015	1.3
2016	1.1
2017	1.3
2018	1.0
2019	1.0

Source: Prequin.
Note: A score > 1.0 indicates a fund year that beat the S&P 500 return. The TVPI does not adjust for credit line usage, vintage year shifting, 40% nonreporting funds, or alleged LBO price-fixing. The scores assume accurate valuation of unsold investments and no penalty for PE illiquidity. Through June 30, 2020; results became available January 5, 2021.

amount of investor money placed into the fund (paid-in capital) to produce (4) the TVPI ratio. A ratio above 1.0 means the fund's total value exceeds the invested capital, and therefore the fund has a profit. A ratio below 1.0 indicates a loss. Since it cannot be easily manipulated, the TVPI ratio is the ratio I prefer to use.

TVPI's principal positive attribute is its easy-to-grasp mechanics. The key negative, as Antonella Puca, senior director of Alvarez & Marsal, explains, "is that it does not account for the timing of cash flows. A critical question is how much actual value the fund has generated for its investors. This includes the unrealized component, or the fair value of the investments in the fund's portfolio as of the measurement date. A TVPI of 1.3 indicates that, based on the current investment valuation, the fund has generated 130 cents for every dollar invested. However, this ratio does not indicate when the cash contributions took place, how long the fund took to generate the 30-cent return, or what the fund's rate of return is on an annualized basis."[18]

"Most private equity managers assert that they are trying to achieve a 2.0 TVPI," or twice their initial investment, indicates Callan Associates—although the managers generally fall short of this goal.[19] Over the last fifteen years, Calpers, the State of California's mega pension fund, had an average 1.5 TVPI for its PE holdings. North Carolina's TVPI was 1.4.

One illustration of translating an IRR into a TVPI is to assume (1) a five-year average life for a fund's investments and (2) a 15 percent annual return. These two assumptions generate a TVPI of 2.0. As one example, the State of Oregon's sizeable PE portfolio produced a 2.0 TVPI for the early-1981–2004 period. After 2004, not one year attained a 2.0 result, and the average over the last fifteen years was 1.5. As average holding periods have crept up to five-and-one-half years, that 1.5 score equals a 7.6 percent IRR. This result is hardly the fantastical return claimed by the industry (see table 4.5).

Table 4.5
State of Oregon pension plan—average TVPI by PE vintage year for selected periods

2019–2005	2019–2010	2019–2015	2014–2010	2009–2005
15 years	10 years	5 years	5 years	5 years
1.5	1.5	1.2	1.7	1.5

Source: State of Oregon pension fund, private equity reviews, 2018, 2019.
Note: The PE inputs assume accurate valuation of unsold investments. A score > 1.0 indicates a fund year that earned a profit.

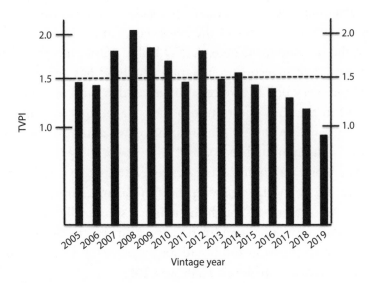

FIGURE 4.4 Buyout fund TVPI results

Another way to analyze TVPI is to review the aggregate industry statistics by vintage year from a PE data service. The result is
like Oregon's (see figure 4.4).

Buyout Industry Tactics for Surpassing
Public Equity Returns

The buyout fund industry emphasizes four tactics that purport-
edly enable it to exceed public stock market returns.

- Using high leverage
- Improving an acquisition's operations
- Attaining critical mass
- Buying right

Using High Leverage

Leverage (or the use of debt) amplifies equity returns, both on the upside and the downside. Take the case of two identical LBO profile companies, one with a debt-to-equity ratio of 2:1 (true LBO) and the other with a debt-to-equity ratio of 1:2. If both companies grow earnings at 5 percent per year and both have a "going in" and "going out" price of 8× operating income, the LBO equity return is four to five percentage points higher with more debt than without. Of course, the opposite relationship occurs when growth falters or M&A prices decline. Then the debt payments "crowd out" equity returns, providing for a substandard result.

Supplementing a buyout's initial leverage is the occasional financial engineering of a portfolio company. If the company's operations have improved but the M&A market is not favorable for a sale, the fund may direct the portfolio company to issue even more debt on top of acquisition loans and to use the proceeds to pay a cash dividend to the fund.[20] In 2019, for example, Sycamore Partners Fund II received a $1 billion dividend from Staples, one of its portfolio companies, in this manner. The dividend returned most of Sycamore's original investment, setting the deal up for an attractive IRR. In 2019, fund manager Leonard Green & Partners sold the real estate of its hospital chain, Prospect Medical Holdings, for $1.55 billion and then leased the real estate back from the new owner. Interest expense declined, but rental costs rose. The sale proceeds were applied to debt reduction and a cash dividend for the Green fundholders. In certain respects, such financial engineering endangers the credit quality of existing loans by piling new loans on top of old ones. From time to time, initial buyout lenders complain about the transactions, failing to recognize that they agreed to have their loan documents written to permit such actions in the first place.

With the American economy and corporate earnings expanding over forty years, the public stock and M&A markets have experienced sustained value gains, so more corporate leverage, in general, has been a successful tactic in enhancing equity returns of listed companies. High leverage is the foundation of the buyout business, but investor returns have been sidetracked in recent years by both high acquisition prices and high management fees.

The leverage tactic is not foolproof. Many portfolio companies do not perform as projected. Earnings fall or valuations collapse. Researchers at California State Polytechnic University deduced that 20 percent of LBO's go bankrupt,[21] and their statistics are corroborated by the bond rating agencies' experience with lower rated junk bond categories (i.e., B and CCC), which comprise firms that have the equivalent of buyout debt or are themselves LBOs.[22] Bankruptcies are disasters for buyout funds, for the return to equity investors is usually zero. By way of corroboration of the researchers and bond rating agency findings, three of the top ten buyout deals, or 30 percent, went bankrupt: Energy Futures Holdings, Harrah's Entertainment, and Clear Channel.

Buyout leverage has waned. As M&A prices rose in the 2010s, LBO lenders were reluctant to raise leverage accordingly, and the debt-to-value ratio declined. "The old days of slapping on 80 percent debt and seeing what happens are gone," one buyout veteran told me in March 2020. Sixty percent to 70 percent ratios are closer to the norm as of this writing.

Operational Improvements

Part of the industry's lore is that acquired companies raise their profit margins once under fund ownership. For the large, publicly traded firms that have gone private, the argument goes that top managers gain a bigger potential ownership interest in the buyout than under the public model. This opportunity for substantial wealth motivates them to work harder and to pinch pennies more than they do under the public model, thus increasing the acquisition's profit margins. For the smaller deals, which are mostly family-owned companies or cast-off corporate divisions, the portfolio firms supposedly foster profit upgrades by using their fund owners' superior networks and resources to bring in top-level experts who assist the incumbent executives in changing ingrained habits, taking sensible risks, and implementing modern management techniques. In a *Harvard Business Review* article, Felix Barber and Michael Gold summed up the concept: "The private equity firms' standard practice is buying businesses and then, after steering them through a transition of rapid performance improvement, selling them."[23]

The logic behind these assertions is compelling, but the actual evidence supporting it is mixed. The challenge for outside analysts is a shortage of available historical accounting data for a sizeable number of LBOs due to the private nature of the asset class. Independent academic researchers have had problems reaching conclusions. The best repositories for the information are the major banks, which arrange and syndicate large buyout loans as well as nonbank lenders, like Antares Capital, that specialize in smaller deals. However, their business is making new loans, not publishing research papers.

One fact that brings skepticism to the operational improvement theory is that a quarter of new LBOs are recycled old LBOs, whereby one buyout fund sells to another buyout fund. Since the first fund supposedly squeezed out the unrealized efficiencies from the portfolio company, there should be few refinements left for the new owner. My experience as an investment banker supports the operational improvement thesis to some degree, but the enhanced margins come at the expense of longer-lived investments in personnel and R&D. That being said, "no operating fix will remedy paying too much for a business," says David Wasserman, partner at LBO fund manager Clayton Dubilier & Rice.[24] Paying an appropriate price for an acquisition target is paramount in achieving fund profit goals.[25]

Attaining Critical Mass

When value is expressed as a multiple of EBITDA, a general rule in the M&A field is that large companies are sold for bigger value multiples than small companies. The reason for the disparity is the fact that small companies carry the perception of greater risk until they become big companies. The small company, in comparison to a similar big company, has a limited product line, more customer concentration, a thinner management team, and other negatives that indicate a greater likelihood of either failure or inconsistency.

As a means to exploit the value differences, many PE funds assemble a collection of small competitors, say, at a 7× EV/EBITDA price. The funds combine the companies into one big competitor, realize the attendant synergies, and then sell the operation at 9× EBITDA either to a *Fortune* 500 buyer, a larger buyout fund, or the IPO market. The higher value multiple assigned to the bigger business, 9× versus 7×, ensures a hefty profit for the LBO fund. The investor community refers to this technique as "buy and build," "roll-up," "consolidation," or "platform build-up." Among many good examples is Caliber Collision, a PE-backed operation that acquired over one hundred auto body shops to become the leader in its industry (see figure 4.5).

The buy-and-build approach works for many buyout funds, but there are no guarantees. The tactic takes time to fully implement, requires the successful integration of many small operations, and depends on finding multiple deals at reasonable prices. John Poerink, partner at Linley Capital, expresses this sentiment well: "Consolidations are incredibly difficult and many fail."[26] Nonetheless, achieving critical mass through M&A dovetails nicely

Platform company acquiring smaller competitors

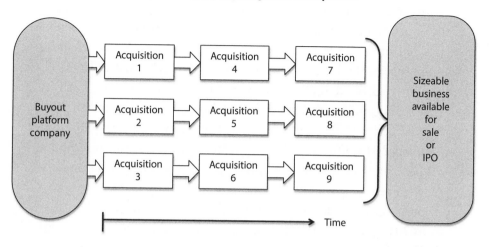

FIGURE 4.5 The buy and build approach

with the skill set of buyout fund professionals, and the technique is immensely popular.

Buying Right

The last tactic for generating better returns than the stock market is buying right. An index fund, by definition, is fully invested and constantly changing in value with the vagaries of the stock market. A PE fund, in contrast, has the flexibility to "pick its spots" when committing money. It can try to time deals when M&A prices are at a low ebb.

Furthermore, unlike an index fund, the buyout fund has access to inside information when it negotiates the purchase of equity. Onsite inspections, management meetings, and detailed financial projections are part of the M&A process. This extra information gives the fund a leg up compared to public stock investors.

In certain public-company to private-company deals, public stockholders have complained that corporate management favored one PE fund over other possible buyers. In the ensuing sale process, the fund did not pay top dollar. The $24 billion Dell buyout registered such protests, as major shareholders, such as Carl Icahn and Southeastern Asset Management, resisted the PE-backed offer. Their protests changed little, and the deal closed in October 2013. One year later, the Silver Lake buyout fund had a 90 percent return on its Dell investment, according to Bloomberg News, even as the stock market rose just 11 percent. The sharp disparity gave credence to the stockholder objections.

In 2014, seven of the largest buyout fund managers settled, for $590 million, a class action lawsuit alleging the funds conspired to drive down takeover prices and reduce competition for numerous deals in the mid-2000s. Economic analyses, outlined in the *University of Cincinnati Law Review*, showed that "the cost to shareholders in the eight litigated multi-billion leveraged buyout transactions approached $12 billion."[27] If the accusations were true and if the estimate was accurate, LBO returns for the period partly resulted from unseemly behavior rather than investment acumen. The number is higher if the calculation includes other deals rumored to have similar issues, and it is possible thirty or forty basis points of the industry's annual return came from such activity, if true, during those years.

M&A price rises have a strong correlation to stock market values. Over the last ten years, the average U.S. M&A deal (including buyouts) increased in size from by 50 percent, and the value multiples rose.[28] Speaking to this topic, a small-market buyout fund manager said, "Our first fund had an average acquisition price of 6× (EV/EBITDA), the second of 7×, and the third (in 2020) is 8×." Private equity prices for larger deals (i.e., over $250 million), expressed as an EV/EBITDA multiple, climbed 35 percent over the same time frame.

The following list illustrates the four tactics for enhancing value.

FOUR BUYOUT FUND TACTICS FOR SURPASSING PUBLIC STOCK MARKET PERFORMANCE

- *Using high leverage:* Maximizing the portfolio company's debt load to enhance the equity holders' return
- *Improving portfolio company operations:* Cutting costs and boosting revenues through efficiencies and sophisticated management
- *Attaining critical mass:* "Rolling up" many small competitors into a big portfolio company
- *Buying right:* Searching for acquisition bargains and schedule purchases for times when M&A prices are relatively low.

Closing

The buyout fund industry's performance results lack the specificity one expects of a trillion-dollar industry. Year-to-year returns are heavily reliant on the managers' estimation of the value of their portfolio companies, most of which are unsold even after holding periods exceeding five years. Cumulative investor profits are influenced by credit lines and cash deposits. Forty percent of funds do not report their results to centralized databases for comparison purposes. Benchmark performance statistics, like the IRR, can be manipulated by fund managers.

My instinct, developed from years in finance, tells me a universal, standardized, above-board performance metric would show returns 2 percent to 3 percent lower on an annualized IRR basis, and 10 percent to 15 percent lower on a TVPI basis, compared to those reported by the industry. Implementing such a metric would require cooperation (or acquiescence) among so many government and industry players as to make the task a practical impossibility.

Acquiring companies at the bottom of the stock market/M&A cycle may be the best approach for LBO funds. One study of buyout returns found that firms acquired at below-average EV/ EBITDA ratios provided the bulk of a fund's profits. Of course, buying at the bottom involves prescient market timing, and few finance professionals are fortune tellers. Adhering to the four tactics set forth herein is no sure thing.

A good rule of thumb in the LBO business is that in a portfolio of ten deals, three provide no return, four make modest profits, and three bring about most gains. The randomness of the big payoffs is unavoidable. Despite the best efforts of buyout fund managers, the goal of consistently beating the stock market for their investors remains elusive, even as the fund managers themselves do very well from a financial point of view.

5

Private Equity and the Holy Grail

IN THE MOVIE *Indiana Jones and the Last Crusade*, the hero assists his father in searching for the Holy Grail, an ancient object with mystical powers that provides its holder with happiness and eternal youth. People risked their lives to attain the grail. If Indiana Jones were to enter the finance profession today, he would hear of another talisman that was long sought after for its significance.

For decades, modern portfolio theory adherents, which include most institutional investors, have engaged in their own quest—a dedicated exploration for an asset that avoids the worst of the stock market's ups and downs yet offers returns that are not only higher than public equities but also substantially greater than those offered by well-rated, fixed-income bonds, which are the traditional haven for risk-averse investors. During the last four decades, the pursuit has ranged far and wide, covering various asset classes, and U.S. institutional investors have traveled to distant lands to seek out such an asset and test it in their portfolios. Candidates for this fabled asset have included convertible bonds, junk bonds, real estate, commodities, international stocks, portfolio insurance, hedge funds, PE, and infrastructure plays. All these asset classes, including buyouts, have encountered problems in fulfilling the goals set out for them.

The marketing of LBO funds relies heavily on their assertion of higher returns versus the stock market. Together with this assertion is a declaration of lower risk, which the industry defines as buyout returns having less variation, or more evenness, than the stock market. Imagine buyouts being a smooth ride in a Cadillac down New York's Fifth Avenue and public company stock prices being an excursion in a pick-up truck on a bumpy country road. If the industry's marketing slogan of "low risk, high return" is true, the combined attributes make buyouts the Holy Grail of the investment business. A graphical representation of the purported risk-return relationship between LBOs and other asset classes appears as figure 5.1.

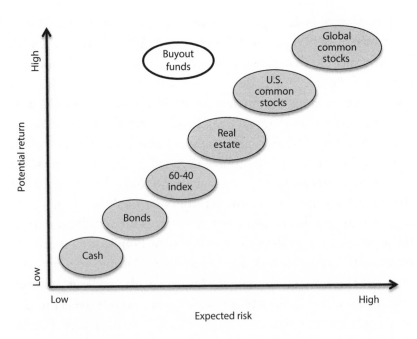

FIGURE 5.1 Asset class: risk return chart. *Note*: Buyout fund industry claims lower risks and higher returns than publicly-traded U.S. stocks.

To calculate the return variations, PE data services compile the year-to-year returns for the industry. The year-to-year returns incorporate a survey of hundreds of LBO funds, which report on their cash distributions and asset value changes over a twelve-month period. The industry calls these one-year returns horizon returns. The determination thus differs from earlier tabulations in this book that focused on a fund's cumulative performance, which was expressed as an IRR, PME, or TVPI statistic. Having examined many buyout fund reports, I retain a high degree of skepticism with respect to this year-to-year data, because it shows that a highly levered asset has a more even performance than an unlevered asset. Table 5.1 shows the latest available Preqin LBO returns (as of this writing) compared to the S&P 500.

Of particular import is the alleged performance of buyout funds during stock market downturns. The results, mostly self-reported, show buyouts losing less than the S&P 500 index, which seems implausible. Using a home-buying analogy, if the real estate market drops by 20 percent one year after purchase, a home buyer employing a 20 percent down/80 percent mortgage financing tactic loses the entire down payment and experiences a 100 percent negative investment return. The all-equity buyer, in contrast, has a minus 20 percent return and retains 80 percent of the home's value. The greater leverage of the first buyer accentuated his or her loss. For stock market and LBO data during downturns, when the differences in results are pronounced, see table 5.2.

Seven years ago, Ted Barnhill and I developed a custom public stock index that mimicked the attributes of those public companies taken private through buyouts. As set forth in the *Journal of Indexes*, the index excluded firms that fell outside of the LBO profile, such as high-tech firms, cyclical businesses, financial companies, money-losers, and those with spotty track records.[1] We found that our index provided good defensive positions during the high-tech rout of 2000–2002, but it offered little protection

Table 5.1
One-year LBO fund horizon returns

Year ended December 31	LBO fund reported results	S&P 500
1999	27.8%	21.0%
2000	2.2%	–9.1%
2001	–12.8%	–11.9%
2002	–3.8%	–22.1%
2003	21.0%	28.7%
2004	28.8%	10.9%
2005	38.3%	4.9%
2006	30.5%	15.8%
2007	24.9%	5.5%
2008	–29.7%	–37.0%
2009	14.6%	26.5%
2010	21.4%	15.1%
2011	9.4%	2.1%
2012	14.6%	16.0%
2013	20.0%	32.3%
2014	14.8%	13.7%
2015	14.9%	1.4%
2016	12.6%	12.0%
2017	20.7%	21.8%
2018	12.8%	–4.4%
2019	21.0%	31.5%

Source: Prequin and Standard & Poor's
Note: the rows in gray are the years in which the stock market dropped considerably, yet the more leveraged buyout fund equity investments dropped less in supposed price. This buyout fund price behavior contradicts fundamental finance theory. With few exceptions, the institutional investment class, the business media, and the finance academy take the PE industry's mark-to-market data at face value.

Table 5.2
Buyout funds versus S&P 500—market premiums

	Buyout reported results	S&P 500	Event
2000–2002	–14.3%	–37.5%	Dot-com internet collapse
2008	–29.7	–37.0	Financial crisis
2011	+9.4	+2.1	U.S. treasury bond credit rating downgrade
2018	+12.8	–4.3	recession fears, China trade war concerns

during the 2008 crash, when the breadth of stock price declines covered both low-tech and high-tech sectors.

As an aside, Barnhill and I tried to sell our buyout replication index methodology to several leading index companies, and we had a few discussions with S&P Dow Jones, the leading index provider offering dozens of stock market indexes on technology stocks, consumer stocks, energy stocks, and other stock sectors. After some investigation, S&P told us, "It's an interesting concept, but we don't think anyone will buy it." The institutional investment community, apparently, did not want an independent benchmark to corroborate their PE investment claims.

In 2017, the *Journal of Private Equity* published a research study titled, "The Curious Year-to-Year Performance of Buyout Fund Returns: Another Mark to Market Problem?"[2] In the study, Ken Yook and I developed a similar mimic index with sophisticated market weightings and industry classifications. One notable data point was 2008, when U.S. stocks had a negative 38 percent return, and our proxy index (before adding LBO-type debt) had a negative 37 percent return. Strangely, the buyout industry itself claimed a more favorable 26 percent return after all fees, *despite its significant debts*. The industry's smaller loss, compared to the two indexes, made little sense and defied classical financial theory regarding leverage and return volatility. An unlikely counterargument might be that, among other matters, (1) PE values, for some reason, deviated sharply from corresponding public stocks; or (2) our proxy was an inaccurate representation of underlying buyout portfolio companies. Indeed, adjusting for buyout leverage, our proxy-index return for public stocks was negative 75 percent in 2008, a remarkable difference with the industry's reported 26 percent. Had anything near the 75 percent been disclosed by the industry, the buyout phenomena would have ended in 2008 (see table 5.3).

An example shows the accelerated drop in value that a highly leveraged firm experiences during an equity market slump. Consider two identical companies: Normal Co. and LBO Co. Both have an enterprise value of $1 billion. Normal Co.'s debt to enterprise value ratio is 35 percent and LBO Co.'s ratio is 70 percent. An economic crisis occurs, and the enterprise value of both firms falls by an equal 20 percent. The impact on Normal Co.'s stock price is minus 31 percent, a steep drop, yet the decline for LBO Co. stock is far worse, 67 percent (see figure 5.2).

Table 5.3
Year-to-year returns during market downturns with proxy index

Year ending Dec. 31	Replication index[1]	Adjusted replication index	Buyout funds[2]	S&P 500	Event
2002	–22.8%	–46.2%	–3.8%	–22.1%	Dot-com crash
2008	–37.6	–75.0	–29.7	–37.0	Financial crisis
2011	–5.0	–9.9	+9.4	+3.1	European debt crisis, U.S. government credit downgrade
2018	–6.7	–11.7	–12.8	–4.4	Recession fears

[1]Our composite buyout replication index was derived, in part, from the Russell 2000 indexes.
[2]Annual returns of buyout funds by Prequin.

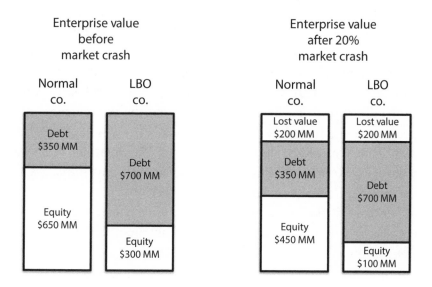

FIGURE 5.2 More leverage: LBO stock should fall 67 percent in price in a downturn

Despite the logic of "more debt means more value drops in a downturn," PE funds professed that the value of their acquisitions during market crashes behaved exactly the opposite—namely, buyout values fell less than those of similar public companies with low debt; and, therefore, according to buyout fund managers, their LBO portfolios were less risky than public stocks. On its face, the "less volatile" contention is ridiculous, and the Holy Grail a mirage. How can a highly leveraged portfolio of companies (i.e., LBOs) be less risky than a similar portfolio of firms with little or no debt? The evidence suggests an industry practice of smoothing its returns, so that the yearly ups and downs of its returns are less than the those of the stock market.[3] By rubbing off the rough edges of their annual results, the industry justifies a low-risk profile and supports its low-risk marketing proposition.

The same circumstance is evident in the real estate PE business. In the 1990s, multiple researchers identified the smoothing phenomenon when comparing the results of publicly traded real estate investment trusts (REITs) to PE real estate funds.[4] The underlying assets of both investment classes were identical, but the real estate PE funds had less pronounced ups and downs in annual returns than the publicly traded property index. Inexplicably, the regulators, like the SEC, ignored the discrepancy.[5] No persuasive argument has ever been offered as to why the volatility of private real estate should be less than the volatility of listed real estate. Return volatility is a trait inherent in investable assets themselves, not in the form of their ownership.

Despite the likelihood of buyout fund smoothing, most observers accept the industry's numbers without question. By way of illustration:

> Our research has shown that returns in private markets are less volatile than in public markets, where both the peaks and valleys of performance are more extreme. Since 2001, PE trailed public markets in 24 of the 28 quarters when the S&P 500 total return was up 5 percent or more. Conversely, PE funds have outperformed in all 21 of the quarters in which the S&P 500 total return was negative over that period. We think this historical pattern will hold in the current environment.[6]
>
> The potential benefits of private equity's structural characteristics are perhaps most evident when markets are under stress. During previous U.S. bear markets, private equity experienced about half of U.S. equities total downturn, on average.[7]

Swinging against the tide of illogic, a growing chorus of analysts have expressed skepticism over this common practice of flattening out year to year LBO results. For example:

> Yet private equity funds represent equity positions in corporates. Hence this low volatility must be artificial, the product of smoothed valuations. Private equity portfolio companies

are influenced by the economic tides just as much as public companies, even if they don't want this reflected in their valuations.[8]

Many pension funds are picking PE because they don't have to mark down the value of the assets as steeply in a downturn, saying "This was a silly reason to buy something."[9]

In 2013, I filed a whistleblower complaint with the Securities and Exchange Commission (SEC) outlining my belief that the smoothing practice was apparent; and, thus, the LBO funds were consciously, or unconsciously, inducing investors to buy-in on the unsound basis of low risk. Providing misleading or inaccurate return data in investor marketing materials is a violation of federal securities laws, and I thought the funds were getting away with submitting fallacious information. Given the billions involved, the complaint, if proven true, could have brought forth noticeable enforcement action. The SEC did not pursue the matter at the time.

Adding evidence to the industry's choreography of private company portfolio values is a 2020 study concluding that "the typical fund experiences a falloff in returns (or performance measures) after it is about seven or eight years old." This study thus indicates that early valuations were uniformly optimistic and then, as time wore on, the funds pushed the values downward when reality set in and the funds sold the companies at fair market prices.[10]

The Mark-to-Market Process for Buyout Funds

To properly document their performance, buyout funds regularly adjust their portfolio company values to reflect financial conditions. This practice is called mark-to-market. Because LBOs, by definition, have long historical track records, funds rely in part on projecting those past results into the future during the mark-to-market exercise. For instance, analysts say, "Amazon has good financial value because the firm's forecast earnings are going to rise quickly."

An equally important valuation approach are comparables, whereby a subject company's worth is determined by the pricing of similar public companies and recent merger deals. Analysts say, "Chevron's $13 billion acquisition of Noble Energy sets a valid foundation for oil sector M&A pricing." For LBO profile firms, the comparable valuation process is straightforward; the comparable companies have long track records and easily understood, low-tech operations. If publicly traded Ingles Markets is valued at 8× EV/EBITDA, then a similar supermarket LBO should have the same ratio. Using this approach, two professionals with the exact same information should not show more than a 10 percent to 15 percent difference in attendant values.

The abuse of mark-to-market accounting has produced notable wrongdoings. The 2001 collapse of Enron, a 1990s stock market darling, and the vaporization of its $70 billion market value, was due principally to Enron's accounting fraud, regarding hard-to-value derivatives, long-term contracts, and private securities. At the same time, the 1990s internet boom saw closely held high-tech companies handing out stock options to senior executives at undervalued prices of pennies per share, depriving the government of tax revenue as executive income was understated. A multitude of such incidents provoked regulatory step ups. In response, the accounting profession issued *Statement of Financial Accounting Standards 157*, a several-hundred-page manual that provided a step-by-step guide for how a financial professional should value a private business.[11] Most LBO funds used mark-to-market accounting before *SFAs 157*, but this guidance (now known as *Accountings Standards Codification 820*) became a useful point of reference for practitioners. The latitude in interpreting the guidelines became an issue and provided some wiggle room in the valuation exercise.

Mark-to-Market in the Real-World

Estimating the value of a private business is part science and part subjectivity. Accounting pronouncements, commercial books, and MBA courses describe the process in chapter and verse. The selection of future growth rates for the subject company earnings, for example, or picking a comparable public business for an analysis, involves a degree of judgment. The problem arises when this judgment consistently favors the buyout community and its school of thought.

At an LBO fund, the mark-to-market process begins internally. An employee and—in the case of large funds—a dedicated valuation team, prepares written valuation reports on each portfolio holding. For small- to medium-sized fund groups, an outside third-party, called a fund administrator, frequently assists in generating the information included in the reports, so there is a degree of independent input. The fund then presents the reports to its certified public accounting firm, which reviews the valuations for reasonableness (see figure 5.3).

The Big Four accounting firms—Deloitte, Price Waterhouse, Ernst & Young and KPMG—perform audits on most of the funds over $250 million in assets, and the Big Four each have their own valuation departments staffed with experts. "We are especially interested in any changes in assumptions in the reports from

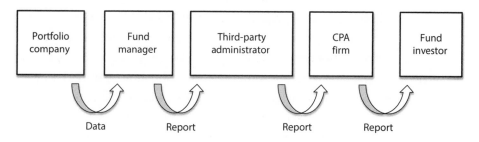

FIGURE 5.3 Portfolio company valuation process

year-to-year," said one Big Four corporate appraiser in May 2020. "Changes, assumptions, and comparables all have to pass a sanity test." Nonetheless, within this framework, there is room for negotiation between the fund and the evaluator, particularly with small funds that cannot afford to pay for intense reviews. "There's definitely some horse-trading," indicated one buyout manager. Another Big Four executive said, "We read the reports carefully. In the end, it is a kind of collaboration, and there is an element of trust between fund and auditor in establishing a valuation."

During market downturns, the published LBO returns thus have a veneer of authenticity, but the custom of highly leveraged firms falling less in value than public companies strains credulity. The accounting rule states that a fund should mark a portfolio company at fair value, or the price it would obtain during an orderly sales process, even if the date in question coincides with a stock market collapse. Yet the industry finds substantial room to operate. With respect to the return smoothing in 2009, one argument I heard was, "The dip was an over-correction; things will bounce back," as if audit firms are soothsayers. Another contention in 2009 was as follows: "Buyout portfolios are protected from stock price fluctuations because fund managers are long-term investors, not short-term speculators." Commenting on the recent March 2020 market dip and the reluctance of funds to knock down valuations significantly, David Larsen, a managing director of valuation advisory firm Duff & Phelps, LLC, said "Taking a severe haircut is a scorched-earth approach. Fair value does not mean fire-sale pricing."[12] Each of these smoothing defenses is overly accommodative to the buyout business, and each prevents investors from seeing a just-in-time snapshot of underlying values. A contrary opinion is expressed by Martin Skancke, the former head of asset management for the Norwegian Ministry of Finance, which controls the massive Norwegian sovereign wealth fund: "For assets like private equity, infrequent valuation gives the appearance of lower volatility, but there might actually be a lot of volatility over the years."[13]

When the stock market fell 19.6 percent in 2020's first quarter, the buyout industry claimed its collective portfolios dropped just 8.9 percent, despite the industry's high leverage. Assuming similar public companies have 35 percent leverage and buyout portfolio firms have 70 percent, the buyout industry's returns for that quarter should have been minus 42.5 percent, not minus 8.9 percent. Attempting to moderate the loss by including M&A deals and discounted cash flow forecasts into the buyout mark-to-market analysis should not convince a sensible evaluator to diminish the minus 42.5 percent and substitute a minus 8.9 percent. In spite of the glaring inconsistency, neither the industry's auditors not its government regulators questioned the March 2020 results. A casual interpretation of this phenomenon writes it off as unmindful valuation processes; a harsher explanation bears the faint smell of securities fraud.

Net Asset Value Practical Expedient

In addition to turning a blind eye to return smoothing, the accounting authorities carve out a special exemption for PE holders. Fund participations are illiquid, hard-to-sell investments with a ten-year lock-in period. The secondary market, should an institutional investor want to sell its share of a fund, is tiny when compared to the industry's total outstandings. This situation causes problems. Suppose a buyout fund has a portfolio of companies with an assigned worth of $1 billion, and a university endowment's share is 10 percent of the buyout fund. In theory, someone should pay the endowment $100 million (10 percent × $1 billion = $100 million) for its share, but in truth secondary buyers demand a discount to the underlying portfolio estimates for a variety of reasons. The pricing protocol is analogous to that of closed-end funds of publicly traded stocks, which historically show a 5 percent to 10 percent discount to the sum of their assets. According to research covering PE secondary transactions, the endowment's $100 million interest likely has a hammer value, of just $86 million, a 14 percent haircut.[14] Moreover, if an accountant follows the Financial Accounting Standard Board's (FASB) own guidelines on appraising nontradeable equities, the revised price is $80 million to $90 million, or a 10 percent to 20 percent discount.

The industry's unusual exemption from normal illiquidity discounts is called the net asset value (NAV) practical expedient convention.[15] It allows PE investors to ignore economic reality and to book their investments at estimated underlying value rather than 10 percent to 20 percent less. No illiquidity discounts make the asset class more attractive to investors than would otherwise be the case. The convention's origins, which date from the mid-2000s, are murky. My curiosity got the better of me, and I called FASB headquarters in Connecticut. When I discussed the matter with a senior analyst, he couldn't recall which outside parties pushed the idea on the FASB, but to me it seemed as if the buyout industry had successfully penetrated the walls of the accounting profession's ivory tower, where the sanctity of principle is meant to be above reproach.

Portfolio Diversification

When the factual basis for higher returns and smoother results appears shaky to sophisticated investors, the industry turns to the last leg of its three-legged marketing stool: diversification. Of the three arguments in support of buyouts—high returns, low risk, and diversification—diversification is the most convincing (see figure 5.4).

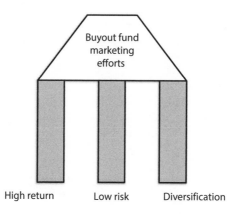

FIGURE 5.4 Three marketing pillars of buyout funds

Diversification is the act of introducing variety. The benefits of diversification to a risk-averse investor are well-known. By owning an index fund with five hundred stocks instead of a highly concentrated portfolio of, say, five stocks, the investor avoids the prospect of the price collapse of just one stock ruining his or her portfolio performance.[16] The risk of one asset or a handful of assets undermining a large portfolio's returns is referred to as idiosyncratic risk. Nonetheless, even the S&P 500 has a degree of idiosyncratic risk, since the top five stocks by index weight—Microsoft, Apple, Amazon, Berkshire Hathaway, and Google—represent 19 percent of its total value. Reducing the idiosyncratic risk of the public stock markets by entering the PE realm is thus a sensible strategy.

The number of U.S. companies with tradeable public stocks approximates four thousand.[17] The number of companies owned by PE, according to the Milken Institute, is seven thousand, with the bulk of them being buyouts.[18] The LBO collective enterprise value is relatively small at $2.5 trillion versus the S&P 500's largest single stock, Microsoft, at $1.4 trillion. By participating in a buyout fund, an institution achieves added diversification through investing

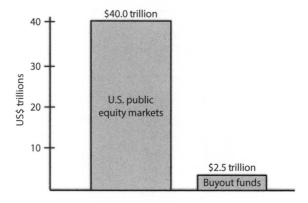

FIGURE 5.5 Public equity markets' enterprise value vs. the buyout industry

indirectly into some of these seven thousand firms. Because of the slight capitalization of these private companies compared to a typical public index component, the benefit may be trivial and perhaps outweighed by management fees, but it is there (see figure 5.5).[19]

A graphical representation of the industry's risk and return claim, versus time-honored investment experience, is set forth above the line in figure 5.6. Slightly below and to the right that historical indicator is the reality that so many institutions and PE fund managers refuse to acknowledge.

Closing

The buyout industry's yearly investment returns are smoothed or ironed out compared to the stock market's returns. This action lowers the perceptible risk of buyouts in comparison to public stock indexes, but the industry's concept of greater leverage entailing less risk flies in the face of financial theory and defies common sense. Adjusting buyout returns for the industry's high debts disrupts the smoothing pattern. Regulators seem to be unfazed

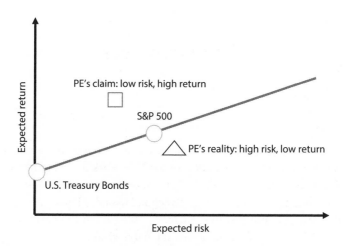

FIGURE 5.6 The PE industry's risk and return claim versus reality

by accounting inconsistencies, and the industry has an interesting mark-to-market pattern. For institutional investors, PE offers a minor diversification benefit when used in conjunction with a public stock portfolio.

6

The High Fees

Once in the dear dead days beyond recall, an out-of-town visitor
was being shown the wonders of the New York financial district.
When the party arrived at the Battery, one of his guides indicated
some handsome ships riding at anchor. He said, "Look, those are
the bankers' and brokers' yachts." "Where are the customers'
yachts?," asked the naive visitor.

THIS APOCRYPHAL STORY ADVANCES the proposition that Wall
Street is in the business of making money for itself, not in generating premium profits for its investors.[1] The idea is easily applied to
the PE industry, where the fund managers own the yachts and similar luxuries, while the investors make do with mediocre returns.
Indeed, independent research shows the investment results of
state pension plans, university endowments, and large foundations
underperform a passive 60–40 public index, despite the tens of
billions in active management fees paid by these institutions.[2] This
fact has never been challenged by Wall Street.

By any measure, buyout fund management fees are extremely
high. Compared to an S&P 500 index fund, where the annual
management fee is three basis points (0.03 percent) of assets under
management, buyout fees are one hundred times higher, at three
hundred to four hundred basis points (3 to 4 percent). With so
much of the investors' money going to the managers, the funds
have a hard time beating the public stock market.

The PE industry, of which LBO funds are the dominant part, does an excellent job of hiding the exact amounts that investors are paying to the managers. To begin the dissection of the fee structure, an understanding of the three fee classifications is necessary (see figure 6.1).

1. Annual fixed fee
2. Performance fee or carried interest fee
3. Monitoring, director, and transaction fees

Annual Fixed Fee

The standard annual fixed fee is 2 percent of the fund's committed capital for the first five years of a fund's life (or whenever the fund is fully invested, whatever comes first), although certain funds have dropped the fee in light of competition. Note that the fixed fee is based off committed capital, not assets under management.[3]

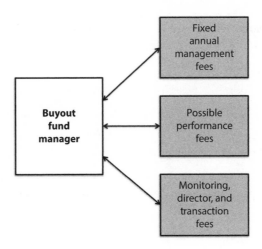

Figure 6.1 Three buyout fund fee categories

Thus, a fund with $1 billion of investor commitments charges $20 million in fixed fees the first year, even if the fund has only invested $200 million of the $1 billion. The first-year fee, therefore, is 10 percent of actual assets under management, or $20 million divided by $200 million. Once the fund had expended the entire $1 billion, the fee typically declines to 1.0 percent to 1.5 percent of the invested amount. Over the fixed, ten-year life of a $1 billion fund, the fixed fees alone represent $145 million of the investors' money (14.5 percent), assuming an annual $200 million drawdown in the first five years, followed by a gradual sale of assets over the next five years (see table 6.1).

Over the same ten-year period, and assuming the same cash outflow and inflow pattern with some acknowledgment for gains, a public stock index fund bills just $1 million in fixed fees. The $144 million difference ($145 − $1 = $144) deprives the buyout investor of profits and subsidizes many PE manager yachts.

Table 6.1
$1 billion fund, fixed fee illustration (in millions)

Year	Committed capital	2% fee	Invested capital	1.5% fee	Total fixed fee
1	$1,000	20	200	—	$20
2	$1,000	20	400	—	$20
3	$1,000	20	600	—	$20
4	$1,000	20	800	—	$20
5	$1,000	20	1000	—	$20
6	$1,000	—	1000	15	$15
7	$1,000	—	800	12	$12
8	$1,000	—	600	9	$9
9	$1,000	—	400	6	$6
10	$1,000	—	200	3	$3

Cumulative total, ten years: $145 million in fees

In the return-generation game, the index fund begins with a clear advantage. Using a football analogy, in an attempt to reach the goal line, the index fund starts at its twenty-yard line, while the buyout fund begins deep in its own end zone. Clearly, all four PE return enhancing tactics set forth in chapter 4—leverage, improving operations, attaining critical mass, and buying right—must click together to surmount the $144 million disadvantage.

Performance Fee

On top of the generous fixed fees, the PE managers receive performance fees to reward them for good results, if any. The standard performance fee is 20 percent of a fund's profits more than an 8 percent internal rate of return. Combined with the fixed fee, this arrangement is called a 2/20/8 structure. If the fund's profits—over and above an 8 percent IRR—are $150 million, for example, the manager's share is $30 million, in addition to the sizeable fixed fees.

Interestingly, the 8 percent benchmark is not keyed to the stock market. If the stock market has a secular, upward run, as has been the case for many years, and corporate values climb by 12 percent annually, investors pay the managers' incentive fees (on the difference between 8 percent and 12 percent) even when the managers' value-creating actions are subsumed by the positive effects of a rising stock market. Fund manager profits essentially piggyback a rising stock market. The largest institutional investors are aware of this incongruity, and they have the power to makes changes. But, they refuse to address the piggyback issue in fee negotiations with buyout funds, clinging to the dubious belief that in doing so the funds will somehow ostracize these same institutions—the funds' biggest customers—from the LBO business.

A portion of the annual performance fee is based on unrealized profits from unsold companies. Owing to the uncertain future outcome of a corporate sale, sometimes a part of the performance fee is placed in a suspension account. After the portfolio companies are sold and the fund's ten-year life has expired, the performance fee is then trued up once the manager and the investors know the actual cash realizations. Excess fees, if any, are returned to the investors.

The industry cloaks the fixed fees and the performance fees in an undertone of mystery, which is supplemented by accounting rules and state laws that obfuscate these expenses. Of thirty-three state pension funds with PE investments and a June fiscal year-end, my research, conducted with a colleague, uncovered just six states that included performance fees in their financial reports.[4] A follow-up forty-two-state survey attempted through the Freedom of Information Act requests saw multiple roadblocks—from state laws prohibiting fee disclosure to hair-splitting denials of same, to accounting systems that did not record such fees, and to secrecy agreements the states signed with the funds.[5] A similar study directed at the top fifty U.S. foundations and their Internal Revenue Service (IRS) Form 990s showed zero foundations disclosing performance fees.[6]

The Government Accounting Standards Board (GASB), which sets accounting principles for state and municipal pension plans, does not require performance fee compilation for accounting records, and neither does the Financial Accounting Standards Board (FASB) for nonprofit entities like foundations and university endowments. Many of America's largest institutions do not know what they are paying. Several years ago, the mammoth California state pension plan, Calpers, admitted that it had no idea how much it paid its PE managers.[7] In 2019, the Texas Education Agency, with a $34 billion endowment, indicated, "We do not maintain data on accrued or estimated carried interest."[8] Overlaying percentage fees paid by entities that do keep track such expenses indicates that U.S. pension plans have paid out tens of billions of such fees in exchange for, as chapter 4 points out, somewhat dubious investment results. David Neal, managing director of Australia's sovereign wealth fund said, "There just are not enough decent private equity managers around to justify the fees."[9] By hiding from the public record these large charges, the regulations and laws impair the public's ability to make rational spending choices.

The State of New Jersey's $75 billion pension plan provides the best fee information among its peer group.[10] (In 2016, I was a paid consultant for the New Jersey State employee unions on pension investments.) For the five years ended June 2020 (the latest information available at this writing), the 8 percent benchmark (of the 2/20/8 structure) for PE was two points lower than the S&P 500's 10 percent annualized return, which meant the PE funds locked in big fees by piggybacking the stock market results. Since private company valuations follow public company share prices—the 2 percent difference provided a windfall for New Jersey's PE managers. On New Jersey's $8 billion PE portfolio over the five years, the managers pulled out $615 million in carried interest fees (see table 6.2) and $1.3 billion in total fees. Surprisingly, in fiscal 2020, when the PE portfolio yielded just 0.2 percent and the S&P 500 returned a much higher 9.5 percent, New Jersey paid out $113 million in PE performance fees.

At a Milken Institute seminar, Robert Smith, chief executive officer of Vista Partner, a $50 billion LBO fund complex, repeated a popular tagline among the buyout set, "We only make money

Table 6.2
State of New Jersey pension plan—PE fixed and performance fees (in millions)

Year ended June 30	2016	2017	2018	2019	2020	Total
Fixed fees	$132	$135	$134	$113	$122	$637
Performance fees	$1096	$90	$146	$156	$113	$615
Stated PE 1-year return, after fees	6.3%	12.7%	17.5%	9.1%	0.2%	
S&P 500 1-year return	1.7%	15.5%	12.2%	8.2%	9.5%	_

if our investors make money."[11] That statement is not entirely true. Given the fixed fees, PE managers make their 2 percent in fixed fees even when the fund loses money. In New Jersey's case, the fixed fees totaled $637 million, slightly greater than the $615 million carried interest. The combined fee total of $1.3 billion, or 16 percent of an $8 billion portfolio, is an astounding amount when you consider the minimal risks taken by fund managers.

A research paper by Yale's Andrew Metrick and UC-Davis' Ayako Yasuda concluded that about two thirds of PE revenue comes from fixed components that are not sensitive to performance.[12] A fee primer, authored by institutional consultant Meketa Investment Group, illustrated the money-making ability of buyout fund managers, even with modest returns.[13] At a modest 10 percent gross IRR, the PE fees, incredibly, represent over one-third of profits (see table 6.3).

Wall Street investment management fees can be a considerable part of state expenditures. For example, Maryland's $496 million in fees in fiscal 2019 was roughly equal to the state's entire budget for higher education financial aid.[14] Because the pension plan's investment expenses are off-budget, a common practice among states, the Maryland legislature does not vote on such fees. States, universities, and foundations should take note of what others are paying. In 2020, New Jersey's stand-alone PE fees as a percent of underlying PE assets were 2.8 percent. Total alternative asset investment expenses (including PE) were 2.6 percent of the underlying assets. Applying this 2.6 percent metric to the Ford Foundation's

Table 6.3
Buyout funds—impact of fees on investor IRR

Gross IRR to investors	0%	5%	10%
Net IRR to investors	(3.6%)	(1.4%)	6.3%
Impact of fees on investor IRR	(3.6%)	(3.6%)	(3.7%)

Source: Meketa Investment Group.

$14 billion endowment, which is 60 percent invested in alternative assets, suggests $215 million in such fees, about 40 percent of Ford's annual grant total. In an email, Ford Foundation's chief investment officer, Eric Doppstadt, disputed this calculation and suggested, without evidence, that the foundation's fees are lower than New Jersey's.[15]

Monitoring, Director, and Transaction Fees

In addition to the 2/20/8 fees, buyout fund managers charge their portfolio companies monitoring, director, and transaction fees.[16] A monitoring fee supposedly compensates the manager for supervising corporate activities, providing strategic guidance, and offering helpful suggestions. A director fee pays the fund for the employee's time when serving as a board member. For assistance in raising financing or closing an add-on acquisition, the manager sometimes receives a transaction fee. The portfolio company deducts the fees on its tax returns, and the fees figure into the fund's overall returns in an indirect manner. Because of the private nature of the companies, exact information is hard to come by. My analysis of what data is available indicates that such fees reduce fund performance by 1 percent annually, although other observers have put forth larger numbers. Generally, the fund manager and investors divide the fees according to a preset formula. The proper accounting for the division of fees can be murky, according to one government report, and buyout investors must be attentive to this matter.

Closing

Buyout fund managers do a good job of extracting fees from their investors and their portfolio companies. The fees are high by any standard, have a heavy fixed component, and dwarf the management fees charged by public-stock index funds. The fees have a hidden quality, and determining their magnitude is challenging, but few institutions take notice. Fees tend to depress investors' returns, and they have a significant impact even at moderate profit levels. The fund management firms receive the generous fee payments despite minor monetary commitments on the firms' part. Fund operating expenses for a large fund operator are in the 50 percent of revenue range, indicating a stunning 50 percent pretax profit margin, as presented by an Apollo Global Management presentation and my own research.[17] Most of the earnings go into the fund managers' pockets because of the minimal capital expense required to run a fund. These attractive economics explain the vast personal wealth accumulated by many buyout fund managers.

7

The Customers

APRIL 1, 1985, WAS a pivotal date for the PE industry and the institutional money management business. On that day, David Swensen began work as the chief investment officer for the Yale University endowment fund. His mission was to modernize the fund's stodgy, conventional tactics—90 percent of its assets were in publicly-traded stocks and bonds—and to consider the new asset categories that Wall Street was developing. A thirty-one-year-old former Lehman Brothers banker, Swensen had no experience as a money manager, and he seemed an unlikely candidate to run a major endowment. However, not coming out of the institutional setting, he had one advantage. He was not tied to the ingrained habits of his peers, and he was ready to try new things. Within ten years, Yale cast off many of its publicly traded securities and replaced them with alternative assets, like PE, hedge funds, commodities, and real estate, all of which promised lower risk and higher returns. The strategy succeeded beyond the trustees' wildest dreams. For twenty years, an incredible run in the finance business, the Yale portfolio recorded a several percentage point premia relative to the returns of its peers and the 60–40 benchmark. Riding a wave of favorable publicity, Swensen became a demigod among institutions. In a 2016 profile, Geraldine Fabrikant of the *New York Times* said, "Mr. Swensen is legendary in the rarefied world of endowment managers."[1] In the preceding two decades, managers by the dozens rushed to emulate his techniques, which the industry coined the Yale model. This unintentional Pied Piper led hundreds of institutions into alternatives with their attendant promises of riches. State pension funds, universities, sovereign wealth funds, and nonprofit foundations stampeded out of conventional securities and into nontraditional investments (see figure 7.1).

This broad and rapid acceptance of alternatives created a Wall Street fee source that, over time, exceeded money from traditional institutional investment advisory work. (Income from buy-out fund fees alone in 2019 were $25 billion.) Accompanying the novel and complex instruments was a need for more analytical staff and increased compensation at institutions. For example, by the mid-2000s, Swensen was the highest-paid employee at Yale,

FIGURE 7.1 Yale endowment as the Pied Piper

earning several million dollars yearly. At the Ford Foundation, the chief investment officer's annual income quintupled in twenty years, from $500,000 in 2000 to $2.5 million in 2019.[2]

Many institutions found Yale's success hard to duplicate. In part, some were late to the party, with the best alternatives already picked over by competitors. Others failed to commit as fully to alternatives as Yale, which, as of this writing, has practically abandoned conventional stocks and bonds by maintaining a 75 percent alternative allocation, including 17 percent to buyout funds. Not all went well with the model. In the 2009 crash, Harvard's endowment, along with Yale an opinion leader among institutions, fell 27 percent in value,[3] despite adhering to the model's diversification guidelines, and Harvard later had a mark-to-market controversy surrounding hard-to-value farmland.[4] By 2020, multiple published studies pointed out that the majority of state pension funds, endowments, and foundations did not beat the passive 60–40 benchmark, despite the ballooning fees and professional staffs,[5] and Yale's prior ten-year returns barely exceeded the 60–40 index, assuming the underlying alternative portfolio was properly priced by the managers.

It mattered little to institutions that the studies showed them leaving billions on the table by not indexing more of their portfolios to public securities. Few institutional people read such research, which usually appears in obscure journals, and those that do often shrug off the conclusions by saying, "If those experts know so much, how come they are not in the private equity business and making millions?" The studies also contradicted the alternative industry's posits of lower risk and diversification away from public markets. A 2020 article by Richard Ennis, an investment consulting pioneer, provides an elaborate analysis of the return volatility, or risk, of institutions using the Yale model.[6] The study, which was reviewed by William Sharpe and Richard Thaler, two Nobel Laureates, found negligible diversification benefit from the use of the Yale model, and it outlined crucial cost savings and extra profits to be gained from an indexing approach. Yet like related research, it was relegated to the trash heap, gaining little traction in the institutional community and zero attention from the business media.

Considering these findings, a cynical view is that Wall Street's embrace of the Yale model was plain-fashioned self-interest—the financial equivalent of putting lipstick on a pig. Banking salespeople, institutional managers, and investment consultants transformed the traditional 60–40 platform into a complicated core/ satellite portfolio with one hundred times the management fees,[7] and no one was the wiser.

What Exactly Is an Institutional Investor?

I have been referring to institutional investors, but what exactly is one? An institutional investor is a large entity with ample cash to invest in a group of assets, which the institution administers in a professional manager. Institutions that participate in private equity come in a wide variety of sizes and shapes. Table 7.1 illustrates this multiplicity. Wall Street considers any entity with under $100 million in assets under management as retail. Thus, to be considered an institution, the investor should have at least

Table 7.1
Principal institutional investors in buyout funds

Pension funds
Sovereign wealth funds
University endowments
Foundations
Fund of funds
Insurance companies
Wealth managers & family offices

$100 million under management. Sissy Cao, coauthor of *Inside the World's Top Institutional Investment Offices*, estimates there are three thousand to four thousand of such institutions in the United States.[8] The principal participants in buyouts are state and municipal pension plans, university endowments, fund-of-funds, nonprofit foundations, and sovereign wealth funds. The largest of these institutions have over $1 trillion in assets under management.

Public Pension Plans

Most state and local governments provide a pension plan to their employees. The plans provide a retirement income based on years of service and annual salary, and many incorporate cost-of-living adjustments to maintain the retirees' purchasing power. The plans are usually a defined benefit where the retirement payments are not adjusted for changes in the market value of the plan's assets. If the plan's asset base drops with a stock market collapse, retirement benefits stay the same. To provide the monies for the payments, the government makes contributions from general tax revenue, the current employees deduct cash from their paychecks, and the plan produces income from its investments. The public plans manage vast sums, around $3 trillion, according to the National Association of State Retirement Administrators,[9] and number more than 5,500 according to the Urban Institute.[10] The large state plans, like California and New York, represent a major share of these assets.

Fund of Funds

A fund-of-funds is a pool of capital that invests in multiple kinds of funds, such as PE funds, hedge funds, and private real estate funds. A fund-of-funds enables smaller institutional investors or wealthy individuals to participate in alternative assets without necessarily having the expertise or resources to investigate multiple managers. The fund-of-funds also provides the requisite diversification among the various vehicles and lets its investors circumvent the high minimum commitment requirements, which can start at several million dollars for a PE fund.

University Endowments

A university endowment represents the savings of a university, sometimes accumulated over many years, through donations or other sources. Dozens of universities have endowments over $1 billion, with the five largest, Harvard, University of Texas, Yale, Stanford, and Princeton, each having over $25 billion.[11] Income from the endowments pays for operating costs, scholarships, and other expenses. Because of their nonprofit status, most endowments must spend 5 percent of their annual assets value each year, according to U.S. tax law.

Nonprofit Foundations

A nonprofit foundation uses income from its investments to support charitable endeavors. The investments often stem from contributions made by a wealthy family or a corporation. Generally, the foundation provides money in the form of grants to other charitable organizations that perform the good deeds, although some foundations administer their own programs. Like a university endowment, a foundation distributes at least 5 percent of its annual asset value each year. The largest U.S. foundation is the Bill & Melinda Gates Foundation, with about $40 billion in assets. Roughly seventy foundations exceed $1 billion in assets.

Sovereign Wealth Funds

Sovereign wealth funds represent a portion of the savings accumulated by a sovereign government or state, usually in the form of financial assets, such as stocks, bonds, real estate, or alternative assets. The governments operate the funds separate from money held in the central bank, and the fund's investment goals are typically long-term in nature. In effect, the government is not spending all the money it is taking in, so a portion is held in trust for future generations. Norway has the largest sovereign wealth fund, totaling over $1 trillion in assets derived from its substantial surplus oil revenues. The next three largest funds are owned by China, Abu Dhabi, and Kuwait, nations that also have a lot of surplus cash.

In general, an institution needs $10 billion in assets to justify an in-house private equity program, which might represent $500 million to $1 billion in commitments. At this level, the institution can afford to hire the five to ten analysts needed to select fund managers, oversee performance, and monitor fees. Below that amount, "They are better off with a small cap public index," says Alex Beath, senior analyst at CEM Benchmarking, "which carries a high correlation with buyout funds, and involves lower fees."[12]

What Are the Primary Objectives of the Institutional Investor?

The primary objectives of the institutional investor are threefold: (1) to preserve capital, (2) to prevent a substantial loss in the portfolio, and (3) to achieve a reasonable rate of return within the confines of the first two objectives. A substantial loss in any given years is 10 percent or more, while a reasonable annualized rate-of-return is 8 percent, although many institutions say 10 percent per annum is the aspiration (see figure 7.2).

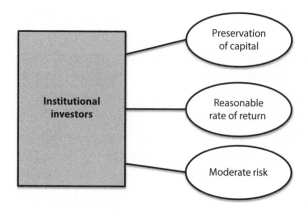

FIGURE 7.2 Institutional investors' portfolio objectives

Institutions attempt to surpass public stock and bond bench-marks, both in terms of better returns and lower price move-ments, through complex modern-portfolio-theory strategies that employ asset combinations in both the public and private invest-ment spheres. For the typical institution, the selection of assets within these allocations and their tactical implementation is left to a small army of third-party money managers, ranging from a few dozen for a smaller institution to over two hundred for a larger one. Supervision of the managers is the responsibility of in-house staffers and, to a lesser extent, outside consultants who may have designed the strategies in use.

The Yale model's early success prompted many funds to recon-sider their traditional asset selections, which had been heavily weighted toward a conventional mix of publicly traded equity and bond portfolios. Initially, institutions saw alternative investments, such as private equity and hedge funds, as exotic niche products—essentially equity-oriented vehicles that could goose up overall portfolio returns in a small way without meaningfully raising portfolio risk. They viewed another major alternative instrument, private real estate, as a means to access an asset category that was underrepresented in the stock market.

Not only did the alternatives appear to offer higher returns, but their historical return variation also seemed lower relative to their publicly traded counterparts (e.g., private equity vs. public common stocks, hedge funds vs. stock-bond combinations, hedge funds vs. a U.S. treasury bonds plus inflation, and private real estate vs. public real estate investment trusts). For example, when the U.S. stock market return was minus 37 percent in 2008, leveraged buyout funds reported a loss of just minus 26 percent.

At the same time, hedge funds promised equity-like returns with bond-like price movements. They intended to either (1) buy the good stocks long and sell the bad stocks short, (2) combine equities with bonds in an optimal manner, or (3) make prudent junk-rated loans for greater net yields compared to normal loans.

Given the apparent low return correlation of alternatives, infusing a traditional stock and bond portfolio with such assets came across as a classic diversification strategy that could maintain (or bolster) returns but lower volatility (or risk). Such were the expectations, ex ante, of many institutions when they doubled alternative asset allocations and thereby increased their third-party investment manager fees accordingly (see the institutional role in a buyout fund in figure 7.3).

Written in investment industry speak, a section of the State of Maryland annual pension plan report is illustrative of institutional fund objectives:

> The mix of asset classes is chosen to provide sufficient growth to meet the long-term return objectives of the System, while providing sufficient diversification to moderate the volatility of that return. For example, a portfolio of equities will likely provide the required return over a long-term horizon but will subject the fair value of the portfolio to unacceptable levels of volatility

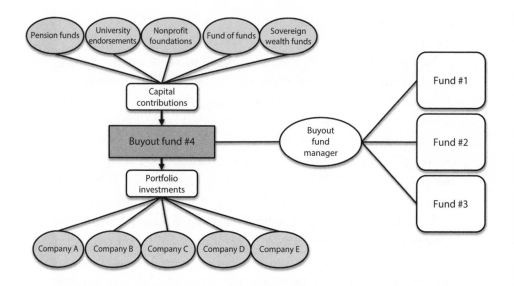

FIGURE 7.3 Institutional investors' position in a fourth buyout fund

such that the goals of minimizing contribution volatility and realizing surplus assets would be difficult to achieve. Combining other asset classes with equities will provide differentiated returns sources, reduce the volatility of returns and help realize those liability-oriented objectives.[13]

In practice, before a fiscal year begins, a typical institution aims to beat the return of a composite passive index. The composite is a weighted average of publicly available benchmarks that mirror the institutions' asset allocation. A consultant, paid by the institution, develops the composite yardstick. Neither the institution nor the consultant routinely discloses the exact methodology used to determine the yardstick. In almost all cases, the institution's executives at fiscal year-end claim to have beaten the composite's returns. A typical quote: "Our benchmark was 6 percent, and the portfolio returned 7 percent." Some executives simply indicate a return percentage without offering any impartial comparator. The system is geared toward institutional executives avoiding unbiased assessments and making themselves look good.

As the Maryland excerpt illustrates, institutional portfolio executives like to cloak their activities in a fog of mumbo jumbo that is indiscernible to the educated layperson. On top of this vernacular, they place a layer of scientific-sounding statistics such as *alpha, beta, standard variance, factor return, c-stat,* and *R squared.* The mathematical list is endless, and so are management's quarterly reports, which, in some cases, exceed one hundred pages of words, charts, numbers, and diagrams that only the most dedicated institutional board member can decipher.[14] These practices form a protective armor around an executive's subpar performance during a yearly salary review, but they are unfair to those senior administrators who try to figure out what is really going on.

Fiduciary Duty

In the United States, many institutions are fiduciaries, which means they are managing assets on behalf of others. As fiduciaries, they owe these entities the duties of good faith, trust, and standard of care. In this sense, the institution and its employees should act first and foremost with the needs of its beneficiaries in mind. The institution should avoid conflicting its own economic interests with those of its beneficiaries, such as retired pensioners, charitable causes, and needy students. For example, a foundation trustee should not steer the foundation to a hedge fund run by one of his or her friends. Moreover, the institution should manage the beneficiaries' money in a responsible way, allocating assets in a prudent manner and conducting the proper due diligence before selecting an investment. The details are tricky, and institutions frequently inject lawyers and financial consultants into the asset allocation and investment selection process to demonstrate compliance with the rules.

Besides offering constructive advice, the outside advisors provide legal air cover to the institution's executives if things go wrong. Thus, if a state pension significantly underperforms a passive benchmark, sits at the bottom of its peer group, or loses big money on a soured buyout deal, the executives and board members can point to the expert advisors and say, "Well, it's not our fault; they recommended it." In any case, the legal system makes it a practical impossibility for a beneficiary to effectively seek redress. A 2017 class action lawsuit filed by Kentucky State retirees against Blackstone Group and Kohlberg Kravis & Roberts, two major buyout firms, was a rarity, because institutions are reluctant to admit mistakes in investment selection.[15] In 2020, a U.S. Supreme Court decision made it harder to bring action against pension plan trustees for alleged violation of fiduciary duty.[16] For institutions like universities and foundations, identifying the exact beneficiaries (and their damages from the misbehavior of asset managers) is a nebulous endeavor in any event (see figure 7.4).

FIGURE 7.4 Fiduciary duties in an institutional investment setting

Consultants

The board members of institutions tend to rely heavily on outside consultants and inside staffers in the private equity commitment process. Both groups have a vested interest in an alternatives-laden portfolio. They want to make a name for themselves, and they do not accomplish this objective by indexing in public stocks. In part, a complex portfolio is a form of job preservation. If PE, hedge funds, real estate, and commodities are ditched by the board in favor of a 60–40 index, the need for these consultants and highly paid employees declines rapidly. Thus, despite the lack of concrete results in the last fifteen years from a Yale model versus a 60–40 passive index, the two groups hail as heroes the PE funds and other alternative asset categories. The consultants push for more alternatives, and the inside staff provides the echo chamber. The lack of professional knowledge about Wall Street among institutional board members does not stop them from voting for more and more buyout fund commitments; however, as fiduciaries, they should at a minimum ask penetrating questions in their oversight role, particularly about past returns and future fees.[17] "We keep scratching our heads [on institutional devotion to the Yale model]," says Chris Philips of index fund provider Vanguard Group.[18] Unfortunately, many board members, who are highly credentialed in their own fields yet ignorant of Wall Street's ways, are too embarrassed to answer questions when faced with a room full of so-called experts. The mutual reinforcement between consultants and staff thus continues unimpeded in the year 2021.

When Wall Street–savvy executives sit on these institutional boards, invariably they are from the PE, hedge fund, and active management spheres. In my survey of the top nonprofit foundations and the largest state pension funds, I could not find one principal involved in index funds. The executives have the societal status, philanthropic resources, or political fundraising ability to secure such sinecures. Their input into portfolio activity may be consciously unbiased, but human nature suggests they support alternatives over public securities either out of true conviction or subliminal perception. The Tellus Institute noticed the issue in saying, "College governing boards have failed to guarantee strong oversight of the Yale Model by relying heavily upon trustees drawn from financial services, many from the alternative investment industry."[19] "On occasion," according to one endowment consultant, "there is some backscratching, if you recommend my PE fund to your endowment, I will put forth yours to mine." For better or worse, the board nomination committees respond to wealth and position, so the situation is unlikely to change.

In any serious discussion of board governance and institutional portfolios, the question of vanity comes up.

– "The board members want to feel important."
– "They want to feel like they are contributing."
– "They want to go back to the country club, and say, 'I approved a $100 million Goldman Sachs buyout fund commitment,' rather than say, 'we ratified an index fund.' "
– "Private equity is more fun than indexing."
– "Private equity provides better lunches."

These comments do not jibe with fiduciary duty, but they summarize the mindset of many a board member.

Standard of Care

In effecting a private equity program, perhaps the biggest offense among institutional investors is not performing the proper standard of care. The level of initial investigation prior to commitment, and the subsequent monitoring of fees and expenses post commitment, is inadequate given the dollars involved.

Imagine a state pension plan considering a $500 million investment in a new $10 billion buyout fund V. The anticipated fees from the $500 million pledge over the fund's ten-year life approximate $75 million, a substantial amount, which, if used in a different way, might help hundreds of poor families pay for better housing. The major dollar commitment deserves careful study. In a merger and acquisition situation, as one basis of comparison, the buyer of a $75 million company, before closing a deal, sends in a SWAT team of accountants, lawyers, appraisers, operations executives, and other professionals to perform an exhaustive due diligence. The idea is for the buyer to verify independently all the seller's information, just as an average person retains a home inspector before purchasing a house. This due diligence exercise comes at great expense to the M&A buyer, as it should to a pension plan.

Despite a similar monetary outlay to the $75 million corporate acquisition, the pension plan's investigation is comparatively lax and unduly trusting for buyout fund V. The state fails to send in a squad of advisors to scour the books of the predecessor fund (i.e., buyout fund IV), fails to meet with fund IV's underlying portfolio companies, and fails to prepare in-depth appraisal reports on these firms so as to verify mark-to-markets. Nor does it attempt to recruit other investors to participate and to share the expense of this greater search effort, which costs perhaps half a million dollars. In fact, the pension plan accepts at face value the fund manager's numbers, a remarkable admission when viewed in the context of a corporate M&A analysis at an identical dollar commitment level. Often the institution farms out a portion of its examination to a third-party consultant, who is conflicted, having made the fund V recommendation to begin with. The third-party consultants independently audit few, if any, of fund IV's numbers. In their defense, the pension plans and the consultants point out that their due diligence budgets lack the room for anything more than a dilatory effort, and besides they explain, "The prominent buyout funds have a brand name to protect. Why would they jeopardize it through deception in order to raise a new fund?" In any case, the fact that a trillion-dollar industry relies on the honesty of hard-bitten Wall Street people should cause disquiet in public policy circles, but to date legislators and regulators are not troubled.

The lenient approach to the industry extends to its fees. Because applicable accounting regulations do not require the recordation of buyout fund performance fees, most investors, in my experience, ignore them and register only fixed fees, although the performance data is obtainable with a simple request to a fund manager. "Don't ask, don't tell" is the institutional motto. The same goes for the monitoring and transaction fees a fund bills to its portfolio companies.

Closing

As someone who has studied the buyout phenomenon, I have been asked by many observers, "Why do so many institutions insist on expensive, actively managed assets, like buyout funds, when the investment results can be duplicated or exceeded by cheaper index vehicles?" The answer comprises several possibilities:

True Believers: It is human nature to believe that your own institution can do better than others by selecting winning and losing investments, such as buyout funds, despite scientific evidence to the contrary. David Villa, executive director of the State of Wisconsin Investment Board, embodies this sentiment, "A big dose of private equity, private real estate, and private debt provides a lot of alpha, a lot of returns."[20]

Career Concerns: Investment executives have built careers and big salaries out of the implementation of complex portfolio strategies rather than passive indexing. Consciously or subconsciously, the investment executives do not want to index themselves out of a job.

Investment Consultants: Institutions hire consultants who provide advice and act as gatekeepers in sifting through buyout managers wanting long-term contracts. The consultants tend to push for alternatives in a portfolio, claiming that alternatives provide better returns and lower risks despite the apparent contradiction with modern finance theory. Institution board members are reluctant to contradict experts.

Stockholm Syndrome: The syndrome relates to a condition whereby hostages develop a psychological bonding with their captors. The concept first gained notice in a 1973 bank robbery in Stockholm, Sweden, when four hostages refused to testify against the two men who held them captive and even raised money for their defense. Institutional executives today deal with so many Wall Street professionals and hear so many PE management marketing pitches, that they become industry captives. The absence of moderating perspectives produces tunnel vision and creates fertile ground for blind conformity within the profession.

Of the four possibilities for why institution executives refuse to consider the substantial indexing of their portfolios, the career concern is clearly the most disconcerting. The executives may very well know that private equity is ineffective, yet they keep pouring money into it to justify a complicated investment portfolio that needs full-time administration. This sordid explanation for active institutional management is almost too terrible to think about. Billions of beneficiary dollars are sacrificed for the career advancement of a few thousand institutional executives. The other motives fall within the bounds of human frailty and behavioral finance and have a less pernicious quality than professional ambition. Board members must be vigilant in policing each of the motives.

8

The Staffs

IT IS OCTOBER 2018, and Carlyle Group's David Rubenstein stands at the podium of the gala annual dinner sponsored by ABANA, a nonprofit organization for U.S. finance professionals with interests in the Middle East. ABANA honors him with its annual achievement award. Held at New York City's Tony Plaza Hotel, the dinner features five hundred movers and shakers from the United States-Middle East investment axis.[1] The group includes the upper crust of American bankers that are tightly connected to the region's oil-rich sheikdoms, such as Morgan Stanley, Blackstone Group, Goldman Sachs, and Citigroup.

As attendees extend polite applause, they know that Rubenstein sits at the pinnacle of the PE industry. He is cochairman of the Carlyle Group, one of the world's largest money managers, with multiple funds, spanning the globe and generating billions of dollars in fees. *Forbes* pegs his net worth at $3 billion and designates him as the 275th richest person in the United States. One of the few business heavyweights in the nation's capital, his well-placed charitable deeds and lofty business status assist with prestigious positions like chairman of the Kennedy Center, chairman of the Smithsonian Institute, and chairman of the Council of Foreign Relations.

His fundraising and marketing efforts on Carlyle's behalf were heroic, and he traveled constantly to speak to investment conferences and meet with possible clients. Unlike many financial titans, Rubenstein exhibited a softer, intellectual side. When, for personal reasons, I was looking to change jobs, a mutual friend set up a meeting with this modern-day Croesus. While he was not helpful on the employment front, Mr. Rubenstein perused one of my books, and asked, "How long does it take to write a book?" I was impressed. Many Wall Streeters would have asked, "How long does it take to *read* one?" Eventually, he authored two books of his own and hosted a nationally syndicated TV talk show. The latter tended to feature fellow business moguls, and the questions were of the softball variety, such as this query directed to Amazon's Jeff Bezos—"Your stock is up 70 percent this year; is there one thing responsible for that?"[2]

At the time of the speech, however, several cracks appeared in Carlyle's carefully constructed image. The firm's PE funds, for the most part, were not beating public equity indexes, and fund returns, when compared to peers, were subpar.[3] Carlyle's common stock, issued in a 2012 initial public offering, was moribund, and its price significantly underperformed the stock market. Embarrassing bankruptcies in the portfolio sullied the firm's public portrayal. Manor Care, the nation's second largest nursing home chain, went under six years after a Carlyle leveraged buyout. The deal loaded the business with $7 billion in debt, but nonetheless Carlyle extracted sizable cash dividends before the bankruptcy. The Manor Care bust followed a decline in healthcare standards for the company's customers, many of whom were poor, disabled individuals, according to a *Washington Post* exposé.[4]

A second black eye came in the form of the bankruptcy of Philadelphia Energy Solutions (PES), a historic oil refinery. Scheduled to shut down in 2012, the refinery was rescued through a $175 million investment by Carlyle, whose efforts were lauded by Pennsylvania politicians as saving 850 well-paying jobs. The subsequent Chapter 11 filing in January 2018 cancelled most of these jobs, but Carlyle escaped with $514 million in cash dividends from PES, thus multiplying its original commitment two times over.[5] This financial legerdemain was a masterstroke given the refinery's downfall.

One of the firm's larger investments—Acosta Inc., a major food broker—experienced operational problems after its 2014 buyout. Changes in consumer buying habits damaged the company's viability, and a year after the ABANA talk the business filed for bankruptcy, saddled with $3 billion in debt. The filing caused Carlyle's biggest one-time loss—$1.4 billion on its Acosta equity investment.[6] These negative items were offset by positives, and they did little to hinder the firm's progress. In July 2018, over three hundred institutions lined up to commit to the new $18 billion Carlyle VII buyout fund.[7] The legacy of Rubenstein and Carlyle thus leaves much for PE professionals to emulate.

Buyout Fund Organization

The structure of small- to medium-size buyout funds comprise two distinct elements: (1) the investment professionals, and (2) the administrative employees. The megafund complexes, like Carlyle, have a third component—(3) operations advisors. The first grouping, investment professionals, is by far the largest segment in terms of personnel (see figure 8.1).

Considering the fee-revenue generating ability of buyout funds, a surprisingly small staff manages the business. The largest fund complexes, with several active funds and annual fees of $1 billion, might have several hundred employees. Vestar Capital, ranked twentieth in investor commitments with $3 billion, runs three active funds and lists a total of thirty investment professionals.[8] Combined with operations advisors, administrators, and support people, Vestar indicates

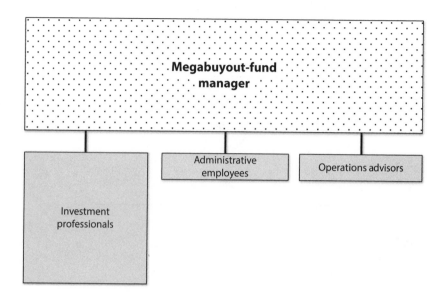

FIGURE 8.1 Megafund organization chart

a sixty-person head count. The PE fund where I worked, Emerging Markets Partnership, employed 140 individuals at its peak, when it managed five funds with $5 billion in collective commitments. Set forth in figure 8.2 is an illustration of a three-fund complex.

The portfolio of a multiple-fund manager comprises typically forty to fifty companies, with thousands or tens of thousands of employees. With majority ownership, the fund manager supervises a portfolio business by installing its own board members, approving the executive team, monitoring results, and offering advice. Operating advisors and third-party consultants supplement the portfolio executives, and fund investment professionals help with financial engineering and add-on acquisitions. Because the LBO fund exercises absolute control by virtue of its controlling interest, its inputs carry greater weight than in a venture capital situation, where the PE investors are in the minority position versus the founders/corporate managers in the majority (see figure 8.3).

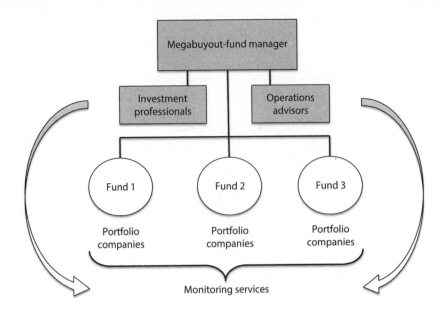

FIGURE 8.2 Fund supervision of portfolio companies

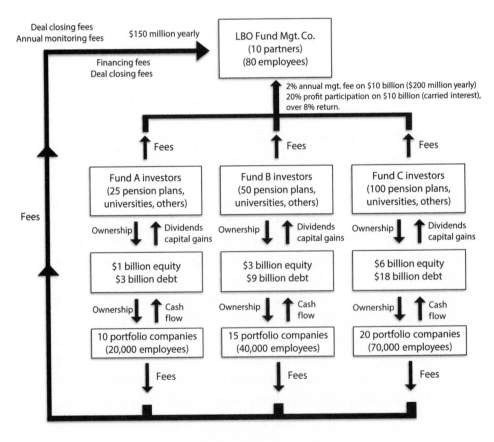

FIGURE 8.3 Three-fund manager illustration, with fees

Administrative Staff

The administrative side of the fund business encompasses diverse functions to varying degrees: overseeing the fund manager's relations with its institutional investors, conducting day-to-day office tasks, completing in-house human relations duties and legal assignments, and driving the accounting for the business.

Operations Advisors

The larger funds employ individuals who were previously executives that ran business operations that fit the LBO profile. For example, two of Vestar Capital's operation advisors are Frank Ingari and Wayne Callahan. Ingari was chief operating officer of Tandigm Health, a major health management firm, and Callahan was an executive with consumer food company H. J. Heinz. These advisors work with portfolio company executives and give them senior-level counsel on how to stimulate sales and improve profits.

Investment Professionals

Investment professionals represent the bulk of a buyout firm's personnel, and they have tremendous responsibilities.

Initially, they look for potential deals, and then they arduously sift through hundreds of opportunities to find a few targets for further study. They analyze this narrow list of selections from both business and financial perspectives. All this time, they interact with outsiders, such as investment bankers, lawyers, and employees at the selling company.

As the merger and acquisition process continues for potential targets, the investment professionals move to the bidding and money-raising phase. They value the target, negotiate with the seller and its advisors, and computer-model the transaction from a financial point of view. These professionals work with buyout lenders and the lenders' lawyers and consultants.

The final steps involve due diligence, legal documentation, additional analysis, and more negotiation. Once the target becomes part of the fund's portfolio, the investment professionals monitor the company and coordinate with its management changes in strategy, finance, and operations.

The investment professionals master a complex set of knowledge, experience, and skill. To succeed, "you probably have to be more investment banker than investor," says John Seitz, a former hedge fund executive now running Foundation Financial Research.[9] The banker's job of getting parties to agree, negotiating a transaction, and exhibiting salesmanship has stark differences with that of a sophisticated public security investor. The latter researches a stock from afar, performs analysis mostly from public documents, and dispassionately considers the security's daily value, all the while weighing the pros and cons of holding it in light of new information. Closing a buyout, in contrast, is a three- to four-month process, and transaction execution over this time is paramount.

Background and Diversity

Predictably, most of the buyout professionals that I have encountered (or researched) have an investment banking background. Wall Street is where they learn the trade of marketing and closing merger deals, debt financings, and equity offerings. The second most representative training is management consulting, where the work experience focuses heavily on business operations. This expertise assists a fund in evaluating a takeover candidate and keeping track of its business. A review of the top twenty funds' employee rosters revealed over 80 percent with either Ivy League undergraduate degrees or top-ten business school MBAs. As a group, they are bright, ambitious, and hard working. They know numbers and business analysis very well, but some leave observers with the impression of cocky overconfidence or a know-it-all mentality. "I didn't like being lectured by a 29-year-old Wharton MBA, who didn't know what was up, in running my company," said one older operating manager. The high pay and job prestige of buyout funds reinforce this attribute, and the lofty attitude also resonates from the fact that many fund employees have enjoyed a gilded upbringing in which their formative years featured a protected life of wealth and privilege.

The homogeneity of the buyout partner class is quite striking. Ten of the eighteen biggest buyout groups provide photographs of their general partners. A review of 358 partners in these ten groups show the vast majority to be white males and, to a lesser extent, Asian Americans. Women comprise less than 10 percent of the list, and blacks encompassed just two individuals (see table 8.1).

The industry's white male dominance has escaped regulatory security entirely. From time to time, the issue surfaces, as it did in a June 2020 *Wall Street Journal* article, but nothing changes.[10]

Table 8.1
Diversity of top buyout fund partners

	Number	Percent
White	323	90.2%
Female	33	9.2
Black	2	0.6
	358	100%

Team Concept

The proper PE transaction process involves a team of individuals, not just one person. The investment professionals foster a team concept for two reasons: (1) to promote deal execution, and (2) to assuage investor concerns about continuity.

On the deal side, the fund assigns five professionals to a typical acquisition team: a general partner, a managing director, a vice president, an associate, and an analyst, with 15+, 10+, 10+, 5+, and 1+ years of experience, respectively. As the acquisition target proceeds through the M&A process, the team stays together, and the younger members learn from the more senior personnel. Because of the limited employee roster at a fund manager, it is important for employees to get along, since they operate in close and regular contact.

Institutional investors are supportive of the team concept at the holistic fund level for pecuniary reasons. If buyout fund I has a good profit history, the institutions believe that keeping the fund I professional group intact enhances the likelihood of successor fund II duplicating this success. In the 1980s and 1990s, the general partners kept the overwhelming majority of the fees, and the junior employees jumped ship either to work for new funds or to join higher-paying competitors. Faced with diminishing returns, the institutions pushed general partners to compensate junior professionals better and to allow their participation in the carried interest. In this manner, the junior people had silver handcuffs and were less tempted to job-hop.

Cash compensation for a first-year associate approximates $150,000–$200,000 per year, for a vice president $300,000–$400,000 per year, and for a managing director/general partner $1 million–$2 million per year. Senior employees share in the fund profits, which is over and above the cash compensation set forth above.

Fiduciary Obligations

Sustained contact with buyout fund executives and their body language leaves the impression that fund personnel have one basic responsibility—to maximize fixed fee income and carried interest for their employer. Under this modus operandi, the occasional unsavory action, such as manipulating returns, unduly leveraging-up companies to extract dividends, or milking investors and portfolio firms for comparatively high fees, is defensible behavior within the legally justifiable bounds of profit maximization. While there is an alignment of interests among PE participants in making money, the fund manager faces a layering of possible conflicts when these interests diverge.

For example, when a buyout fund executive becomes a board member of a portfolio company, he confronts a dual fiduciary situation. He owes a fiduciary duty to the fund and its investors, as well as to the company's stakeholders. In practice, the executive may be called upon to take actions that do not benefit the company. He also has obligations to the fund's investors, which may be incompatible with what is best for the fund's manager, of which he is part owner (see figure 8.4).

Consider another illustration. The fund directs a portfolio company to borrow more money and to use the proceeds to pay a cash dividend to the fund's investors (one variation of financial engineering). The cash distribution enhances the fund's immediate returns, but based on the executive's experience with the company, which the new lenders lack, she believes the debt heightens the danger of near-term insolvency. What is the executive to do? To which side does she owe the greater loyalty? A strict legal interpretation says she owes a duty to all sides, but this reading of the law places the executive in an untenable position.

Another example. The fund uses a subscription line to acquire a company in advance of its investors' capital infusion. The action

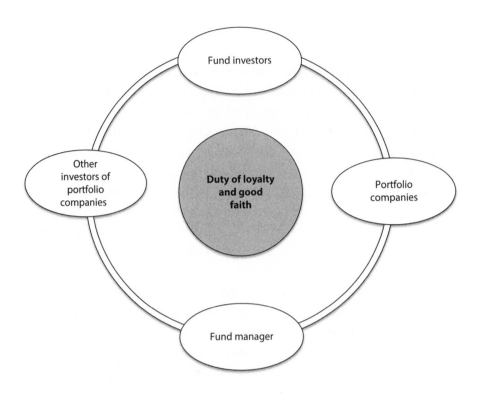

FIGURE 8.4 The fiduciary obligation of a senior buyout fund executive

boosts the fund's IRR calculation and pleases the fund's investors, many of whom lack the expertise to interpret the credit practice, which pushes the fund's returns in the top-quartile performance ranking. This ranking helps the fund manager recruit new investors. Should the executive object to the subscription line because it artificially inflates the IRR?

Not infrequently, a buyout fund's investment is in the form of convertible preferred stock, which has preferential rights compared to common stock that portfolio company employees hold. The economic interests of these two ownership classes can separate in matters like voting power, refinancing, and bankruptcy. How does the fund executive navigate this conflict?

Lawyers provide guidance to the funds for navigating these conflicts between portfolio company stakeholders, investors, and fund partners. Senior fund executives, at least, are aware of their duties in wearing several fiduciary hats. Legal and other experts can be called in to paper over indeterminant activities; however, the plurality of conflicts within the system makes adhering to a straight-and-narrow ethical line difficult, as noted above. Even for the most honorable executive, the temptation to push the envelope in favor of their employer may be too great. The shortage of enforcement, either through regulatory actions or aggrieved party lawsuits, makes boundary stretching easier. In June 2020, the Securities and Exchange Commission issued a "Risk Alert: Observations from Examination of Entities Managing Private Funds."[11] The publication catalogued a laundry list of conflict abuses that the SEC encountered in reviewing hundreds of fund managers. Nonetheless, few such managers suffered financial penalties from incurring infractions over the years.

Closing

Buyout fund professionals are a hardworking, highly educated bunch. They possess a complex mix of skills that is hard to find outside of Wall Street, and their knowledge base covers an impressive combination of deal making, finance, business analysis, and operations. The professionals have been unable to beat the stock market by any objective measure, but they have built a better mousetrap for obtaining lucrative fees from institutional investors. Legally sanctioned secrecy provisions and lax accounting standards have perpetuated the business long past a reasonable shelf life.

9

The Enablers

DRIVING DOWN A STEEP road set into a hillside, you may notice a guardrail on one side of the street. The guardrail keeps your car from straying into a hazardous area, like a sharp vertical drop. The guardrail provides a safety zone and establishes a boundary. The U.S. regulatory system has guardrails to define a range of acceptable behaviors by financial actors, to inform investors of the risks of various assets, and to protect financial market participants from an abundance of malpractices.

Wall Street moguls argue for free markets and unfettered capitalism, but governments have installed limits on mercantile excesses almost since the start of large-scale industrialization. Child labor laws, food safety oversights, and monopoly restrictions are just a few legislative initiatives designed to curtail abuses and to protect the capitalist system from itself. In the United States, the private sector and the democratic order pursue an ongoing partnership, with some friction, whereby the government outlines ground rules for proper commercial activity and business owners operate within the confines of those laws to maximize profit. Despite their

FIGURE 9.1 Key buyout fund industry rulemakers, regulators, and referees

allegiance to the free market side of this model, Wall Streeters are not above asking for government interference when it suits their interests. The 2009 and 2020 federal bailouts of the financial system provide ample evidence of this dichotomy. Inside the buyout fund business—a subset of the financial markets—the guardrails are bent, if not broken. The rule makers and referees are inattentive, if not indifferent, to possible mischief. This chapter looks at the inaction of those in authority (see figure 9.1).

State Legislatures

State and municipal pension plans are walled off from overt legislative interference. When the plans were set into motion, the designers wanted the safety of retiree assets to be of principal importance. The designers did not want a plan's asset quality being endangered by legislators placing investments with favored constituents and awarding management contracts to campaign contributors. A plan's governing board was to have zero or limited legislative representation, and a plan's money management fees were off budget, meaning the legislature lacked the ability to weigh in during the plan's annual expense approvals. "So many state legislators think of pension plans as a single line item in the operating budget," says Jean Pierre Aubrey of the Boston College

Center for Retirement Research.[1] That being said, the legislature is not powerless to influence a plan's investment policy.

Legislatures can implement guidance on maximum fees, and they can, if they have the desire, supervise the staff, particularly when investment returns fall below an objective benchmark, like the 60–40 index. The legislature can require a plan's trustees, investment executives, and consultants to sit for embarrassing public testimony and to answer for substandard results. They can require the plan to gather data on performance fees and, in official reports, to post the plan's annualized returns against an objective measure. In this way, legislators and constituents have a fair basis for comparing the plan to peers rather than the legislators having to refer to some made-up in-house measurement. Sadly, most legislatures fail to exercise this minimal oversight. A shortage of financial sophistication, an ignorance of the fiscal damage done by high fees and low returns, and a sense of inertia about how things change at a multibillion plan, contribute to the neglect. Chris Tobe, a former trustee of the State of Kentucky Retirement Systems, adds another line of thinking, pointing out, "One of the largest private equity firms had thirty-five lobbyists on retainer in the state."[2]

As one example, a senior Maryland legislator, now retired, in a private discussion, admitted to knowing of the state plan's poor investment record. Convincing his fellow legislators of the same and moving them to impose oversight for optimizing investment results was "too much heavy lifting," he said a couple of years ago. "The educational process among the legislature would be overwhelming." Since that conversation, the plan has spent over $1 billion in fees, while returns stay in the bottom quartile of its peers.

Public Sector Union Leaders

Unlike university endowments and nonprofit foundations, state and municipal pension plans have an easily identifiable group of beneficiaries—government employees who will retire with a pension and existing retirees who receive a pension. Most of these individuals are represented by unions that have the resources to hire experts who can tell whether plan executives are managing assets wisely. For many public plans, union officials, by statute, occupy board seats and have a first-hand view of the expensive Yale-model tactics adopted by investment staffers.

Given that most state and municipal plans are not beating passive-index yardsticks, union officials should (1) protest and (2) seek ways for the plan to better preserve and enhance retiree benefits. But they remain strangely silent, even as PE fund managers siphon off billions in fees, with the plans having little to show for the expense. Indeed, research shows that the average state and municipal plan has underperformed a low-cost, 60–40 index fund over the last twenty years. Echoing this fact, the American Federation of Teachers published a key research report that alerted its member unions to the vagaries of the Yale model,[3] but there was little buy-in among state officials. In one rare occurrence, a collection of New Jersey state employee unions openly rebelled at their pension plan's costly use of alternative managers. The situation featured an unusual spectacle—the fund's investment staffers and the board's political appointees uniting to fight beneficiaries for the right to purchase buyout funds.

Several print reporters who cover the retirement plan beat and who reviewed organized labor's passivity with me, ascribe the indifference to Wall Street's wining and dining of union officials. My impressions are different. I believe those union officials, who are in a position to know, believe that state and municipal legislatures, where they exercise a high degree of political influence, will make up future pension plan cash shortfalls by increasing the existing levels of government cash contributions. As a result, in their collective opinion, substandard investment performance is not something for union members to worry about.

Accounting Authorities

The Financial Accounting Standards Board (FASB) and the Government Accounting Standards Board (GASB) are private, non-profit organizations that source the accounting principles used by institutional investors. The main purpose of these principles is to present fairly the financial condition of the institutions to investors, lenders, and other stakeholders. A secondary objective is to ensure transparency and consistency among the financial reports of these entities. The Securities and Exchange Commission (SEC) and the Municipal Securities Rulemaking Board have input into the development of accounting principles codified by FASB and GASB.

These accounting authorities comply with the PE industry's penchant for secrecy, allowing institutions to exclude performance fees or carried interest as an expense item on their financial reports. Accordingly, institutional stakeholders, including beneficiaries, are left in the dark about the true costs of these investments.

Moreover, the accounting authorities are overly solicitous about the industry's longing to administer, for its own benefit, the mark-to-market process for its portfolio companies. Fund managers generate the individual valuation reports and control the information flow for third-party administrators, if any, and the fund's independent auditors. Because so much money hinges on the accuracy of these valuations, the procedures have need of more rigor to ensure integrity. Independent third-party appraisers should play a larger role, with access to portfolio company executives and the related data. The auditors should require that the appraisers be rotated annually to avoid their getting too cozy with fund managers. The present circumstance, where funds are allowed to grade their own homework, is an unsuitable arrangement for what is now a trillion-dollar industry.

Along the same lines, the accounting authorities allow the industry to highlight internal-rate-of-return results, but investors

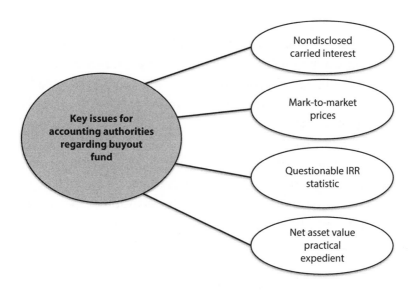

FIGURE 9.2 Accounting authorities: key issues regarding buyout funds

are not given the appropriate warnings about the weaknesses of the IRR and its susceptibility to manipulation. The FASB's endorsement of the Net Asset Value Practical Expedient makes the institutional bookkeeping of PE investments simpler, but it undermines the long-accepted treatment for closed-end funds. Finally, the practice furthers the illusion that holders can sell their fund participations easily at the stated net asset value, when, in fact, such is not the case (see figure 9.2).

Private Equity Databases

The five dominant PE databases—Pitchbook, Preqin, Burgiss, Thomson Reuters, and Cambridge—provide a wealth of information. Of key concern is their compilation of return measurements and quartile rankings. These five data services take the funds' mark-to-market assumptions at face value when independent corroboration is necessarily called for. The assumptions have a critical impact on year-to-year fund results, and there is a need for independent validation. The databases fail to warn investors about both (1) the substantial proportion of unsold companies included in buyout returns and (2) the undependability of the IRR computation that is often used in comparisons. The databases should mention that 56 percent of buyout fund investments over the last fifteen years remain unsold, and they should highlight the fact that their services encompass only 60 percent of the funds. The latter point leaves an open question regarding how the inclusion of the missing 40 percent might affect the industry's performance statistics.

Federal Government

The federal government has coddled the buyout industry for so long and in so many ways that is difficult to know where to begin a discussion. The best place to start is the carried interest loophole.

Carried Interest Loophole

Carried interest is the buyout fund manager's performance fee. The federal government characterizes these fees as capital gains to the manager rather than what they truly are—wage-like cash payments. The differential in federal tax rates, 20 percent for capital gains and 37 percent for wages, is thus 17 percent, and the 17 percent represents an unjust subsidy to a small group of wealthy people. The loophole is worth billions every year, and preserving it is the top legislative priority of the American Investment Council, the industry's lobbying arm. Every few years, legislators under both Democratic and Republican administrations propose closing the loophole, but it stays untouchable, a lasting testament to PE's political power.

As an aside, Wall Street wants the average Joe to think the tax differential between capital gains—the profit from selling an asset or investment—and wages is enshrined in the Constitution, but the differential has come and gone since the United States first instituted income taxes. The individuals deriving the most advantage from the differential are those who have sizable assets to buy and sell, and they are a small percent of the population.

Interest Tax Deduction

For decades, buyout companies reduced their taxable income through the 100 percent interest expense deduction on their hefty debt loads. The federal government, in effect, subsidized the buyout business compared to operations with low leverage. However, debt-like instruments at the bottom of an LBO's capital layer cake are not debt in the truest sense of the word. They are deeply subordinated to other creditors, have sky-high interest rates that do not befit real debt, and often carry complex profit participations. The Internal Revenue Service should properly define these loans as preferred stocks, and thus their coupon payments would not be tax deductible.

In 2017 Congress placed a limit on interest deductions expressed as a percent of a company's earnings.[4] Depending on the industry's inventiveness in circumventing the limits, the new laws have the potential to reduce the interest deduction benefit for a typical buyout by 20 percent to 30 percent.

Corporate Veil

A buyout fund has multiple operating businesses that are under common ownership and common control. There is a legal argument that the buyout fund is a holding company that abuses the

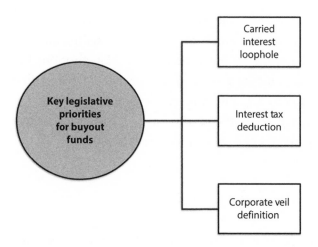

FIGURE 9.3 Key legislative priorities for buyout funds

corporate veil principle. If the principle is modified by legislation, as several have suggested, creditors and employees of a bankrupt portfolio company could then go after the assets of other buyout portfolio companies, and even the fund manager itself, in order to seek redress. This action collapses the corporate veil and consolidates the fund's businesses. Such legislation would prompt a more conservative debt approach by buyout funds to avoid defaults that might initiate such activity (see figure 9.3).

Nonprofit Foundations and Endowments

Many large foundations and university endowments have sizeable alternative asset portfolios. The prospect of a tax-exempt institution spending 2 percent to 3 percent of its assets annually on PE and hedge fund fees raises questions about how well the institution fulfills its charitable mission. The December 2017 tax legislation imposed a tiny income tax on the thirty wealthiest universities, but it ignored the base question of portfolio management fees. Foundations and universities are important buyout-fund customers, so changes to their status impacts the industry.

Monitoring Fees

LBO funds bill their underlying companies monitoring fees. The Internal Revenue Service treats monitoring fees as a tax-deductible expense at the company level, thereby reducing corporate tax payments.[5] The fees can be substantial. According to the *Wall Street Journal*, over a five-year period, the four biggest buyout firms, Blackstone, Carlyle, Apollo, and KKR—collectively reported $2.1 billion in transaction and monitoring fees (after rebating part of the fees to investors in their funds). How much monitoring must be done to justify $2.1 billion? In an eight-year period, the buyout fund owners of Univision, a $14 billion deal, extracted $193 million in management fees.[6] Monitoring fees have the flavor of a nontax-deductible cash dividend, and their current expense classification is another tax subsidy.

Securities and Exchange Commission

The SEC is a federal government agency that is primarily responsible for overseeing the U.S. securities markets, including the PE industry. As stated on its website, the mission of the SEC is "to (1) protect investors and (2) to maintain fair, orderly and efficient markets." The combination of (1) and (2) promotes a third objective—(3) investor confidence in the markets.[7] The combination supports capital formation and the efficient use of capital, two critical elements of the U.S. financial system. The government does not want investors placing money into businesses based on faulty or misleading information, nor does it want investors to be

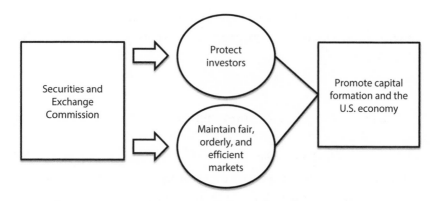

FIGURE 9.4 Securities and Exchange Commission: key objectives

cheated through the use by others of market manipulations, hidden fees, or excessive fees (see figure 9.4).

The SEC has a broad mandate, but it has insufficient resources to properly carry out its objectives. The agency employs only 4,500 people to oversee a huge securities market, which functions reasonably well but is also a happy hunting ground for all manner of charlatans, tricksters, and smooth operators who prey on retail and institutional participants alike. With a trillion dollars in equity commitments and thousands of active funds, the buyout industry is a thin slice of the SEC's portfolio, and the agency's resources are inadequate for the task of close supervision, given its other responsibilities. After all, the four thousand active PE funds are roughly equivalent to the four thousand active publicly traded companies, but the agency's budget was never increased to reflect the PE industry's growth.

Compounding the problem is the fact that the PE business is principally private in nature and the investors are almost all institutions. Accordingly, the investors are supposedly sophisticated enough to investigate the merits of a buyout fund without the need for SEC handholding. Because of this premise, the agency regulates the buyout business with a light hand; lacks a dedicated, full-time, interdisciplinary team for the industry' supervision; and its PE enforcement actions are few and far between. "The SEC does not regulate the private equity business and has never wanted to regulate the private equity business," said a former SEC attorney who still works in government.

There is no public outcry for regulation, for the bulk of investors are unaware of the blurriness of the profit measurements and fees. For those that harbor suspicions, there is a reluctance to speak out, either for fear of being blackballed career-wise or for fear of being singled-out as having made a bad investment that requires scrutiny. One airline pension plan executive said, "Why say anything? I won't even be here in ten years when the results of the buyout funds we hold are really known."

Certainly, with the rife of irreconcilable conflicts among fund managers and the spate of questionable numbers, one expects the SEC lawyers, even on a limited budget, to have a field day with buyout funds and their dubious claims. Pointing out the smoothing of annual rates-of-return would be a notable effort. Imposing a minimum standard of disclosure for profit measurements and portfolio valuation procedures would be useful to investors. Restraining specious declarations by fund managers on the positive attributes of PE in marketing documents, TV appearances, and YouTube videos fall within the agency's power. The SEC restrains public company executives who hype a company's prospects but, in an inexplicable double standard, remains silent when PE executives pump up the industry.

Setting maximum annual fees, as a percent of assets under management, is within the SEC's purview, and a sensible cap might help public pension plans and charitable institutions to steer clear of paying 3 percent to 4 percent yearly just because a rising stock market boosts buyout values. Yet the SEC has done none of this, despite the industry's prominence.

The solicitous attitude toward buyout funds and its lack of enforcement action stems partly from a "culture of association" between financial regulators and Wall Street interests.[8] This phenomenon first drew notice after the 2008 financial collapse, when the government bailed out the money-center banks with hundreds of billions of dollars, and subsequently the Justice Department declined to prosecute any bigwigs for the misdoings that led to the crisis. A lone midlevel bond trader, Kareem Seragelden of Credit Suisse, was the only Wall Streeter to see jail time, even as the New York banks paid billions in fines that were ultimately borne by shareholders, not executives. The culture of association continues to this day. The buyout fund employees, their outside attorneys, and the SEC personnel all go to the same schools, and all occupy the same strata of society. "They feel they belong to the same club," said one former SEC attorney on May 12, 2020, "The enforcers may be up against their prior employer or a possible future employer. Unconsciously, perhaps, the richer way to do it is to leave no sore feelings at the end." Howard Fischer, a partner with Moses & Singer who served as a trial counsel with the SEC under two administrations, expressed the situation differently. Commenting on the departure of SEC chairman Jay Clayton in November 2020, Fischer said, "I don't think he made any enemies. Even cases brought against large institutions were all settled on lenient terms."[9] A true crusader, and the SEC has its share of such people, feels outflanked in this environment.

Exhibit A of this governmental phenomenon is the curious case of Robert Smith, the aforementioned CEO of Vista Equity Partners. In October 2020, Smith admitted to hiding a reported $200 million in partnership income, in part by using multiple offshore accounts.[10] Nonetheless, he escaped a felony conviction, avoided jail time, and paid $139 million in taxes and penalties (a tiny 2 percent of his net worth). Compare this charitable treatment with that of a little person—like Mike (the "Situation") Sorrentino, a cast member of the *Jersey Shore* reality TV show. First accused of not paying taxes on $9 million of income, Sorrentino admitted to evading taxes on a lesser amount and wound up being a convicted felon and served eight months in Otisville, New York's federal prison.[11]

A secondary difficulty at the SEC is the agency's self-perception of its chances of winning a case against a wealthy buyout fund that has vast legal resources to fight an enforcement action. Unless a case is a slam dunk with videos, inside emails, and whistleblower testimony, the SEC may well conclude the probability of victory is remote, even when a losing case still provides a deterrent factor to the industry's indiscretions. Lastly, enforcement actions that rely on an evidentiary foundation of convoluted numbers and expert opinions, which is the situation for complex buyout financings—may give the agency pause. "They lack the self-confidence to think they can win a case against the big firms," said one former SEC attorney.

In July 2020, Jay Clayton, the SEC chairman, gave a full-throated endorsement to a new policy at the Department of Labor. The department now allows 401(k) sponsors to introduce buyout funds into the $7 trillion individual retirement market, saying such a move increases investor choice.[12] As the preceding narrative demonstrates, exposing widows and orphans to this largely unregulated, illiquid, and secretive investment option lacks prudence.

Four months after advocating for buyout funds' inclusion in IRAs, Mr. Clayton announced his resignation from the SEC. Six weeks after he departed the SEC, he joined Apollo Global Management, one of the largest PE fund complexes, as lead independent director, a part time job paying half a million dollars per year.[13] One month later, he assumed the role of non-executive chair of the board.

After an interview with two SEC staffers, the author submitted a list of written questions to the SEC regarding its regulation of the private equity industry. As of this writing, the SEC has declined to respond to the questions.

Closing

The legislative, audit, and regulatory machinery covering buyout funds is accommodative to the industry's growth. This collective posture is tremendously beneficial to fund managers, who enjoy special tax treatments, lax accounting rules, and governmental kid gloves.

10

The Fellow Travelers

FEW PEOPLE KNOW THE story of Energy Future Holdings—at $45 billion, the largest leveraged buyout ever. The deal represented the pinnacle of the LBO business in the mid-2000s, and the transaction was poised to be a shining example of how the PE model enhances the operations and profits of even the biggest well-run firms. Instead, playing against type, the transaction was a debacle, and the company went bust in 2014. The $8 billion outlay from equity investors, including prominent buyout funds KKR and Texas Pacific, was completely wiped out. Warren Buffett's Berkshire Hathaway was a lender to the deal, and it lost $900 million on its $2 billion debt participation, prompting Buffett to tell his shareholders, "Most of you have never heard of Energy Future Holdings. Consider yourself lucky. I certainly wish I hadn't."[1]

A little-known fact is that Energy Future Holdings was not a one-off occurrence. In fact, three of the top ten leveraged buyouts went bankrupt despite all the expert business analysis, financial engineering, and operations advice poured in by the PE owners. Participants lost billions. Another three of the top ten buyouts were breakeven, even as the funds held onto the companies for over a decade, waiting for fortunes to change. The investors in those six deals would have been better off staying in the stock market; accordingly, the remaining four of the top ten deals were left as winners. A 0.400 batting average is outstanding in baseball but a mediocrity in investments. One would think a success rate of just 40 percent on its marquee deals—the industry's most noteworthy transactions—would be a black eye for the PE action model and consequently an insurmountable obstacle to its ability to secure commitments for successor funds. With other asset classes, when investment managers seek new money, prospective finance sources would point out the six of ten failures and resist calls for additional dollars. Yet none of this happened in the buyout business. The institutions dismissed the losses, brushed aside the debacles, and embraced the industry's request for more cash. As a result, the six foundering megadeals were relegated to the dustbin of history, and the industry's reputation for infallibility lived on. Hundreds of billions moved into LBO coffers during subsequent fund-raising efforts (see table 10.1).

Buyout titans portray themselves as big, tough guys, installing strict discipline on their acquisitions and laying off thousands of employees without blinking an eye. Even though they sit alone at the top of the PE pyramid, they are not loners, and they recognize the need for friends to keep the money train in motion. Providing help to them is an influential group of fellow travelers, individuals who are sympathetic to the buyout business and who engage with business media, academic centers, investment consultants, service providers, and wealth management firms. Their assistance is not a frontal endorsement but rather a tacit complicity, whereby the fellow travelers downplay competing investment tactics, such as replication indexing, that are better than buyouts yet cheaper (see table 10.2).

Table 10.1
Top ten leveraged buyouts

Company	Enterprise value (billions)	Results
Energy Futures Holding	$45	Bankrupt
Hospital Corporation of America	$33	Good return
Harah's Entertainment	$30	Bankrupt
Kinder Morgan	$29	Good return
First Data	$29	Neutral
Clear Channel Communications	$27	Bankrupt
Alltel	$27	Good return
Hilton Hotel	$26	Good return
RJR Nabisco	$24	Neutral
Freescale Semiconductor	$18	Neutral

Sources: Prequin, author research.

Table 10.2
Fellow travelers in the buyout business

Business media
Investment consultants
Academic centers
Service providers
Financial advisory firms

The Business Media Coverage

The media coverage of the PE industry is divided into three categories:

- Manager oriented
- Stenography
- Investor protection

Manager Oriented

The manager-oriented reporting focuses on new transactions, existing investments, industry expansion, fundraising, and purported returns, along with PE-manager personalities and deeds. Readers gain a good knowledge of industry activity and the current state of affairs, and the reporting provides interpretations of events and interesting stories on the players. The coverage offers little or no critical analysis of the industry's operating methods and success claims, which are taken as a given. The secrecy of the buyout industry, the expense of investigative work, and the risk of alienating information sources makes it all but impossible for a reporter to dissect the industry's frailties on a systematic level. Manager-oriented content is the bulk of the media coverage for these reasons.

Stenography

Rehashing press releases with no independent research or storyline is a mainstay of the business media. This approach covers a sizeable portion of what is reported on the industry, and it provides basic information that media consumers want to know. Media firms ask their employees to write many stories for a given block of work time; therefore, the employees have little ability to complete rigorous research on most developments in the financial markets. In-depth reporting, if any, is thus on a highly selective basis, and it is sometimes lost in the shuffle of the daily grind. A solid investigative piece requires a few months of effort backed by a reporter with extensive PE knowledge, and these requirements stretch the resources available to media outlets.

Investor Protection

Investor protection write-ups incorporate elements of both manager reporting and stenography, but the content includes a measure of skepticism about buyout methods, profits, and leaders. In some cases, the content is a full-blown exposé, usually about a buyout bankruptcy and its repercussions or about the unprincipled means by which a PE firm strips a company of its assets after loading it with debt. Of note are high-profile bankruptcies of companies well known to the public, like Toys "R" Us. The validity of the industry's benefits to its investors receives less scrutiny, in part due to the confidential nature of the relevant data, the multiplicity of evaluation criteria, and to the media's resistance in challenging the current consensus.

The Business Media

The business media comprises four groupings:

1. Traditional print
2. Television
3. Trade publications
4. Bloggers

Traditional Print

Newspapers and magazines represent the traditional print media. A few major newspapers provide sustained coverage of PE, such as the *Wall Street Journal*, the *New York Times*, and the *Financial Times*. Prominent business magazines, such as *Fortune, Forbes,* and *Institutional Investor*, follow the business regularly. At $1 trillion in equity commitments, the industry is not peanuts, but it remains a niche subject in the context of larger financial and economic matters. Print journalists offer reasonably balanced reporting, but the PE stories tend to have a positive spin, with buyout executives often coming off as geniuses in beating the odds and conquering the public indexes. Thus, these publications have been supportive, perhaps inadvertently, of the industry's expansion.

Because of the media's problems in collecting hard information, the industry's penchant for secrecy, and the plausibility of purported investment results, even experienced journalists fall victim to the buyout funds' public relations efforts, as evidenced by this 2019 paean to the industry, penned by ex-reporter and business commentator Steve Pearlstein for the *Washington Post*:

> The reason private equity has become as big as it has is because, for the past 30 years, it has consistently delivered higher returns than the public stock markets—and that after taking into account the outlandish fees paid the private equity managers.[2]

Of course, this statement is not true, and a diligent research effort exposes its fault lines. The mellowing of the business press with respect to tough reporting is part of a trend. Dean Starkman, former business reporter and author of *The Watchdog That Didn't Bark: The Financial Crisis and the Disappearance of Investigative Journalism*,[3] tracks the evolution of journalistic priorities that has shifted from accountability reporting, which is costly and sometimes offensive to industry sources, to access reporting, which is inexpensive and inoffensive. Clearly, this shift in priorities contributed to delays in the unmasking of the mortgage-lending mess and the 2008 economic crisis. Wall Street and its regulators could not be counted on to provide forewarning, and the press warnings appeared too late in the game for the crisis to be contained.

As time goes on and the number of unsold LBO deals piles up, the industry's shortcomings will be difficult to hide. The traditional print media will play closer attention to funds' usefulness to institutional portfolios, and to the funds' deleterious impact on the rank-and-file beneficiaries of the prominent institutions that bankroll the PE industry.

Television

With a small window of content compared to print media—a half hour of TV equals one page of newsprint—business television networks tailor their content to a wide audience. A wide audience is the antithesis of the PE market, whose participants are few (i.e., a roster of sophisticated institutional staffers and wealthy individual investors). The millions of employees at the funds' underlying portfolio firms are unlikely viewers for buyout TV segments, although this dynamic may change as 401(k) accounts find PE in their asset mix, encouraging more stories. What little coverage there is mostly relates to big deal announcements, large buyout bankruptcies, and fund manager interviews. The latter lean toward the softball variety, and TV anchors are more prone to ask billionaire managers about the general state of the economy or financial markets rather than to pose pointed questions about fund performance. Some anchors, such as CNBC's Melissa Lee, exhibit a healthy skepticism when faced with a tub-thumping PE player, such as Triago's Antoine Drean,[4] whom she interviewed for CNBC's *Power Lunch* program. A useful counterpoint is more interviews with the likes of index pioneer John Bogle, who avoided fads and never changed his investing philosophy.

Business TV anchors do not perform semi-cross-examinations of prominent guests, as is the case on Sunday morning public affairs talk shows. Unlike political leaders who believe they need the media exposure to advance agendas, financial executives can decline invitations to appear on business TV with little negative consequence. Tough questions make them reticent to take part in interviews, and access becomes problematic for the network. A print reporter covering PE summed up the situation to me as follows: "Business TV is about giving the guests a soapbox." A doubting reporter grilling a fund manager makes little economic sense for a TV network that needs a steady stream of prominent quests to attract viewers.

Trade Publications

As the LBO industry grew, media firms and entrepreneurs started fund-focused publications, like *Alt Assets Daily Private Equity Newsletter*, *Buyouts Insider*, and *Private Equity International*. Typically set up as subscriber-paid websites, they provide a lot of information on what is going on and who is doing what. Reporters frequently scrutinize industry trends and patterns, but they avoid fund performance research. "The numbers are too complicated," says one trade journalist. "Our editors are paranoid about getting it wrong." The publications accept paid advertising, and some earn additional revenue sponsoring seminars where investors can learn from experts and mingle with fund managers.

The five principal PE database services—Preqin, Pitchbook, Burgiss, Thomson Reuters, and Cambridge—offer online newsletters that are like the fund-focused publications. Their proprietary databases also supply the foundation for industry analyses in numerous ways: investor types, managers, subsector class, geographic location, and news category. The database services make portions of their news and fact-finding available to the public, but they are fundamentally subscription models where customers pay thousands of dollars per year to access the information and analysis.

Bloggers

In 2014, the Ninth Circuit Court of Appeals ruled in *Obsidian Financial Group v. Crystal Cox* that bloggers are journalists and entitled to the constitutional protections of journalists.[5] Obsidian is a financial advisory firm that sued blogger Crystal Cox for defamation. Only a handful of blogs focus on PE, and most of them have an educational bent, telling the reader how the business works rather than offering opinions. There is a far wider universe of Wall Street–oriented bloggers, and these individuals touch on buyout-related subjects from time to time, again with an emphasis on education and events rather than critical thinking.

Investment Consultants

The broad popularity of the Yale model and the blanket acceptance of modern portfolio theory among institutions necessitated an increase in in-house staff dedicated to the investment function. The staffers deal with the growing complexity of asset composition and portfolio analysis at their institutions. These developments provided the impetus for the expansion of the institutional investment consulting business. As of this writing, virtually every public pension plan has an outside consultant, as do many endowments and foundations. Many institutions employ multiple consultants. These consultants almost universally promote the use of PE (and other alternatives) in institutional portfolios, so they are a key component in the industry's progress.

Consultants assist the in-house staff and supply resources and expertise that the staff lacks. Depending on the institution's needs, the advice might start with high-level issues—such as future cash flow requirements—to granular matters—such as individual asset manager selection. In my opinion, the in-house staff can handle this work credibly, particularly at the larger institutions. But as the University of Oxford's Howard Jones said about the prevalence of consultants at institutions, "It's backside covering. It's easy to say you took expert advice."[6] Here is a brief overview of potential consulting assignments:

INVESTMENT CONSULTANTS—POTENTIAL ASSIGNMENTS FOR INSTITUTIONAL INVESTORS

High Level

- Review of future cash flow, liquidity, and rate-of-return needs.
- Evaluate the institution's time horizons and risk-tolerance levels.
- Develop an asset allocation model, indicating percentage of stocks, bonds, and alternatives in the portfolio.

Secondary Level

- Screen third-party money managers that fit the asset allocation model and make specific manager-hiring recommendations.
- Review overall portfolio performance against predetermined goals and benchmarks.
- Monitor third-party manager results and costs and advise on monetary commitments for each manager.

For public pension plans, the biggest customer segment of the buyout industry, the asset allocation game is all about forecasting a 7 percent annual portfolio return. The higher the return, the better the plan looks. Below 7 percent, a plan shows a larger unfunded pension deficit than with a greater number like 8 percent. With a lower number like 6 percent, the pension beneficiaries might get nervous about upcoming cash shortages and press for higher employer contributions to the plan. If the state or municipal employer pours more money into a pension plan, the larger contribution crowds the government's budget. However, if the plan's investment staff forecasts a greater yield, like 10 percent, the plan's actuaries and the state's bond rating agencies will express reservations about undue optimism at the plan. Where do investment consultants come in? They design portfolios that justify the 7 percent forecast by injecting into its assets a moderate dose of PE, which supposedly supercharges the portfolio's profit prospects. A representative table of capital market assumptions, as of January 2021, from Callan Institute, a premier consultancy, appears as table 10.3. Note how PE has the greatest forecast return.[7]

Like other actors in the buyout fund ecosystem, investment consultants accept a fund manager's self-reported performance as a given. Consultants rarely send their own valuation experts to verify unsold portfolio company mark-to-markets, nor do they send their own accountants to inspect fund financial records. Exceptions to this rule might be made if a fund's returns deviate sharply from the norm, but in general the consulting fees are

Table 10.3
Ten-year capital market assumptions, January 2021

Asset class	Projected annualized return
U.S. equities	6.60%
Global equities, ex U.S.	6.80%
U.S. core bonds	1.75%
High-yield (junk) bonds	4.35%
Real estate	5.75%
Private equity	8.00%
Hedge funds	4.00%

Source: Callan Institute, January 2021, "2021 Capital Market Assumptions," Jay Kloepfer, Adam Lozinski, and Kevin Machiz

too small to warrant a thorough diligence during a run-of-the-mill manager selection process. In other words, consultants face a perverse situation: institutions are willing to sign up for a $200 million fund commitment, for example, and guarantee $30 million in fees to the manager, yet they refuse to spend $500,000 on a proper due diligence process that may or may not signal the investment's rejection. The consultant's inclination, therefore, is to cut risk and to recommend an experienced brand-name manager with a long history in the hope the PE manager will safeguard its legacy by hitting the industry averages. "If a consultant has the option of a multi-billion-dollar fund manager that has successfully raised multiple prior funds, they will recommend them almost every time, instead of a new or smaller fund manager that might be more difficult to scale within their network," says Jason Lamin, chief executive of Lenox Pack, a networking platform for institutions and emerging managers.[8]

There is no statistical foundation for thinking big, older managers outperform small, newer managers, but that actuality does not stop the practice. Then as well, consultants study fund track records intensely, ignoring the documented evidence that managers are unable to repeat positive performance on a consistent basis. Consultants' suggestions on LBO fund managers, therefore, have little probative weight. The most adverse action by consultants over the last few decades has been to support PE's inclusion into the asset allocation model, even when proper indexing can duplicate PE's results. Consultants' repeated endorsements of individual managers and the entire asset class are influential and are therefore beneficial to the buyout business (see figure 10.1).

Consultants never seem to tire of beating the drum for old-line managers, like TPG Capital, as well as for the occasional newcomer that holds the promise of being the next Carlyle Group. Through this assistance to the buyout business, the consultants have done untold harm to institutions—and the beneficiaries—by pretending that buyout fund selection is a scientific exercise or

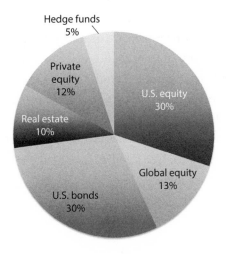

FIGURE 10.1 Typical consultant asset mix proposal

something more than rolling the dice in a rigged crap game where the fund managers have a distinct advantage over the investors.

Neither the institutional clients nor the regulatory agencies have attempted to solve the consultants' dilemma. If the consultants take the high road and admit the truth—that a 60–40 stock-bond index beats the Yale model and that costly alternative assets, like PE, are inappropriate for most clients—then they put themselves out of business. Armed with such candid advice, institutions will no longer pay millions of dollars to review a multitude of third-party managers and asset allocation plans. The institutions will revert to simpler times when publicly traded securities comprised 90 percent of their investments.

Service Providers

The buyout industry has many service providers that post information, news, and research on their websites. Service providers include management consulting firms, law firms, and accounting firms. The website posts are noncritical and educational in nature—how buyout deals are done, here are recent legislative rulings, set forth are current transactions—and the posts demonstrate a service provider's expertise in the business. A few service providers supply links to lengthy research reports developed by the service provider and covering trends, statistics, deal summaries, and fund performance results.

Academic Centers

As the buyout industry expanded, it attracted the academic community's attention. Finance professors created university courses on PE; sponsored related conferences for students, alumni, and guests; and published research papers on the industry.

The courses are descriptive, providing an outline of how the industry functions, how a deal gets done, and how a few transactions turned out. Most business schools consider PE to be a niche segment of the capital markets, so course offerings are limited. As a result, many fledgling deal-doers make do without formal instruction. Yet, despite the meager exposure for students, the industry's mystique is unmistakable. In my merger and acquisition classes at Johns Hopkins Carey Business School, which does not have a PE course, about half of the students want to join the industry upon graduation. They see it as an interesting business and a one-way ticket to a good living.

Business school–sponsored seminars, which might last a couple of days, take a different tack. With the help of a moderator, panels of practitioners review aspects of the buyout business, and attendees ask questions of the panel after the formal discussion. The panelists' presentations occasionally devolve into chest pounding, as the practitioners tell everyone within earshot how terrific their respective profits are. Despite the quasi-academic involvement, the seminars avoid certain topics, and an attendee does not hear a dialogue, for example, on whether buyout funds beat public stock indices. A notice for the popular Wharton Annual Private Equity Conference is illustrative:

> Following the incredible success private equity managers have experienced in delivering market-beating returns, building leading companies, and attracting fundraising from investors, the bar has been set higher than ever, and firms must continue to innovate to stay ahead of the pack.[9]

In the early 2000s, researchers at prominent business schools released studies on performance that concluded that buyout funds decisively beat the stock market.[10] Due to their timing, these seminal studies focused on the buyout industry's golden years, and the professors relied heavily on the now somewhat discredited internal-rate-of-return measurement. No matter. The notion that buyouts provided higher returns quickly became "settled law," to borrow a legal phrase, and over a decade passed before the academic community, following the footsteps of a few dissenters, looked seriously at private versus public returns. In the meantime, the industry's fellow travelers cited the academic studies as an independent, unbiased imprimatur of the industry's profit-making abilities.

Wealth Management Firms

Buyout funds are principally directed at large institutions, but high-net-worth individuals and small institutions—namely, the retail market—have access to the product indirectly. The retail market participants do not have full-time in-house investment managers, and in their place many use financial advisors to guide them through the web of portfolio options. As Martin Krikorian of Capital Wealth Management writes, "Today there are financial advisors everywhere you look. Banks, brokerage firms, insurance agencies, credit unions, and accounting firms all seem to offer financial advice."[11] Their typical portfolio recommendation is a mix of publicly traded stocks, bonds, mutual funds, and passive index funds.

For wealthier clients who meet regulatory guidelines for purchasing alternative assets, many of the advisors offer the ability to obtain a moderate PE exposure. A friend of mine who works as an advisor for one of the wirehouse brokerage firms—five of the largest wirehouses are Morgan Stanley, Bank of America, Merrill Lynch, Wells Fargo, and UBS—sat in on a PE sales pitch, but not a hard sell, in mid-2020. Here is the gist of the presentation:

> Compared to the stock market, private equity funds provide higher returns, greater diversification, and a low correlation to public markets. The client cannot expect cash distributions for five years, and the product furnishes a five-year commission tail for the advisor, on top of fees for the fund-of-fund managers and PE managers.

As described in the sales pitch, PE fits well within the modern maxim that clients should seek diversification and low market correlation across a portfolio. The claims embedded in the wirehouse's explanation are open to question; yet, at the very least, the placement of PE on its product platform, alongside the more traditional offerings, is a tacit endorsement of the asset class.

The big-ticket fee reputation of the asset class is not lost on the advisor community. "Fees are always first and center for advisors on any strategy, but especially on alternatives," says Donal Mastrangelo, head of U.S. iFunds for Mercury Capital Advisors, "The second layer is how much of the fees are disclosed. That becomes the enigma for advisors to solve for. Some firms are reticent, others are more transparent, but it can take a little bit of forensic accounting, to understand what the total cost of ownership is over the life of the fund."[12]

Closing

The buyout fund industry would not be as large as it is today without the implicit support and benign neglect of a host of fellow travelers. These compadres include individuals employed by business media, investment consultants, service providers, academic centers, and financial advisory firms. A truth seeker may be frustrated by the breadth and diversity of this grouping. Alas, such a seeker might find comfort in the kindred plight of Diogenes, the Greek philosopher, who roamed the streets of Athens with a lantern in a futile attempt to find an honest man.

11

In Closing

WHEN A PUBLISHER RECEIVES a book proposal, it is not unusual for the publisher to ask outside authors, experts, and academics to review the proposal and to make comments on the book's content and marketability. One reviewer for a prospective publisher of this work had this to say about my proposal:

> Mr. Hooke can't be right about the leveraged buyout industry. If he were, the participants in this part of the capital markets would be suffering from a mass hallucination!

This reviewer's opinion is simply wrong. The buyout phenomenon, which has taken hold of numerous educated and experienced businesspeople, is not a hallucination. Rather, it is a manifestation of the irrationality that grips Wall Street from time to time. Consider the following.

On a macro scale, the United States exhibited two financial manias over the past twenty years. In the run-up to the great financial crisis (2007–2008), mortgage-backed-securities were all the rage. Institutions, banks, investment firms, and government agencies stuffed their portfolios with these securities, the value of which had been then affirmed by countless analysts, experts, appraisers, lawyers, accountants, bond rating agencies, and regulators. The eventual realization that many of these securities had the equivalent worth of wallpaper led to a calamity that cost the economy trillions. Likewise, a decade earlier, investors poured money into internet stocks with an unbridled enthusiasm, and the dot-com bubble was born. Speculative excess was everywhere. High-tech companies with little more than a business plan raised billions in capital, completed hot IPOs, and closed billion-dollar merger deals. When the dot-com music stopped in March 2000, the tech-heavy Nasdaq stock index began a gut-wrenching 76 percent drop, extending over a tortuous two and a half years. Wall Street became awash in valueless stock certificates of internet companies that, only a few years earlier, had been touted by thousands of sophisticated players as the next big thing.

The buyout business is not what it was twenty years ago, and it is living off a reputation for high returns that is now undeserved. This conclusion contradicts accepted Wall Street wisdom—but as one bond trader said about commonly held beliefs in financial markets, "It's the accepted wisdom, until it isn't." Such became the case with the abrupt endings to the mortgage-backed-securities and dot-com stock crazes. For now, despite any number of statistical studies that show buyout funds do not perform as advertised, the industry still has positive buzz. Over the last eighteen months, for example, six new $10 billion-plus funds have opened, and 2020 was the best year ever for buyout fundraising. In June 2020, Calpers, the $400 billion California pension plan that is the bell cow for hundreds of institutions, announced that it will increase its allocation to PE funds to get a better yield.[1] Yet the plan's total-value-to paid-in ratio for PE investments over thirty-five years is only a modest 1.5×, which puts the plan's PE portfolio in neutral territory compared to stocks.

How has the industry's mystique gone unchallenged for these many years, enjoying a lifespan that is two to three times longer than other investment fads? In part, the secrecy of the industry and the complexity of its data have blocked the most intrepid doubting Thomas from confirming suspicions. The mortgage-backed-securities and dot-com investments were publicly traded, and, over time, skeptics were able to point repeatedly at adverse information to build up credibility. In contrast, the rates of return, fees, and diversification attributes of the buyout asset class are shrouded in a numbers fog. An investigation surrounding the last fifteen years' of performance remains dependent on what the industry says its unsold companies are worth, even as the high proportion of unsold investments—56 percent at last count—suggests that few portfolio firms have willing buyers at reasonable prices. Otherwise, the funds would have sold the investments and moved on.

Meanwhile, a self-perpetuating feedback loop allows the industry to operate in a parallel universe where the laws of financial physics do not apply. To illustrate, buyout managers sell their product as a way to beat the stock market; however, for the last fifteen years, the average fund underperformed the S&P 500. The managers say the product has less risk than the stock market and low correlation to it, but both assertions are refuted by the proven impact of leverage on corporate value movements. The established relationship between debt and equity is based on sixty years of classical finance theory and is endorsed by Nobel laureates such as William Sharpe, Harry Markowitz, and Merton Miller. Special accounting rules, approved by the appropriate authorities, permit PE managers to mark-to-market their own portfolios with minimal oversight and empower institutional investors to ignore expensive carried interest fees. Compounding this oddity is that the carried interest can kick in even when a fund underperforms the stock market. "Don't ask, don't tell" becomes the institutional refrain with respect to such elevated fees. A lack of regulatory standards provides the funds with the latitude to choose among multiple yardsticks for performance assessment and top-quartile ranking. The reliance on easily manipulated IRR measurements, instead of the more neutral total-value-to-paid-in ratio, distorts actual economic returns at a time when investors need accuracy. The industry's principal customers—state and municipal pension plans, university endowments, fund-of-funds, and nonprofit foundations—have administrators who commit their employers to PE for career preservation, since the logical investment choice—a low-cost public stock index fund—obviates the need for their own jobs. Regulatory agencies, such as the IRS, SEC, and Department of Labor are noticeably absent, and thus, the feedback loop is complete (see figure 11.1).

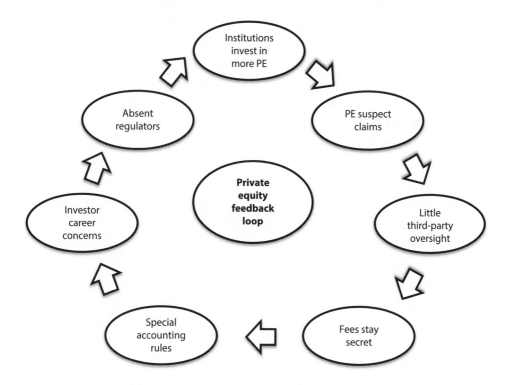

FIGURE 11.1 PE industry feedback

The demonstrated longevity of the feedback loop rests on one key underpinning, according to one observer: "Everyone makes money except the beneficiaries (of the institutions), so the system lives on." Private equity managers, investment consultants, and institutional executives make good livings at the expense of state and municipal retirees, university students, fund-of-funds clients, and foundation grantees, so no one wants to blow the whistle. The question then becomes one of societal priorities. Which is more important—the purchase of luxury items, such as pent-houses on Park Avenue, beach houses in the Hamptons, and villas on the Cote d'Azur, or the support of public pensions, college scholarships, and nonprofit charities? Economists of the doctrinaire school argue with this simplistic characterization, and they respond, "Who is to say one expenditure is better than the other? It is the free market at work." In the end, the nations' political and economic actors must decide through action what avenue is appropriate going forward. Alternatively, these actors can shrug their shoulders, avoid the money decision, and echo the words of Ross Johnson, the chief executive of LBO target RJR Nabisco. Reflecting on the deal's inequities to various RJR stakeholders, he pondered, "What does a few billion dollars matter in the sands of time?"[2]

When the buyout industry began in earnest forty years ago, many business commentators viewed the transactions as a force for good, bringing discipline, professionalism, and modernity to a sluggish hidebound U.S. industrial base ravaged by nimble foreign competitors. By the late 1990s, two eminent professors, Harvard's George Baker and NYU's George David Smith, went on to say, "As both prod to action and example, the management buyout has helped restore American business to its vital promise."[3] The industry's rapacious financial and governance techniques never quite lived up to this laudatory image, but at least the average fund of that distant time recorded a string of market-beating returns—albeit with attendant bankruptcies and high fees. Such is not the case today. While much of the business media lionizes buy-out titans as investment demigods with a Midas touch, the truth is less glowing. Recent results are pedestrian, and market-beating buyout funds are a random occurrence rather than a predictable event. Managers have a tough time duplicating prior success, and big funds do about the same as small funds. Median annual rates of return, using a total-value-to-paid-in metric, are in the 8 percent to 9 percent range, and the TVPI ratio itself is a humdrum 1.5, if the funds' mark-to-market reporting is to be believed. The track record is hardly divine, only human. This book therefore welcomes the buyout managers' return to the world of men.

That being said, there is much to marvel at in the way buyout managers have conducted their business. They have taken a simple concept—borrowing money to increase equity returns—and shaped it into a massive commercial empire with little accountability. They have cloaked middling investment returns in a mass of confidentiality and misinformation, and they have secured the acquiescence of numerous outside third parties in furthering their industry's growth. Most importantly, they have convinced the institutional world that PE is an integral part of modern portfolio theory; and, consequently, it must be included in all institutional asset allocations, thus ensuring themselves a revenue stream for years to come. These are remarkable accomplishments without proper recognition, and acknowledgement is long overdue.

Some intellectuals lament that the 2000s have produced few master painters compared to the previous century, which had Picasso, Pollock, and Mondrian, among others. However, this complaint takes a narrow view of those who practice the imaginative arts. Note the words of the Count of Monte Cristo, a literary figure of immense wealth, as he talked to his affluent Parisian banker, Baron Danglars, "My dear baron, he who handles money well is also an artist."[4] Viewed in this light, the last twenty years have put forth artists of a different kind—Henry Kravis of KKR,

Leon Black of Apollo, and David Rubenstein of Carlyle Group—to mention a few. Their uncanny skill in weaving a tapestry of success through the investment world is commendatory; they are the cultural icons of this time in history.

Typically, a book of this nature, which exposes an industry's shortcomings and a market failure, ends by presenting a laundry list of suggested reforms. In present day America, such a list is pointless. The buyout industry is woven into the fabric of American business, political, and charitable institutions, and it has the power and influence to forestall meaningful change. The subservience of elected officials to wealth is well chronicled, and before expending significant effort, would-be reformers should reflect on the words of Roman governor Pontius Pilate to the rebellious Ben Hur, prince of ancient Judea: "A grown man knows the world he lives in, and, for the present, that world is Rome."[5] The phrase encapsulates the futility of today's institutional beneficiaries in asking their financial advisors to buck the status quo. Giving in to cynicism and despair is the only rational option for those beneficiaries, many of whom consider the buyout business to be unfair on any number of levels.

The industry's arguments against reform are easily anticipated. Set forth below are well-worn claims that Wall Street trots out when faced with restrictive legislation.

"Such changes will set back the financial markets for a hundred years."

"New regulation will kill any hope of financial innovation."

"Additional laws will disrupt free markets and will strangle the businessman."

Still, even Adam Smith, the Scottish economist, who coined the term "the invisible hand" and who is referred to as the father of capitalism, did not mean the words *free markets* to be a market free of government interference and ground rules, particularly when one side—in this instance the buyout funds—gains from an asymmetry or an imbalance of information.

Furthermore, the definition of a businessman, in this context, refers to the senior executive or the business owner. Even so, the definition is both too narrow for broad application and too self-serving of commercial interests. In a landmark speech, William Jennings Bryan, a famous populist of the early 1900s, critiqued the dominance of business by Wall Street interests, a theme that has resonated since the Founding Fathers. Without being condescending to the average American, Bryan tried to convey to average people that they too are part of the economy, and not just the bigwigs in the fancy suits and the large offices.

> The man who is employed for wages is as much a businessman as his employer. The attorney in a country town is as much a businessman as the corporate counsel in a great metropolis. The merchant at the crossroads store is as much a businessman as the merchant of New York. The farmer who goes forth in the morning and toils all day . . . is as much a businessman as the trader who bets upon the price of grain. The miners who go 1,000 feet into the earth and bring forth precious metals are as much businessmen as the financial magnates who in a backroom corner the money of the world.[6]

Obviously, a miner or a farmer is not a businessman. That hyperbole aside, these individuals have a stake in what goes on in the investment markets. To varying degrees, their goals conflict with those of Wall Street, yet they depend on effective financial advice to support retirement payments, children's college scholarships, and charitable good deeds. The capital pools to which they entrust their money—public pension plans, university endowments, nonprofit foundations—can ill afford to commit more dollars to buyouts when the profit prospects of this asset class are questionable. For institutions, chasing the PE magical elixir diminishes the financial hopes and dreams of the beneficiaries they purport to serve.

Institutions keep getting reports on how great everything is in the buyout business—and, as a result, they suggest that all the beneficiaries should be content with the asset class. Yet they should be aware that these reports are laced with elements of self-interest, self-preservation, and pied piper conformism. Beneficiaries like to think that institutional investors are serious people—with Wharton and Harvard MBAs—and that the managers are being scientific and looking out for beneficiaries during the investment process. In the private equity sphere, what the beneficiaries get instead is a ruse carried out by experts, where decision making is fraught with a lack of independent thinking, an inability to achieve objectives, and a whiff of duplicity.

Notes

1. A Day in the Life

1. Louis Peck, "State Treasurer Nancy Kopp Not Slowing Down," *Bethesda Magazine*, September/October 2015, 24.

2. This and other unsourced quotes throughout the book are from confidential interviews conducted by the author.

3. Details on the state's private equity investment is set forth in Maryland State Retirement and Pension System, Private Equity Commitment List, ,https://sra.maryland.gov/sites/main/files/file-attachments/investment_section_2020 _cafr.pdf?1609772692

4. Actuarial and investment information for the Maryland State Retirement and Pension System is available from the Comprehensive Annual Financial Report prepared on a yearly basis, https://sra.maryland.gov/sites /main/files/file-attachments/2020_msrps_cafr-web_final.pdf?1609769114.

5. "Georgetown Endowment had 0.8 percent Minus Return on Pooled Endowment," *Moody's Credit Opinion*, January 9, 2019.

6. Michael Cooper, "Musicians' Pension Plan Seeks Benefit Cuts in Face of Shortfall," *New York Times*, January 7, 2020, 19.

7. Preqin Alternative Assets Database provides information on Green Equity Investors private equity funds.

8. See *Maryland Public Employees and Retirees Benefit Sustainability Commission*, 2010 interim report, dated January 2011, and the *Maryland Legislative Joint Committee on Pensions* report. Both provide background on changes to the Maryland pension plan.

9. Noah Buhayar, "Buffett Says $100 Billion Wasted Trying to Beat the Market," Bloomberg News, February 25, 2017, https://www.bloomberg.com /news/articles/2017-02-25/buffett-says-100-billion-has-been-wasted-on -investment-fees.

10. Teddy Grant, "Maryland Backs Two Leonard Green Funds," *Buyouts Insider*, December 2, 2019, https://www.buyoutsinsider.com/maryland -backs-two-leonard-green-funds-2/.

2. The Private Equity Industry

1. Jerry Knight, "KKR Using Only $15 Million of Its Own in Nabisco Buyout," *Washington Post*, December 2, 1988, https://www.washingtonpost .com/archive/politics/1988/12/02/kkr-using-only-15-million-of-its-own-in -nabisco-buyout/1e733dd9-9b4e-432e-85c6-5fc594668a0a/.

2. The 2009 buyout vintage year following the 2008 crash featured low acquisition pricing and premium buyout returns years later. Studies showed that a principal factor in certain buyout returns being more than public markets is low buy-in acquisition prices. See: https://www.morganstanley.com/im /publication/insights/articles/articles_publictoprivateequityintheusalong termlook_us.pdf?1596549853128; https://www.institutionalinvestor.com/article /b17xwqqjjf71c9/one-young-harvard-grad%E2%80%99s-quixotic-quest -to-disrupt-private-equity; and https://verdadcap.com/archive/explaining -private-equity-returns-from-the-bottom-up.

3. Jeff Hooke and Ted Barnhill, "Replicating Buyout Funds Through Indexing," *Journal of Indexes* (November/December 2013): 36–39.

Jeff Hooke and Ken Yook, "The Curious Year-to-Year Performance of Buyout Fund Returns: Another Mark-to-Market Problem?" *Journal of Private Equity*, Winter 2017.

4. J. F. L'Her, R Stoyanova, K. Shaw, W. Scott and C Lai, "A Bottom-Up Approach to the Risk-Adjusted Performance of the Buyout Fund Market," *Financial Analysts Journal* 72, no. 4, July/August 2016; 36–48; Daniel Fisher, "Young Hedge-Fund Manager Cracks The Private-Equity Code: Small Stocks And Leverage," https://www.forbes.com/sites/daniel fisher/2016/08/29/young-hedge-fund-manager-cracks-the-private-equity -code-small-stocks-and-leverage/?sh=17ca03e267df.

5. Academic studies that discuss replicating buyout funds through the purchase of public stocks include:

Hooke and Barnhill, "Replicating Buyout Funds Through Indexing,"

Brian Chongo and Dan Rasmussen, "Leveraging Small Value Equities" (working paper, University of Chicago, Chicago, IL, August 1, 2015), https://papers.ssrn.com/sol3/papers.cfm?abstract_id=2639647.

Alexandra Coupe, "Assessing the Risk of Private Equity: What's the Proxy?" *Alternative Investment Analyst Review*, CAIA Member Contribution (Quarter 3, 2016), file:///C:/Users/owner/Downloads/AIAR_Q3_2016.pdf.

Erik Stafford, "Replicating Private Equity with Value Investing, Homemade Leverage, and Hold-to-Maturity Accounting" (working paper, Harvard Business School, Boston, MA, September 18, 2020), https://papers.ssrn.com/sol3/papers.cfm?abstract_id=2720479.

Jeff Hooke and Ken Yook, "The Curious Year-to-Year Performance of Buyout Fund Returns: Another Mark-to-Market Problem?" *Journal of Private Equity* (Winter 2017), https://jpe.pm-research.com/content/21/1/9.abstract.

J. F. L'Her, R. Stoyanova, K. Shaw, W. Scott, and C. Lai, "A Bottom-Up Approach to the Risk-Adjusted Performance of the Buyout Fund Market," *Financial Analysts Journal* 72, no. 4 (July/August 2016): 36–48.

6. Neal Triplett compensation available at: https://paddockpost.com/2018/05/19/executive-compensation-at-duke/.

7. A description of Good Buy Gear and its venture capital transaction is found at Christine Hall, "Good Buy Gear Rises $6M Series A for Second-Hand Baby, Children's Gear," Crunchbase News, October 6, 2020, https://news.crunchbase.com/news/good-buy-gear-raises-6m-series-a-for-second-hand-baby-childrens-gear/.

8. For a review of the State of New Jersey pension plan's experience with hedge funds, see Jeff Hooke and Ken Yook, "Alternative Asset Fees, Returns and Volatility: A Case Study of the New Jersey Pension Fund," *Journal of Alternative Investments* 22, no. 3 (2020): 33–41. See also the New Jersey pension fund annual investment report for 2019, page 29, https://www.state.nj.us/treasury/doinvest/pdf/AnnualReport/AnnualReportforFiscalYear2019.pdf.

9. A good discussion of modern portfolio theory is found at Kenneth R. Solow, *Buy and Hold is Still Dead*, 2nd ed. (New York: Morgan James Publishing, 2016), 135–139.

10. Prudent man review in Josh Lerner, Ann Leamon, and Felda Hardymon, *Venture Capital, Private Equity and the Financing of Entrepreneurship* (Hoboken, NJ: John Wiley, 2012), 9.

11. The loosening of pension plan investment restrictions is summarized well in Pew Foundation, "The State Pension Funding Gap," 2016. https://www.pewtrusts.org/en/research-and-analysis/articles/2017/04 /state-pension-funding-gap. See also "CEM Benchmarking, Asset Allocation and Fund Performance of Defined Benefit Pension Funds in the United States, 1998–2011," June 2014. https://www.cembenchmarking .com/ri/insight/4.

12. For a discussion of the corporate veil, see Gordon H. Broogh, *Private Limited Companies: Formation and Management* (London: Sweet and Maxwell, 1990).

13. Susan Faludi, "The Reckoning: Safeway LBO Yields Vast Profits but Exacts a Heavy Human Toll," *Wall Street Journal*, May 16, 1990, A1. https://www.pulitzer.org/winners/susan-c-faludi.

14. For a discussion on the number of new funds in the 1990s, see Guy Fraser-Sampson, *Private Equity as an Asset Class* (Hoboken, NJ: John Wiley, 2007), 102–103.

15. Bruce Wasserstein, *Big Deal: The Battle for Control of America's Leading Corporations* (New York: Warner Books, 1998), 88–93.

16. Information on the number of discrete active LBO funds, available at https://www.preqin.com.

17. Nicolas Shaxson, *The Finance Curse: How Global Finance Is Making Us all Poorer* (New York: Grove Press, 2019), 56.

18. Stephen Pagliuca, "Bain Capital CEO Stephen Pagliuca on the State of Private Equity, #CNBC, January 23, 2020, YouTube video, 6:54, https:// www.youtube.com/watch?v=kWFJU8jeVHA.

19. Bethany McLean, "Finance Is Supposed to Serve the Economy—Not Harm It," *Washington Post*, December 27, 2019, B5.

20. Noam Chomsky, *Manufacturing Consent: The Political Economy of the Mass Media* (San Francisco: Pantheon Media, 1988).

21. Phil Erard, interview with the author, January 10, 2020.

22. A profile of Steven Klinsky is found at: https://www.forbes.com/profile /steven-klinsky/?sh=56d1321513af.

23. Investopedia, s.v. "bond," last updated February 2, 2021, https://www .investopedia.com/terms/b/bond.asp.

3. How Does the Private Equity Industry Work?

1. Ady Adefris, chief operating officer, Ion Pacific Funds, interview with the author, January 23, 2020.

2. For a Pitchbook Benchmarks reference that only 25 percent of PE funds beat the public markets, see Paul Sullivan, "3 Investments That May Have Hit Their Peak," *New York Times*, September 14, 2018, https://www .nytimes.com/2018/09/14/your-money/investment-private-equity-venture -capital.html.

3. A notable academic study on quartile persistence was authored by Robert S. Harris, Tim Jenkinson, Steve N. Kaplan, and Rudiger Stucke, "Has Persistence Persisted in Private Equity?" (working paper no. 2304808, Darden School, Charlottesville, VA, 2014).

4. For a discussion of top quartile persistence, see McKinsey Global Private Market Review, February 2017, Quartile performance discussed in Morgan Stanley Investment Management, "Public to Private Equity: A Long Term Look," August 4, 2020.

5. See also Ji-Woong Chung, "Performance Persistence in Private Equity Funds," (working paper, Korea University, 2012); Greg Brown, Raymond Chan, Wendy Hu, Kelly Meldrum and Tobias True, "The Persistence of PE Performance," *Journal of Performance Measurement* (Fall 2017).

6. Reiner Braun, Tim Jenkinson, and Ingo Stoff, "How Persistent Is Private Equity Performance?" *Journal of Financial Economics* 123, no. 2 (February 2017).

7. Eric Zoller, "Spin-Out Firms Are High on LP's Wish List," *Private Equity International*, February 17, 2016.

8. Duena Blomstrom, " 'No One Gets Fired for Hiring IBM.' But They Should," *Forbes*, November 30, 2018, https://www.forbes.com/sites /duenablomstrom1/2018/11/30/nobody-gets-fired-for-buying-ibm-but-they -should/?sh=7740433948fc.

9. Jeff Hooke and Ken Yook, "The Relative Performance of Large Buyout Fund Groups," *Journal of Private Equity* (Winter 2016).

10. Julia Creswell, "The Private Equity Firm (Providence) That Grew Too Fast," *New York Times*, April 4, 2015.

11. Darren Foreman and Luke Jacobs, Commonwealth of Pennsylvania Public School Employees' Retirement System, Public Investment Memorandum, Bain Capital Fund XII, LP, May 19, 2017.

12. Arleen Jacobius, "General Partners Putting Money Where Investment Are," *Pension and Investments*, March 20, 2017, 1.

13. Andrew Gunther, managing director, Darby Private Equity, interview with the author, April 28, 2020.

14. Mike Gaffney, Bancroft Group LLC, interview with author, April 28, 2020.

15. Felix Barber and Michael Goold, "The Strategic Secret of Private Equity," *Harvard Business Review*, September 2007, 57.

16. For Steve Denis quote, see Sapna Maheshwari and Vanessa Friedman, "Debt Burden Joins Virus as a Killer of Retailers," *New York Times*, May 15, 2020, B1, https://hbr.org/2007/09/the-strategic-secret-of-private-equity.

4. The Poor Investment Results

1. Mario Gianni, presentation at Hamilton Lane seminar, March 5, 2018. https://www.hamiltonlane.com/news/409681255/2017-Market-Overview-Performance and Mario Gianni, "NASDAQ Signature Series, September 2018," Hamilton Lane, September 11, 2018, YouTube video, 12:16, https://www.youtube.com/watch?v=48Cgx0P2qjk.

2. H. MacArthur and Josh Lerner, "Public vs Private Equity: Is PE Losing its Advantage?" *Bain 2020 Private Equity Report*, February 24, 2020.

3. Antti Ilmanen, Swati Chandra, and Nicholas McQuinn, "Demystifying Illiquid Assets: Expected Returns for Private Equity," *Journal of Alternative Investment* 22, no. 3 (winter 2020): 8–21.

4. For a discussion on post 2005 returns, see Robert Harris, Tim Jenkinson, and Steven Kaplan, "Private Equity Performance, What Do We Know?" *Journal of Finance* 69, no. 5 (2014): 1851–1882.

5. The following notes present research and articles on PE performance, including buyouts falling behind public equities either straight up or adjusted for leverage and specific attributes.

Goldman Sachs & Co., "Historical Distributions of IRR in Private Equity," *Investment Management Research* (November 2001).

Ludovic Phalippou, "Performance of Buyout Funds Revisited?" *Review of Finance* 18, no.1 (March 2013): 189–218.

Steven Kaplan and Bert Sensoy, "Private Equity Performance: A Survey," *Annual Review of Financial Economics* (2015): 597–606.

Robert Harris, Tim Jenkinson, and Steven Kaplan, "How Do Private Equity Investments Perform Compared to Public Equity?" *Journal of Investment Management* (June 2016).

J. F. L'Her, R. Stoyanova, K. Shaw, W. Scott, and C. Lai, "A Bottom-Up Approach to the Risk-Adjusted Performance of the Buyout Fund Market," *Financial Analysts Journal* 72, no. 4 (July/August 2016): 36–48.

Oregon State Treasury, "OPERF Private Equity Review & Annual Plan," February 1, 2018, February 1, 2020. Other states have reached similar conclusions on their PE portfolios.

A. Ang, B. Chen, W. N. Goetzmann, and L. Phalippou, "Estimating Private Equity Returns from Limited Partner Cash Flows," *Journal of Finance* (May 10, 2018).

Hema Parmar and Sonali Basak, "Private Equity's Returns Questioned, This Time by Buffett," Bloomberg.com, May 6, 2019, https://www.bloomberg .com/news/articles/2019-05-05/private-equity-s-returns-questioned-again -this-time-by-buffett.

Jonathan Ford, "Private Equity Returns Are Not All They Seem," *Financial Times*, September 15, 2019, https://www.ft.com/content/2812c2c6 -d634-11e9-a0bd-ab8ec6435630.

Jonathan Ford, "Pension Funds and Private Equity: A Puzzling Romance," *Financial Times*, February 2, 2020, https://www.ft.com/content /fc16cdec-45ba-11ea-aee2-9ddbdc86190d.

Dan Primack, "Private Equity Returns Fell Behind Stocks over the Past Decade," Axios.com, February 24, 2020, https://www.axios.com/private-equity -returns-stock-market-47519044-0087-4863-a9cd-0dd9dc8b57bd.html.

Ludovic Phalippou, "An Inconvenient Fact: Private Equity Returns and the Billionaire Factory," *Journal of Investing* (forthcoming 2021).

6. Gregory Brown and Steven Kaplan, "Have Private Equity Returns Really Declined?" *Kenan Institute of Private Enterprise Report*, April 2019.

7. Oregon State Treasury, "OPERF Private Equity Review & Annual Plan," February 1, 2018, February 1, 2020.

8. Goldman Sachs & Co., "Historical Distributions of IRR in Private Equity," *Investment Management Research* (November 2001).

9. Ford, "Private Equity Returns"; Ford, "Pension Funds and Private Equity."

10. Primack, "Private Equity Returns Fell Behind Stocks."

11. David Hunn and Susan Carroll, "Broken Trust, School Fund Investment Returns Don't Measure Up," *Houston Chronicle*, March 3, 2019.

12. Dan Ilisevich, chief financial officer, Unison Global Inc., interview with author, February 4, 2020.

13. For a brief discussion on the use of credit lines, see Antonella Puca, "Private Equity Funds: Leverage and Performance Evaluation," Enterprising Investor, CFA Institute (blog), July 1, 2018. https://blogs.cfainstitute.org /investor/2018/07/16/private-equity-funds-leverage-and-performance -evaluation/.

14. Parmar and Basak, "Private Equity's Returns Questioned."

15. Robert Harris, Tim Jenkinson, and Rüdiger Stucke, "Are Too Many Private Equity Funds Top Quartile?" *Journal of Applied Corporate Finance* 24, no. 4 (December 2012). See also:

"Top Quartile Status Doesn't Tell Us Much," PERACS.com, newsletter, January 9, 2017; related podcast: "How Can 75 percent of Private Equity Firms Rank in Top Quartile?" https://peracs.com/top-quartile-status-doesnt -tell-us-much/

Conversation with Professor Oliver Gottschalg: https://peracs.com/podcast -how-can-75-of-private-equity-rank-in-top-quartile-conversation-with-dr -oliver-gottschalg/; https://www.privatefundscfo.com/study-77-of-gps-could -claim-top-quartile-status/.

For a tabulation of the dispersion between top and bottom quartile funds, see exhibit 1, J. P. Morgan Asset Management, "Addressing the Benchmark-ing Challenge, Private Equity," June 2018, as well as reports by Cambridge Associates, https://www.cambridgeassociates.com/answers/ca-answers-are -private-equity-returns-doomed/; https://www.sec.gov/files/cambridge-associates -private-investments.pdf.

16. For the Apollo IRR calculation, see https://www.apollo.com/~/media /Files/A/Apollo-V2/documents/events/2018/apollo-global-management-llc -may-investor-presentation-vfinal.pdf, 19. Leon Black quote: David Ruben-stein in conversation with Leon Black at SuperReturn International 2019, https://www.youtube.com/watch?v=bTrJYJ69dPg.

17. A paper by Alexandra Albers-Schoenberg, at INSEAD, "Measuring Private Equity Performance," 2019, provides helpful background on mea-surements https://www.insead.edu/sites/default/files/assets/dept/centres/gpei /docs/Measuring_PE_Fund-Performance-2019.pdf.

18. Author interview with Antonella Puca, May 27, 2020.

19. Callan Associates, *Private Equity Measurement*, https://www.callan .com/callan/blog-archive/pe-measurement/.

20. For older, well-described examples of financial engineering, see Eileen Applebaum and Rosemary Batt, *Private Equity at Work* (New York: Russell Sage Foundation, 2014).

21. Brian Ayash and Mahdi Rastad, "Leveraged Buyouts and Financial Distress," (working Paper, July 20, 2019). They tracked a sample of 484 public to private LBO's for ten years and found a 20 percent default rate. https://papers.ssrn.com/sol3/papers.cfm?abstract_id=3423290.

22. A good discussion of B and CCC-rated bond default rates appears in Arturo Neto, "Sliding Down High Yield for Greater Returns," Seeking Alpha, October 2, 2019, https://seekingalpha.com/article/4294484-sliding -down-high-yield-for-greater-returns.

23. For a discussion on operational improvements, see Felix Barber and Michael Gold, "The Strategic Secret of Private Equity," *Harvard Business Review*, September 2007.

24. David Wasserman, partner Clayton Dubilier & Rice (speech at a Milken Institute Seminar, Creating Value Against Competition, July 6, 2018). https://milkeninstitute.org/videos/private-equity-creating-value-against -increased-competition.

25. For a discussion of a study that showed the lowest-priced deals produced the bulk of Bain Capital buyout returns, see Paul Sullivan, "3 Investments That May Have Hit Their Peak," *New York Times*, September 14, 2018, https://www.nytimes.com/2018/09/14/your-money/investment -private-equity-venture-capital.html; see also Preqin.com, or McKinsey & Company *Global Private Market Review 2020*, for data on the low-priced years of 2008 and 2009 tending to produce the best buyout returns. https:// www.mckinsey.com/~/media/mckinsey/industries/private%20equity %20and%20principal%20investors/our%20insights/mckinseys%20private %20markets%20annual%20review/mckinsey-global-private-markets-review -2020-v4.ashx.

26. John Poerink, Linley Capital, "Private Equity: The Consolidation Play and Due Diligence," Wharton School, February 10, 2011, YouTube video, 1:17:35, https://www.youtube.com/watch?v=thyxopgzG4k&t=3114s.

27. Christopher Burke et al., "Masters of the Universe: Bid Rigging by Private Equity Firms in Multibillion Dollar LBOs", *University of Cincinnati Law Review* 87, no. 1 (October 2018): https://scholarship.law.uc.edu/cgi /viewcontent.cgi?article=1254&context=uclr.

28. IMAA Institute, "Number and Value of M&A Activity in North America," 2020, https://imaa-institute.org/mergers-and-acquisitions-statistics/. For a discussion of M&A deal multiples in various years, see Preqin.com or McKinsey & Company *Global Private Market Review 2020*, https://www.mckinsey.com /~/media/mckinsey/industries/private%20equity%20and%20principal %20investors/our%20insights/mckinseys%20private%20markets %20annual%20review/mckinsey-global-private-markets-review-2020-v4.ashx.

5. Private Equity and the Holy Grail

1. For a seminal discussion on how a buyout fund can be duplicated through the purchase of public stocks and how buyout funds results should correlate, see Jeff Hooke and Ted Barnhill, "Replicating Buyout Funds Through Indexing," *Journal of Indexes* (November/December 2013), https:// www.etf.com/publications/journalofindexes/joi-articles/20196-replicating -buyout-funds-through-indexing.html.

2. For a discussion on how buyout fund returns are reported as less volatile than equity market returns, see Jeff Hooke and Ken Yook, "The Curious Year-to-Year Performance of Buyout Fund Returns: Another Mark-to-Market Problem?," *Journal of Private Equity* (Winter 2017), https://jpe.pm-research.com/content/21/1/9.abstract.

3. Kyle Welch and Stephen Stubben, "Private Equity's Diversification Illusion: Economic Co-Movement and Fair Value Reporting" (working paper, November 1, 2018), https://papers.ssrn.com/sol3/papers.cfm?abstract_id=2379170.

4. Multiple researchers observed return smoothing in the private real estate equity fund business when compared to REITs. A good review of the literature is in David Gelter, Bryan MacGregor, and Gregory Schwann, "Appraisal Smoothing and Price Discovery in Real Estate Markets," *Urban Studies* 40 (May 1, 2003): 1047–1064. A good quantitative review is in J. Diaz and M. Wolverton, "A Longitudinal Examination of the Appraisal Smoothing Hypothesis," *Real Estate Economics* 26, no. 2 (1998): 349–358.

5. NEPC investment consulting research,"A Primer on US Equity REITs and Their Role in an Institutional Investment Portfolio," April 1, 2015, 9–10, https://cdn2.hubspot.net/hubfs/2529352/Blog/2015_04_nepc_a_primer_on_us_equity_reits_and_their_role_in_an_institutional_investment_portfolio.pdf.

6. Nizar Tarhuni, "Covid 19 Impact on Private Market," Pitchbook 2020 Private Equity Database, analyst note.

7. Ted Dinucci and Fran Kinniry, "Benefits of Private Equity in a Volatile Market," Vanguard Inc., May 7, 2020, https://institutional.vanguard.com/VGApp/iip/site/institutional/researchcommentary/article/InvCom BenefitsPrivateEquityVolMkt.

8. Nicolas Rabener, "Private Equity: Fooling Some of the People All of the Time?" Enterprising Investor, January 20, 2020, https://blogs.cfainstitute.org/investor/2020/01/20/private-equity-fooling-some-of-the-people-all-of-the-time/.

9. For a Munger quote on private equity smoothing, see "Buffett Slams Private Equity for Inflated Returns, Debt Reliance," *Economic Times*, last updated May 5, 2019, https://economictimes.indiatimes.com/buffett-slams-private-equity-for-inflated-returns-debt-reliance/articleshow/69180905.cms?from=mdr.

10. Greg Brown, W. Hu, and J. Zhang, " The Evolution of Private Equity Fund Value," Working Paper, June 11, 2020, sponsored by Private Equity Research Consortium and The Institute for Private Capital, https://www.burgiss.com/applied-research-blog/the-evolution-of-private-equity-fund-value, page 1.

11. For a review of mandated valuation techniques for private corporations, see Financial Accounting Standards Board, "Fair Value Measurements," statement of Financial Accounting Standard 157 (accounting standard codification 820), 2006.

12. For David Larsen quote, see Chris Cumming, "Market Swings Likely to Hit Private Equity Valuations," *Wall Street Journal*, April 2, 2020, B3.

13. For Martin Skancke quote, see Anna Hirtenstein, "State-Run Investors Shun Stocks, but Embrace Risk," *Wall Street Journal*, July 25, 2020, B10.

14. Taylor Nadauld, Berk Sensoy, Keith Vorkink, and Michael Weisbach, "The Liquidity Cost of Private Equity Investments: Evidence from Secondary Market Transactions," *Journal of Financial Economics* 132 (November 2018): 158–81, https://papers.ssrn.com/sol3/papers.cfm?abstract_id=2802625.

15. For a review of the net asset value expedient convention, see Financial Accounting Standards Board, Accounting Standards Update 2015–07, Fair Value Measurement (topic 820), "Disclosures for Investments in Certain Entitles That Calculate Net Asset Value per Share," May 3, 2015.

16. For a seminal study on equity portfolio diversification, see Lawrence Fisher and James Lorie, "Some Studies of Variability of Returns on Investments in Common Stocks," *Journal of Business* 43, no. 2 (April 1970): https://www.jstor.org/stable/2352105?seq=1.

For an updated study on diversification, see Ronald Surz and Mitchell Price, "The Truth About Diversification by the Numbers," *Journal of Investing* (Winter 2000): http://ppca-inc.com/Articles/DiversByNumbers.pdf.

See also Eric Critlendon and Cole Wilcox, "The Capitalism Distribution: Fat Tails in Motion," Blackstar Funds research paper, 2008, https://seeking alpha.com/article/108867-the-capitalism-distribution-fat-tails-in-motion.

17. For the U.S. stock market capitalization, see Edward Yardeni, Joe Abbott, and Mali Quintana, "Stock Market Briefing: Market Capitalization," Yardeni Research, March 19, 2021, https://www.yardeni.com/pub/marketcap.pdf.

18. See: https://milkeninstitute.org/sites/default/files/reports-pdf/WP-083018-Companies-Rush-to-Go-Private-FINAL2.pdf

19. The following two articles indicate that private equity's addition to an institutional portfolio has historically not provided diversification: Kyle Welch and Stephen Stubben, "Private Equity's Diversification Illusion: Evidence From Fair Value Accounting," SSRN, November 1, 2018, https://ssrn.com/abstract=2379170; Richard M. Ennis, "Institutional Investment Strategy and Manager Choice: A Critique," *Journal of Portfolio Management* 46, no. 5 (2020): 104–117.

6. The High Fees

1. Fred Schwed, "Where are the Customers' Yachts? A Good Hard Look at Wall Street," (Hoboken, NJ: John Wiley, 1955 [2006 reprint]).

2. The inability of state pension funds to beat a 60–40 index with the inclusion of alternative assets is set forth in two recent papers, Jeff Hooke and Ken Yook, "The Grand Experiment: The State and Municipal Diversification into Alternative Assets," *Journal of Investing* 27 (supplement; Fall 2018): 21–29, https://joi.pm-research.com/content/27/supplement/21 .abstract; and Richard Ennis, "Institutional Investor Strategy and Manager Choice," *Journal of Portfolio Management* (February 28, 2020): https://jpm .pm-research.com/content/early/2020/02/28/jpm.2020.1.141.abstract.

The following paper shows that large foundation investment underperformed a 60–40 index: Jeff Hooke, Ken Yook, and Wenqi Chu, "Top Foundations' 10-Year Plunge into Alternatives Yields Mixed Results and High Fees," *Non-Profit Leadership and Management*, September 2018.

The next two papers also concluded that university endowments have not outperformed a 60–40 index:

Dennis Hammond, "58 Years of Endowment Performance," *Journal of Investing* (June 2, 2020): https://joi.pm-research.com/content/early/2020/06/02 /joi.2020.1.138.

Richard Ennis, "Endowment Performance," 2021, https://richardmennis .com/blog/endowment.

3. For a review of the fee structure, see Eileen Applebaum and Rosemary Batt, *Fees, Fees and More Fees: How Private Equity Abuses its Partners and US Taxpayers* (Washington, D.C.: Center for Economic and Policy Research, May 2016), https://cepr.net/images/stories/reports/private-equity -fees-2016-05.pdf.

4. The fact that only six of thirty-three states that had June 30 year ends and supplied performance fee information is set forth in Carol Park and Jeff Hooke, "2018 State Pension Fund Investment Report" Maryland Public Policy Institute, April 26, 2018, https://www.mdpolicy.org/research /detail/2018-state-pension-fund-investment-performance-report.

5. Jeff Hooke and Yunya Shen, "Survey of 42 State Pension Funds and Private Equity Performance Fee Disclosure, with the Use of Freedom of Information Act filings (FOIA)" (working paper, 2020), Johns Hopkins University Carey Business School.

6. Jeff Hooke, Ken Yook, and Wenqi Chu, "Top Foundations' 10-Year Plunge Into Alternatives Yields Mixed Results and Higher Fees," *Non-Profit Leadership and Management* 29, no. 3 (September 18, 2018): 449–460, https://onlinelibrary.wiley.com/doi/abs/10.1002/nml.21338.

7. For information that Calpers did not know its PE performance fees, see Chris Ford and Chris Newlands, "Calpers Private Equity Problems Pile Up," *Financial Times*, July 11, 2015, 12.

8. Susan Carroll and David Honn, "Broken Trust Texas' Huge School Endowment Pays Out Less and Less for School Children," *Houston Chronicle*, March 2, 2019.

9. For Neal quote, see Chris Newlands, "Low Tax and High Fees Consume Future Fund," *Financial Times*, July 11, 2015, https://www.ft.com /content/dbf7f11e-2632-11e5-bd83-71cb60e8f08c.

10. For information on New Jersey fees and alternative asset performance, see State of New Jersey Investment Council, *2019 Annual Report*, https://www.nj.gov/treasury/doinvest/pdf/AnnualReport/AnnualReportfor FiscalYear2019.pdf.

11. #MIGlobal, "Global Private Equity Outlook," Milken Institute, July 9, 2018, YouTube video, 58:32, https://www.youtube.com/watch?v =TpFOPHUhRBg.

12. For information on the proportion of private equity fees that are unrelated to performance, see Andrew Metrick and Ayako Kasuda, "The Economics of Private Equity Funds," *Review of Financial Studies* 23 (August 2010): 2303–2341, https://papers.ssrn.com/sol3/papers.cfm?abstract_id=996334.

13. Blaze Cass, Andrew Gilboard, and John Haggerty, "Private Markets Frees Primer," Meketa Investment Group, October 2019, https://meketa .com/wp-content/uploads/2012/10/Private-Markets-Fees-Primer-FINAL .pdf.

14. State of Maryland Higher Education Commission, Fiscal 2019 Operating Budget, page 341. https://dbm.maryland.gov/budget/Documents /operbudget/2019/agency/Maryland-Higher-Education-Commission.pdf.

15. Email exchange with author, September 2020. See also Marc Gunther, "Ford Releases Investment Return, More Grant Makers May Be on the Way," *Chronicle of Philanthropy*, October 2, 2017, https://www.philanthropy .com/article/Ford-Releases-Investment/241353.

16. For a review of portfolio company fees, see. Ludovic Phalippou, Christian Rauch, and Marc Umber, "Private Equity Portfolio Company Fees" (working paper 2015-22, Said Business School, University of Oxford, December 15, 2015), https://papers.ssrn.com/sol3/papers.cfm?abstract_id =2703354.

17. For a review of the business model of the buyout fund business and its profit margins, see Marc Rowan, Apollo Global Management presentation, September 12, 2011, https://www.apollo.com/~/media/Files/A /Apollo-V2/documents/events/2011/barclays-conference-slides-12-sep-11 -final-.pdf.

7. The Customers

1. Geraldine Fabrikant, "The Money Management Gospel of Yale's Endowment Guru," *New York Times*, November 5, 2016, https://www.nytimes.com/2016/11/06/business/the-money-management-gospel-of-yales-endowment-guru.html.

For more on Mr. Swensen's background, see "Yale's Financial Wizard, David Swensen, Says Most Endowments Shouldn't Try to be like Yale," Propublica, February 18, 2009, https://www.propublica.org/article/yales-financial-wizard-david-swensen-says-most-endowments-shouldnt-try-to-b.

David Swensen, "Guest Lecture by David Swensen," YaleCourses, April 5, 2019, YouTube video, 1:11:23, https://www.youtube.com/watch?v=AtSlRK0SZoM.

Information on the Yale endowment portfolio and performance history is available at www.investments.yale.edu.

"Investment Return of 5.7 percent brings Yale Endowment value to $30.3 billion," *Yale News*, September 27, 2019, https://news.yale.edu/2019/09/27/investment-return-57-brings-yale-endowment-value-303-billion.

2. Ford Foundation CIO compensation is disclosed on the Foundation's IRS Form 990, 2000 and 2018, available at Economic Research Institute website: http://www.erieri.com/form990finder/details?ein=936026156.

3. "Endowment Value Declines 29.5 percent as Investment Return Is Negative 27.3 percent," *Harvard Magazine*, September 10, 2009, https://harvardmagazine.com/2009/09/sharp-endowment-decline-reported.

4. "The Harvard Endowment: Mark-to-Make-Believe," Charles Skoring, March 21, 2018, available at www.charlesskorina.com/?p=5411.

5. The endowment, state pension plan, and foundation investment returns have underperformed a 60–40 index. See the following studies articles, none of which have been refuted by Wall Street or institutional managers:

M. L. Walden, "Active versus Passive Investment Management of State Pension Plans," *Journal of Financial Counseling and Planning* 26, no. 2 (2015): 160–171.

Richard S. Warr, "The Cost Savings Associated with Indexing the North Carolina Pension Fund," unpublished manuscript, 2016.

E. Tower, "Should the Equities in the North Carolina State Employee Pension Fund Be Indexed or Actively Managed?" (working paper No. 210, Economic Research Incentives at Duke (ERID), 2016).

Jeff Hooke and Ken Yook, "The Grand Experiment: The State and Municipal Pension Fund Diversification into Alternative Assets," *Journal of Investing* 27 (supplement; Fall 2018), 21–29, https://joi.pm-research.com/content/27/supplement/21.abstract.

Jeff Hooke, Ken Yook, and Wenqi Chu, "Top Foundations' 10-year Plunge into Alternatives Yields Mixed Results and High Frees," *Non-Profit Leadership Journal* (September 2018).

Pew Foundation, "State Public Pension Funds' Investment Practices and Performance," September 26, 2018.

"An Examination of State Pension Performance, 2000 to 2017," Cliffwater, LCC, September 2018, https://www.psers.pa.gov/About/Investment/Documents/PPMAIRC%202018/2%20An%20Examination%20of%20State%20Pension%20Performance%202000-2017.pdf.

Julie Segal, "Ivy League Endowments Fail to Beat a Simple 60–40 Portfolio-Again," Institutional Investor, November 29, 2018, https://www.institutionalinvestor.com/article/b1c1c4tq2bjm3c/Not-One-Ivy-League-Endowment-Beat-a-Simple-U-S-60-40-Portfolio-Over-Ten-Years.

"Public Pension Performance, Company Pension Investments to Passive Index Portfolios," Institute for Pension Fund Integrity, August 2019.

Richard Ennis, "Institutional Investment Strategy and Manager Choice: A Critique," *Journal of Portfolio Management, Fund Manager Selection* (July 2020): 104–112.

Dennis Hammond, "58 Years of Endowment Performance," *Journal of Investing* (August 2020): https://joi.pm-research.com/content/early/2020/06/02/joi.2020.1.138.

Richard Ennis, "Endowment Performance and the Demise of the Multi-Asset-Class Model," https://richardmennis.com/blog/endowment-performance.

6. Ennis, "Institutional Investment Strategy and Manager Choice."

7. A brief discussion of fees and fee disclosure among top foundations and state pension funds appears in two papers: Hooke, Yook, and Chu, "Top Foundations' 10-Year Plunge," https://onlinelibrary.wiley.com/doi/abs/10.1002/nml.21338; Hooke and Yook, "The Grand Experiment," 21–29. https://joi.pm-research.com/content/27/supplement/21.abstract.

8. Sissy Cao and Ian Floyd, *Inside the World's Top Institutional Investment Offices* (New York: Trusted Insight, 2017). Interview with author, July 1, 2020.

9. Public plan asset totals available at National Association of State Retirement Fund Administrators: https://www.nasra.org/retirementsystemdata.asp.

10. Number of state and municipal retirement plans available at Urban Institute: https://www.urban.org/policy-centers/cross-center-initiatives/program-retirement-policy/projects/urban-institute-state-and-local-employee-pension-plan-database.

11. Mark J. Drozdowski, "Should Endowments Influence Your College Decision," Best Colleges (website), September 29, 2020, https://www.bestcolleges.com/blog/university-endowments-college-decision/.

12. Alex Beath, senior analyst, CEM Benchmarking, interview with author, June 26, 2020.

13. Maryland State Retirement and Pension System, *Comprehensive Annual Financial Report 2019*, investment section, https://sra.maryland.gov/sites/main/files/file-attachments/investment.pdf?1585750415.

14. Vermont's quarterly pension investment report is a good example of length and complexity. The annual reports are even more lengthy. https://www.vermonttreasurer.gov/sites/treasurer/files/VPIC/PDF/2019/FYE%20Q4%202019%20State%20Employees%20Retirement%20System%20Full%20IPA.pdf.

15. An update on the State of Kentucky lawsuit appears in Mark Vandevelde and Billy Nauman, "Kentucky Sues Blackstone and KKR over Fund Performance," *Financial Times*, July 22, 2020, https://www.ft.com/content/dcc74348-07a4-4757-a94b-77b9ea5ad23a.

16. "Supreme Court Holds That ERISA Defined-Benefit Pension Plan Participants Do Not Have Article III Standing To Sue For Fiduciary Breach," Gibson & Dunn (website), June 1, 2020, https://www.gibsondunn.com/supreme-court-holds-that-erisa-defined-benefit-pension-plan-participants-do-not-have-article-iii-standing-to-sue-for-fiduciary-breach/.

17. A brief discussion of fees and fee disclosure among top foundations and state pension funds appears in two papers: Hooke, Yook, and Chu, "Top Foundations' 10-Year Plunge"; Hooke and Yook, "The Grand Experiment," 21–29.

18. Chris Philips quoted in James Stewart, "College Endowments Opt for Alternative and Less Lucrative Route," *New York Times*, February 22, 2018, https://www.nytimes.com/2018/02/22/business/college-endowments.html.

19. Center for Social Philanthropy, Tellus Institute, "Education Endowment and Financial Crisis," May 27, 2010, https://www.tellus.org/pub/Tellusendowmentcrisis.pdf.

20. David Villa, executive director State of Wisconsin Investment Board, speaking at 9th Annual Delivering Alpha Summit, New York City, September 19, 2019, https://www.cnbc.com/video/2019/09/19/heres-where-the-opportunities-are-for-pension-funds.html.

8. The Staffs

1. "2018 ABANA Achievement Award Dinner Honoring David Rubenstein," ABANA, October 2018, https://www.abana.co/events/all/2018-abana-achievement-award-dinner-honoring-david-rubenste.

2. David Rubenstein, "Amazon CEO Jeff Bezos on the David Rubenstein Show," September 19, 2018, YouTube video, 48:11, https://www.youtube .com/watch?v=f3NBQcAqyu4.

3. Carlyle Group, confidential marketing document for Carlyle Direct Access Fund, Q1 2019.

4. Peter Whorisky and Dan Keating, "Overdoses, Bedsores, Broken Bones, What Happened When a Private Equity Firm Sought to Care for Society's Most Vulnerable," *Washington Post*, November 25, 2018, https://www .washingtonpost.com/business/economy/opioid-overdoses-bedsores-and -broken-bones-what-happened-when-a-private-equity-firm-sought-profits -in-caring-for-societys-most-vulnerable/2018/11/25/09089a4a-ed14 -11e8-baac-2a674e91502b_story.html.

5. Jarrett Renshaw, "Refiner Goes Belly-Up After Big Payouts to Carlyle Group," Reuters, February 20, 2018, https://www.reuters.com/article/us -usa-biofuels-pes-bankruptcy-insight/refiner-goes-belly-up-after-big -payouts-to-carlyle-group-idUSKCN1G40I1#:~:text=The%20Carlyle %2Dled%20consortium%20collected,thirds%20stake%20in%20the %20refiner.

6. Nathan Vardi, "Carlyle's 1.4 Billion Folly: Inside the Biggest Buyout Loss in Washington D.C. Firm's 33-Year History," *Forbes*, March 4, 2020, https://www.forbes.com/sites/nathanvardi/2020/03/04/carlyle-groups -14-billion-folly-inside-the-biggest-buyout-loss-in-washington-dc-firms -33-year-history/#2cb4722d25b4.

7. "The Carlyle Group Raises $18.5 Billion for U.S. Buyout Fund," Carlyle Group, news release, July 20, 2018, https://www.carlyle.com/media -room/news-release-archive/carlyle-group-raises-185-billion-us-buyout -fund-largest-fund-firm.

8. Information on Vestar Capital executives available at www.vestarcapital .com.

9. John Seitz, president of Foundation Financial Research, interview with author, June 27, 2020.

10. Miriam Gottfried, "Blackstone to Bypass Scramble for Investment-B Talent in Bid to Diversify Hiring," *Wall Street Journal*, June 24, 2020, https:// www.wsj.com/articles/blackstone-to-bypass-scramble-for-investment-bank -talent-in-bid-to-diversify-hiring-11592996401

11. Securities and Exchange Commission, "Risk Alert: Observations from Examinations of Entities Managing Private Funds," June 2020, https://www .sec.gov/files/Private%20Fund%20Risk%20Alert_0.pdf.

9. The Enablers

1. Jean-Pierre Aubrey, assistant director of state and local research, Boston College, Center for Retirement Research, interview with author, July 7, 2020.

2. Chris Tobe, former trustee of Kentucky Retirement Systems, interview with author, July 8, 2020.

3. *The Big Squeeze: How Money Managers Crush State Budgets and Workers Retirement Hopes* (Boston: American Federation of Teachers, 2017), https://www.aft.org/sites/default/files/bigsqueeze_may2017.pdf.

4. 2017 interest tax deduction changes are summarized in: Wolf Richter, "The GOP's New Tax Law Punishes the Riskiest Companies in America," *Business Insider*, December 24, 2017, https://www.businessinsider.com/what-trump-tax-law-means-for-companies-corporate-interest-expense-2017-12.

5. Transaction and monitoring fees covered in: Eileen Applebaum and Rosemary Batt, "Fees, Fees and More Fees: How Private Equity Abuses Its Limited Partners and U.S. Taxpayers," Center for Economic and Policy Research, May 2016; and Simon Clark, "Private Equity's 'Hidden' Fees Totaled $20 Billion," *Wall Street Journal*, December, 13, 2015, https://www.wsj.com/articles/private-equitys-hidden-fees-totaled-20-billion-1450051201.

6. Mark Maremant, "Fees Get Leaner on Private Equity," *Wall Street Journal*, December 28, 2014, B1.

7. See Securities and Exchange Commission website for explanation of its responsibilities: https://www.sec.gov/about/what-we-do.

8. The following books shed light on why regulators often fail to prosecute: Jesse Eisinger, *The Chickenshit Club: Why the Justice Department Fails to Prosecute Executives* (New York: Simon & Schuster, 2017); John Coffee, "*Corporate Crime and Punishment, The Crisis of Underenforcement* (San Francisco: Berrett-Koehler, 2020).

9. Paul Kierman and Dave Michaels, "SEC Boss's Exit Makes Way for Rules Push," *Wall Street Journal*, November 17, 2020, A1.

10. For information on the Robert Smith case, see https://www.justice.gov/opa/pr/private-equity-ceo-enters-non-prosecution-agreement-international-tax-fraud-scheme-and-agrees; and a long article on the Robert Smith case is in: Peter Whoriskey, Yeganeh Torrati, and Keith Alexander, "A Dodgy Deal Made Him Rich. It Worked Until Now," *Washington Post*, November 18, 2020, G1.

11. For more information on Sorrentino's tax case, see https://www
.usatoday.com/story/entertainment/celebrities/2019/09/11/mike-the-situation
-sorrentino-look-into-his-time-behind-bars/2139556001/ and https://www.justice
.gov/usao-nj/pr/michael-situation-sorrentino-and-his-brother-marc-sorrentino
-sentenced-federal-prison-tax.

12. For Jay Clayton's comments on private equity and 401(k) plans, see
"Clayton Wants Retirement Investors to Have More Access to Private Funds,"
InvestmentNews, April 9, 2019, https://www.investmentnews.com/clayton
-wants-retirement-investors-to-have-more-access-to-private-funds-79000.

See also: "Statement on the Department of Labor's Investment Advice
Proposal," Chairman Jay Clayton, June 29, 2020, https://www.sec.gov/news
/public-statement/clayton-dol-investment-advice-proposal-2020-6-29.

Edward Siedle, "Trump DOL and SEC Keep Tossing 401-K Investors to
the Wolves of Wall Street," *Forbes*, July 5, 2020, https://www.forbes.com
/sites/edwardsiedle/2020/07/05/trump-dol-and-sec-keep-tossing-401k-investors
-to-the-wolves-of-wall-street/#100d1882bb90.

13. Clayton's Apollo compensation can be found at Noor Zainab Hussain,
Jessica Di Napoli, and Chinuike Oguh, "Apollo Taps Ex-SEC Chief Clayton
in Board Overhaul," February 8, 2021, Reuters, https://www.reuters.com
/article/us-apollo-global-clayton/apollo-taps-ex-sec-chief-clayton-in-board
-overhaul-idUSKBN2AI1HB.

10. The Fellow Travelers

1. Josh Kosman, "Buffett Is a Two-Time Loser in Texas Energy Bid,"
New York Post, August 21, 2017, https://nypost.com/2017/08/21/buffett
-is-a-two-time-loser-in-texas-energy-bid/.

2. Steven Pearlstein, "Senator Warren's Plan for Private Equity Has Good
Aims but Misses the Mark," *Washington Post*, July 27, 2019, https://www
.washingtonpost.com/business/economy/sen-elizabeth-warrens-plan-for
-private-equity-has-good-aims-but-misses-the-mark/2019/07/26/f66d6652
-af1b-11e9-8e77-03b30bc29f64_story.html.

3. Dean Starkman, *The Watchdog That Didn't Bark: The Financial Crisis
and the Disappearance of Investigative Journalism* (New York: Columbia
University Press, 2015).

4. "Private Equity Booming Due to Its Resilience, Strong Performance:
Triago Founder," CNBC Television, November 13, 2019, YouTube video,
4:06, https://www.youtube.com/watch?v=UAz7U09KHGw.

5. Robinson Meyer, "U.S. Court: Bloggers are Journalists," *Atlantic*, January 21, 2014, https://www.theatlantic.com/technology/archive/2014/01/us-court-bloggers-are-journalists/283225/.

6. The Howard Jones quote is in Andrew Ross Sorkin, "Pension Funds Fees are Wasting Money on Consultants," CNBC, October 1, 2013, https://www.cnbc.com/2013/10/01/study-pension-funds-are-wasting-money-on-consultants.html.

7. Callan Institute, "2020 Capital Market Assumptions," January 2021, by authors Jay Kloepfer, Adam Lozinski, and Kevin Machiz https://www.callan.com/uploads/2021/01/f70a4ed4a43ef1c9e5babf544d79e0ea/2021-capital-market-assumptions-webinar-final.pdf.

8. Amy Whyte, " Allocators Need Them, Asset Managers Resent Them, and Everyone is Afraid of Them," *Institutional Investor*, March 4, 2019, https://www.institutionalinvestor.com/article/b1dd82391ds6sz/Allocators-Need-Them-Asset-Managers-Resent-Them-And-Everyone-Is-Afraid-of-Them.

9. Wharton Private Equity and Venture Capital Conference, 2021, accessed March 1, 2021, https://whartonpevcconference.org/.

10. Prominent academic studies indicating high buyout fund returns in the late 1990s and early 2000s had authors from prestigious universities, like University of Chicago, MIT, University of Virginia, Duke University, London Business School and Oxford University. See the following articles.

Steven N. Kaplan and Antoinette Schoar, "Private Equity Performance: Returns, Persistence, and Capital Flows," *Journal of Finance* 60, no. 4 (August 2005): 1791–1823, https://onlinelibrary.wiley.com/doi/full/10.1111/j.1540-6261.2005.00780.x.

Chris Higson and Rüdiger Stucke, "The Performance of Private Equity," London Business School Collier Institute on Private Equity research paper, https://papers.ssrn.com/sol3/papers.cfm?abstract_id=2009067.

Robert S. Harris, Tim Jenkinson, and Steven N. Kaplan, "Private Equity Performance: What do We Know?" Journal of Finance 69, no. 5 (October 2014): 1851–82, https://onlinelibrary.wiley.com/doi/abs/10.1111/jofi.12154.

Steven N. Kaplan and Berk A. Sensoy. 2015. "Private Equity Performance: A Survey." *Annual Review of Financial Economics* 7 (2015): 597–614.

11. Martin Krikorian, " How to Protect Yourself from Another Bernie Madoff," *Lowell Sun*, December 15, 2019, https://www.lowellsun.com/2019/12/15/how-to-protect-yourself-from-another-bernie-madoff/.

12. Donal Mastralangelo quoted in "Lower Fee Private Equity Feeders Aim for Advisor Market, Mercury Capital Advisors, November 30, 2017, https://mercurycapitaladvisors.com/lower-fee-private-equity-feeders-aim-for-advisor-market/.

11. In Closing

1. Erik Schatzker, "Calpers CIO Seeks More Private Equity Leverage to Boost Returns," Bloomberg, June 15, 2020, https://www.bloomberg.com/news/articles/2020-06-15/calpers-cio-eyes-more-private-equity-leverage-to-boost-returns.

2. Bryan Burrough, "RJR Nabisco, An Epilogue," *New York Times*, March 12, 1999, https://www.nytimes.com/1999/03/12/opinion/rjr-nabisco-an-epilogue.html.

3. George Baker and George David Smith, *Kohlberg, Kravis and Roberts and the Creation of Corporate Value* (Cambridge: Cambridge University Press, 1998), 206.

4. See, *The Count of Monte Cristo*, directed by David Greene (London: ITC Entertainment, 1975).

5. See, *Ben Hur*, directed by William Wyler (Beverly Hills, Metro-Goldwyn-Mayer, 1959).

6. Quotes from William Jennings Bryan, "Cross of Gold" speech, History Matters, July 9, 1896, http://historymatters.gmu.edu/d/5354/.

Index

Page numbers in *italics* indicate figures or tables.

Lambeth Equity Fund III, 51–52
Larsen, David, 110
LBOs. *See* leveraged buyouts
Lehman Brothers, 45
leveraged buyouts (LBOs):
  academic centers favoring,
  182; accountability in, 15–16,
  24, 34, 59–60, 71–72, 76, 78;
  accountability rejected by, 103;
  administrative staff of, 147;
  bankruptcy of, 35, 39, 92,
  169–170; as blind pools, 29–30;
  capital structure of, 22, 22; cash
  flow of, 69, 118; Clayton on,
  167; corporate veil in, 161–162,
  162; data services capturing, 78;
  deal flow in, 61; debt-to-equity
  ratio in, 21–22; Dennis on, 70;
  developments promoting, 34;
  EBITDA of, 68, 68; EV of, 114;
  as favored, 33; fund formation
  of, 53–54, 54; fund managers of,
  21, 66, 66–67; Gibson Greetings
  as, 17; growth capital compared
  with, 25; hedge funds compared
  with, 26, 133; as high leverage,
  105; historical track record of,
  54–57, 55, 56; history of, 29–30;
  index fund contrasted with, 95;
  institutional investors in, 128,
  128; investment professionals of,
  147–148; by IRR, 183; as job-
  killer, 14; Johnson on, 190; at
  Lambeth Equity Fund III, 51–52;
  Manor Care bankrupt by, 143;
  marketing of, 15, 20, 52, 62–63,
  73, 75, 85, 100, 184–185; mark-
  to-market for, 107–108; mutual
  fund contrasted with, 71–72,
  72; operational improvements
by, 92–94; Oregon and, 77,
  77; organization of, 144–146,
  145; PE contrasted with, 73; PE
  likened to, 35; pension fund and,
  40; performance improvement
  by, 70; portfolio diversification
  and, 112–114, 113, 114; public
  model contrasted with, 92–93;
  raising money for, 53–54, 54;
  rate-of-return of, 73; recycling
  of, 93; regulations on, 31–32,
  154–155, 155; RJR Nabisco as,
  18, 18, 33, 75; self reporting
  shielding, 188; service providers
  of, 181–182; sifting process
  of, 64, 64–67; smoothing
  practice for, 114–115; S&P
  500 compared to, 20, 75, 188;
  stockholder objections to, 96;
  stock picking compared with,
  70–71; target profile of, 22–23,
  24; in television, 175; timeline
  of, 53; top quartile funds of,
  55, 83–84; top ten, 170, 171;
  treatment of, 33; types of, 36;
  valuing of, 67; venture capital
  contrasted with, 57, 69; of Vista
  Equity Partners, 36–37; Wall
  Street cherishing, 186; Warren
  against, 38; Wasserstein on, 36;
  year-to-year returns of, 80, 101,
  103, 104, 104, 105. *See also*
  alternatives; fund managers;
  performance, of LBOs; top
  quartile funds; validity, of
  buyout industry
line of credit: accountability
  circumvented by, 80; buyout
  return and, 80–83; IRR and,
  80–83, 81, 82